THE WASHINGTON HISTORICAL ATLAS

Who Did What When and Where in the Nation's Capital

Laura Bergheim

WOODBINE HOUSE
1992

58,976

Published by Woodbine House
5615 Fishers Lane, Rockville, MD 20852
301/468–8800; toll free 800/843–7323

Cover illustration & design: Adrienne Beck

Maps on pages 3, 30, 72, 108, 130, 176, 226, 247, 288, 300 from Washington D.C. Visitor's Map © 1991 by Rand McNally, R.L. 91–S–96. Maps on pages 223, 232, 239, 262, 170, 295 from Champion's Washington D.C. Street Map © 1991 by Rand McNally, R.L. 91–S–96. Maps on pages 150, 206, 217, 257 from the D.C. Transportation Map prepared by the D.C. Department of Public Works.

Library of Congress Cataloging-in-Publication Data

Bergheim, Laura, 1962–
      The Washington historical atlas : who did what when and where in the nation's capital / by Laura Bergheim
          p. cm.
      Includes bibliographical references and index.
      ISBN 0–933149–42–5 : $15.95
      1. Historic sites—Washington (D.C.) 2. Historic sites—Washington (D.C.)—Maps. 3. Washington (D.C.)—History. 4. Washington (D.C.)—Guidebooks. 5. Washington (D.C.)—Maps.
I. Title.
F195.B47   1992   90–50502
975.3—dc20   CIP

Manufactured in the United States of America

10   9   8   7   6   5   4   3   2   1

To my parents, Mel and Donna Bergheim,
with love, admiration, and thanks

Table of Contents

Acknowledgements

So many people contributed their time, effort, knowledge, skills, and support for this book that thanking them could take up an entire chapter by itself. Instead, let me just express my gratitude to the historians and archivists of Washington's historical societies and organizations, historic sites and memorials; the librarians and researchers at the Washingtoniana Collection of the Martin Luther King, Jr. Library, the Library of Congress, the National Archives, and the USGS; and all the people whose dedication to the preservation and documentation of history have helped make my job that much more delightful and fascinating.

Beth Wood was a tremendous help, both as a researcher and a friend, and for that I give her my deep thanks. Thanks to Jack Looney and Mia Bergheim (and driving Donna) for their photographic excursions. Thanks, also to Bill Adler, Jr. and Beth Pratt Dewey at Adler and Robin Books, for taking the time and energy to see the book through from inception to its rather overdue delivery. Ditto for the folks at Woodbine House, whose patience and understanding allowed me to write the book as it should be, not as it had to be. And thanks to the people at RTR Production Company (including Beth Stephens, Bob Gaudian, and Mike Pengra) for their support in giving me the time I needed to finish this book even as our launch date breathed down our collective necks. And thanks to Rand McNally for their wonderful maps.

Special thanks to my family, who have seen me through book after book (this being the most difficult yet) with love and support. My parents, Mel and Donna Bergheim, who raised me in the Washington area, are a living illustration of how, when good people come together, they can do even greater good, through activism and informed discussion. Special thanks are due my mother, Donna, who in the final days of this book spent her every waking hour (and there were more than usual) backtracking and fact-checking and phone calling and hand-holding. And feeding me Hershey's Kisses with Almonds.

Most of all, thanks to Jim Medwid for putting up with me through all this yet again. Love truly does have the power to conquer all, even frayed nerves and late nights and caffeine jags.

Preface

When I was a kid travelling out west, we went to one of those Western towns that cater to what tourists think the Wild West was—shoot-'em-up gun-fights, contests to catch a squealing greased-pig, and square-dance barn-raisings. Writing a history of Washington, D.C., for some reason brought that trip to mind (especially the greased-pig catching part), because no matter what you think you know (or know you don't know), you find that the shiny, slippery surface of legend, while sparkling, can also blind you with its glare.

There is more than enough history in Washington to go around, and frankly, this book could be ten times as long as it is and still not cram it all between two covers. But maybe that is as it should be, for the more one tries to tame and encapsulate the history and cultural legacy of any place and time, the greater the sense of ultimately adding to that blinding glare of collective legend.

Think of this book as a trail map rather than as a complete history or as a simple tourist guide. Let it lead you into foreign territory in your own back yard, let it re-introduce you to vistas and sights you have seen a hundred times but never understood. And let the voices of the past, the diaries and journals and advertisements and social notes whisper in your ear and tell you stories and read you poems. Most of all, let Washington waltz you about the dance-floor of time; but leave your own dance-card at home.

Introduction

A CITY OF MAGNIFICENT COMPROMISES

Charles Dickens once derided Washington, D.C., as being "a city of magnificent intentions," meaning it had not yet begun to live up to the hubris it was already developing in the middle of the nineteenth century. But more aptly, he might have called it a city of magnificent compromises: From the selection of its site, to the still-pungent battles over development, Washington has been a city in a state of persistent paradox.

Until the decision was made to build a city for the nation's government, the Continental Congress had floated all over the Atlantic seaboard, spending time in Philadelphia, Princeton, Annapolis, Trenton, and New York City. Indeed, one wag suggested that a proposed statue of George Washington be mounted on wheels to follow the migratory Congress around.

Both the North and the South wanted the capital, but New York's Alexander Hamilton and Virginia's Thomas Jefferson struck a compromise. They agreed that the South would give the North the money to pay the Continental Army soldiers their back salary, in exchange for which the capital would be located a bit to the south. Not too far, mind you—but at least, not in New England, either.

In 1789, Congress gave President Washington the authority to select a capital location. The following year, Washington (personally partial to the Virginia countryside, having grown up near Fredericksburg and building his estate at Mount Vernon) selected a spot at the fork of the eastern and western branches of the Potomac. The site was on the upper crust of the Piedmont Plateau and the lower lip of the coastal plain below, at the spiritual boundary of north and south—the states of Maryland and Virginia.

Surveyor Andrew Ellicott and mathematician Benjamin Banneker laid out the boundaries of the diamond-shaped capital, "ten miles square," which included real estate in both Maryland and Virginia. To plan the city itself, Congress hired Pierre Charles L'Enfant, a French architect and planner who had served on Washington's staff in the Continental Army.

For the design of this, one of the world's first planned capital cities, Pierre L'Enfant drew upon his love for the broad boulevards and park-like circles of Paris. Though pleased with the plan, Congress found the planner himself to be a difficult and uncompromising man. L'Enfant was dismissed in 1792, after he ordered the destruction of the foundation for a house being built on Capitol Hill (then Jenkins Hill) by wealthy land baron Daniel Carroll. Carroll's house was being built in the way of L'Enfant's plan, it seemed.

L'Enfant indignantly refused the paltry $2,500 Congress voted to give him for his city plans, instead suing the legislature for $100,000, which he never recovered. He died a pauper, and went unmourned at his death; but in 1909, L'Enfant's remains were finally reburied, with ceremony fitting the planner of the city, at Arlington National Cemetery.

The land on which Washington was built was not, as legend has it, a swamp. Most of the land consisted of dense forests, wide fields, and rural farmland. But much of it was a flood plain, which meant that the waters of the Potomac River (which then came up to where modern-day Constitution Avenue runs) and the Tiber Creek (which flowed south from Maryland) often turned parts of the city into soupy bottom lands.

The area was already populated by Native American tribes and tobacco farmers who lived in peace and often traded goods. The Town of George (now Georgetown) was a flourishing port city. So, too, was the City of Alexandria across the river. (The oldest major community in the area, Alexandria had been surveyed by George Washington himself in his youth.) Alexandria was swallowed up by the new nation's capital, only regaining its freedom in 1846, while the Town of George did not become an official part of Washington until 1871.

Andrew Ellicott's map of the Territory of Columbia, submitted to George Washington on June 25, 1793. (National Archives)

The same year that L'Enfant was dismissed, work began on the President's House (now called the White House). In 1793, work commenced on the Capitol. Construction workers became the first new inhabitants of Washington, setting up camps and brick kilns in the park across Pennsylvania Avenue from the President's House which they were building.

Although the Capitol was still incomplete in 1800, President John Adams insisted that Congress move down to Washington and into its new home. Adams followed soon afterwards, becoming the first president to take up residence at 1600 Pennsylvania Avenue. The house was not yet finished, however, and drove First Lady Abigail Adams to fits of despair.

The newly arrived legislators and other federal employees soon filled up the hotels and boarding houses that sprang up around the Capitol and President's House. The inns and townhouses of the Town of George became popular with those who could stomach the bumpy carriage roads into the new city.

Civilization came slowly to Washington. The effort of building massive federal structures ate up time and money, leaving little left over for such amenities as paved streets. For many decades, Pennsylvania Avenue was the only "paved" street, and at that was only covered with wooden planking.

In 1814, when British troops attacked Washington and burned most of the federal buildings (including the President's House and the Capitol), some Americans saw this destruction as a blessing. Congress debated whether to desert the capital and start fresh somewhere else—anywhere else—where a longer tradition of civilizing comfort had been established, where the threat of malaria and cholera did not hang like a cloud of mosquitoes over the city's lowlands.

But too much political and emotional energy had already been devoted to the establishment of the city on the banks of the Potomac. In 1815, the rebuilding of the city commenced.

Over the next forty years, the capital city grew in fits and starts. It developed a healthy port trade, and, despite its still-unfinished qualities (such as dirt roads and open sewers), drew many a prominent figure to set up a house in the city or an estate in the suburbs.

The city's black population increased rapidly as Washington gained a reputation for being a place with northern sentiments south of the Mason-Dixon Line. The practice of slave trading was abolished in Washington in 1850, as part of the famed Compromise of 1850. This compromise warded off the Civil War for another decade by allowing slavery to continue in the South while giving new states the option to ban the institution.

By the mid-century, the strained relations between North and South were felt keenly in Washington. In 1861, when Abraham Lincoln arrived for his first inaugural, the tense city was so rife with rumors of an assassination plot that Lincoln snuck into the city by train and was secretly ensconced at the Willard Hotel downtown.

Within months, the nation was at war with itself, and Washington was instantly compromised by its own location. Soon, forts surrounded the city and Washington swarmed with Union soldiers. As the war pressed on, the wounded and dying began pouring into the city from the nearby battlegrounds in Virginia and Pennsylvania. Washington became a

During the Civil War, the 8th Massachusetts Volunteers were billeted in the unfinished Capitol Rotunda. (*Harper's Illustrated History of the Civil War*)

city-wide hospital ward, with every public building from the Capitol to the Patent Office transformed into makeshift hospitals.

Throughout the war, rumors often surfaced that the Confederates were at the city limits, although the only real danger of invasion occurred in July of 1864, when Confederate General Jubal Early and his troops besieged Fort Stevens, five miles north of the (then) city boundaries. President Lincoln rode out to watch the battle, standing atop the ramparts as the cannons blasted and the bullets whizzed all about him.

The Civil War may well have been the greatest test of the Union's strength and spirit, but its aftermath was perhaps the harshest strain yet on the capital city's endurance. The assassination of President Lincoln at Ford's Theater on April 14, 1865 was a bitter herald of the difficult years to come.

Following the Civil War, Washington's black community nearly tripled. Census figures from 1870 show that the city's total population of 109,199 included some 35,392 blacks, whereas the 1860 census had reported a black population in the city of only 10,983, of whom 9,209 were freedmen and women.

By the 1870s, there were as many crowded alley neighborhoods, with their rough-hewn shacks and tents, as there were communities of built housing. As overpopulation and poor sanitation plagued the city, Congress once again began whispering that perhaps the capital city should be moved. Some representatives were even bold enough to scout out potential sites in the Midwest.

Before plans to move the capital could get past the talking stage, Congress struck at the root of Washington's problems: its city government. Cast adrift within the larger firmament of the national government, the local government was often at a loss for self-regulation. In April of 1871, Congress passed legislation creating the Territory of Washington, giving the city an official status in and of itself, including a non-voting delegation of one to Congress. The Territorial Act also provided for the creation of several oversight boards, including a health commission—whose responsibilities included getting farm animals out of the roads—and a five-member Board of Public Works.

Under the iron rule of the irrepressible Alexander "Boss" Shepherd, the Board of Public Works almost singlehandedly changed the face of Washington. Shepherd literally overhauled the city, overseeing street grating, paving, and lighting projects, the enclosure of open sewers, and the planting of thousands of trees throughout Washington. During his two-year reign, the Boss ensured the best jobs for his own contracting companies or their subsidiaries, had the areas where he owned real estate cleaned up first, and in the process, spent millions more than was budgeted for his projects.

In 1874, President Ulysses S. Grant appointed Shepherd Territorial Governor. Shepherd's municipal spending spree, however, had already caught up with the Territory of Washington, which found itself broke and a national laughingstock. That same year, Congress called for an investigation, and Shepherd's shady methods were exposed. Congress called him up on allegations of corruption, and even some of Shepherd's close associates supplied evidence against the man who had made Washington livable. Shepherd was practically run out of town, although he did return years later to a hero's welcome. The federal government bailed out the wayward city that year, but took away its territorial status (including home rule). It was not until 1964 that citizens of Washington were allowed the right to vote in national elections, and the city itself did not regain home rule until 1975.

The city's size changed dramatically in 1890 when the northern boundaries (as designated by Boundary Road, now called Florida Avenue) were extended northward to absorb the well-established suburban communities of Mount Pleasant, Cleveland Park, Glover Park, and a number of others.

The city was further transformed at the turn of the twentieth century through the efforts of Senator James McMillan of Michigan, Chairman of the Senate's District Committee. In 1901, McMillan convinced Congress to appoint a Park Authority that would bring Washington into the mainstream of the "city beautiful" movement sweeping the nation. The McMillan Commission (including architect Charles McKim, landscaper Frederick Law Olmsted, Jr., and sculptor Augustus Saint-Gaudens), toured the great cities of Europe, and, in 1902, reported their suggestions. These included: a return to the roots of L'Enfant's original plan (including making the Mall a ceremonial space); the construction of new memorials on the parkland claimed by the Army Corps of Engineers' dredging of the Potomac River from the 1880s until 1900; and a Beaux-Arts transformation of most of the federal city buildings.

View of the suburbs, circa 1794–1795. (Library of Congress)

In 1910, Congress appointed the permanent Fine Arts Commission, which soon became the arbiter of architectural direction and taste that the McMillan Plan had set forth. Before much redevelopment could take place, however, two world wars and the Great Depression claimed the city's attention. Yet, the ceremonial city of monuments that includes the Mall and the Tidal Basin, as well as such planned federal office parks as the Federal Triangle, were built as a result of the McMillan Commission's suggestions.

Just as the Civil War did, World War I transformed Washington into a camp—but this time, with the war a continent away and communications technology permitting swifter transmittal of battle plans, fewer soldiers trained in Washington's parks, and far more clerks scribbled away in temporary buildings set up along the Mall and up and down Pennsylvania Avenue. The bureaucratization of warfare reached a new high during World War II. The Mall and its surrounding areas were once again built up with temporary offices, while the thousands of clerks and secretaries, officers and spies who came to work for the war effort crawled the city, hunting for scarce apartment space. Private homes and townhouses throughout the city were turned into boarding houses, and one-bedroom apartments suddenly became home to three or more occupants. Of all the wartime transformations, that of World War II had the most lasting effect on the city's development and society. Never again would Washington be called a sleepy southern town.

Washington has gone to war numerous times, but more often, the war has been brought home to the city by citizens anxious to air their grievances before an audience of

Congressmen and the national media. Famous as a protest capital of the world, Washington has seen a stunning array of marches and sit-ins, riots and arrests. Who can forget the image of the Rev. Dr. Martin Luther King, Jr., standing on the steps of the Lincoln Memorial in 1963 to deliver his "I have a dream" speech before a crowd of 400,000 civil rights marchers?

Every decade has its causes; every generation, its reason to be heard. Today's protests focus on issues of abortion and race relations, on military intervention in South America, on gay rights, the environment, and the problems of the hungry and the homeless.

Sadly, some protests have turned violent. Indeed, one of the cruelest forces to change the face of Washington in the past century has been the power of the riot. The most famous riot to strike Washington began on April 4, 1968. As news spread that the Rev. Dr. Martin Luther King, Jr., had been assassinated in Memphis, a wave of riots engulfed American cities from New York to Los Angeles. Washington was one of the hardest hit cities, with the neighborhoods of Shaw and the 14th Street corridor bearing the brunt of four violent days. Ten people were killed; $15 million in damages was sustained by the city. Some areas have yet to fully recover.

Violence is nothing new to Washington streets, but as a city besieged in recent years by "crack" cocaine houses and drug-related murders, Washington has gained a dangerous reputation as America's "Murder Capital." The city may have hit its lowest point when Mayor Marion Barry was arrested on charges of cocaine possession in 1990, having been videotaped in a local hotel smoking a crack pipe. Yet, also in 1990, Washington regained its position in the graces of the nation when it elected the first black woman mayor of a major city, Sharon Pratt Dixon (now Sharon Pratt Kelly). Kelly promised to help build community coalitions and tackle the city's entangled governmental problems. But these things take time, and the capital is, in the scheme of civilization's span, a young city yet.

When Americans think of Washington, they think of the Washington Monument and the Smithsonian, the Congress and the president. But Washington is also a hometown to those who live and work here. Unique among the nation's cities, Washington is a national arena set amidst local neighborhoods. The people of Washington continue to leave their mark on world history and local lore. This intermingled legacy of international consequence and everyday life makes Washington a city well worth preserving, exploring, and saluting.

How to Use This Book

The Washington Historical Atlas is designed and written for browsers, researchers, city dwellers, and tourists alike. Each chapter includes an introduction that describes the basic history of the area, followed by entries (keyed by numbers to maps) that give the history and flavor of a site and its occupants. At the end of each entry, where appropriate, there is a "See Also" referral that guides the reader to other relevant entries throughout the book. Those referrals typeset in **bold** appear in the same chapter as the original entry; all other referrals include a chapter title to further guide the reader to the site of relevant entries. Referrals that appear in "quotation marks" are sidebars—short, thematic entries that appear throughout the book. Sites that are considered public places (such as museums, parks, galleries, restaurants, certain government buildings offering regular tours, etc.) are designated with the symbol ⟨ Open to the Public ⟩ . Keep in mind that many local and federal government buildings are not meant for wandering, even though they are technically within the public domain. Inquire about public tours of such buildings if you have no official business inside, but want a closer look. The appendices at the back of the book include a bibliography, historic timeline, and a special section on Homes of the Great.

There is no right or wrong way to use *The Washington Historical Atlas*; it was fun to write, and is meant to be fun to read, whether to dip in for a few morsels at bedtime or to keep in the backseat when driving around the city looking for specific sites. The best way to use the book is to let your curiosity lead you where it may. The city's history will happily follow along for the ride.

Chapter 1

THE WHITE HOUSE AND ENVIRONS

There is far more history (from naughty to haughty) in this regal little enclave of Washington than one-stop tourists know. Here some of the city's great leaders struggled to avert the Civil War—as Secretary of State Daniel Webster and Henry Clay did, if only temporarily, by hammering out the Compromise of 1850 in Webster's home, now the site of the **U.S. Chamber of Commerce.** Here, too, they plotted to win that war—not only in the salons of the White House, but in homes like **Blair House,** where Robert E. Lee was offered, and refused, the command of the Union Army. Murders were committed here (in **Lafayette Park,** where the district attorney was slain by a jealous husband), and attempted (at **Blair House,** where a foiled assassination left a secret serviceman and an assassin dead; and at the **Rodgers House,** where Lincoln's Secretary of State, William Seward, narrowly escaped being murdered in his bed). If ghosts walk anywhere in Washington, they may well roam this area; not only in the halls of the White House, but along the paths of Lafayette Park late at night, or in the chambers of the ornate **Old Executive Office Building,** where more than a thousand treaties were signed. For here, history lives on even as the fables of the past are replaced by the foibles of the present.

As planned by Pierre L'Enfant, this was one of the first areas of Washington to be developed for use as the nation's capital. Indeed, several of the city's oldest remaining public buildings are found within a few blocks of each other in this powerful neighborhood. David Burnes, a Scottish country gentleman, originally owned the land in this area—including the broad sweep of field that traipsed down to the banks of the Potomac (which at the time extended up to modern-day Constitution Avenue). At first, Burnes was reluctant to give up his land, but he finally agreed to sell—after much haggling and a few implied threats about the government's right to condemn the land and then buy it at a deeply discounted rate. Legend has it that President Washington visited the recalcitrant Burnes at his home and emerged several hours later, holding the deed to the land upon which many of Washington's most important buildings and monuments would someday be built.

Work on the President's House commenced in 1792, while the land between it and the planned Capitol grounds was still a muddy expanse of woods and fields watered by Tiber Creek and the Potomac River. Pennsylvania Avenue, as designed by Pierre L'Enfant, was laid out to run in a diagonal line between the President's House and the U.S. Capitol so that the Executive and Legislative Branches could lock their gazes upon each other with unobstructed vision. L'Enfant's master plan was, however, later detoured when the Treasury Building was constructed next door to the White House, forcing Pennsylvania Avenue into an awkward right angle around the building before continuing its path to the Capitol.

The White House dominates this section of town (as it does the entire city, at least as a source of symbolic power). In front and behind the mansion are two major parks—

Burning of Washington by the British, 1814. (*Our First Century*)

Lafayette Park to the north and the **Ellipse** to the south—both of which were originally designed to be part of the president's estate. The Ellipse has managed to retain its intended role as the "backyard" of the White House in spirit if not in privacy, acting as a stately grass buffer between the presidential residence and the chaotic doings of the Mall and its galleries and monuments. Lafayette Park, however, has led a far different existence: Its usages ranged from racetrack to campground (even zoo animals found a home in the park in the mid-eighteenth century). But as the center of power radiated out from the President's House, savvy new citizens transformed the park north of the executive mansion into a virtual Hyde Park, lined with elegant townhouses and soon rife with intrigue and powerplays.

When British forces burned the city in 1814, this area was one of the hardest hit. Having triumphed at the Battle of Bladensburg, Rear Admiral George Cockburn's troops marched into Washington. They burned the Capitol, using Library of Congress books as kindling. Then they marched up Pennsylvania Avenue and lit a torch to the President's House, after first dining on the fine victuals set out earlier by Dolley Madison in preparation for a dinner party.

The White House and the city itself were rebuilt after the British attack; ironically, however, twentieth-century efforts of developers and planners almost managed to wipe the face of Washington clean of its early architecture more effectively than the best efforts of the British attackers.

In 1901, Congress appointed the McMillan Commission to develop a solution to seemingly runaway planning problems of the city, which, by the turn of the twentieth century, had long-since derailed from L'Enfant's original vision. This committee recommended the homogenization of federal city architecture into a single Beaux-Arts style. Although this redevelopment doomed a number of fine Victorian buildings in Washington (particularly in and around the Mall area), the commission only saw its dream realized in one building near the White House: The **U.S. Chamber of Commerce,** completed in 1926. Depression and war managed to keep most of the planned McMillan redevelopment of the area at bay until the city had begun to cherish the eclectic older architecture that was slated for destruction.

Nevertheless, the progress of normal development did take its toll on the area. The delightful old

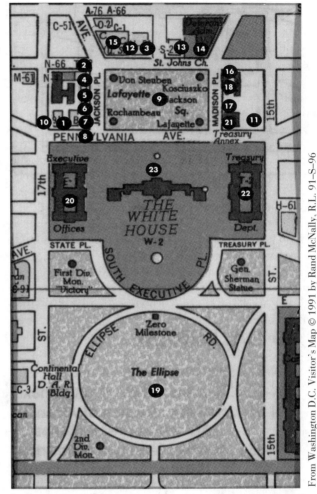

mansions and townhouses that once lined the nearby K Street area in new downtown have now given way to glass box buildings. Modern office buildings also threatened to encroach on some of the most historic houses around Lafayette Square. Luckily, President John F. Kennedy inaugurated a preservation program in 1963 that protected the older homes and buildings in the area. Through his efforts, many of the homes of Madison Place, along the east side of Lafayette Square, were preserved by the use of "fill-in" architecture that surrounds but does not surmount the original buildings.

PLACES: North of Pennsylvania Avenue

❶ Blair House Complex (1650 Pennsylvania Avenue)

The Blair House complex is run by the federal government as guest quarters and a ceremonial site for foreign VIPs. **Blair House** was purchased by the federal government in 1948—supposedly at the suggestion of Eleanor Roosevelt, who had once come upon White House guest Winston Churchill wandering about in the middle of the night, searching for the president so that they could continue an earlier meeting. Mrs. Roosevelt thought that having heads of state out of the family's hair at night might afford the president a better chance to rest.

In 1950, President Harry S Truman and his family moved into Blair House while the White House underwent renovations. Oscar Collazo and Grizelio Torresola, a pair of Puerto Rican Nationalists who hoped to draw attention to the plight of their nation, saw in the president's temporary quarters a less-secure window of opportunity. At 2:15 on the afternoon of November 1, 1950, as the president was napping before a planned visit to Arlington Cemetery, Collazo and Torresola approached the front entrance of Blair House. Guns blazing, the pair stormed the secret service agents out front, wounding several and killing one, Leslie Coffelt—but not before Coffelt killed Torresola. Collazo was also badly wounded in the assassination attempt, which never made it beyond the front steps, although he recovered enough to stand trial. Convicted on March 7, 1951, of attempted murder, Collazo was sentenced to death. His sentence was later commuted to life imprisonment by the very president whom Collazo and his compatriot had tried to murder. A plaque by the door to Blair House commemorates the ultimate sacrifice made by Coffelt, a guardian to the end.

Blair House was built in 1824 by Dr. Joseph Lovell, the nation's first Surgeon General. Upon Lovell's death in 1836, the house was sold to Francis Preston Blair. Blair, a newspaper editor who became a confidante of presidents from Jackson to Grant, served on Jackson's ill-fated "kitchen" cabinet. Aside from Blair, five other cabinet members were to live in the house before the property was purchased by the federal government.

In April 1861, Francis Blair met at Blair House with Robert E. Lee to offer him the command of the Union Army. Lee had previously discussed the same matter with General Winfield Scott, across 17th Street at the War Department (then housed in the Winder Building), and was now being pressed by Blair, at President Lincoln's behest, for an answer.

At the time, Lee was Commandant of West Point, and one of the most highly respected and genteel military men in Washington. Torn between his commitment to the Union as an American and a loyal soldier, and his allegiance to his deep Dixie roots, Lee agonized over Lincoln's request. He finally decided he could not lead an army against the Confederacy, and, sadly, rejected the president's offer. Then he rode back over Long Bridge to his Arlington estate, to ruminate over his decision. A few days later, Lee bid farewell to his wife, Mary Ann Randolph Custis Lee (great-granddaughter of Martha Washington), and children, and headed South to Richmond to offer his services as the commander of the Confederate Army. Soon after the war began, the federal government seized Lee's Arlington estate. After serving as a hospital and then a freedman's camp, the grounds were eventually transformed into Arlington National Cemetery.

Another fateful Civil War leadership move also took place at Blair House. Here, in December of 1861, the decision was made to place Admiral David Farragut in command of the Union's crucial naval attack on New Orleans.

The adjoining Lee House was built in 1859 by Admiral Phillips Lee as a gift for his bride, Elizabeth, the daughter of Francis P. Blair. The house was purchased by the federal government in 1942 for use as guest quarters for visiting dignitaries.

Although Blair House is mainly used for visiting foreign dignitaries, President-Elect Ronald Reagan and his wife, Nancy, frequently stayed at Blair House during his pre-inauguration transition period. A mini-scandal was sparked on October 2, 1981, when then-Washington *Post* gossip columnist Diana McLellan whispered in her "Ear" column that, according to a close associate of Rosalyn Carter's, Blair House had been bugged by the Carter White House during the Reagans' stays. The Carter people vehemently denied the charge and threatened to sue the *Post*, which printed an apology on October 23rd, noting that, although their source was credible, the story was likely a false rumor. Nevertheless, it's likely that visiting dignitaries have been peering behind paintings and looking up lampshades ever since.

See Also: The White House; "Blood in the Chambers" (Chapter 3); The Winder Building (Chapter 5)

Decatur House. (Jack Looney)

Cutts-Madison House. *See* U.S. Court of Claims Complex

2 Open to the Public **Decatur House (748 Jackson Place, NW; 202/842–0920)**

Designed by the famed architect Benjamin Latrobe, Decatur House was the first private residence built at Lafayette Square. When completed in 1818, the house was considered a home to rival the importance and power of the neighboring President's House. This had as much to do with its elegant and popular residents as with its architectural splendors.

Commodore Stephen Decatur and his lovely bride, Susan Wheeler Decatur, were the talk of Washington. With their youth, beauty, wealth, and fame, they seemed destined to have a lengthy reign at the top of the city's social ladder. Already, the Commodore's heroism in battling the British Navy and Barbary pirates had made him a star in the firmament of drawing rooms and private clubs. In 1820, the couple had been living barely a year in their new dream house when a disgruntled fellow naval officer, Commodore James Barron, challenged Decatur to a duel. Court-martialled for his absence during the War of 1812, Barron had recently sought to wipe clear his record by seeking a new naval command, but his reinstatement was denied by the Navy (an act supported by Decatur and many fellow officers).

Despite his repugnance for the barbaric ritual of dueling, Decatur agreed to meet Barron on the dueling field in Bladensburg, Maryland, on March 22, 1820. Both men's pistols found their marks, but only Barron's shot inflicted a mortal wound. Borne home to his young wife and their new home, Decatur died there that evening. On March 24, as the funeral procession wound its way through Washington, citizens lined the streets to pay tribute to their hometown hero in one of the city's earliest funerary spectacles.

The young widow, Susan Decatur, was left behind to try to run the large and expensive household while still in a state of intense grief. Within a few years, Susan Decatur's reduced finances forced her to move to a smaller Georgetown residence. In 1836, local tavern-keeper John Gadsby purchased the home, and for some time, he ran a profitable slave market behind the house. Decatur House later was home to a roster of other powerful Washingtonians, including Martin Van Buren and Henry Clay. At different times, it also served as the British, French, and Russian Legations.

At the end of the Civil War, the house was purchased by a local adventurer, Edward Fitzgerald Beale, who is perhaps best known for trying to get the U.S. Army to import and adapt camels to the winning of the West. Sadly, the American Camel Corps he worked to promote couldn't make it over the hump of ill-humor the animals instilled in Army handlers, and the project was disbanded in 1864. Paintings with camel motifs can still be seen in Decatur House, which remained in Beale's family for eighty-four years. The home is now run by the Trust for Historic Preservation as a historic house museum. The Decatur Carriage House (next door to the house, on H Street) has been transformed into office space and a gift shop featuring crafts, memorabilia, and references on historic preservation.

See Also: Site of National Hotel (Chapter 2); Susan Decatur House (Chapter 6); "Slavery in Washington" (Chapter 12)

---

3 | Open to the Public | **Hay-Adams Hotel (800 16th Street, NW; 202/638–6600)**

Since opening in 1927 as the Manger Hay-Adams Hotel, this Harry Wardman creation has remained one of the most elegant, refined hotels in the city. Ethel Barrymore, Sinclair Lewis, Amelia Earhart, and Charles Lindbergh are but some of the guests to have graced the hotel hallways. In the early 1980s, Lt. Col. Oliver North frequently entertained potential donors to the Contra money pipeline at the bars and restaurants of the hotel, which was an easy commute from North's office at the National Security Council's **Old Executive Office Building** headquarters.

This site had an illustrious (and even scandalous) career long before the hotel was built. During the Civil War, the home of a woman who would later be called the Mata Hari of the Civil War—Rose O'Neal Greenhow, a Confederate spy—was located at approximately this location. Mrs. Greenhow was an attractive and sociable widow who had a talent for entertaining Union officers and other powerful gentlemen. The secrets that passed from their lips to hers ended up as coded messages sent across the lines to enemy generals. She is said to have warned Confederate General Beauregard of Union Army movements in time for him to prepare for what would become the Second Battle of Bull Run. Mrs. Greenhow was put under house arrest on August 23, 1861, and her house was transformed into an armed prison (some jokingly called it Fort Greenhow) for other loose-lipped ladies with Southern leanings. In early 1862, Mrs. Greenhow was transferred to the Old Capitol Prison (where the Supreme Court now stands), and she and her young daughter Rose were subsequently deported to Richmond.

In 1885, the site regained its respectability when the twin homes of two powerful men were built at the site. The wrap-around homes belonged to John Hay (Secretary of State under Presidents William McKinley and Theodore Roosevelt) and Henry Adams (grandson of President John Quincy Adams, and statesman, historian and author best known for his autobiography, *The Education of Henry Adams.)* Adams was widowed shortly before moving into his new H Street home when his wife, Marian, bereaved over the loss of her father, apparently took her own life.

A crowd in front of the Hay and Adams houses awaits news of the Boxer Rebellion in 1901. (Library of Congress)

The Hay and Adams houses, both designed by H.H. Richardson (a classmate of Adams's at Harvard), once dominated the corner of 16th and H Streets, wrapping around the block with a single facade. Yet both homes provided complete privacy for their residents, and the twin houses became symbolic of the powerful pair of men who occupied them. The houses were destroyed in 1927 to make way for the Hay-Adams Hotel.
See Also: Roger's House Site and **Old Executive Office Building**

Jackson Place Houses (On Jackson Place between H Street and Pennsylvania Avenue)

Most of the historic nineteenth-century houses that once lined Jackson Place, on the western border of Lafayette Square, have been destroyed, and artificial facades have been put in their place. A few, including the best known, **Decatur House** (at 748 Jackson Place) remain. (The houses of Madison Place, on the eastern border, fared somewhat better, although many are now part of the **U.S. Claims Court Complex.**) Aside from Decatur House, the other houses of note that stand (or once stood) along Jackson Place include:

❹ 736 Jackson Place: Franklin Pierce's Secretary of State, William Marcy, called 736 Jackson place home, as did The (Republican) Man from Maine, James G. Blaine, who served in the House, Senate, and on the Cabinet, but never managed to be elected President. And President Theodore Roosevelt and his family lived here in 1902 during one of the White House restorations. While in residence here, Roosevelt slipped on the front steps and fractured his leg.

See Also: Blaine House (Chapter 7)

❺ 734 Jackson Place: Local businessman Charles C. Glover lived at this residence. Glover served in the late nineteenth century and early twentieth century as Riggs Bank President, and in that position of power led other prominent citizens in petitioning Congress for the charter that led to construction of the National Cathedral. Glover and his followers also pushed Congress to appropriate money for the purchase and preservation of Rock Creek Park; in fact, the Rock Creek Park bill was drafted here, at Glover's townhouse, in late 1888. Glover's name is still attached to another park project: Glover-Archbold Park. Glover and another prominent citizen, Mrs. Anne Archbold, donated the land for the park which still bears their names.

See Also: Glover-Archbold Park (Chapter 8)

❻ 730 Jackson Place: This was the home of Daniel Sickles, who murdered District Attorney Philip Barton Key in 1859 in Lafayette Park, after discovering the young lawyer was having an affair with his wife, Teresa. The scandal rocked Washington, and led to one of the greatest murder trials in the city's history.

See Also: Rodgers House; Key's Lovenest Site (Chapter 2)

❼ 722 Jackson Place: Often called the Ewell House, this now-gone mansion was built in 1820, and served as the home to two very powerful, very different men. Elihu Root lived here while serving as William McKinley's secretary of war. Root then leased the house to William Randolph Hearst, the king of yellow journalism, who served two terms in Congress as a representative from New York.

❽ 712 Jackson Place: The most notable resident of this townhouse was Major Henry R. Rathbone, an aide to President Lincoln. Rathbone and his fiancee, Clara Harris, were invited to join the presidential party at Ford's Theater on the evening of April 14, 1865. They took the place of General U.S. Grant and his wife, who had unexpectedly left town at the last minute. Rathbone and his intended were in the box with the Lincolns when John Wilkes Booth shot the president. When Rathbone tried to stop Booth from escaping, Booth slashed him in the arm. Rathbone did not lead a happy life thereafter. He and Clara married and moved to Europe, and in 1885 Rathbone tried to kill his children, murdered his wife, attempted suicide, and died years later in an insane asylum.

See Also: Ford's Theater (Chapter 2)

---

❾ | Open to the Public | **Lafayette Park (Pennsylvania Avenue across from The White House)**

"Lafayette Square was society. . . . Within a few hundred yards of [the Jackson statue] . . . one found all one's acquaintances as well as hotels, banks, markets and national government. Beyond the square the country began." So wrote historian and author Henry Adams in *The Education of Henry Adams*, about this self-contained enclave of high society that grew up around Lafayette Park in the nineteenth century. Proximity to the White House was a lure that drew many a mover and shaker to build a townhome on the park's outskirts, and thus the park's boundary streets formed the most powerful quadrant of society in the city. The list of those who lived in the homes that ringed the park reads like a manifest of destinies: Henry Clay, Daniel Webster, Henry Adams, Dolley Madison, James G. Blaine, Stephen Decatur, and, of course, the White House occupants, to name a few. Their elegant drawing rooms became breeding grounds of political intrigue, social drama, and military intelligence. Their church, **St.**

John's Episcopal (at the northeast corner of the park), became the house of worship for presidents and cabinet members, diplomats and generals alike.

Now famed as a camp-out site for protesters hoping to catch the president's eye and conscience from across Pennsylvania Avenue, the area that now includes Lafayette Park and its surrounding square was originally envisioned by L'Enfant as seven acres of lawn, trees, and gardens that would sweep gracefully up to the president's front door. But Thomas Jefferson, hoping to free the new nation of imperial pretenses, insisted the land be designated a public park. To immortalize the point, Pennsylvania Avenue slices decisively between the square and the White House grounds, forever dividing the two into separate presidential and public domains.

One of the greatest spectacles of the young city's history took place at the park in 1824, when Revolutionary War hero the Marquis de Lafayette was honored at the President's Park, as it was called at the time. During his stay, the city welcomed Lafayette with an outpouring of gratitude—holding dinners and receptions for him, and giving him a place of honor at the first commencement of Columbian College (now George Washington University). To further honor the Marquis, the park where some of the festivities took place was re-named in his honor, although for a time it was also called Jackson Park (for the statue of Andrew Jackson that long dominated the park).

The park itself, an orchard at the time it was purchased by the federal government, saw scant development as a real park until the mid-nineteenth century. Instead, it was used for a variety of projects: During construction of the President's House, the park served as an encampment and worksite for the laborers; the park also served as military encampments and staging areas during both the War of 1812 and the Civil War. At other times, the park was a horse-racing track, and even an open-air zoo.

In 1851, landscape architect Andrew Jackson Downing finally developed a planting program. As the century wore on, the memory of the park as a barren parade ground faded as trees and statues began dotting the landscape. For a number of years in the mid-to-late nineteenth century, the park was surrounded by a high iron fence that was locked at night. This fence very nearly caused an international incident during the Lincoln years, according to author Fred J. Maroon. In *Washington: Magnificent Capital*, Maroon noted that one of President Franklin Roosevelt's favorite Washington tales involved a dangerous liaison in Lafayette Park. According to FDR, Secretary of State William Seward was walking home late one evening, when he heard embarrassed cries of help coming from behind the locked gates of the park.

Upon investigation, Seward discovered that the British minister and the wife of the Spanish minister had become trapped inside the fence because they had been too—er—preoccupied to notice the gatekeeper locking them inside. The diplomatic duo begged Seward for his discreet assistance, so Seward set off in search of the gatekeeper. Happening upon President Lincoln, who was out for a late night stroll, Seward solicited the president's aid. Lincoln and Seward then carried over ladders from the White House grounds, and extricated the flustered pair.

The park continues to evolve. As recently as 1970, brick walkways and fountains were installed to help unify the park's atmosphere. The park features five major statues, each honoring a war hero. The Andrew Jackson Statue in the center of the park was, for nearly forty years, the only statuary to grace the park. Installed in 1853 to honor Jackson's role at the Battle of New Orleans during the War of 1812, the tribute was the first equestrian statue to be cast in the United States by an American. The sculptor, Clark Mills, earned instant renown for his then-remarkable accomplishment of balancing the statue's weight upon the hind legs of Jackson's rearing horse. The four cannon at the statue's base were captured by Jackson from the Spanish at Pensacola, Florida. The four other statues, one at each corner, pay tribute to foreign heroes who fought for America's freedom during the Revolutionary War. Those honored with statues are the Marquis de Lafayette; Comte Jean de Rochambeau, head of the French Expeditionary Force; General Frederick Von Steuben, a Prussian Baron who whipped the troops into form at Valley Forge; and Thadeus Kosciuszko, a Polish general who defended Saratoga and West Point.

Lafayette Park also features The Bernard Baruch Bench of Inspiration. This bench was well known to be the outdoor office of Bernard Baruch, social philanthropist and advisor to President Franklin Roosevelt. Baruch often spent hours in Lafayette Park, pondering the problems of the day from his favorite bench. A plaque memorializing Baruch and his bench, a gift from the Boy Scouts of America, is displayed on a short pedestal next to the bench. Another bench in the park is a historic footnote to the machinations of the CIA: According to the authors of *Washington Confidential* (a 1951 guidebook to the seamier side of the city), the Central Intelligence Agency maintained a bugged bench in Lafayette Park so they could listen in on the conversations of park-goers.

---

10 | Open to the Public | **Renwick Gallery (Pennsylvania Avenue at 17th Street, NW; 202/357–2700)**

John F. Kennedy saved this glorious building from the wrecking ball in 1963 by recommending it for inclusion in the Lafayette Square restoration he supported. The Renwick Gallery was designed by James Renwick, architect of the Smithsonian "Castle," to serve as the home of the **Corcoran Gallery.** Construction began in 1859, but before the building had gotten very far, the Civil War erupted, and Lincoln's Army Quartermaster Montgomery Meigs took over the unfinished gallery as his headquarters. After the war, the building was finally finished and the Corcoran collection installed. When the collection grew too big for its home, it moved to new quarters, also designed by Renwick, just around the corner on 17th Street. In the interim, the building served as the U.S. Court of Claims. Then in 1965, it was acquired by the Smithsonian Institution. In 1971 it re-opened as the Renwick Gallery, which exhibits American artwork and crafts.

See Also: Corcoran Gallery (Chapter 5)

---

11 | Open to the Public | **Riggs National Bank (1503 Pennsylvania Avenue, NW)**

Since its completion in 1901, the Riggs Bank building has housed one of the city's most prestigious financial institutions. Riggs has gained a symbolic status as the bank of official Washington, at least in part due to its happy proximity to the White House (most presidents maintained an account or two here) and the Treasury Department. As Riggs and Company, the pre-eminent private financial institution in Washington, D.C., the bank lent $500,000 to army contractors in the first year alone of the Civil War. So powerful was the firm that the Riggs president even kept a desk in the main Treasury Building until banking reform under the Wilson Administration forced the company to stay in its own building across the street.

Riggs Bank and its next-door neighbor, the American Security Bank, stand at a site that was previously occupied by two buildings designed by George Hadfield: the W.W. Corcoran Office Building, and the Branch Bank of the United States, built on this site in 1825. Riggs Bank made its earlier home at the Branch Bank Building, and it was here that President Lincoln deposited his pay in a Riggs checking account during the Civil War. Later tenants of this pair of buildings included the *Chicago Times-Herald* and the *Chicago Evening Post.* The Hadfield buildings were torn down in the early 1900s and replaced with their current currency tenants.

See Also: U.S. Treasury

Rodgers House. *See* **U.S. Court of Claims Complex**

12 Slidell House Site (1607 H Street, NW):

Slidell House was razed in 1922, but before its demise it counted among its famed occupants Senator John Slidell and Gideon Welles, Secretary of the Navy under Lincoln. The home's greatest notoriety, however, was gained from its reputation as a haunted house. It was said that the spirit of Marian "Clover" Adams, the wife of statesman and author Henry Adams, could be seen standing at the windows or wandering the hallways of the house for years after her (supposed) suicide in the house.

Henry Adams and his wife had moved into Slidell House upon their arrival in Washington in 1877, and they lived there until Marian's death six years later. Grief-stricken by her father's death, Marian Adams died alone in her sitting room, probably by her own hand, on a December day. Her husband was away on business at the time. Henry Adams was devastated by his wife's death, but refused to comment despite the whispers of Washington society that swirled around him. He commissioned the sculptor Augustus Saint-Gaudens to create a statuary marker for his wife's grave in Rock Creek Cemetery, insisting that no words or other commemoration mark the burial site. That statue, often called "Grief," is now recognized as one of Saint-Gaudens's most graceful and moving works.

See Also: Hay-Adams Hotel; Rock Creek Cemetery (Chapter 9)

13 Open to the Public St. John's Episcopal Church (1525 H Street, NW; 202/347–8766)

"Church of Presidents" is the historical nickname awarded St. John's Episcopal Church, and this title is aptly chosen. Built in 1816, St. John's is the second oldest building on Lafayette Square (the White House is the oldest), and has been the church of choice for many U.S. Presidents. Indeed, Pew 54 bears a plaque dubbing it the "President's Pew." Since the church opened, every U.S. President has visited at least once to offer his prayers to a higher authority. Windows in the north gallery honor presidents who were communicants in the church, including Madison, Monroe, Van Buren, Harrison, Taylor, and Tyler. And another window—facing the White House—was a gift to the church by then-President P. Chester Arthur, who met his wife, Ellen Lewis Preston, here when she was a choir member. (Arthur liked to look out at the window from the Executive Mansion and remember his courtship).

The church was designed by Benjamin Latrobe and renovated and enlarged by James Renwick in 1883. St. John's was Latrobe's own house of worship, and in building it he made himself so proud that he wrote to his son, Henry, shortly after finishing the project: "I have completed a church that has made many Washingtonians religious who had not been religious before."

The bronze bell in the tower, made in 1822 by Paul Revere's son, once served as more than a summons to services: In Washington's early years, it was the firefighters' bell, rung to call the area volunteer firefighters (some of the city's finest gentlemen) to action.

See Also: St. John's Parish House

14 St. John's Parish House (1525 H Street, NW)

The Parish House, purchased by St. John's in 1954, was built in 1824 by St. Clair Clarke. The house served as the British Embassy during the 1840s and, during this tenure became known as Ashburton House, in honor of Lord Alexander Baring Ashburton, who served as British Minister to the United States.

It was here that one of the longest-standing territorial disputes between the U.S. and Great Britain was finally resolved, with the signing of the Webster-Ashburton Treaty in 1842. Negotiated by Lord Ashburton and Daniel Webster (a Lafayette Square neighbor himself), the treaty at last formed an agreement about the northeastern boundary between Canada and the United States.

In 1849 the Ashburton House became the British Legation. A famed diplomat who resided there then is now known more for his literary skills than his diplomacy: Poet Robert Bulwer, Earl Lytton, aka Owen Meredith, author of the famed novel in verse, *Lucile*. Son of the novelist Edward Bulwer-Lytton, Bulwer served in Washington as private secretary to his uncle, the British Minister Sir Henry Bulwer.

See Also: St. John's Episcopal Church

Tayloe House. *See* U.S. Court of Claims Complex

15 Open to the Public **U.S. Chamber of Commerce (1615 H Street, NW; 202/659–6000)**

Here at 1611 H Street stood the mansion of Daniel Webster, which was given to him as a token of respect by his admirers. It was at this house, now lost to time, that Webster, then Secretary of State, and Henry Clay forged the deal for the 1850 Compromise that staved off the imminent rebellion of the Southern States. The Webster house was later home to William W. Corcoran, the art collector who fathered the art gallery by the same name. The house was demolished in 1922 to make way for the U.S. Chamber of Commerce building. Completed in 1926, the Chamber of Commerce building was the only McMillan Plan building to wedge its way into this neck of the woods.

See Also: U.S. Capitol (Chapter 3)

U.S. Court of Claims Complex (Madison Place)

This was once one of Washington's most historic blocks, before the structures here were swallowed by the block-long U.S. Court of Claims complex. Some important structures were lost (notably the **Rodgers House**), while some (notably the **Cutts- Madison House** and the **Tayloe House**) were saved due to President Kennedy's support of preservation efforts. Among the buildings that remain are:

16 **Cutts-Madison House** (1520 H Street, NW): Constructed in 1820, this was once the famed home and social salon of the ultimate Washington hostess, Dolley Madison. Until her death in 1849, the former first lady lived in this house built by her brother-in-law. The year before her death, Dolley Madison survived a fire at the house, even managing to save her husband's papers from the flames.

According to Richard M. Lee's *Mr. Lincoln's City*, the Cutts-Madison House was of particular importance during the Civil War, for it may have been the site of the headquarters of the Army of the Potomac. After President Lincoln gave General George McLellan command of the city defenses on September 2, 1861, the general settled into new offices, from which he controlled the hordes of military units pouring into Washington to battle the South, oversaw the forts ringing the city, and mapped out battle plans for the Army of the Potomac. McLellan was removed from his post in March of 1862, barely six months after taking the command. The definite site of the headquarters is disputed among historians, some of whom place the offices at a now-lost building that stood at the site of the U.S. Treasury Annex.

Later, the Cutts-Madison House served as the first headquarters of one of Washington's most famous clubs, the Cosmos Club (which soon sprawled next-door

The murder of Philip Barton Key II by Daniel Sickles. (*Our First Century*)

into the **Tayloe House** as well), and later still as an early headquarters of the National Aeronautics and Space Administration (NASA).
See Also: Tayloe House and **U.S. Treasury Annex;** Octagon House, Seven Houses Site (Chapter 5); Cosmos Club (Chapter 7)

17 **Rodgers House/Belasco Theater Site** (17 Madison Place): Built in 1831, the Rodgers House seemed a magnet for murder and mayhem during its sixty-odd years of existence. On February 27, 1859, one of the most scandalous murders of the nineteenth century took place on its steps. The victim was Philip Barton Key II (the son of *Star Spangled Banner* composer Francis Scott Key), the dashing District Attorney who was said to be carrying on with a certain Teresa Sickles during trysts at a nearby lovenest in Downtown, and even on the grounds of the Congressional Cemetery. The killer was her husband, Congressman Daniel Sickles. Having heard more than enough rumors to stoke his jealous rage, Sickles stalked Key through Lafayette Park. Upon turning to see his wife signalling to Key from the window of the Sickles house at **730 Jackson Place** (probably as a warning), Sickles confronted Key as he climbed the steps to the Washington Club (at the **Rodgers House**). Once upon his prey, Sickles fired three deadly shots into the lawyer's chest at close range.

Teresa Sickles became a social pariah because of her infidelity, and underwent the added scandal of divorce from her murderous husband. Daniel Sickles was tried and acquitted, the first person in a U.S. court to use the newfangled plea of temporary insanity. He went on to serve as a Major General in the Civil War, and gained later fame when he donated the leg he had lost in battle to the Army Medical Museum (now housed at the Walter Reed Medical Center).

Another near-slaying took place within the house itself on April 14, 1865, when resident William Seward, Lincoln's Secretary of State, was attacked in his bed by Lewis Payne, one of John Wilkes Booth's co-conspirators. As Booth was assassinating President Lincoln at Ford's Theater, Payne lied his way into the Rodgers House to carry out his portion of the murderous masterplan. Seward, bedridden from injuries sustained during a carriage accident, received three serious stab wounds (a neck brace he was wearing because of the accident helped save his life). Seward's son awakened during the commotion, and in coming to his father's aid, was also wounded. Legends have it that the young man was in fact roused by the ghost of Philip Barton Key II, which raised a ruckus to avert another heinous murder at the house.

But the Rodgers House was far more than a murderers' mecca—indeed, some of the great minds of the time resided there. The site for the house was purchased from Henry Clay (actually bartered, in exchange for a prized jackass) in 1829. The house was built for Commodore John Rodgers, a prominent naval officer, whose descendants also became prominent Washingtonians. His son, John Rodgers, Jr., served as Superintendent of the Naval Observatory, and indeed suggested placing the Observatory on Observatory Hill in the first place. His daughter, Louisa, married Major General Montgomery Meigs, Lincoln's quartermaster. Following Rodgers's death in 1838, the house was home to James K. Paulding, a writer and Naval Secretary under President Van Buren. The house was then converted into The Washington Club, an upscale boarding house and meeting place for powerful men. In 1845, the house served as a home-away-from-home for President James K. Polk and his family during the renovation of the White House. Later occupants included President Grant's Secretary of War, William Belknap, who was forced to resign during a major political scandal revolving around his selling of a public office, and James G. Blaine, the powerful and acerbic Republican standard bearer who never quite made it to the White House. In 1894, the house was destroyed and the Lafayette Square Opera House was built in its place.

The opera house opened in 1895 with a gala premier performance featuring Lillian Russell. It was re-named the Belasco Theater in 1905. The Belasco Theater survived until 1964, when it was torn down to make way for the U.S. Court of Claims. During its heyday (from about 1905 to 1930) the stage of the lavish Belasco Theater

The Bulfinch Gatehouses (Jack Looney)

was trod by such luminaries as Sarah Bernhardt, Al Jolson, Ethel Barrymore, Enrico Caruso, and Will Rogers. It was here at the Belasco that a little girl named Helen Hayes made her stage debut at the age of five, singing "Down by the Zuider Zee." Converted to a movie palace in 1935, then returned to a stage theater in 1937, the Belasco briefly regained its days of theatrical glory during two wars, and was used in between to store Treasury Department records. Purchased in 1940 by the federal government, the theater was refurbished in 1942 as the local Stage Door Canteen. Here American servicemen, as well as movie stars like Rita Hayworth, high-society locals like Washington doyenne Evalyn Walsh McLean, and jet setters like Duchess of Windsor Wallis Simpson came to mix and mingle. The theater was again called to duty during the Korean War, as the USO Lafayette Square Club. In 1964, the mansion-theater-turned-nightclub was destroyed by the federal government to make way for the completion of the U.S. Court of Claims.

See Also: Jackson Place Houses: 730 Jackson Place and **Lafayette Park;** Ford's Theater and Key's Lovenest Site (Chapter 2); Walter Reed Army Medical Center (Chapter 9); Congressional Cemetery (Chapter 11)

18 **Tayloe House** (21 Madison Place, NW): Referred to by President William McKinley as the "Little White House" when it was home to his principal advisor, Mark Hannah, the house was once considered a center for socializing second only to that big white house at the end of the park. Tayloe House was built in 1828 by Benjamin Ogle Tayloe, who also built the Octagon House. It later served as an annex for the Cosmos Club, which was housed next door at the **Cutts-Madison House.**

See Also: Cutts-Madison House

PLACES: South of Pennsylvania Avenue

19 | Open to the Public | **The Ellipse (Park south of the White House, bordered by 17th Street and Constitution Avenue, and 15th Street)**

Truly the president's extended backyard, the Ellipse has long served as a ceremonial stage setting for such symbolic elements as the National Christmas Tree. Known during the nineteenth century as the White Lot (probably because it was enclosed by a white fence), the Ellipse was often used to bivouac various military units as they passed through Washington during the Civil War. It continued to make history as one of the country's earliest baseball parks, for the newfangled game was played on diamonds here during the Civil War.

Today, these one-time play and parade grounds are frequently home to a range of non-government-sponsored political activities, including protests and mock memorials that are often related to rallies on the Mall.

The Ellipse has a variety of special memorials and unique structures. The Bulfinch Gatehouses (at the southwest and southeast corners of the park) are often mistakenly thought to be lock keepers' houses. But these gatehouses originally served a totally different function: Architect Charles Bulfinch placed them on the grounds of the Capitol, where they did duty as guard-houses until being put out to pasture at the Ellipse. The high-water marks on the gatehouses show just how far up the Potomac used to come at this point!

Other Ellipse monuments include the little-known Boy Scout Memorial (on the eastern fringes of the Ellipse), and, nearby, the equally overlooked Settlers Memorial, a simple little monolith memorializing the eighteen original landowners of the city. The Zero Milestone, in the section nearest the White House, designates the point from which city planners were supposed to start all measurements, so as to keep the White House ever at the center of the city. The Ellipse is also adorned with two lesser-known military monuments: The First Division Monument

The State, War, and Navy Building, circa 1886. (*Picturesque Washington*)

(between E Street and State Place), also known as "Victory," was created by Daniel Chester French to honor the men of the First Armored Division of the U.S. Army who fought and died during World War I. The Second Division Monument (in the southwest section of Ellipse, facing Constitution Avenue) was originally erected in 1936, and, with additional elements installed after World War II, now honors those who fought in both World Wars with the Second Division.

See Also: The White House; Capitol Grounds (Chapter 3); Lock Keepers House (Chapter 4)

20 Old Executive Office Building (17th Street and Pennsylvania Avenue, NW)

Originally the State, War and Navy Building, the Old Executive Office Building (OEOB) was constructed on the site of the previous Navy and War Department Buildings. It was built over a period of seventeen years, beginning in 1871, and has since been the scene of some of Washington's most important (and even covert) diplomatic events.

Today the OEOB is considered a landmark of amusingly outrageous ornamentation and has been listed on the National Park Service's National Register of Historic Places since the 1960s. But in its early days, it was thought to be a hideous aberration. Mark Twain once called it "The ugliest building in America," a sentiment later echoed by Harry S Truman, who decried it as "The greatest monstrosity in America." And monster it may have been, for it eventually killed its original architect, Alfred Bult Mullett. After trying unsuccessfully to sue the government for nearly $160,000 due him for his work, Mullett committed suicide in 1890. This final insult (coupled with the public disdain for the building) simply proved too much for Mullett, who had resigned from his post as chief architect in 1874 after the government refused to allow him to pay contractors.

Mullett, who had also been one of the Treasury Building architects, had been selected for this project by Grant's Secretary of State, Hamilton Fish. Like Mullett, Fish was starry-eyed over France's palatial architecture of the Second Empire period. The resulting building, which ended up costing some $10 million dollars, was the country's largest office building when it was finally completed in January of 1888.

Even before the building was complete, the Departments of State, War, and Navy took up occupancy. Indeed, one main reason for the endless construction was a battle for grandeur among the occupants. Hamilton Fish, whose State Department moved in in 1875, crowed about his opulent Diplomatic Reception Room, which incited the Navy Department (taking up occupancy in 1879), to build the marble and onyx Library Reception Room. Not to be outdone, the War Department (which moved in in 1888), had the walls of the Secretary of War's office covered with a tooled-leather-like decorative material. And all around the outside of the building, cannons and guns captured in various wars were planted as deadly decorations. (The presence of President Taft's pet cow, Pauline, who grazed on the south lawn of the OEOB between 1909 and 1913, must have had a softening effect on this otherwise belligerent facade.)

Perhaps such opulence was justified. After all, much of America's diplomatic business was conducted in the elegant rooms of the OEOB. In 1898, the Spanish Ambassador was given his walking papers (and thus a declaration of war) here by Secretary of State John Hay; the peace treaty for the same war was signed here two months later. The Treaty of Versailles, which ended World War I, was also signed at the OEOB in 1919, and the United Nation's Declaration was signed here as well in 1942. In all, more than a thousand treaties of war, peace, and economic or political alliance were signed at the Department of State's offices in the OEOB (most in the elegant Indian Treaty Room).

Somewhat less diplomatic was the event that led President Franklin Roosevelt to demand that all swinging doors be removed from the premises: A bustling clerk accidentally smacked visiting British Prime Minister Winston Churchill with the flipside of one of the swinging doors. Churchill landed on his Great British behind, and Roosevelt ordered a permanent end to the open-and-close door policy at the OEOB.

In 1943, the Army, Navy, and Air Force were combined as the Department of Defense and were moved to the newly constructed Pentagon. In 1947, the State Department vacated the premises for its new headquarters in Foggy Bottom. The outdoor arsenal that had bristled around the building for so long was already gone by then, ordered removed in 1943 by Secretary of War Henry Stimson. (Some duplicate pieces were melted down for the war effort.) Today, only a pair of cannon taken during the Spanish-American War decorate the front (Pennsylvania Avenue) entrance to the building.

Newer tenants of the OEOB have included every vice president since Lyndon Johnson, the Office of Management and Budget, and the Council of Economic Advisors. In 1986 the building became renowned for another tenant—the National Security Council (NSC), whose basement headquarters were the site of much of the Iran-Contra machinations undertaken by Lt. Col. Oliver North and his cohorts. It was here, in North's NSC office (Room 392, to be exact), that the square-jawed Marine led covert efforts to raise funds for the Nicaraguan Contras. When investigators began closing in on North's operations, he and his secretary, the photogenic Fawn Hall, went on a shredding binge to destroy classified—and damning —documents about their operations. What they couldn't shred, North and Hall smuggled out of the building through the 17th Street exits. (Hall titillated the media and spectators at the Congressional hearings when she revealed she had concealed classified documents in her bra and boots to smuggle them out of the building.) In 1989, North was convicted on three counts: destroying documents, obstructing Congress, and illegally accepting a gratuity—a home security gate). His sentence was later overturned, however, by a federal judge who declared North had been unfairly tried based on his testimony before the Senate investigative committee. In exchange for her testimony, Fawn Hall was not indicted.

See Also: Hay-Adams Hotel and **"White House Pets"**; State Department Building (Chapter 5)

21 U.S. Treasury Annex (Pennsylvania Avenue at Madison Place, NW)

This was once the site of the Freedman's Savings Bank, erected here in 1869 as the main headquarters of a banking system set up for blacks during the Civil War. The last president of the bank, abolitionist leader Frederick Douglass, wrote of the institution in his autobiography, ". . . when I came to Washington and saw [the building's] magnificent brown stone front, its towering height, its perfect appointments and the fine display it made in the transaction of business, I felt like the Queen of Sheba when she saw the riches of Solomon. . . ."

Unfortunately, the bank's grandeur seemed to promise more stability than it could eventually deliver. Despite Douglass's best efforts, the continuing economic chaos caused by the Depression of 1873 led the institution to go belly up in 1874. The bank's depositors, thousands of blacks who had been working to create a new life for themselves, lost all of their savings.

Purchased by the federal government in 1882, the building was employed as office space before being razed in 1899 to make way for the Treasury Department Annex. A plaque at the Madison Place entrance describes the site's importance as a black history landmark.

Some sources also identify this as having been the location of the Army of the Potomac Headquarters, where General George McLellan plotted the city's defenses and mapped out his rarely enacted strategies for enemy battles. Other sources place headquarters at the Cutts-Madison House.

See Also: Frederick Douglass Home (Chapter 3); Cedar Hill (Chapter 11)

22 U.S. Treasury Building (1500 Pennsylvania Avenue, NW)

Washington was far from surprised when the British burned the first Treasury Building in 1814. After all, the enemy also razed the Capitol, the White House, and most of the other official buildings in the city.

But some in Washington began to wonder whether the American economic system was cursed after the second Treasury Building burned to the ground in 1833. (Even President John Quincy Adams had joined the water-bucket brigade trying to save the building.) Afterwards, just *deciding* where to put the new Treasury Building took more than a year.

U.S. horse barracks on Treasury Building grounds, as sketched for _Harper's Weekly._

Finally, fed up with haggling among his own staff and on Capitol Hill, President Andrew Jackson stormed out of the White House and slammed his walking cane into the spot where he declared that construction of the new Treasury Building would begin immediately. Although it was approximately in the same location as the old Treasury Building, the plans called for a much more massive structure than the previous models. This added bulk effectively destroyed a key element of city planner Pierre L'Enfant's vision: the diagonal line of Pennsylvania Avenue, originally designed as a straight visual link between the White House and the Capitol.

Even with the hurdle of site-selection so gracefully overcome, it took four architects and more than three decades before the building was completed. Robert Mills, one of the architects of the Capitol, designed the east wing of the elegant Greek Revival building (completed in

A Different Kind of War Hero

Over the years, officers of the Treasury have had to deal with many an economic crisis—but never one as hilarious or horrifying as the one in which the Register of the Treasury nearly signed his life away to help save the Union. The incident, which occurred while the South had the upper hand in the conflict, involved a pair of war ships the Confederates had ordered from a British naval yard. The Union government got wind of the scheme, which would have given the Confederacy the naval muscle it lacked—a major weakness that the Union Army had been exploiting. In desperation, American envoys begged the British government not to allow the war ships to leave the country. The British were no friends to the Union, but a private London financier agreed to put up the one million pounds required to hold the ships in their port—if the Americans could send $10 million in American treasury bills out on the next steamer to England.

The lively book *Thirty Years in Washington,* edited by Mrs. John R. Logan and published in 1901, picks up the curious tale from here: "At 11 o'clock that Friday night the Register of the Treasury was called to the White House, where he found Lincoln, Seward and Chase in consultation. Great danger threatened the Union, they said, if these vessels should leave England, and they wanted to know if $10,000 [in bonds] of $1,000 each could be signed and sent on next Monday's [New York] steamer. The Register thought it could not be done unless he should sign as long as he possibly could and then resign so that the President could appoint another Register to continue the task without a break.

"But this plan might make the bonds irregular and was considered only as a last resort, so the Register set to work signing the bonds. He signed for seven hours steadily, a messenger taking each new bond as quickly as it was signed and leaving a new bond under the Register's pen. Saturday morning his hands began to inflame, acute pains set in, but still the work went on, always the same mechanical repetition of the same movements of hand and arm in writing his own name. A physician was constantly at hand; prepared foods were given and stimulants were administered at intervals; but weakness crept apace, and the task was proving too much for human endurance.

"At four o'clock on Sunday morning the physician informed the Register that if he signed any more bonds it would endanger his life; but he kept on, signing more and more slowly and laboriously, he could not remain in one position for any length of time, and the bonds were carried from table to table to break up the dreadful monotony. His fingers and hand were drawn and twisted. Finally, at noon on Sunday the last bond was signed, the last hundred taking longer than the first thousand. They were hurried to New York and were placed on the steamer, arriving in London in due time. The Register collapsed completely after the task was finished, and it was months before he recovered from the strain."

1842). The other three wings were designed by other architects from 1855 to 1869, with a very long pause for the Civil War. Not only was construction stopped on the Treasury Building during the Civil War, but the site was selected as an emergency fortress should the rebels take

Washington. The incomplete interiors were fortified with beams, manned with soldiers, and supplied for a siege, should such an event occur. (It never did.) At the same time, the grounds of the building were transformed into stables and a drilling ground for the U.S. Cavalry.

Until after the Civil War, the Treasury Building shared its site with the stolid little brick State Department Building, which had been constructed at the site of the original Treasury Building (burned by the British). This building held the offices of Secretary of State William Seward, and President Lincoln stopped by frequently to meet with his friend and cabinet member. Once the construction of the Treasury Building re-commenced, the old State Department Building was destroyed to make way for the Treasury's north wing. In 1875, the State Department hopped halfway up the block to the ornate State, War and Navy Building (now the **Old Executive Office Building**), which was still under construction at the time.

Another building that once shared the site was the temporary foundry of Clark Mills. Here the sculptor cast his masterpiece bronze equestrian statue of Andrew Jackson, which was unveiled in 1853 and still graces Lafayette Park.

The Treasury Department was an innovator in a number of seemingly disparate areas. It was the birthplace of the U.S. Secret Service, which was created on July 5, 1865 to foil counterfeiters who were making money faster than the government could prove it was fake. The building once had a wonderful exhibit on the art of the counterfeiter, but had to remove it for fear it would provide inspiration to future fake money-makers. A few remnants are still displayed at the Bureau of Engraving and Printing.

It was also the birthplace of the G-girl—for the Treasury Department was the government's first large-scale employer of young women (mainly as clerks and secretaries). This then-radical move was necessitated by the extraordinary growth in government work during the Civil War, at a time when all able-bodied men were fighting. On a less-pleasant note, recently uncovered letters discovered by historian James Goode indicate that, during Reconstruction and later, the Treasury Department may have been a leader in what is now referred to as sexual harassment. The letters, written by Architect of the Capitol Thomas Walter to his wife, include the revelation that about twenty young women were prepared to testify before Congress that their boss at the Treasury, S.M. Clarke, had required sexual favors in exchange for their obtaining or keeping their jobs. "Col. Provost informs me that between 40 and 50 of the women employed in Mr. Clarke's department are about to increase the population . . . it is a perfect Sodom," Walter wrote to his wife on May 6, 1864.

The Treasury Building has also served as the site for grand inaugural events, and even as a temporary Oval Office. In April of 1865, while the nation mourned the death of President Lincoln, the new president, Andrew Johnson, turned the reception rooms of the Treasury Secretary into his temporary office to give Mrs. Lincoln a chance to pull herself together before the new executive staff descended on the White House. From this short-term oval office, Johnson planned Lincoln's funeral and set in motion the plans for the post-war era.

The rooms used by Johnson were restored in 1991 as part of a large-scale restoration of historic Treasury rooms that began in 1985. Another recently restored room is the elegant Cash Room, where President Grant's first Inaugural Gala was held in 1869.

Tunnels run beneath the Treasury from the **White House** and to the **Treasury Annex** across the street, enabling the president to come and go with greater secrecy. Another underground installation for the president was constructed in the early 1940s, when the atomic bomb was first developed: An underground vault was specially outfitted to serve as a bomb shelter for President Franklin Roosevelt in case of an atomic attack on the city.

See Also: Old Executive Office Building and **U.S. Treasury Annex;** Clark Mills Home and Foundry Site (Chapter 10); Bureau of Printing and Engraving (Chapter 12)

The White House Telegraph Room during the Spanish-American War. (Library of Congress)

㉓ Open to the Public | **The White House (1600 Pennsylvania Avenue, NW; 202/456–7041)**

What other residence in America could have letterhead that simply states its name and its city, without so much as a street number, zip code, or even state abbreviation? Only the White House, the most famous house in America, the oldest federal building in Washington, and the most prevalent symbol of the presidency. All a television reporter has to do is stand in front of the North or South Portico, and viewers from Argentina to Zimbabwe can identify the site as: The White House, Washington.

Yet, this famed presidential palace startles tourists daily with its accessibility. Turning west onto Pennsylvania Avenue at 15th Street and New York Avenue, it is suddenly there. No fanfare, no beating of drums (with the exception of the occasional cacophony from protestors staked out at Lafayette Park). Just a pleasant, porticoed mansion in the middle of the city, surrounded by office buildings and monuments. One needs a different vantage point—looking down 16th Street from Meridian Hill, or up 17th Street from the Tidal Basin—to fully appreciate the simple and evocative beauty of the executive mansion.

The first visual impression that most visitors gain of the White House is an anachronistic revelation out of place and time with the modern reality of the high-security, high-technology White House. But the modern mansion was indeed once a simpler home where children played in the halls and livestock grazed on the lawn. In the nineteenth century, the White House was

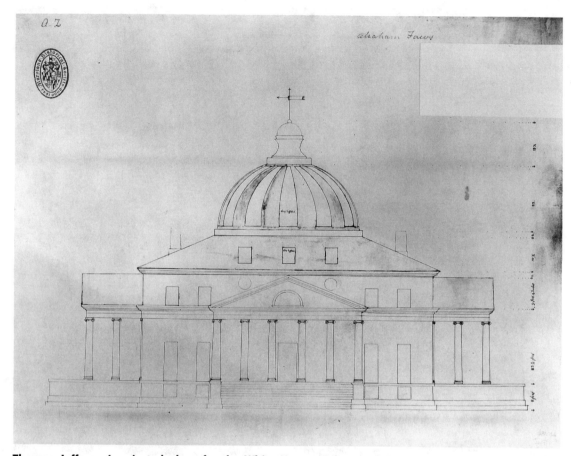

Thomas Jefferson's rejected plans for the White House. (Library of Congress)

just another stop on the social circuit; ladies and gentlemen making the rounds would stop by and leave their cards with the butler to inform the occupants they had dropped in for a social calls. Likewise, the president and his wife embarked almost daily on similar social rounds, often strolling together from home to home to return a call paid to them the previous day.

The accessibility of the presidency of the past is revealed in this matter-of-fact entry that appeared in the diary of Washington wife Elizabeth Lomax. Dated Tuesday, June 19, 1855, the entry relates how Lomax obtained a letter from President Franklin Pierce in answer to her request. The entry reads: "[A] Pleasant day. . . . I wrote a note to the President, asking him to appoint a time when I could see him. He replied that he could see me about three o'clock . . . I donned my best bonnet, and went to the Executive Mansion at the appointed time. I was received with great courtesy . . . The President listened with interest to my request, then gave me a strong letter to Secretary McClellan, which I took at once to his residence on "E" Street."

Even up through the administration of Franklin Roosevelt, strangers could bravely drop off their cards at the White House and find themselves invited to a state dinner within the month. The attempt on the life of President Truman in 1950, during which would-be assassins stormed the temporary presidential homestead of **Blair House,** undoubtedly contributed to a change in policy. Theaters and train stations were no longer the only hunting grounds for assassins.

Naturally, the tenor of life in the White House has, in large part, been a reflection of the inhabitants of the executive mansion. The boisterous White House family life of Theodore Roosevelt's brood (with their menagerie of pets and affection for indoor roller skating) was a

A White House Sampler

Herein lie some tasty tidbits about the life and times of the White House, from weddings to wakes and gossip to ghosts:

The Pot-Luck Mansion: How Presidents Have Changed the White House

President John Adams may have been the first president to decorate the White House to his own liking, but he certainly wasn't the last. In fact, to this day, the White House is an ongoing collaboration between its tenants and history, with modern technology and taste constantly being introduced by the rotating residents. Thomas Jefferson, who lost the competition to design the house in the first place, later got his chance to alter the architecture after all. During his presidency, he and Benjamin Latrobe designed and installed the terraces on the east and west sides of the house.

As the nineteenth century progressed and the house gained a roster of former inhabitants, it slowly gained other amenities as well, including a billiard table and landscaped gardens (courtesy of John Quincy Adams), chandeliers and French furnishings (tastefully imported by James Monroe), running water (piped in thanks to Andrew Jackson), gas lighting (the bright idea of James Polk), and central heating (Franklin Pierce's warmest legacy). Presidents in the twentieth century contributed such additional niceties as the house's first bathroom and telephone (although not in the same location), which were installed at the behest of Rutherford B. Hayes. The house got a major lift when its first elevator was put into place, thanks to James Garfield, while Benjamin Harrison was responsible for the first electric lights in the building.

Sometimes a president's physical problems were also manifested in the White House additions—notable examples include Franklin Roosevelt's swimming pool (which he needed for therapeutic exercise), William Howard Taft's oversized bathtubs (for his oversized body), and John F. Kennedy's rocking chair (a necessity for his agonizing back pain). Not all presidential additions were well-received by the locals, however. The sitting porch on the second-story of the south portico, a homey midwestern touch added by Harry S Truman, raised the hackles of quite a few Washingtonians when it first appeared on the house's facade. But the city learned to take such country manorisms in its stride, for when George Bush installed his backyard horseshoe pit, nary an eyebrow was arched.

Joyous Occasions

Rutherford B. Hayes was the only president sworn in at the White House, in a surprise ceremony in the Red Room following a dinner party given in his honor by outgoing President U.S. Grant on March 3, 1877. The White House has, however, seen quite a few marriages, although Grover Cleveland was the only *president* married at the White House. Snagged by pretty young socialite Frances Folsom, the president was married on June 2, 1886 in the famed Blue Room.

The house has more frequently been the nuptial scene for presidential offspring. In the nineteenth century, the mansion's East Room was the site for the marriage of U.S.

(Continued)

Grant's daughter, Nellie, while twentieth-century brides included Theodore Roosevelt's impetuous oldest daughter, Alice; Woodrow Wilson's daughter, Jessie Wilson; and Lyndon Johnson's daughters, Lucie Baines and Lynda Byrd. (Lucie Baines Johnson was married in 1966 to Patrick Nugent, and Lynda Byrd Johnson married Virginia's Charles Robb, now a Senator, in 1967). Only four years passed before the next marriage took place at the house, the much-publicized Rose Garden wedding of Tricia Nixon to Edward Finch Cox in June of 1971.

Children at the White House

The White House has witnessed the births of eleven babies during its two hundred years, although most of the children who gained fame for their White House escapades were imported. The most famous kids to run wild at the White House were the rough-riding brood of Theodore Roosevelt. Visitors to the Roosevelt White House came away with tales of ponies in the hallways and roller skating in the East Room. Of only children, Amy Carter was certainly a headliner, setting tongues wagging with such precocious habits as reading at the table during state dinners.

One day a year (the Monday after Easter Sunday), the White House grounds are literally overrun with children, most if not all of whom are not presidential offspring. The annual White House Easter Egg Roll has been a tradition since the days of "Lemonade Lucy" Hayes. The opening of the grounds to young egg-rollers began after a horde of distraught children, denied their usual access to the Capitol grounds for the annual (if unofficial) event, descended on the White House in 1887. President Hayes and his wife allowed the children to use the White House grounds for their hunt. Ever since then, with the exception of the period between 1941–53, the eggs have rolled right along the lawns of the Executive Mansion. Today, the event has become a major media blitz, complete with cartoon characters roaming the lawns and sports stars autographing eggs for fans young and old. (One caveat: All visiting adults must be accompanied to the event by a child.)

Death—and Afterlife?—at the White House

Seven presidents have died while in office and subsequently lain in state in the East Room. But only two have actually died in the White House itself: William Henry Harrison, who succumbed in 1841 to pneumonia he acquired during his long-winded inaugural address; and Zachary Taylor, who died in 1850 of a severe gastro-intestinal disruption, caused by the apparently lethal combination of ice milk and cherries, consumed at an Independence Day celebration. In 1892, Caroline Harrison, wife of Benjamin Harrison, became the first First Lady to die at the White House; her funeral was held in the East Room.

Several children have also died while occupants of the house, including little Willie Lincoln, whose death from a cold and fever at the age of twelve devastated his father, Abraham Lincoln. And Calvin Coolidge's namesake died at the age of sixteen, after stubbing his toe while playing tennis with his brother on the White House courts. A streptococcal infection was diagnosed, but no treatment could be found to save the boy.

With such a morbid history, it is no wonder that the house is said to be haunted. The most famous ghost in the White House is that of Abraham Lincoln, who (according to sources as varied as Eleanor Roosevelt and Harry S Truman) has been seen numerous times in the Lincoln Bedroom. (The Lincoln Bedroom was actually Lincoln's study in his lifetime, and the room in which he signed the Emancipation Proclamation). Even presidential dogs are said to have been spooked by the ghost. Lincoln would be a good candidate for the afterlife in any case, as he reportedly had a premonition of his own murder several days before the event. While posing for the young sculptress Vinnie Ream (for a bust commissioned for the Rotunda), the president told his friends of a dream he had had the night before, in which he walked into the East Room of the White House to find a casket there, surrounded by mourners. When he inquired who had died, he was told that it was the president.

Lincoln's son, Willie, has also been identified as a resident ghost, as have Abigail Adams, Dolley Madison, and a mixed slate of former servants and other White House workers.

White House Pets

While the human occupants of the Executive Mansion have always commanded the lion's share of media attention, four-legged tenants have often made headlines as well. White House dogs have led the pack of pets. It seems every American knew FDR's sweet little terrier, Fala, on sight, and most knew long before Nixon made it into the White House that they wouldn't have his pup, Checkers, to kick around anymore once he was in office. An in-town (and tongue-in-cheek) battle over beauties of the beast ensued when the *Washingtonian* magazine labeled

Sheep grazing on the White House lawn around 1880.
(Library of Congress)

the Bushes' beloved spaniel, Millie, the "ugliest dog." But Millie had the last word (or bark) when her book about a dog's life in the White House, *Millie's Book,* hit the best-seller list. The book was ghost-written by Millie's mistress, Barbara Bush, who had previously collaborated with another (then-vice-presidential) pooch on a similarly dog-eared volume.

Other pets to grace the White House have included Caroline Kennedy's pony, Macaroni, who, although usually boarded in Virginia, made frequent White House lawn appearances. Theodore Roosevelt's children were notorious pet-lovers, and legend has it that at least once they snuck a favorite pony into the White House via an elevator. Sheep were often set to graze on the White House lawn in the nineteenth century, as a way to keep the lawns groomed. Another barnyard buddie, a dairy cow named Pauline, was a favorite of William Howard Taft, who had her graze next door on the south lawn of the Army, War and State Building (now the Old Executive Office Building.)

(Continued)

Not all presidents were as open about their animal passions: While it was known that Andrew Jackson kept racehorses in the White House stables, the president kept secret the fact that he entered them in local heats under the name of an employee.

White House Whispers

As long as there has been a president, the walls of the Executive Mansion have had ears to set tongues wagging. Thomas Jefferson, who used the Green Room as his formal dining room, even instituted a special serving device he had invented himself, which rotated food to the various guests, so as to keep snooping servants from hearing the dinner table conversation.

As the presidency has matured, a formula for White House gossip seems to have emerged that goes as follows: The glamour factor (highest with the Kennedys and the Reagans) generates the juiciest rumors about the private lives of presidential families, while the powergrip factor (high with Andrew Johnson, Nixon, and Taft) seems to generate the most damning in-house political gossip. Likewise, the more respected a president, whatever his foibles (Abraham Lincoln and Franklin Roosevelt fit the mold), the less willing society—and history—is to make much of either private or political follies. On the other hand, if a president gains little public respect while in office (the fate of Jimmy Carter and Gerald Ford), every wrong move he and his family make is subject to ridicule.

The alleged legions of ladies (including Marilyn Monroe), who were supposedly snuck in for afternoon romps with President Kennedy, provoked whispers galore, although it took years before tongues had loosened up enough to wag about it openly. Franklin Roosevelt, too, generated much discussion, yet sparse condemnation, for his long-term romance with former secretary Lucy Mercer (in whose presence he died). Grover Cleveland, the only president to move into the White House while still a bachelor, was the talk of the town for his flirtations before marrying Frances Folsom. Warren G. Harding reputedly fathered a child out of wedlock with paramour Nan Briton (the conception was said to have occurred in his Senate office), a rumor that haunted him throughout his presidency.

Nor are first ladies immune to such gossip. Edith Bolling Galt Wilson, whom President Wilson married soon after the death of his first wife, was much whispered about before her marriage to the president, for their romance had supposedly been born before the first Mrs. Wilson's death. The second Mrs. Wilson continued to generate rumors when she served as de facto President following her husband's debilitating stroke on October 3, 1919. Mary Todd Lincoln's frail mental health, and her frequent, volatile arguments with her husband, were the subject of much discussion, although society took pity on her after Lincoln's assassination and her subsequent institutionalization. Some first ladies even generated gossip by their excessive morality—Lucy Hayes got the nickname "Lemonade Lucy" by banning all alcohol at the White House. President and Mrs. Polk invoked quiet disdain among Washington's social set with their ban on alcohol and refusal to allow dancing at the White House. Even at his own inaugural ball, Polk demanded that the dancing cease when he arrived with his wife.

Perhaps the most gossiped-about first lady in history was Nancy Reagan, whose clashes with everyone from White House staffers to Raisa Gorbachev were legendary, and whose taste for designer clothes and expensive china earned her the label of

America's Marie Antoinette. The rumors reached a feverish pitch after the Reagans left the White House, when Kitty Kelley's unauthorized biography of Nancy Reagan alleged that the first lady had carried on with singer Frank Sinatra during long White House "lunches."

Mrs. Reagan's successor, Barbara Bush, successfully quashed early rumors about her sharp tongue by projecting a kinder, gentler image when she moved into the White House. During the 1988 presidential campaign, Mrs. Bush made headlines with her poetic notation that a term rhyming with "witch" described vice-presidential candidate Geraldine Ferarro. Barbara Bush's public outspokenness has since been softened to focus on issues such as literacy.

sharp contrast to the solemn lifestyle of President Polk, who banished such frivolities as alcohol and dancing from White House functions. Yet, even as society in general has relaxed its formal rules of etiquette, the image of the White House has grown exponentially more elegant and subdued in the second half of the twentieth century. Imagine sheep grazing on the grounds of the White House. A preposterous thought today, yet a common sight during the First World War, when President Wilson proudly displayed his home's sheepish lawn maintenance technicians, whose low-cost, non-mechanical methods were praised as aiding the war effort.

Indeed, as the legend of the White House grows ever older, it has taken on a life and history of its own. The figures of history, powerful or pathetic, who have passed through its doorway are but a cast list of players on this stage. Nixon kneeling in prayer the night before his resignation . . . Kennedy standing at the window during the Cuban Missile Crisis . . . Lincoln in his study, signing the Emancipation Proclamation . . . Roosevelt beside the fireplace to address the nation . . . All are scenes from an ongoing production that constantly encompasses new audiences, new actors, new world orders. Only the theater stands unchanged.

The White House was only adopted as the site's official name during the administration of Theodore Roosevelt, although it had carried the moniker "White House" since early in its existence. Some legends say it gained the name following the British attack in 1814, when the house was white-washed to brighten up the smoke-damaged masonry. But other accounts seem to point to the house's color as a reference point almost from the time it was built, for its creamy limestone was a pale contrast to the red brick of the nearby edifices.

And what a time that was: The President's House (as it was first called) was the first official building of official Washington, constructed before the Capitol, before the monuments—before the city itself was much more than woodland, fields, and rutted roads. George Washington chose the site for the President's House, for he loved the view offered by the downhill swoop to the Potomac. Originally the house was to be a regal estate with sweeps of landscaped lawns and gardens to the north and south. Thomas Jefferson vetoed the northern lawn, however, and that real estate was developed into **Lafayette Park** instead. The Ellipse was retained in the final plans, and still serves as the closest thing to an executive parkland.

A competition was held to find the perfect design for the new executive mansion, and among the entries received (and rejected!) was a simple Roman (palladian) design submitted by none other than Thomas Jefferson. Perhaps had Jefferson signed his own name rather than the pseudonymous initials A.Z. to his entry, his design might have won the competition. But Jefferson wanted to see whether his design could win on its own merits, not on the basis of his political clout. The man who won the competition (and the $500 prize money) was James

Hoban, a little-known, self-taught craftsman from Ireland, who had based his winning design on the simple lines of a crisp, classical Irish manor near Dublin.

Despite having chosen its location, George Washington never got the chance to sleep—much less live—at the White House. But all other presidents, from John Adams to George Bush, have lived at the executive residence. Yet, most early presidential families would undoubtedly have preferred to continue living in the comforts of their own homes. During the first twenty years or so, the White House was a chilly and barren mansion, and it was once considered nearly a penance for any man foolish enough to want to lead the country. The first First Couple to live in the White House—John and Abigail Adams—probably had the toughest tenure of any White House occupants. They officially took up residence at the President's House on November 1, 1800, and, despite the blessing Abigail reportedly gave to the house as she entered, she soon found herself cursed with a dank, drafty building devoid of furnishings and far from the comforts of her home in Boston. Perhaps to assuage his wife's discomfort, her husband had bell-pulls for servants installed, along with some decent furniture that made the house a livable place. But Abigail never quite developed the sense of respect for the mansion that its later residents felt: Legend has it that she would hang the family's wash out to dry in the East Room.

The White House has certainly seen some alterations, and not all have been pleasant. When the British burned the mansion in 1814, it caused what was perhaps the most dramatic forced re-modelling. The interior was completely gutted and the mansion was not reopened until 1818. But a close second goes to the near-riots of Andrew Jackson's inaugural celebrations, in which the general public literally trashed the place. And undoubtedly the Union troops who were bivouacked in the East Ballroom during the Civil War left their mark on the mansion as well.

As early as 1926, President Calvin Coolidge was warned that the roof would cave in unless major renovations were undertaken to shore up the sagging structure. But the president ignored the engineers' warning, and the rotting infrastructure was overlooked until a piano partially fell through a floor in the mansion. In 1950 a drastic overhaul saved the White House from virtual collapse. The renovation gutted most of the interior, leaving only the famous masonry and a few small sections. President Truman and his family moved across Pennsylvania Avenue to **Blair House** for the duration of the renovation. When the White House was again livable, the alterations were barely visible from the outside; but inside, it was a whole new house. Today, preservationists shake their heads in shock when they discuss how most of the historical interior pieces, from the wallpaper to the mantlepieces, were dumped in a landfill or given away as souvenirs. Little of the original interior was restored to the renovated house. The best that later curators could do was approximate the look of the original house and recreate the decor with modern reproductions.

Up until the early 1960s, quite a few White House furnishings came (and quite a few more went) with the changing of administrations. But in 1961, Jacqueline Kennedy, dismayed at the state of the hodge-podge palace, set about making the White House into a true showplace. She sent out a world-wide request for original furnishings from the house, and banished the hideous leftovers of past administrations. To show off her changes, Mrs. Kennedy led the nation on the first-ever televised tour of the White House. To preserve the historical integrity and decor that the Kennedys had at last established at the house, Congress passed an act declaring all furnishings and decorations to be property of the White House, and not subject to the whims of the world leader. Today if the president or someone in his household want to dispose of any White House item, it must be donated to the Smithsonian Institution.

See Also: Lafayette Park, The Ellipse, and **Blair House Complex;** U.S. Capitol (Chapter 3); "The Burning of Washington" (Chapter 10)

Chapter 2

DOWNTOWN

The once (and, developers hope, future) center of the urban life of Washington, this section of the city sprawls just east of the White House, just northwest of the Capitol. When the city first rose from muddy fields and thick woodlands, the location of this area made it the ideal spot for the boarding houses, hotels, and taverns that were the social center of most working cities. And not surprisingly, such typical recreational facilities as bawdy houses and faro clubs arose in the vicinity. When a society is built, often the first level of the foundation is its lowest common denominator, and this was certainly true of Washington's downtown area, which was soon home to Congressmen and pick-pockets alike.

By the mid-nineteenth century, however, Downtown Washington had evolved into the city's main public area, with fine milliners and tailors, shoemakers and dressmakers, photographic studios and tobacconists lining the dusty avenues. Seventh Street was Washington's Park Avenue, a boulevard for strolling and being strolled about (if one was still of a pram-able age), for dressing up and stepping out for lunch with the ladies or the lawyers. The dining rooms of hotels like the **Willard** drew a ready-made clientele of high-society shoppers for high tea, and political powerbrokers for dinner and cigars. The hotel lobbies drew another sort of society—a gathering of hangers-on, office-hunters, and favor-seekers.

Its proximity to the powers that ran the country also made Downtown a perfect location for the pavement-pounding press. So many news bureaus and papers set up shop in the downtown quadrant (running roughly from Pennsylvania Avenue north along 14th Street, then east on H and south again at 11th Street) that the area gained the nickname "Newspaper Row." The area remains the central quarter for the city's print media, with most news bureaus maintaining offices in or near the **National Press Building** at 14th and F Streets.

The wedge of real estate now known as Federal Triangle was, originally, a muddy field often flooded by the perpetually overflowing Tiber Creek. Then in 1816, the flooding was finally controlled by the construction of the Canal of Tiber Creek. Following the canal's stabilizing presence, the land was quickly swamped anew, this time with commercial development. **Center Market,** a thriving marketplace much like Capitol Hill's Eastern Market, became the anchor for a wave of businesses, hotels, restaurants, and publishers that filled the triangle.

The area deteriorated during the Civil War, as the city became an armed camp and dangerous characters swarmed into Washington to prey on the overcrowded citizens. The small police force (only eighty-eight members strong in 1861) and the military police were overwhelmed by the level of crime and prostitution, especially in the downtown area. In an effort to contain the ribald revelry of gambling salons and prostitution houses which had become Downtown's major growth industry during the war, these establishments were encouraged (often forced) to concentrate in the area now known as Federal Triangle.

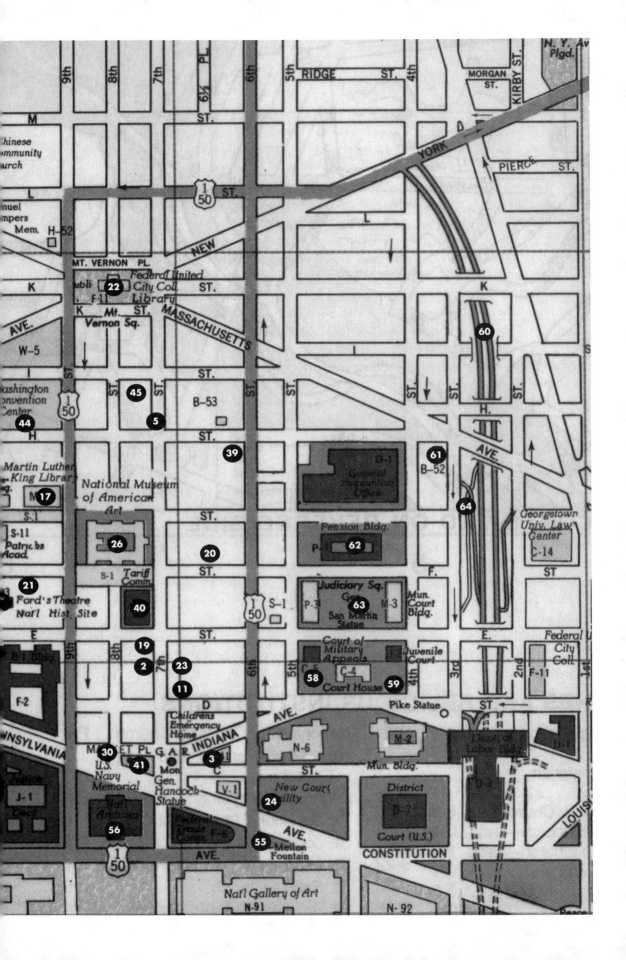

Downtown never quite pulled itself back out of the red-light district formed in the triangle. But the triangle itself was developed as federal office space when the McMillan Commission's recommendations for a homogenized planning design began being implemented in the early twentieth century.

The rest of Downtown was left in a bit of a rut as the century turned: With trolley cars creeping upward into the fashionable and ever-expanding neighborhoods of Upper Northwest, and with the advent of motor cars making Georgetown and Alexandria all the more accessible, the proximity that had made Downtown a natural social center lost its importance. As if kissed by an ugly toad, much of the area began to fade magically, tragically, back into the rough and rowdy neighborhood from whence it had been transformed. By the middle of the twentieth century, upper 14th Street was one of the best-known and most dangerous "strips" in town—burlesque houses, cheap liquor stores, floating crap games, and houses of prostitution had taken back much of Downtown.

There were a few remnants of respectability. The National and Warner Theaters still drew middle- and upper-class audiences to the road-show productions of New York shows. The Willard, although down, was not out; it still catered to wealthy and powerful visitors. The ink still flowed along Newspaper Row. And the federal and local government buildings on the fringes of Downtown were more or less immune to the decay setting in around and along the 14th Street Corridor.

The race riots of 1968 only made matters worse for downtown Washington. The burnt-out shells of bordering neighborhoods to the northeast cast a pall over the whole city. By 1970, much of the area swarmed with peep shows, XXX neon signs promising LIVE GIRLS, and adult bookstores that catered to an amazing array of humanity. More than one politician was ensnared in this seedy booby-trap of a neighborhood. Former Mayor Marion Barry was renowned for his forays to the THIS IS IT nightclub, where he allegedly indulged in illegal substances with friends and party girls, and Congressman Wilbur Mills was exposed as a regular at the Silver Slipper, where his sometime-sweetheart Fanne Foxe was a main attraction (and where Mills had been known to jump on stage and shimmy with her).

Since the low point of the early 1970s, substantial redevelopment has taken back much of Downtown from the skin trade and the mean streets of Downtown have been pushed into neighboring neighborhoods. The Shops at National Place (at the National Press Club building), Metro Center, the Convention Center, and Techworld have all brought a polished, if somewhat homogenized, new commercialism to old Downtown. The Willard Hotel underwent a spectacular renovation, as did its smaller and less-well-known neighbor, the Hotel Washington. The rollercoaster ride is far from over, however. Even as Old Downtown got its act together, the national recession spawned a local economic downturn. Garfinckel's department store went bankrupt in 1989, and other major Washington retailers also went out of business or found themselves on shaky financial ground. Now the glitzy glut of new retail and office space that transformed Downtown to an upscale commercial district threatens to turn it into a ghost-town instead. Only time will tell.

Suffragette parade on Pennsylvania Avenue, March 13, 1913. (Library of Congress)

PLACES: Central Downtown

From 15th Street east to Judiciary Square, and from Pennsylvania Avenue north to Franklin Square, central Downtown was and is now becoming again the heart of the city's commercial district. This was where the hotels and restaurants, taverns and shops drew people from throughout the city to socialize and conduct business. Although the character has changed over the years, vacillating wildly from the genteel days of 7th Street shopping to the red lights and hot nights of the 14th Street strip, Downtown remains a lively commercial district.

❶ John Quincy Adams House Site (1333 F Street, NW)

John Quincy Adams lived at a fine brick townhouse here from 1817 to 1825 while serving as secretary of state to President James Monroe. He returned to this house in 1834, and lived here until his sudden death in 1848. The house had previously been the home of another secretary-of-state-turned-president, James Madison, who lived here from 1801 to 1809 while serving in Jefferson's cabinet. During Madison's residency, his wife, Dolley, lit up the neighborhood with her frequent soirees; in fact, her skills as a hostess so impressed the widowed president that Jefferson often had Dolley Madison act as hostess at the White House during his tenure.

See Also: The White House and Cutts-Madison House (Chapter 1); U.S. Capitol (Chapter 3); Octagon House (Chapter 5)

A Stroll to Old Downtown

Let us take a walk, into Downtown Washington along the Pennsylvania Avenue of 1902, when the century was new and the city was just old enough to have a true sense of its own place and time. Our guide today is Thomas Fleming; our guidebook, his delightfully irreverent tome, *About Washington*. The tour begins at the Capitol and takes us down America's Main Street to Sixth Street:

"There is no street in all the world like Pennsylvania Avenue. It is so wide that only skyscrapers on both sides could give it a definite sky line. On a bright morning it affords a most entertaining promenade, with its hurrying crowd bent upon reaching the Capitol to secure points of vantage in the galleries of Congress, or to meet members in the committee rooms, or perhaps to wander aimlessly about the great structure, peering into its numberless recesses and corridors, and admiring its historical chambers rich in reminiscence.

"Leaving the Capitol grounds, the first thing to catch the eye is a quaint old second-hand bookstore on the right hand side on fifth street, the proprietor of which stands in his cave of volumes like a hibernating bear. . . .

"Across the street are the Botanical Gardens, where the Congressman and his lady friends frequently stop to secure the charming little boutonnieres with which to adorn a lapel or a corsage before entering the Halls of Legislation on the Hill.

"It will be noticed that this part of the avenue looks somewhat run-down at the heel. Small shops with cheap signs abound. Shoe-shining "parlors," souvenir shops, five cent barber shops and three cent lunch rooms monopolize this section. A well-conducted barber shop in this vicinity gives a shave for a nickel with a "clean" towel to every customer. . . .

"A little further along the street is the "Official Photographer of Washington," or rather the photographer of the officials of Washington, for his windows seem to contain portraits of all the notabilities of the Capitol. This is one of the places where the new member gets even with the old members—for his picture, it will be observed, is just as large as those of his influential colleagues. Strangers in the city never pass these attractive windows without endeavoring to pick out their respective representatives in Congress.

"We now come to the National Hotel, at the corner of Sixth Street, the resort of the Southern member of Congress and his many friends. On the opposite corner, across the avenue, is another equally well-known hotel—the St. James.

"Sixth Street at this point is a sort of port for entry for the Capitol. Crowds of travelers are constantly passing in both directions, for closely adjacent is the Baltimore and Potomac depot, which is the Union Station of the Pennsylvania Railroad system, the Chesapeake and Ohio, the Southern Railway, the Seaboard Air Line, and the Norfolk and Western."

—**Thomas Fleming**, *Around the Capitol* (1902)

❷ Clara Barton's Boarding House Site (488½ 7th Street, NW)

Like most of the boarding houses that were once jumbled in among the stores, restaurants, saloons, and hotels of Downtown, the rooming house that once stood here is long gone. During the Civil War years, Clara Barton lived here while she nursed wounded soldiers at area hospitals. Barton helped revolutionize battlefield medicine by improving sanitization and surgical methods, and the unforgettable experiences she took with her from her years as a Civil War nurse led her to found the American Red Cross in 1882. In 1886, she purchased a house at 947 T Street, NW; the house still stands today.

See Also: American Red Cross Headquarters (Chapter 5); Clara Barton House (Chapter 9)

❸ Matthew Brady's Gallery Site (627 Pennsylvania Avenue, NW)

In 1858, famed Civil War photographer Matthew Brady opened his Photographic Art Gallery and studios on the upper floors of this office building (gutted for renovation in 1967 but still standing). The great leaders of America came here to be photographed, and it was from these headquarters that Brady worked when not in the field photographing Civil War scenes. Brady, and his less well-known assistant, Alexander Gardner, changed the face of war reporting with their photographs of corpses and blood-soaked fields. Many of these photographs are preserved at the National Archives.

Alexander Gardner, who actually photographed many of the shots credited to Brady (all were identified as coming from Brady's studios) later angered his former boss by opening up his own successful portrait studio. During Brady's years at this site, the first floor of the building held one of downtown's more popular and raucous pubs, Thompson's Saloon, and, until 1967, one of Washington's most beloved pharmacies—Gilman's Drug Store. Brady himself lived at the upstairs gallery from 1880 to 1881, although his residence during most of his years of glory in Washington was the National Hotel.

See Also: Alexander Gardner's Photographic Studio Site, National Hotel, and National Archives

❹ Frances Hodgson Burnett First House Site (1219 I Street, NW)

Now lost to time, the home of popular authoress Frances Hodgson Burnett once stood here. Burnett wrote her most famous work, *Little Lord Fauntleroy* (1886), in this house. According to David Cutler's 1989 book, *Literary Washington*, Burnett's house was a famous literary salon, and was visited one day in 1882 by Charles Dickens, who was again touring America's lucrative lecture circuit.

See Also: Brookings Institution and Frances Hodgson Burnett's Second House Site (Chapter 7)

❺ Chinatown Friendship Arch (Over H Street between 7th and 8th Streets)

As a ceremonial entryway to the Chinatown section of Washington, this gloriously baroque arch provides an exotic gateway to this little enclave of Chinese-Americans. In 1990, a central section collapsed onto the roadway during afternoon rush-hour. Fortunately, no injuries occurred, and the arch was repaired to stand ceremonial guard once again within a few days. It is the largest Chinese arch in the world.

❻ `Open to the Public` Epiphany Church (1317 G Street, NW; 202/347–2635)

Built before the Civil War, this Episcopal church has been attended by some of Washington's more prominent citizens, among them General John "Black Jack" Pershing, Mrs.

Alexander Hamilton, and Chief Justice Morrison R. Waite. Lincoln's Secretary of War, Edwin Stanton, had a pew-for-life at the church. As legend has it, Stanton took this pew after the Church's rector, accused of loyalty to the South, sought out Stanton and proclaimed his loyalty to the Union with such passion that Stanton decided to join the church. The loyalty of Epiphany's parishioners went unquestioned, especially in July of 1862, when cartloads of wounded soldiers were brought into the church and laid out on the pews, transforming the sanctuary into a surgical ward and the Epiphany faithful into angels of mercy.

7 | Open to the Public | **Ford's Theater (511 10th Street, NW; 202/426–6924)**

Ford's Theater was built in 1863 by John Ford on the ashes of Ford's Atheneum, a Baptist-church-turned-music-hall that had burned down in 1862. The theater quickly became a center stage for much of Washington's political and social powers, sharing these honors with the **National Theater** a few blocks to the west. But on the night of April 14, 1865, the theater gained a notoriety that extended far beyond its fame as a nice place to see a play.

On the fateful evening, President Abraham Lincoln and his entourage arrived at the theater to see a performance of the play, *Our American Cousin*, a lightweight tragi-comedy starring the popular actress, Laura Keane. It was to be the last performance of the play, and Lincoln, a fan of Keane's, didn't want to miss her performance. He was to have been accompanied by General and Mrs. U.S. Grant, but they cancelled at the last minute, having to leave town suddenly. The

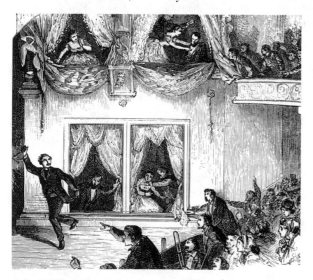

Lincolns invited the president's aide de camp, Major Henry Rathbone, and his fiancee, Clara Harris, to take their places.

The play had already begun when the presidential party slipped quietly into their box. The play stopped mid-act, and the band struck up "Hail to the Chief" to honor Lincoln's presence. He acknowledged the audience with a bow before settling in to enjoy the show.

As the second act commenced, a bitter and deranged Southern actor, John Wilkes Booth, slipped past Lincoln's bodyguard and entered the Presidential Box. Taking aim at the back of Lincoln's head, Booth fired two shots, which struck Lincoln in the skull and smashed into his brain. The theater froze as Mary Todd Lincoln rose in horror, howling that the president had been shot. Major Rathbone

John Wilkes Booth leaps to the stage after shooting Abraham Lincoln. (*Our First Century*)

tried to stop Booth, who slashed the aide before leaping out of the box toward the stage. Catching his boot spur in the American flag draped in front of the box as he fell, he tumbled to the stage, breaking his leg. Legend has it that he stood for a moment upon the stage to proclaim "Sic Semper Tyrannis" (Thus Ever to Tyrants—the motto of the Commonwealth of Virginia), although actual eyewitness accounts claim he shouted "The South Is Avenged."

This was not the president's first encounter with John Wilkes Booth at Ford's Theater—in fact, Lincoln had twice attended productions at the theater to see Mr. Booth perform on stage.

After the shooting, President Lincoln was carried across the street to a boarding house, the **Petersen House**, where for twelve hours he clung to life. He never regained consciousness. Lincoln died early in the morning on April 15, 1865.

In the days before the assassination, Booth and six co-conspirators had gone over and over their plan. Booth cased Ford's Theater in advance of the performance Lincoln was to attend. A hermit who lived in the alley next door to the theater testified that he saw Booth enter and leave the theater several times before the evening of the killing, and that on that April night he saw Booth arrive on horseback and slip in the back door. The other conspirators, who had joined with Booth in a pact to murder the top executives of the land, studied their targets as well. But George Atzerodt, assigned to murder the vice president, grew frightened at the appointed hour and failed to carry out his part of the plan. Lewis Payne, assigned to kill Secretary of State William Seward, did indeed attack his target at his residence, The Rodgers House in Lafayette Square as he lay in bed. But Seward eventually recovered from his stab wounds. Only John Wilkes Booth, mastermind of the plot, fulfilled his portion of the conspiracy.

In the chaos that followed the shooting, Booth escaped from the theater and led pursuers on a convoluted hunt through the Maryland and Virginia countrysides before he was flushed out of a burning barn and shot to death at the Bartlett Farm near Bowling Green, Virginia.

Ford's Theater stage entrance and alley down which Booth escaped. (*Walks about Washington*)

Four other conspirators—Samuel B. Arnold, Edward Spangler, and Michael O'Laughlin—as well as Dr. Samuel Mudd (the doctor who set Booth's broken leg)—were sentenced to hard labor in the Dry Tortugas. O'Laughlin died of yellow fever while in prison. The other three were later pardoned by Andrew Johnson during the last days of his embittered, embattled presidency. (In the midst of his impeachment hearings, he felt nothing but sympathy for the folks who did in Old Abe.)

The other conspirators were not so lucky. They were imprisoned at the U.S. Penitentiary, where they were tried for conspiracy to murder the president, and hanged in the outside yard before a crowd of onlookers.

Following the assassination, Ford's Theater was saved from angry mobs intent on burning the place down, and seized by the federal government. The owner was jailed on suspicion of conspiracy, but was later cleared of any involvement with the Booth gang.

Over the next century, Ford's was used for a variety for purposes. At first, the federal government used the building for office space and records storage. In 1893, another fatal tragedy took place at the building when a floor collapsed, killing twenty-two people and injuring more than sixty others, and the federal government moved most of the workers to other sites. For a time, it was home to the recently formed Army Medical Museum, which now resides at Walter Reed Medical Center, and still exhibits artifacts from Lincoln's assassination. The theater was also used for the storage of War Department records in the early twentieth century.

But for a century, the stage remained dark as a brooding reminder of one of the city's most galvanizing tragedies.

On February 13, 1968, the theater was reopened after a $27 million restoration. Matthew Brady photos were used to ensure that the theater was restored to the way it appeared on the night Lincoln was assassinated. The only major change since that time has been the installation of more comfortable seating than the original caned, ladder-backed seats (which were auctioned off at a fundraiser in the late 1980s). Ford's Theater has regained its place in the cultural life of Washington, becoming a particularly popular venue for productions of one-man shows and plays treating American themes and issues. The National Park Service operates the building as a historic site, and the theater itself with its restored presidential box can usually be viewed during the day.

The Lincoln Museum (in the basement of Ford's Theater) features memorabilia from the assassination of the president, including the murder weapon, the boots worn by Lincoln on the night of the shooting, and other artifacts. The history of the theater itself is explored here as well.

The State Box (in the first box tier, above and to the right of the stage) was restored to appear as it did the night of the assassination. The box where Lincoln sat is draped in a reproduction of the flag on which John Wilkes Booth snagged his boot spur. The furnishings in the box are also reproductions, with the exception of the red damask settee and a steel-engraved portrait of George Washington, both of which decorated the box on the night of the shooting.

See Also: The National Theater, Petersen House, and **Mary Surratt House;** Jackson Place Houses: 712 Jackson Place, and Rogers House (Chapter 1); National Air and Space Museum (Chapter 4); Walter Reed Medical Center (Chapter 9); Fort McNair (Chapter 11)

---

8 Foster Home Site (1401 I Street, NW)

Now the site of the Franklin Tower, an office complex, this was once the site of the home of John Watson Foster, a diplomat whose grandson, John Foster Dulles, was born in this house in 1888.

See Also: John Foster Dulles House (Chapter 8)

---

9 Franklin School (13th and K Streets, NW)

Adolph Cluss, one of the best school architects in the country, designed this wonderfully wise building in 1868. He built the equally magnificent Sumner School as a sister school (for black students; the Franklin was then for whites only). Children of rich and powerful Washingtonians, including those of Presidents Chester Arthur and Andrew Johnson, attended classes here. But its true claim to fame is as the site where Alexander Graham Bell—The Pa of Ma Bell—reached out and touched someone on purpose. Bell placed the first telephone call from the Franklin School on June 3, 1880. On the other line was a building one block away on L Street (perhaps a portent of the heavy-duty collection of phone-working lobbyists and lawyers who now work the L Street corridor).

See Also: Sumner School (Chapter 7)

---

10 Open to the Public Freedom Plaza (Pennsylvania Avenue between 14th and 13th Streets)

A ceremonial plaza installed in 1980 as part of the National Capital Planning Commission's urban renewal and redevelopment plans, Freedom Plaza is a flat park with an inlay detailing Pierre L'Enfant's plan of the city of Washington. Parades and fundraising events are often held at the plaza, which is also a prime viewing area for inaugural parades and other Pennsylvania Avenue pageantry.

⓫ Alexander Gardner's Photographic Studio Site (Northeast corner of 7th and D Streets, NW)

Billboard-sized signs on the large brick building that once stood at this corner used to advertise GARDNER'S GALLERY and VIEWS OF THE WAR to passersby. Most Washingtonians, however, would have known without the screaming headlines whose photographic gallery the site was. Alexander Gardner began as Matthew Brady's assistant; but after countless numbers of his battlefield scenes were reproduced and credited to Brady, Gardner decided to strike out on his own.

After opening his gallery here, he soon had a list of powerful clientele. In fact, Alexander Gardner took the famous "Last Photograph" of Abraham Lincoln. After taking the photograph on April 10, 1865, Gardner was surprised to find that the glass plate of the negative had a mysterious crack running along the side of the president's head. At the time, Gardner was not really distressed by the damaged negative, as he had already photographed Lincoln on several occasions, and expected to do the same in the future. As fate (and John Wilkes Booth) would have it, though, the president was assassinated in Ford's Theater four days later, on April 14. Oddly, the crack in the negative crosses the president's head at about the same place where Booth's bullet ripped into his skull.

See Also: Matthew Brady's Photographic Studio Site

⓬ Garfield Home Site (Northeast corner of 13th and I Streets, NW)

James Garfield, the twentieth president of the United States, built a home at this site that served as his Washington residence from 1869 until his departure for the White House in 1881. He had planned to return to the house after his presidency, but he survived barely six months in office before being slain by Charles Guiteau at the Baltimore and Ohio Railway on the Mall (now the site of the National Gallery of Art). Garfield's widow sold the home in 1895, and the house was demolished in 1964.

See Also: Old City Hall; The White House (Chapter 1); National Gallery of Art (Chapter 5)

⓭ Garfinckel's Site (1401 F Street, NW)

Garfinckel's once was the city's quintessential urbane department store. Founded by Julius Garfinckel as a clothing shop for the carriage trade in 1905, the store slowly grew too big for its own business at 13th and F Streets and moved over a block to this address in 1930. For nearly 60 years, the department store expanded its reach, competing successfully with the Hecht Company, Woodward and Lothrop, and the Lansburgh Department Store in the downtown area and at other Washington area locations. But in 1989, much to the shock of the cave dwellers (as the highest of Washington high society are known) and other city residents, Garfinckel's went bankrupt and closed its doors. Several other major Washington retailers soon followed, as the economy weakened further.

See Also: Lansburgh Building

⓮ Halls of the Ancients Site (1312 New York Avenue, NW)

Once upon a time, this was the site of a magical museum devoted to ancient cultures and arts. Built here in 1898 by art collector, merchant, and big-time dreamer Franklin W. Smith (with funding from local department store maven S. Walter Woodward), the Halls of the Ancients was an elaborately staged sampling of ancient artifacts and architecture, which included Egyptian, Roman, and Saracen halls. The owners hoped to parlay the museum into a massive complex funded by Congress, but Smith went bust within a few years. The Halls of the Ancients continued to operate as a tourist attraction under different management until 1926, when it was torn down to make way for another local landmark, the Capital Garage—the nation's largest parking garage when it was built. (It was torn down in 1974 to make way for new office space).

THE HALLS OF THE ANCIENTS

FOR PROMOTION OF

National Galleries of History and Art in Washington

1312, 1314, 1316 and 1318

NEW YORK AVENUE.

Admission, 25 Cents.

THE Halls of the Ancients are constructed for illustration of the art, architecture, religion, and life of the ancient Egyptian, Assyrian, Graeco - Roman, and Saracenic peoples. The design for the Egyptian portal is a section of the Hypostyle Hall of Karnak in exact size of the original: columns 70 ft. high and 12 ft. in diameter. It enters the Hall of Columns, more grand in dimensions and beautiful in color, than the Saulenhof built by Lepsius at Berlin.

Ad from the Washington *Standard Guide,* 1903.

(15) | Open to the Public | **Hotel Washington (15th Street at Pennsylvania Avenue, NW; 202/638–5900)**

Built in 1918 by Carrere and Hastings in the Italian Renaissance style, the Hotel Washington is one of the oldest continually operating hotels in Washington. A favorite with U.S. presidents and other VIPs, the hotel was refurbished and updated in the late 1980s.

This site was previously occupied by the five-story brick Corcoran Building, where a number of federal offices were located. Among these was the Washington Military Department's Pay Department, which was located on the top floor. This meant that many a disabled military man was required to hobble up five flights of stairs to collect his pay—a plight that did not go unnoticed by a young clerk here named Walt Whitman, who witnessed the daily struggles of the Civil War wounded both here and at the hospitals where he nursed the soldiers.

See Also: Walt Whitman's Boarding House(s)

(16) Key's Lovenest Site (383 15th Street, NW)

The Department of Commerce now stands at what was once the site of a small house used by District Attorney Philip Barton Key II, the son of *Star Spangled Banner* composer Francis Scott Key. The younger Key used the residence as a lovenest for trysting with his beloved, a married woman named Teresa Sickles. Teresa, who lived a few blocks away in a Lafayette Square mansion, had a jealous husband, Daniel Sickles, who murdered the young DA in Lafayette Park on February 27, 1859. During his subsequent trial, Daniel Sickles got off on the first-ever plea of temporary insanity in an American court.

See Also: Jackson Place Houses: 730 Jackson Place and Lafayette Park (Chapter 1); Congressional Cemetery (Chapter 11)

(17) | Open to the Public | **Martin Luther King, Jr. Library (901 G Street, NW; 202/727–1111)**

Ludwig Mies van der Rohe, king of brilliant boxy bauble buildings, designed this downtown public library in 1972. The library features outstanding research facilities for the study of African American history. It also houses the Washingtoniana Collection on the history of Washington, which includes oral history collections and the morgue from the now-defunct *Washington Star* newspaper.

In the nineteenth century, this area held Mausoleum Square, the burial grounds of such prominent families as the Van Nesses and the Burnes. When the prime downtown real estate was developed, most of the gravesites were moved to the Rock Creek Cemetery in upper Northwest.

18 Kirkwood House Site (Northeast Corner of Pennsylvania Avenue and 12th Street)

Like most of the Civil War-era hotels in Washington, the Kirkwood House is long gone. But in its heyday, it rivalled Willard's or the National for its elegant accommodations. Lincoln's second-term vice president, Andrew Johnson, had a third-floor suite at the Kirkwood House; and it was here, at 7:30 a.m. on April 15, 1865, that he was informed of the president's death by Army Chief of Staff General Henry Halleck. At 10 a.m. that day, with the members of Lincoln's cabinet gathered around in the parlor of the new president's hotel suite, Chief Justice Salmon P. Chase administered the oath of office to Andrew Johnson.

19 Open to the Public | Lansburgh Building (450 7th Street, NW)

This building was originally home to the locally famous Lansburgh's Department Store. Lansburgh's opened here in 1916, and remained one of the major downtown stores until it finally went out of business in 1970, when downtown Washington was at its lowest point. After serving as a home to local government agencies arts groups from 1980 to 1987, the site was re-developed as a retail center that now houses the Shakespeare Theater, previously at the Folger Shakespeare Library.

20 Belva Lockwood's House Site (619 F Street, NW)

The parking lot that fills this side of F Street between 6th and 7th Streets once held the home of Belva Lockwood, the first woman to run for president. (She headed the ticket of the National Equal Rights Party in both 1884 and 1888). In a notoriously male-dominated city and profession (law), Lockwood gained renown with her equal rights-oriented legal practice, which she ran out of her basement. Belva Lockwood furthered the cause of women's rights through legal channels, counting among her successes a law requiring that female federal employees be paid at the same rate as their male counterparts. Lockwood is memorialized at the National Women's Party Headquarters (the Sewall-Belmont House) on Capitol Hill.

See Also: Sewall-Belmont House (Chapter 3)

21 Metropolitan Theater Site (932 F Street, NW)

Right next door to the 930 Club once stood a theater that drew equal if not greater audiences for its performances. The Metropolitan Theater was one of Washington's premier movie palaces. When it opened in 1918 along with two other movie palaces (the Palace and the Rialto), downtown was given its first taste of cinema theaters. The Metropolitan had a Greek temple facade complete with a Doric frieze spelling out the theater's name in carved lettering. Like the Knickerbocker Theater and B.F. Keith's Theater, the Metropolitan was built by local theater maven Harry Crandall. The Knickerbocker Theater's architect, Reginald Wycliffe Geare, also designed the Metropolitan.

Metropolitan Theater marquee, 1927. (Library of Congress)

Local boy Al Jolson's first "Talkie" film, "The Jazz Singer," had its Washington debut at the Metropolitan Theater in 1927, ushering in the age of sound for the city's movie-goers. The theater was also used for stage performance until the Second World War, and it was here that soon-to-be big band leader Fred Waring got his first break a year out of college, playing the theater for a full season before moving on to national stardom.

The 1,400-seat theater was sold in 1928 to the Warner Brothers chain, which remodeled the theater twice—once in 1954 and again in 1961—in vain attempts to continue attracting the large audiences needed to keep the theater open. In the end, the lure of television won out and the Metropolitan Theater was razed in 1968.

See Also: Old Ebbitt Grill and **Lillian and Albert Small Jewish Museum/Adas Israel Synagogue;** Knickerbocker Theater Site (Chapter 8)

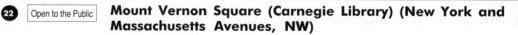

22 | Open to the Public | **Mount Vernon Square (Carnegie Library) (New York and Massachusetts Avenues, NW)**

The beautiful Beaux-Arts Carnegie Library, endowed as so many across the country were by millionaire and literacy philanthropist Andrew Carnegie, was built in 1902. The building was restored by the University of the District of Columbia (UDC), and is used as part of its Mount Vernon Campus.

Before the library was built at the site, Mount Vernon Square was a public marketplace. It was here that the infamous Know-Nothing Riots of 1857 occurred, when members of the anti-foreign, anti-Catholic political party known as the Know Nothings brought out a loaded cannon

during a fight at a polling place. President James Buchanan called out the Marines, who shot into the crowd, killing six people and injuring many more.
See Also: "Washington Riots" (Chapter 9)

㉓ *National Era* Site (427 7th Street, NW)

This site was home to Washington's first (and only major) abolitionist paper, the *National Era*, which first went to press in 1847 at a site near the old Patent Office. Within a year, the paper was nearly shut down by the so-called "Pearl Riot," in which angry mobs attacked the paper after a band of abolitionists tried to spirit seventy-six slaves out of Washington aboard the schooner *Pearl*. Becalmed at the mouth of the Potomac River, the ship and its passengers were hauled back to Washington where its captain, Daniel Drayton, and his cohorts were immediately put on trial. The escaped slaves were re-sold to owners in the harsher slavery states of the South.

Blaming the *National Era* for provoking the attempted escape, infuriated whites attacked the newspaper offices and threatened to lynch its publisher,

Turn-of-the-century sketch of philanthropist Andrew Carnegie. (*Around the Capital*)

Gamaliel Bailey. But Bailey and his paper persisted, and the attempted escape and its ugly aftermath eventually became the turning point for Washington's social conscience. Within two years, the slave trade was abolished in the District as part of the Compromise of 1850. In 1851, the *National Era* began serializing an anti-slavery melodrama by Harriet Beecher Stowe. That work was later published in book form as *Uncle Tom's Cabin*.
See Also: "Slavery in Washington" (Chapter 12)

㉔ National Hotel Site (Northeast corner of Pennsylvania Avenue at 6th Street, NW)

In 1826, one of the area's most prominent innkeepers, John Gadsby (of Alexandria's Gadsby's Tavern) opened the National Hotel here. His site was a row of six Federal houses called Weightman's Row, after the builder, Roger Weightman, who had run the city's most frequented bookstore out of a corner town-house in the row before going on to serve as the Mayor of Washington. Gadsby's National Hotel was quickly established as one of the most eminent and graceful lodgings in town, and it became a particular favorite with Southerners.

In 1836, Gadsby passed the reins of hotel management on to his son John so that he could devote more time to the profitable slave market he was operating behind his home, the famous Decatur House. Under the younger Gadsby's management, the National Hotel continued to draw political, commercial, and literary leaders. Among the guests at the hotel were Abraham

Lincoln, Andrew Jackson, James Buchanan, and Henry Clay (who literally checked out—of his earthly existence, that is—in his room at the hotel in 1852). Civil War photographer Matthew Brady spent his most productive years in Washington as a resident at the National Hotel. And in 1829, Andrew Jackson made the hotel his pre-inaugural headquarters, causing a near-riot by offering to meet with any citizen who wanted to talk with him. The crowds who descended on the hotel to meet the president-elect were overwhelming, and Jackson was forced to turn them away. The gathered throng awaiting his inaugural at the Capitol (to which he walked from the National Hotel), was even more boisterous—and the skittish Jackson ended up scaling a back wall of the Capitol to sneak in for his oath-taking. Later in the day, the same raucous citizens ran rampant through the White House, causing extensive damage.

One of the most famous guests to grace the hotel was Charles Dickens, who stayed here during his tour of the nation. He recorded his residence at the National Hotel in his 1841 book, *American Notes*, thus: "The hotel in which we live is a long row of small houses fronting on the street and opening at the back upon a common yard . . . clothes are drying in this yard; female slaves, white cotton handkerchiefs twisted around their heads, are running to and fro on the hotel business; black waiters cross and recross with dishes in their hands. . . ."

The hotel later fell into "ill" repute after an outbreak of a mysterious disease swept through the premises during James Buchanan's inaugural festivities in 1857. The president's own nephew died before the hotel was closed on account of the deadly disease it seemed to be spreading. It reopened a few months later after remodelling, and the mystery illness was no longer evident.

At the outset of the Civil War, the hotel was the scene of a mass exodus, when many Southern leaders who roomed at the hotel departed Washington as quickly as possible to take up their new posts in the Confederate government. But the National remained popular throughout the conflict, and is said to have swarmed with Southern spies during the war years. Also located at the National Hotel was the Federal Censor's office, where the journalists of near-by Newspaper Row had to have all dispatches, stories, illustrations, and other reports of war activity cleared for publication. Those newspaper men tromping in and out never suspected the story brewing beneath their noses at the National Hotel: John Wilkes Booth, a regular guest when in town, is believed by historians to have hatched much of his plot to kill the Lincoln while staying at the National Hotel. Booth stayed at the hotel on his final visit to Washington, in room 228, and slept there the night before he killed the president.

The hotel remained a fixture in Washington until 1921, when it was too badly damaged in a fire to continue operating at its previous levels of occupancy. It then became federal office space, serving a long stint as the National Guard Armory and as the headquarters for the Selective Service System in 1941. The building was razed in 1949. The District's Employment Services Building now stands at this site.

See Also: Matthew Brady's Photographic Gallery Site, Ford's Theater, Petersen House, and **Mary Surratt House;** Decatur House (Chapter 1)

---

25 Open to the Public **National Museum of Women in the Arts (1201 New York Avenue, NW; 202/783-5000)**

Locating the National Museum of Women in the Arts in what was once the Town Theater, a renowned burlesque/movie house, was a delightful stroke of irony indeed. The museum, funded through grants and donations, is the only such collection in the world dedicated solely to the artistic endeavors of women. Founded by Wilhelmina Holladay, the museum opened in 1987. It stages rotating exhibits and houses a permanent collection of works by women artists. The Waddy Wood-designed building, completed in 1911, was originally used as a Masonic Temple.

26  **National Portrait Gallery and National Museum of American Art (F Street, between 7th and 9th Streets, NW; 202/357-2700)**

The building that today holds the National Portrait Gallery and the National Museum of American Art began life as the Old Patent Office. In 1836, the original patent office and all of its holdings, housed in Blodgett's Hotel (now the site of the **Tariff Commission Building**), perished in a fire. Construction on the new building began three years later and lasted on and off until 1866.

President Lincoln's second inaugural reception was held in the gallery of the Patent Building in March of 1865, the month before his assassination. The event was a boisterous and bountiful social occasion in a city just emerging from the darkest war in the nation's history. But things got a little out of hand at the reception. As journalist Noah Brooks recounted the evening, ". . . its beauty was marred by an extraordinary rush of hungry people, who fairly mobbed the supper tables, and enacted a scene of confusion whose wildness was similar to some of the antics of the Paris Commune."

This site was also host to far more somber scenarios during the Civil War, when, like most public buildings in the city, the Patent Building was drafted into military service. First providing space for troop barracks, the building also soon took on the role of makeshift hospital for the wounded. As the death toll rose, its chambers were used as a morgue as well. It was at the Patent Office hospital ward that Red Cross founder Clara Barton and Yankee poet Walt Whitman nursed the wounded and the dying brought in by trains and barges from the battlefield. The human suffering that Whitman witnessed during his work at the hospital haunted him and his writing ever after.

At the time it was erected, the building was the largest in the country. The architect was Robert Mills, who was also a major contributor to the Capitol and Treasury buildings. Mills designed the building in the style of the Parthenon, and the classical style is echoed throughout the structure with its marble hallways and Doric columns.

When the Patent Office moved to the Department of Commerce headquarters in 1932, the Civil Service Commission took up residence in the vacated building until it moved to new quarters in the early 1960s. Once again deserted, the building was slated for demolition (to make way for a parking lot). The Commission of Fine Arts, however, procured a presidential pardon for the building. The site was turned over to the Smithsonian, which eagerly established two galleries at the site.

The two museums that now reside here share the building and delightful inner courtyard, but they also share a deeper bond with the soul of the building. For there was once an earlier museum here as well—the Patent Model Museum, where the finest attempts at invention and discovery, the truest tries at elaboration on imagination, were put on display for the world to see. The patent model museum no longer exists as a whole, although bits and pieces go on display at the Patent Office, now located in Rosslyn, Virginia.

The National Museum of American Art (on the north side of the building) is the country's oldest collection of art, although this is its first permanent home. Originally known as the Museum of Fine Arts, the collection focuses its full attention on American artists throughout history. The art is arranged chronologically so that visitors move from room to room through the story of American art. The historic Lincoln Gallery, where President Lincoln's second inaugural reception was held in 1865, is now hung with works of such twentieth-century artists as William de Koonig and Robert Rauschenberg.

The National Portrait Gallery (on the south side of the building) is the only such museum in the country, concentrating on the art of portraiture in all its forms, from *Time Magazine* covers to pop sculpture. The collection is heavily weighted toward the political life, with countless presidential portraits and representations of representatives. Artists whose works are displayed here run the gamut from John Singer Sargent to Augustus Saint-Gaudens.

See Also: Tariff Commission Building; "The Burning of Washington" (Chapter 1)

㉗ National Press Club (14th Street at the southeast corner of F Street)

The thirteenth floor of this office and shopping complex is the gathering place, watering hole, and press-conference haven for much of Washington's working press, the National Press Club. The National Press Building, which houses dozens of news bureaus from around the country, is perhaps the most compact remaining bastion of the old Newspaper Row which once sprawled up and down 13th and 14th Streets and along Pennsylvania Avenue, with major newspapers like the *Washington Times-Herald*, the *Washington Star*, and the *Washington Post* holding court in their own buildings. (Out-of-towners were also well represented, and included the Chicago *Tribune* at 1319 F Street, the New York *Times* at 1330 F Street, and Cincinnati *Gazette* at 513 14th Street. Today, only the *Post* still maintains its own building, a mile north of the National Press Club.

The National Press Club was founded in 1908, and was both renowned and castigated for its all-white male membership policy. Female reporters were virtually barred from fully reporting on the important news conferences and luncheon speaking appearances by national and international leaders because women were relegated to a balcony above the main floor, and banned from passing down questions to the speakers. That policy changed in 1964 when female journalists were at last allowed to cover the events from the main floor; but women were still denied the right to join the elite press corps until 1971. In 1985, the National Press Club further added to the ranks of its female membership when it merged with the Women's National Press Club.

Not that women weren't welcome at the old boys' Press Club from time to time. In fact, one of the most famous photographs of Harry S Truman shows the president tickling the ivories of an upright piano at a Press Club event, while Lauren Bacall lounges atop the instrument. The picture, taken in 1948 by Washington *Star* photog Gus Chinn, was used as a campaign photo. No wonder Dewey didn't beat Truman.

The site where the Press Club Building stands was once the location of another Washington establishment of note: the Ebbitt House, a once-fine hotel and saloon that was a favorite with politicians and newspapermen alike. The Ebbitt lives on, in a fashion, as the Old Ebbitt Grill (the original bar is still there), a block over on 15th Street.

See Also: Old Ebbitt Grill, The Washington *Post* Building, The Washington *Star* Building, and The Washington *Times-Herald* Building

---

㉘ | Open to the Public | The National Theater (1321 Pennsylvania Avenue, NW; 202/628–6161)

Along with **Ford's Theater**, the National was a theater of choice for the city's social and political elite. In fact, the night of April 14, 1865, Abraham Lincoln was originally slated to attend a performance at the National rather than at Ford's Theater. As one legend has it, John Wilkes Booth, who had friends at the National Theater, was in the theater that afternoon to pick up some mail, and by chance overheard news of the president's last-minute change of plans. He hurried away to case Ford's Theater to implement an alternate plan of attack. Another legend has haunted the National Theater since the mid-nineteenth century. The story goes that two actors became quite angry with each other during a Shakespearian production. Backstage, one of the actors killed the other, and discarded the body in the foundation of the theater. Ever since that alleged murder, there have been reported sightings of a tragic, ghostly figure dressed in Shakespearian garb, stalking in the wings in a fit of perpetual rage. During excavation of the theater following one of its many fires, workmen supposedly found the murder weapon—a pistol—and skeletal evidence of the victim, although the veracity of the legend has never been proven.

The National Theater has had a long run in Washington, although at times it has performed to mixed reviews. The theater was established in 1835, and became a mainstay of the young city's somewhat thin early cultural life. It also did double duty as a ballroom during the larger of two inaugural balls for President James K. Polk in 1845. Less than two months after the party, the theater burned to the ground. It was rebuilt and reopened four years later as the New National Hall ("Swedish Songbird" Jenny Lind warbled at the grand reopening). Within two years of the re-opening, a wall collapsed. Rebuilt once again, the theater became the New National Theater. It suffered another four fires over the next seventy years, and was finally rebuilt in its present incarnation in 1922.

The history of the National Theater's use parallels the history of American theater in the past two centuries. It was a popular venue for both travelling theatrical troupes such as the one to which John Wilkes Booth and his famous brother, Edwin, belonged, as well as for theatrical spectacles of world-famous performers. When vaudeville was all the rage, the National presented popular troupes and performers whom they felt were appropriate for the delicate sensibilities of Washington's high society. The National was, in a very real sense, the arbiter of theatrical taste for the upper-class masses.

Like other theaters of its ilk, the National Theater was segregated by race. Only whites were allowed to sit in the orchestra seats; blacks were relegated to the bal-

The National Theater. (Jack Looney)

conies, if they were allowed in at all. During the 1950s, the actors of Theater Guild struck against the National for its segregation policies, and the theater was forced to transform itself into a movie house to keep its doors open. The theater desegregated shortly thereafter, and has continued to bring the road companies of popular broadway shows to Washington ever since.

See Also: Ford's Theater, Warner Theater

㉙ National Telephonic Exchange Site (1413 G Street, NW)

This was the home of the National Telephonic Exchange, the embryonic Bell Telephone Company's Washington operation. By 1878, according to Charles Ewing's 1976 book *Yesterday's Washington*, the exchange was publishing a directory of those with telephone exchange numbers in Washington. This first real phone book listed 190 numbers in Washington; not surprisingly, the White House exchange number was simply "1."

See Also: Franklin School; Alexander Melville Bell House, Alexander Graham Bell Laboratory, and the Volta Bureau (Chapter 6); Alexander Graham Bell House Site and Bell-Morton House (Chapter 7)

㉚ Open to the Public Navy Memorial (in front of the Market Square complex at Pennsylvania Avenue between 7th and 8th Streets, NW)

A courtyard memorial to America's naval forces, the Navy Memorial is the world's largest grid map of the world. The focal point of this big, flat earth is the statue of the "Lone Sailor," created by sculptor Stanley Bleifeld and installed in 1987.

31 Open to the Public ### New York Avenue Presbyterian Church (1313 New York Avenue, NW; 202/393–3700)

Sometimes referred to as the "Lincoln Church," the earlier version of this house of worship was the Lincoln family church. During the Civil War, the rector even provided the president with a private entrance and sitting room so he could covertly attend Wednesday night services at the church. Lincoln's secret attendance was uncovered, however, when some curious children followed the footsteps in a new-fallen snow from the side door of the church all the way back to the White House.

During the Civil War, the army planned to take over the New York Avenue Presbyterian as much needed hospital space, as it had done with other Washington churches (including the **Epiphany Church**). But Lincoln insisted his church remain a house of worship throughout the war. The original Lincoln Pew (where U.S. presidents are still seated when in attendance at the church) and the hitching post out front that was used by the president have been preserved and remain at the church.

See Also: Epiphany Church

32 Open to the Public ### Old Ebbitt Grill (675 15th Street, NW; 202/347–4801)

This brasserie dates back to 1856, when its original proprietor, William E. Ebbitt, opened a boarding house in Downtown (probably near where the Washington Convention Center now stands) that featured a stand-up bar. In various incarnations and at various locations, the Ebbitt was a popular watering hole with future presidents U.S. Grant, Grover Cleveland, and Theodore Roosevelt. William McKinley lived at Ebbitt House when it was located at its most famous site, a building at the corner of 14th and F Streets (now the site of the **National Press Building**).

In 1983, the Ebbitt, which had slowly evolved into a restaurant saloon, moved to its present site. The restaurant had changed ownership in 1970 when the owners of the Clyde's Restaurant chain (then just a single Georgetown location) tried to buy the Ebbitt's collection of antique beer steins, and ended up bidding on the entire saloon. (They bought it for $11,200.) The Ebbitt Grill was in sorry shape at the time, but the young entrepreneurs transformed it back into a popular dining spot by sprucing up the interior and re-establishing an excellent kitchen staff.

Previously on this site was the wonderful Beaux-Arts vaudeville theater, B.F. Keith's. George Burns and Gracie Allen performed their star-making "Lambchops" routine here; the Barrymores took the stage (and only barely gave it back); indeed, virtually all the great vaudevillians performed here from the late teens through the 1920s.

The owner of the theater, Harry Crandall, also owned several other theaters, including the **Metropolitan Theater**, five blocks east of B.F. Keith's on F Street, and the Knickerbocker Theater at Columbia Road and 18th Street. The Knickerbocker was the site of one of Washington's most deadly disasters when, on a winter evening in 1922, the theater's snow-laden roof caved-in, killing ninety-six people and injuring dozens of others. Soon after the Knickerbocker Disaster, the B.F. Keith's programs began highlighting in **bold type** the fact that the theater featured **EMERGENCY EXITS INDICATED BY RED LIGHTS**.

B.F. Keith's Playbill Tidbits

L eafing through old B.F. Keith's playbills gives a charming peek at the social and commercial world of Washington in the heady post-World War I period. The pages of the programs also include full-page advertisements for such long-gone Washington establishments as the Peerless Motor Company's Washington Branch at 14th and P Streets, and Dikeman's Beverage Stores. Smaller advertisements promote hairstyling salons ("French Process Oil Permanent Wave with shingled bob . . . at Emile, 1221 Connecticut Avenue"), dining establishments ("Pomona's Restaurant, 1307 E Street, NW—'The Home of Regular Dinners'"), and even mediums ("Rizpah Eldon, the world's noted Medium and Palmist. She stands alone in her profession. As a Scientific Palmist she is accurate. As a Medium she gives names and descriptions of spirit friends, messages; information on all affairs of life, family information, business deals, mining; inventions. Office hours 10 a.m. to 10 p.m. 514 F Street, 2nd Floor.")

See Also: **"B.F. Keith's Playbill Tidbits,"** **Metropolitan Theater,** and **National Press Club;** Knickerbocker Theater Site (Chapter 8); Lincoln Theater (Chapter 9)

---

33 | Open to the Public | **Old Greyhound Bus Terminal (1100 New York Avenue, NW)**

This bus terminal is one of the classic examples of Art Deco architecture still standing in Washington. Built in 1939–40, and gone to seed in the 1960s and 1970s, the Greyhound Super Terminal as it was first called, was nearly torn down before being saved by the Art Deco Society of Washington, in conjunction with the D.C. Preservation League and the Committee of 100 on the Federal City. In September of 1991, the fully-realized renovation was unveiled to critical applause. The historic importance of the city bus station has been preserved through displays of artifacts and photographs.

---

34 **Old Washington *Post* Building Site (1337 E Street, NW)**

From 1895 until 1954, the original Washington *Post* Building was located here, just to the west of the National Theater. The paper, founded in 1877, had moved around quite a bit before taking up residence at the stately castle-like building that once stood here. According to James M. Goode's *Capital Losses* (1979), the *Post* had previously called three other locations home: 919 Pennsylvania Avenue (in its first year), 337 Pennsylvania Avenue (from 1878–1880), and the corner of 10th and D Streets (from 1880 until 1895).

See Also: Washington *Post* Building

---

35 | Open to the Public | **Pershing Park (Pennsylvania Avenue at 13th and 14th Streets)**

This small, inviting park honors the World War I heroics of General John "Black Jack" Pershing, Commander of the Army Expeditionary Forces. A statue of the general stands in the park, silhouetted against a wall inlaid with campaign maps of his greatest battles. A small ice-skating rink also draws a crowd in winter months.

At approximately this site there once stood an enormous red brick building constructed in 1884 as an armory for the Washington Light Infantry Corps. The Corps occupied the lower levels of the brick building, while the upper portions were rented to east-coast theater king John Albaugh for his Grand Opera House. Albaugh also operated or managed other local stages, including the National Theater. During its nearly three-decade run as Albaugh's, the 2,000–seat auditorium also served as a great convention hall, hosting such events as the 1888 International Council of Women meeting (with Susan B. Anthony presiding).

In 1901, the theater became known as Chase's Opera House, and took on its final form under Sylvester Poli as Poli's Theater in 1913. According to Constance McLaughlin Green's seminal history, *Washington: A History of the Nation's Capital (1879–1950)* (1962), Poli's was a favorite of President Wilson. To protect the president from would-be assassins, the manager of Poli's had a special hole cut in the alley wall behind the theater, so Wilson could arrive in secrecy at the presidential box in the balcony. For added security on evenings that the Wilson was in attendance, the manager also filled the balcony with presidential supporters by giving away tickets to desireable guests. The president was evidently unaware of the freebie seats, for he once remarked how glad he was that his attendance helped sell out the Poli's balcony on those evenings. The theater was destroyed in late 1930 to make way for the planned construction of federal buildings in the Federal Triangle project.

Not far from this park, at the corner of Pennsylvania Avenue at 15th Street, once stood the Pershing Victory Arch. The enormous decorative woodwork arch that stretched across Pennsylvania Avenue was erected to serve as a ceremonial gateway for the massive victory parade held on September 17, 1919. General Pershing led some 25,000 troops and fifteen bands in a four-mile long procession up Pennsylvania Avenue and under the arch as a crowd of 400,000 on-lookers wildly cheered. President Wilson, however, in San Francisco to promote the League of Nations, missed the festivities. The arch was gone before the year was out, but the parade and its spectacular gateway made headlines around the nation.

---

36 | Open to the Public | **Petersen House (House Where Lincoln Died) (516 10th Street, NW; 202/426–6830)**

The Petersen House has engraved its place in history as the house where President Lincoln was taken after being shot. The house was built in 1849 by Swedish emigrant William Petersen, a tailor who worked in the first floor of his little house and rented out the upstairs rooms. On the evening of April 14, 1865, Petersen provided a room to a down-and-out actor named John Wilkes Booth. The next night, President Lincoln was shot during the second act of a play he had been attending across the street at **Ford's Theater.** After being carried across 10th Street, the president was placed on a small bed in a guest room. Throughout the night, Secretary of War Edwin Stanton worked in a nearby parlor, questioning witnesses to the crime. The president never regained consciousness, and died early in the morning of April 15, 1866, while his wife, son, and friends stood mournful watch in the salon of the house.

In 1896 the federal government purchased the Petersen House, and in 1932, with the aid of a coalition of women's groups, the house was refurnished with authentic pieces and re-opened as a museum. It is now operated by the National Park Service as "The House Where Lincoln Died." On exhibit are a number of authentic period pieces and artifacts from the assassination, including the bloodied pillow upon which the dying president rested his head for the last time.

See Also: Ford's Theater, Mary Surratt House

---

37 **Rhodes Tavern Site (601–603 15th Street, NW)**

After the British had set fire to the White House, virtually destroyed the Capitol, and wreaked general havoc on most of official Washington in 1814, it was time for a beer. They headed for what was to become known as "Rum Row" (for the number of saloons along the strip), for a drinking binge at the nearby Rhodes Tavern. Legend has it they drank late into the evening, emptying casks of ale as they toasted their handiwork that had left the city badly crippled. They may have had a hangover the next day, but it was surely not so bad as the one they encountered upon their return to Britain, when public opinion lambasted the soldiers for destroying America's capital city.

Rhodes Tavern also played several important roles in Washington history, and most were unrelated to drinking. The Tavern had originally stood at 1431 F Street, but some time between 1807 and 1814, this site was converted to a storefront, and the tavern moved to its 15th Street location. The original site served as a polling place during the first municipal election, in 1802. The site was also operated as one of Washington's first bookstores by Roger Weightman, who served as the Mayor of Washington from 1824 to 1826. In 1814, the Bank of the Metropolis opened at the site, with Andrew Jackson as an original stockholder, and one of the city's original land-owners, John Van Ness, as bank president.

Another bank with a far more recognizable name—Riggs Bank—also got its start at the Rhodes Tavern (15th Street) building. On April 15, 1840, the Corcoran and Riggs banking and deposit partnership opened here. While at this location, the bank helped finance the first telegraph line in the U.S. (built between Washington and Baltimore).

Rhodes Tavern remained a popular drinking establishment throughout the nineteenth century, especially with merchants and businessmen. Rhodes was a particular favorite with slave dealers, who often settled their sales over a drink at the bar. It was also a popular hotel for many years. In the twentieth century, the building fell into disrepair. Other tenants, including a fruit market, moved in, and Washingtonians soon forgot that the famous place still stood in the heart of Downtown. Despite being listed on the National Register of Historic Places, in September 1984 Rhodes Tavern fell to the wrecking ball, to make way for the office and shopping complex that stands in its place today.

See Also: Old Ebbitt Grill; White House and "The Burning of Washington" (Chapter 10); The Octagon House (Chapter 5); Washington Navy Yard (Chapter 11)

---

38 Edwin Stanton House Site (1323 K Street, NW)

President Lincoln's short-tempered secretary of war, Edwin M. Stanton, lived in a house, now gone, that once stood at this address (now an office building). The house was Stanton's last home in the capital; he died in 1869.

---

39 Mary Surratt House (604 H Street, NW)

Now home to Go-Lo's (Chinese) Restaurant in the heart of Chinatown, this nineteenth-century townhouse was once the boarding house owned and operated by the notorious Mary Surratt. It was here that the Lincoln Conspirators met and mingled during the planning stages of the plot to kill the president and his cabinet.

Mary Surratt's boarding house was a simple place—frequented by theater folk and down-on-their-luck political hopefuls who often stayed for a week or a month. The genteel southern hostess of the house made it a haven for alienated Confederates in the heart of the Union capital, and thus a natural magnet for the band that would become known as the Lincoln Conspirators. Led by John Wilkes Booth, an actor who could never quite live up to his brother Edwin's fame, the other conspirators included George Atzerodt, Lewis Payne, David Herald, Edward Spangler, Michael O'Laughlin, and Samuel B. Arnold.

For several months before the assassination, the Lincoln Conspirators met at the boarding house, plotting to take revenge on the Union for what they perceived to be the rape of the South. The original plans called for the kidnapping of President Lincoln. But as the plan

The Surratt Boarding House. (*Harper's Pictorial History of the Civil War*)

President Lincoln's second inauguration. John Wilkes Booth is standing, hatless, on the balcony above the man leaning on the corner post. Co-conspirator George Atzerodt is the bearded man standing directly below Lincoln; to his left are Edward Spangler and Lewis Payne.

progressed, they realized that a mere kidnapping would still result in conviction and hanging for treason. Better to aim high if they were to give their own lives anyway. So they settled on murder instead—not just of the president (whose assassination Booth willingly took as his assignment), but also of Vice President Andrew Johnson and Secretary of State William Seward. In other words, the annihilation of the top level of the executive branch.

The conspirators planned their moves carefully, watching the workings of the Lincoln administration and learning the habits of the men they planned to murder. A photograph taken at Lincoln's second inauguration at the Capitol (less than three months before his death) reveals three of the conspirators—Booth, among them—standing in the crowd around the president as he spoke. It is an eerie photo, ripe with prescience and a sense of pre-history.

Mary Surratt, a self-professed Southern sympathizer, was among those accused of the crime. Three days after Lincoln's assassination, Mrs. Surratt was arrested at her boarding house and carted off to the Old Capitol Prison for interrogation. Her level of involvement in the plot has never been definitively proven (or disproven), although her son, John, who escaped overseas, was clearly a conspirator. Nevertheless, Mary Surratt was jailed, tried, and hanged for her role in one of the city's most heinous crimes. She lies buried in the Mount Olivet Cemetery. A plaque placed on the building by a Chinese-American Lions Club notes the historic significance of the house.

See Also: **Ford's Theater** and **Petersen House;** Organization of American States (OAS) Building (Chapter 5); Mount Olivet Cemetery (Chapter 10); Fort McNair (Chapter 12)

40 | Open to the Public | **Tariff Commission Building (Northeast corner of 8th and E Streets, NW)**

Designed by Robert Mills and built between 1836 and 1867, the Tariff Commission Building was the city's Old Post Office until the "new" Old Post Office building was completed in

1899. In 1845, Samuel Morse opened the first telegraph office in America at the Old Post Office building. The location made perfect sense, as the telegraph was rightly envisioned as the latest technological version of the good old mail service. During the Civil War, the Post Office building's basement became the site of a major Union Army commissary. This commissary was stocked, among other goods, with bread baked down the road, at the basement bakeries of the U.S. Capitol.

But the history of the site predates this magnificent building, for it was here that the city's famous Blodgett's Hotel once stood, and here that the original Patent Office was located.

The city's earliest and grandest "hotel," even if it never served as such, was Blodgett's Hotel. Designed by White House architect James Hoban, the building was completed in 1794 by New England merchant Samuel Blodgett, Jr., one of the city's first real-estate magnates. Blodgett financed the hotel, a stately marble structure complete with Ionic columns, with plans to raffle it off, along with a variety of lesser buildings he was erecting in the newborn city. But he overextended himself and ended up in debtors' prison in Philadelphia. Even while jailed, Blodgett promoted plans for a national university in the nation's capital. Blodgett died in 1814 in Baltimore, his schemes and dreams all but forgotten.

His lottery hotel had been used as everything but a hotel—a Philadelphia theater company had opened the United States Theater, the first in the city, at the building in 1800, and the site was also used as a temporary meeting place for Congress after the British burned the Capitol in 1814.

The British would have destroyed Blodgett's Hotel as well, for by then it was serving as the Patent Office. Only the brave act of Dr. William Thornton, then the director of the Office of Patents, saved the place from destruction. Throwing himself in front of the British cannon that were poised to fire into the building, Thornton delivered an impassioned plea about the sanctity of human genius and creativity, embodied, he proclaimed, in the models and records of the Patent Office. Although they had already burnt virtually every other federal building in the city, the British backed off, and the Patent Office was saved.

But what the British couldn't find in their hearts to do, a clerk accidentally did in 1836 when he mistakenly placed still-glowing fireplace ashes in a wooden garbage box, setting off a spectacular conflagration that destroyed the building. The collection of the Patent Office, including its models and records, was lost. A grand new building was erected beginning in 1839, which went on to serve as a Civil War hospital and now holds the collections of the **Museum of American Art** and the **National Portrait Gallery**.

See Also: National Portrait Gallery/Museum of American Art; U.S. Capitol and Supreme Court Building (Chapter 3)

---

41 Temperance Fountain (Pennsylvania Avenue at 7th Street)

Perhaps one of the most obscure and most easily overlooked memorials in Washington is this odd little water fountain. It was erected in 1880, a gift to the city from a philanthropic, teetotaling dentist named Henry Cogswell, who was wont to donate such drinking fountains to cities so that the citizenry would have a non-alcoholic beverage always at the ready. The fountain, gracefully topped with a statue of a crane, no longer offers its H_2O to slake the thirst of pas-

**Temperance Fountain.
(Jack Looney)**

sersby—a pity, since the good dentist Cogswell would have probably been delighted at the advent of fluoridated drinking water.

---

42 Open to the Public **The Vista Hotel International (1400 M Street, NW; 202/429–1700)**

**The Vista Hotel International.
(Jack Looney)**

The Vista has long been a favorite hotel with the business community, but it gained new fame when it became the site for Mayor Marion Barry's startling fall from grace on January 18, 1990. There had been years of innuendo and gossip about Mayor Barry's love of women and drugs, but no proof was ever found to bring him to trial, until the truth was put on video tape.

Barry was lured to the hotel by an old girlfriend, Rasheeda Moore, who was working with the District Attorney's office to catch the mayor in the act of using drugs. Under the eye of surveillance cameras, he proceeded to make passes at her while she was offering him crack cocaine. The mayor at last graciously accepted the crack pipe and smoked a few hits before federal marshals burst in and arrested the mayor. As he was cuffed and led from the room, Barry could clearly be heard mumbling epithets like "The bitch set me up." The cameras had recorded the whole event. The city and the nation watched, stunned and bitter, as the mayor attempted to explain away his problems in media interviews.

Rasheeda Moore is writing a book with the working title of *Coming Clean: The Feds, the Mayor, the Drugs and Me*, which is due to hit the stores in the fall of 1992.

See Also: The District Building

---

43 Open to the Public **Warner Theater (513 13th Street, NW; 202/626–1050)**

An Art-Deco classic in downtown Washington, the Warner Theater first opened in 1924 as a movie palace and theater. It could never quite compete with the larger and more elegant **National Theater** around the corner, but it managed to stay in business as a cinema, and as an occasional stage for concerts and travelling musicals.

The area behind the Warner Theater was once one of Washington's major "alley" neighborhoods, Slate Alley (so-named for a slate factory located in the alley during the 1850s). Like most Washington alley neighborhoods, Slate Alley was populated by poor blacks and whites who lived in ramshackle huts and make-shift homes. The life of Slate Alley was all but forgotten until 1989, when excavation behind the theater was undertaken in preparation for building a parking garage. Digging uncovered a surprisingly rich cache of artifacts beneath the modern alleyway area. Urban archaeologists hailed the find as a major advance in the study of the mainly lost world of Washington's alleys, noting that the number of bottles and containers discovered backed up a long-held theory among social historians that alley dwellers helped support themselves by "junking"—collecting and re-selling items scoured from other alleys and the richer neighborhoods. Everything discovered in Slate Alley, from the tobacco pouches to the wine bottles (both of which were found in great numbers) helped fill in gaps of knowledge

The Alley Life

Up until World War II, Washington's low-income neighborhoods were most commonly found in the city's alleyways and long-backyards. These alleys, Washington's version of slums, were largely populated by poor southern blacks and white Eastern European immigrants. The neighborhoods developed thanks largely to L'Enfant's plan, which, unlike the typical grid plan of most American cities, was diagrammed as a series of radiating lines—creating plenty of irregularly sized lots with long, narrow backyards. Early in the nineteenth century, landowners discovered that it was more profitable to rent the odd-lot space as cheap housing than to plant gardens. Shacks and makeshift homes were put up in seemingly every available alleyway and yard, especially following the Civil War, when the city's black population tripled almost overnight.

By the turn of the century, alley life was a deeply ingrained social problem, and soon the government began looking for ways to end the scourge of slum life in Washington. A variety of legislative and social measures were attempted, but none made a difference until 1934. In that year, Congress created the Alley Dwelling Authority, with the mission of eradicating the alley neighborhoods through the construction of quality public housing and other relocation efforts within a decade. The commission, together with a variety of other urban renewal projects, was so successful at erasing the neighborhoods that little is known or remembered about the city's alley life.

The following description, which appeared in the Works Projects Administration (WPA) American Guide *Washington: City and Capital* (1937), describes the crisis of alley life in the city, even as progress was being made in eradicating it: "Living conditions in the alley 'dwellings' have been, and still are, extremely bad. For the most part the houses have no heat, electricity, running water, gas or sewage connections. A single privy may serve twenty or more families. There is no place for children to play, and the overcrowding, in the opinion of social investigators, exceeds the limits of decency. . . . In 1934, some 10,000 Negroes and 500 whites live in alley dwellings. The number has been higher. In 1872, during the post-Civil War alley boom, 22,000 negroes and 3,000 whites were counted in the police census of the alleys." The 1870 government census counted 35,392 blacks in Washington, which means that nearly two-thirds of the city's blacks were living in the hellish conditions of the alleys in the late nineteenth century.

about the everyday life of Washington's ordinary people. The artifacts are earmarked for a lobby display in the newly refurbished Warner Theater, which re-opens in 1992.

See Also: The National Theater and **"The Alley Life"**

---

44 | Open to the Public | **Washington Convention Center (900 9th Street, NW; 202/789–1600)**

Among the historic buildings thought to have once stood where conventioneers now tread are the original Ebbitt House and numerous boarding houses and gambling dens.

Although the cold, gray, cavernous convention center has been viewed as an architectural wasteland, it is deemed a great improvement over the previous sites for conventions and other large gatherings. For years, conventioneers had to settle for the likes of the **D.C. Armory,** the Washington Coliseum, or hotel ballrooms for their get-togethers. And the Washington Convention Center helped pull Downtown back around the corner of respectability again, sparking construction of hotels and restaurants, as well as the huge Techworld development. The Convention Center opened in 1983, and since that time has hosted over a thousand events ranging from the enormous conventions of the American Booksellers Association (which have since outgrown the center) to the "World of Wheels" car and truck shows.

See Also: Old Ebbitt Grill

---

45 **Washington Hebrew Congregation Building (816 8th Street, NW)**

This glorious romanesque building was built in 1898 for the city's oldest Jewish congregation, which had been formed in 1852 by twenty-five mainly German Orthodox Jews. In 1855, they received the first federal charter allowing a Jewish congregation to hold property in Washington, and began worshipping at a former Methodist Church. In 1870, there was a split between the orthodox and more liberal factions. The orthodox members formed the **Adas Israel** congregation, and in 1873 began construction on their own synagogue (the city's oldest synagogue built for that purpose). In 1898, President William McKinley and his cabinet officiated in the laying of the cornerstone for this building.

The Greater New Hope Baptist Church is now located at the site, while the Washington Hebrew Congregation worships in a modern temple on Macomb Street in upper Northwest.

See Also: Lillian and Albert Small Jewish Museum/Adas Israel Synagogue

---

46 **The Washington _Post_ Building (1150 15th Street, NW; 202/334-7969)**

Now the grand old lady and leading paper in Washington, the _Washington Post_ has struggled through some of the darkest passages and withstood the brightest spotlights in the history of American journalism.

The paper that has served as the backdrop for a family dynasty and a journalistic legend was founded in 1877 by Stilson Hutchins, and spent the next twenty years struggling to gain a respectable foothold among the crowd of papers large and small, local and national, that jostled for position along the area known as Newspaper Row (around and along Pennsylvania Avenue, from approximately 14th Street to 9th Street).

The paper's first building was in the heart of that journalistic jungle. It stood shoulder to elbow grease with competing papers such as the _Washington Star_ (the city's oldest daily paper, founded in 1855), the _Daily News_, and the _Herald_. By the turn of the century, the _Post_ had gained an educated readership and a vaunted reputation. But when it was purchased by John McLean in 1905, the yellow journalism so prevalent in the Hearst-drawn days of the new century took over. Soon, the paper read like just another juicy, sleazy rag. It continued to sell well, however, because most of the other papers had also sunk to the same low level of journalistic integrity.

The paper hit bottom after John McLean's death in 1919. The _Post_ was passed on to his son, Edward Beale McLean, who quickly ran his own fortune into the ground while he drove what remaining dignity the paper retained into the mud. Edward McLean had become a close friend of President Warren G. Harding's. He even built a golf course at his Wisconsin Avenue estate, Friendship, so he could tee off in privacy with the president. This friendship was the publisher's undoing. He got too close to the president and too close to his associates to be able to shield himself from the brewing tempest that was to become known as the Teapot Dome Scandal. As the tales of the Harding Administration's involvement in the illegal sale of oil-rich public lands in Tea Pot Dome, Wyoming, spread like a slick of Texas tea, Edward McLean was ruined. He had been too close to the cozy coverup to pull out.

The paper nearly folded. McLean himself went bankrupt. He was declared insane in 1931, and carted off to an asylum in Maryland, where he died a decade later. The *Post* was sold at a bankruptcy auction in 1933. The buyer was Eugene Meyer, a businessman who saw in the em-battled newspaper a risky but potentially brilliant investment, and he worked hard to rebuild the once solid reputation of his new acquisition.

The tale of how Meyer and his family turned the *Post* into the newspaper of the century reads like something the paper itself might have written in its days as a tabloid. Meyer quickly brought the standards of the paper up from the gutter by hiring a respected and experienced staff, setting new ground rules for journalistic integrity, and cleaning up the editorial philosophy of the paper. In 1954 he purchased the Washington *Times-Herald*, merging it with the *Post*. By the time he handed the reins of the *Post* over to his son-in-law, Philip Graham, the paper was the strongest in Washington and a national leader on par with the *New York Times* and the *Chicago Tribune*.

Philip Graham had married Meyer's daughter Katharine, and he joined the family business determined to continue the paper's ascent to greatness. But he suffered from severe depression, an illness that drove him to take his own life in 1963. Katharine Graham had until then remained in the shadows, little suspecting she would be expected to take over the paper herself. But the woman known as Kay was tougher and smarter than most onlookers imagined. She took the helm of the paper with a firm hand, bringing in a growing roster of top talent, includ-ing the news-hound par excellence, Ben Bradlee, who joined the paper as an assistant editor.

Bradlee became the paper's Executive Editor in 1967. Three years later, in 1970, the *Post* shocked the nation when it published excerpts from the "Pentagon Papers," the damning, secret account of U.S. policy and military action in Vietnam that President Nixon attempted to squelch. The courts had slapped a restraining order on the *New York Times* (which had actually gotten the documents first) in time to stop that paper from publishing, but the *Post* managed to beat the court order heading its way. Both papers were later vindicated in a federal court ruling that allowed the full public disclosure of the Pentagon Papers. In the meantime, the Washington *Post* had made a big splash in a big pond, but its greatest moment of glory came fast on the heels of the Pentagon Papers.

In 1972, reporters Bob Woodward and Carl Bernstein found themselves on the trail of a surprisingly hot story when they began covering what appeared to be a simple break-in at the Democratic National Committee's McGovern campaign headquarters. But that break-in, which occurred at the Watergate Complex, was the reporters', and the paper's, biggest break in his-tory. Woodward and Bernstein's tireless, relentless, and sometimes fruitless investigation even-tually unmasked a coverup that led all the way to the Oval Office. That, in turn, led to the White House exit of President Richard Nixon, and a Pulitzer Prize for the *Washington Post* (but not for Woodward and Bernstein individually).

The *Post* came down to earth fairly hard after the brilliance of the Watergate years. In 1975, blood mixed with ink when a pressman's strike became a violent protest over modern methods of publication. And less than a decade later, *Post* reporter Janet Cooke was forced to return a Pulitzer Prize when it was discovered that her prize-winning story about a boy named "Jimmy" living a life of poverty-stricken heroin-addiction, was actually a composite profile rather than the genuine inner-city portrait of shame it had been billed as. Cooke left the *Post*, and the paper continued on, a bit humbled but still at the top of its class. The 1981 folding of the city's only other major paper, the *Washington Star*, gave the *Post* a monopoly in the city. The emergence of the Unification Church-funded *Washington Times* in 1982 has failed to cut into the circulation of the *Post*, which now steams ahead with Donald Graham, Katherine's son, at the helm. Ben Bradlee announced his retirement in June of 1991, leaving the job of Executive Editor to Managing Editor Leonard Downey, who will have both a tough act to follow and the coverage of a new century to lead.

The Washington *Post* Building stands on the site of St. Augustine's Catholic Church, the city's first black Catholic church, which was formed in 1858 by freed slaves. The congregation built its church at this site in the 1870s, and Saint Augustine's remained here until it was demolished in 1948 to make way for the *Post* building. The church has since re-located to the Shaw neighborhood.

See Also: Old Washington *Post* Building Site, Washington *Star* Building, and Washington *Times-Herald* Building; Russell Senate Office Building (Chapter 3); Watergate Complex and Kennedy Center for the Performing Arts (Chapter 5); McLean House (Chapter 7); Mclean Gardens (Chapter 8); Meridian House International/White-Meyer House and St. Augustine's Catholic Church (Chapter 9)

---

47 Washington *Times-Herald* Building (1317–1321 H Street, NW)

Often thought of as Washington's upscale paper because it was renowned for employing young society folk, the *Times-Herald* was created in the late 1930s when Cissy Patterson merged two Hearst papers, the evening *Times* and the morning *Herald*. Patterson, a member of the powerful Dupont Circle Patterson family, had edited the *Herald* for Hearst since 1933. The *Times-Herald* was eventually purchased by Eugene Meyer in 1954 and merged with the **Washington** *Post*.

The *Times-Herald* employed several once and future Kennedys. In 1941, Kathleen Kennedy, JFK's younger sister, worked at the paper doing "girl-on-the-street" interviews with passersby about current events and social topics. A decade later, the paper hired young Jacqueline Bouvier upon her arrival in Washington in 1951 (she had just turned down a coveted *Vogue* award of a year in Paris working at the fashion magazine). Bouvier's job, similar to Kathleen Kennedy's, paid very little, but it did get her out on the street to learn about Washingtonians. While at the *Times-Herald*, Bouvier met the (also coveted) bachelor Senator from Massachusetts, John F. Kennedy.

JFK seemed to have a taste for the ladies of the *Times-Herald*, for, during his sister's stint at the paper, he became involved with one of her co-workers, Inga Arvad. The year was 1941, and Lieutenant Jack Kennedy was stationed in Washington at the Office of Naval Intelligence. The dalliance soon had eyebrows raised—not only was the blonde bombshell older and (having been married twice already) wiser than her young beau, but rumors began to swirl that she was a German spy. Arvad had covered German affairs for a Danish newspaper in the 1930s, and had become friendly with Hitler when her reportage of Hermann Goering's wedding brought her into the inner circles of the Third Reich. The FBI began investigating Arvad, and JFK's powerful father, Joseph P. Kennedy, pulled some strings and saved his son's threatened naval career by having the young man swiftly reassigned out of Washington. The relationship lasted barely a year, but it was rumored that Kennedy's affection for the woman he called his "Ingabinga" continued for years afterward.

See Also: The Washington *Post* Building; Kennedy Houses (Chapter 6); Patterson House (Chapter 7)

---

48 Washington *Star* Building (1201 Pennsylvania Avenue, NW)

Although now transformed into a regular office building, this building still bears the name of its once-illustrious occupant. The Washington *Star*, for years the major competing newspaper to the Washington *Post*, was founded by a print-shop owner named Joseph Burrows Tate. The original offices of the *Evening Star* (as it was first known) were in Tate's tiny print shop at 8th and D Streets, but Tate promised the city he would soon be publishing one of

Washington's grandest papers. The first issue of the *Evening Star* rolled off the presses on December 16, 1852. The last issue left the presses on August 7, 1981.

Tate had originally launched the paper to support the Whig party presidential campaign of Mexican War hero General Winfield Scott. But the paper was transformed from a propaganda tool to a real newspaper when William Douglas Wallach bought the *Evening Star* in 1853. Crosby Noyes purchased the paper in 1867 (although the Wallach family continued to have some stake in the paper). The

Crowd watching the Washington *Star* scoreboard during the 1925 World Series, won by the Senators. (Library of Congress)

Noyes and Kauffman families maintained the paper until 1974, when it was sold to Joseph Albritton, who in turn sold the *Star* to Time, Inc. in 1978. Time, Inc. owned the paper until its final issue went to press three years later.

One thing for which the *Evening Star* was rarely credited, but for which it deserves recognition, is its innovation in the field of White House communications: In the late 1870s, the paper set up an experimental phone system which linked it directly to the U.S. Capitol, the first such direct connection between the press and the powers-that-be.

See Also: The Washington *Post* Building

---

49 Walt Whitman's Boarding House Site(s) (1407 L Street)

Now occupied by the American Medical Association Building, this site once held one of the hundreds of rooming houses in Washington that served the over-crowded city during the Civil War. Walt Whitman lived in this and a number of other boarding houses (including ones at 1405 M Street, and at 502 Pennsylvania Avenue).

Whitman first passed through Washington in the winter of 1862 on his way to the Virginia front, where his brother George lay wounded from battle. Two weeks later, Whitman returned to Washington to offer his services in caring for the wounded and dying soldiers pouring into Washington daily. Much of Whitman's ministrations took place at the old Washington Armory (which once stood at the site of the Hirshhorn) and at the Old Patent Office, both of which were used as military hospitals during the Civil War.

Upon his arrival in Washington, Whitman stayed in the home of a friend, William Douglas O'Connor, before finding a room at this boarding house for $7 a month. He left Washington for six months after the stress of caring for the wounded brought on an emotional breakdown, then returned to the city and spent the next twelve years working at various low-level government positions (including, during the Civil War, a job at the Paymaster's Office, then located in a building where the **Hotel Washington** now stands). While living here, Whitman is believed to have written a number of poems inspired by the Civil War which were published in 1865 as *Drum Taps*. The sequel to this work, also largely written in Washington, included some of Whitman's most famous poems. Two of the most notable were about the death of Lincoln: "When Lilacs Last in the Dooryard Bloomed," and "O Captain, My Captain."

Although Whitman had published his most famous and controversial work, *Leaves of Grass*, in 1860, two years before coming to Washington, he was little known outside radical and literary circles. Nevertheless, the book caught up with him in 1865 when his boss at the Indian Bureau, Interior Secretary James Harlan, found out about the scandalous volume of poems. Whitman was fired, but was soon hired to work for the Attorney General's office—a post he held until a debilitating stroke in 1873 forced him to retire and leave Washington. At the time of his stroke, Whitman was living in a little attic room in a house at 535 15th Street.

See Also: Clara Barton's Boarding House, Hotel Washington, and **National Portrait Gallery/National Museum of American Art;** National Air and Space Museum (Chapter 4)

---

50 | Open to the Public | **Willard Inter-Continental Hotel (1401 Pennsylvania Avenue, NW; 202/628–9100)**

Named for hotelier Henry Willard, the current hotel stands on or near the site of two earlier Willards—the Willard Hall, a popular nineteenth-century theater that fronted on 14th Street, and the "Old" Willard Hotel, a considerably smaller but equally elegant hotel where presidents-elect traditionally slept on the eve of their inauguration. The first Willard, opened in 1816, had been converted from a row of private houses. The present-day Willard was built in 1901 by Henry Hardenburgh, and was refurbished with much fanfare in 1986.

Not surprisingly, intrigue sometimes followed close on the coat-tails of the Willard's prominent guests. In the days before his inauguration, Abraham Lincoln was spirited undercover into his rooms at the Willard (after secretly entering Washington) because his aides feared for his life. But no sooner had he settled in than Lincoln was whisked away to appear before Congress, which was rife with rumors that he had already been assassinated. Lincoln left for his inaugural in such a hurry that he checked out of the Willard without paying his tab, and later sent a note promising payment and apologizing for his deadbeat exit. Warren G. Harding also kept his aides on their toes during his pre-inaugural stay, but for entirely different reasons. In *Washington Tapestry* (1946), Olive Ewing Clapper, the wife of a prominent Washington journalist, describes the scene at the Willard the night before Harding's inauguration:

"The President-Elect and Mrs. Harding were occupying the presidential suite at the Willard Hotel [on the evening before his inauguration]. Harding's friends were worried about the arrival that night at the hotel of one of his lady friends. They didn't want any scandal on the eve of his inauguration. They cautioned Harding to stay in his room. But apparently they didn't trust him where a pretty woman was concerned, for they kept a vigil out in the hall all night. Sure enough, before the night was over, the President-Elect tiptoed out into the hall. His friends pushed him back into the room. Then they went upstairs, knocked on the lady's door, and ordered her to pack and get out of town, threatening to put the FBI on her trail if she didn't go at once. She was so frightened she left immediately."

The Willard Inter-Continental Hotel. (Jack Looney)

Harding's vice-president, Calvin Coolidge, kept a suite at the Willard, and it was there that he took the oath of office on August 21, 1923, for the second time. The constitutionality of the first oath, administered three weeks earlier by Coolidge's father in Vermont after Harding's sudden death, had been questioned.

The Willard was not only a favorite of the rich and powerful; its lobby also swarmed with a large contingency of hangers-on and hangers-around. So many, in fact, that U.S. Grant is said to have coined the term "Lobbyists" to describe the office- and favor-seekers in constant attendance.

The dangers to be found at the Willard went beyond the lobbyists lying in wait. In one episode in the mid-nineteenth century, a California Congressman showed just what he thought of the service at the hotel by shooting a Willard waiter dead on the spot (an act which, for all we know, could be the source of the phrase "stiffing the waiter").

On a higher plain, the Willard also played a role in musical (and patriotic) history as the site where Julia Ward Howe penned the famous lines that were to become the words to the "Battle Hymn of the Republic." The inspiration came to Howe in 1861, when she and her husband were visiting Bailey's Crossroads in Virginia and witnessed a Union battalion march by, singing "John Brown's Body." Legend has it that Mr. Howe turned to Mrs. Howe and declared that he thought she could write more fitting lyrics to the song than those they had just heard. Upon her return that day to The Willard Hotel (where the couple was staying while in Washington), she sat down and wrote out the first lines of what would become the nation's best loved military anthem, "Mine eyes have seen the glory. . . ." A plaque at the hotel notes this historic event.

PLACES: Federal Triangle

The area now known as the Federal Triangle was once the anchor of the shopping district, with 7th Street, the major commercial route, ending at the Center Market at Pennsylvania Avenue. The market, which filled several blocks, was the largest and most diverse market in the city. It was as often frequented by the members of Congress who lived in the nearby boarding houses as it was by more questionable elements of society sifting in from the nearby, naughty Swampoodle (in the area of present-day Union Station) and other areas. Despite the draw of the market, much of the area now called Federal Triangle had a basically nasty reputation. It partially comprised the dangerous area along the Canal of Tiber Creek between 15th and 13th Streets that was known as Murder Bay, a pestilent shanty town that ran along a narrow strip to the east of the Ellipse.

During the Civil War, the area became seamier still, as the triangle area became a badlands known as "Hooker's Division." (Some say the name comes from General Joseph Hooker, who may have ordered the containment of prostitutes here, while others note that the ladies may have already been called Hookers because they were regular camp followers of Hooker's army.) The neighborhood was jammed with saloons, gambling dens, and houses of prostitution. Among the whorehouses, according to Richard M. Lee's *Lincoln's City*, was an Ohio Avenue (a street no more) establishment called Nellie Starr's, where John Wilkes Booth's mistress, Ella Starr, plied her trade. Legend had it that Ms. Starr was so distraught over her lover's evil deed that she tried to kill herself soon after Lincoln's assassination. Although the Murder Bay/Hookers Division area was perhaps the city's worst, it became even more dangerous as another nearby neighborhood of criminal acts, Swampoodle, was slowly absorbed into the more proper surrounds of Capitol Hill; the pick-pock-ets and cut-throats of Swampoodle were pushed east to Murder Bay.

As the century turned, hopes were high that the magnificent new Post Office Building (now called the **Old Post Office**), built in 1899 at Pennsylvania Avenue and 12th Street, might spawn new, reputable development. Yet, despite McMillan Plan recommendations to turn the triangle into a municipal office park, only one major government building was constructed in the area over the next two decades—the **District Building** at 14th and Pennsylvania, erected in 1908. The seedy side of life continued to thrive in the Federal Triangle until the late 1920s, when, fortified with federal funds provided by the Public Buildings bill of 1926, the U.S. government bought the triangle. At long last, it was hoped that the McMillan Commission's dreams of a formal collection of ornamental buildings might be fulfilled. The National Commission of Fine Arts took a keen interest in investing the space with a grand, neo-classical architectural scheme, and plans and models were drawn up with these elegant hopes in mind. But construction commenced at the advent of the Depression, which was followed by a world war that demanded speedy building. The up-shot was that the Federal Triangle never fulfilled the majestic scheme envisioned for it. Instead, it is a tidy, graceful collection of curvaceous buildings that provide workable office space for a range of federal needs.

Major construction is now underway to try to finish the job started decades ago, or at least fill in the blank spots. The Pennsylvania Avenue Development Commission (PADC), for one, is determined to bring the triangle full-circle, and has supervised a renewed planning and development of the area.

Center Market. *See* National Archives

51 Commerce Department Building (15th Street to 14th Street, between E Street and Constitution Avenue, NW)

The Commerce Department Building covers approximately half of the area that was once the city's nastiest slum, Murder Bay. (The other half is covered by the Departmental Auditorium/Bureau of Customs Buildings). It seems somehow fitting that the department charged with promoting tourism, consumer spending, etc. should have been built on the site of some of the city's most notorious casinos and prostitution houses, and later, the site of a popular tourist attraction: The Battle of Manassas Panorama Building. The panorama building, built in 1885, housed a giant round mural that depicted famous Civil War battle scenes (a similar panorama mural building still stands in Gettysburg). The attraction was destroyed in 1918 to make way for a one of the city's first downtown parking garages.

In the basement of the elegant Commerce Department Building is one of Washington's least-known attractions, The National Aquarium (202/377–2825). The country's oldest aquarium looks its age, especially in this era of aquarium amusement parks. But this odd little treasure is true to its history—opened in 1873 (in this location since 1923) it still merely displays some 200 tanks of fish, turtles, and other amphibious creatures.

A graceful giant, the Commerce Department complex was the world's largest government office structure when it was built in 1932 according to a design by Stephen Ayres. The European influence is visible throughout the building, from the 14th Street facade (based on the Louvre's Perrault facade) to the six courtyards that allow light to filter into the depths of the complex.

See Also: Federal Building Complex

Departmental Auditorium. *See* Federal Building Complex

52 | Open to the Public | **District Building (Pennsylvania Avenue and 14th Street, NW)**

At two o'clock on the afternoon of March 12, 1977, groups of angry Hanafi Muslims attacked the District Building as well as the B'Nai B'Rith headquarters and the Islamic Center. The scene inside the District Building melted into chaos as the terrorists fired their weapons in the hallway outside the chambers where the city council was in session. Maurice Williams, a twenty-four-year-old radio reporter, was killed in the melee. A security guard was seriously wounded, as was Marion Barry, on the city council at the time, who took a bullet in the chest. (Years later, Barry associates recalled how the future mayor began forging a new political coalition from his hospital room after the shooting. Near martyrdom, it seemed, had its rewards after all.) The siege went on into the night, finally ending early in the morning on the 13th, when envoys from the embassies of Iran, Pakistan, and Egypt negotiated an end to the violent attack.

Built in 1908 by the firm of Cope and Stewardson, the District Building serves as the city government's seat of power; but when this Beaux-Arts edifice first rose up along the triangle, many citizens were horrified by its arrogance, and for years people argued about whether to tear it down. Now, like so much of Washington's earlier architecture, the District Building is recognized as a gem of turn-of-the-century design.

See Also: B'Nai B'Rith Headquarters (Chapter 7); Islamic Center (Chapter 8).

53 Federal Building Complex (Constitution Avenue between 12th and 14th Streets, NW)

Murder Bay and Hooker's Division were once firmly encamped here, where sedate federal office buildings now stand. The centerpiece of the Federal Triangle complex of inter-related buildings, the building group was designed by Arthur Brown who used himself as the facial model for Maj. General Nathanael Greene, as he appears in the Departmental Auditorium's second-story relief panel.

The enormous parking lot that for years filled the courtyard of the complex was originally envisioned as "The Great Plaza," a formal garden that would serve as a central park for the Federal Triangle environment. Instead, it became an oasis for autos. I.M. Pei is now constructing the $650 million International Cultural and Trade Center there, and even if the Great Plaza garden will never be realized, at least the wasteland that once was will soon be replaced by a viable building.

> **The Departmental Auditorium** (Constitution Avenue between 12th and 14th Streets): The Departmental Auditorium, long a ceremonial meeting hall whose beauty belies the string of dull names it has endured, was the site of two historic events, one which heralded war and the other which demanded peace. In October of 1940, as the prospect of a second world war loomed ever larger on the political horizon, a crowd gathered in the auditorium to watch President Franklin Roosevelt launch a renewed Selective Service lottery by which young men would once again be called up for military duty. Up until this time, many Americans had still believed that the country would not be going to war in Europe again. But as Germany swept across the Continent and the American military began examining its own readiness, advisors

urged the president to move forward and renew the draft. More a ceremonial, patriotic event than a major draft pick, that first lottery at the Departmental Auditorium nevertheless sent ice water coursing through the veins of American mothers and fathers of teenaged sons. Within a year and a half, America was at war again.

Less than a decade later, the Departmental Auditorium was again the site of an historic gathering when the foreign ministers of eleven European nations attended the 1949 signing ceremonies of the NATO (North-Atlantic Treaty Organization) Treaty, held within this hall. The ceremony was presided over by President Harry S Truman and Secretary of State Dean Acheson, the architects of the alliance that continues to control nuclear proliferation and military force among its member nations.

The federal building complex also includes the U.S. Customs Service Building (northeast corner of 14th Street and Constitution Avenue), and the Interstate Commerce Commission (12th Street at Independence Avenue).

---

54 | Open to the Public | ## Internal Revenue Service Building (111 Constitution Avenue, NW)

Your tax dollars are at work in a building where once stood a somewhat cheerier institution—Carusi's Assembly Rooms. An amalgam of social halls, Carusi's was the site of the inaugural balls from Presidents John Quincy Adams through James Buchanan. Indeed, the mammoth IRS Building, which takes up a full city block, stands in the heart of what was once Hooker's Division, where many an illicit act took place. In particular, the site was once home to one of Washington's most beloved eating establishments: Harvey's Oyster Salon. Harvey's was founded in 1858 at a former smithy by a pair of brothers, the Harveys. When the armed forces of the wartime capital developed a taste for oysters, Harvey's became one of the main purveyors of the mollusk. According to Richard M. Lee's *Mr. Lincoln's City*, Harvey's was often deluged with orders from the Army demanding 100 to 500 gallons of oysters. The Harvey brothers kept their oyster boats running to the Chesapeake Bay throughout the war, despite the dangers of sailing past Confederate Army strongholds, where the shores were lined with cannon that could (and often did) sink passing merchant vessels. Harvey's was the precursor to the recently closed restaurant at 1001 18th Street known for many years by the same first name.
See Also: Harvey's Restaurant (Chapter 7)

---

55 ## Mellon Memorial (6th Street at Constitution Avenue, NW)

Across Constitution Avenue from the National Gallery of Art which Andrew Mellon donated to the nation, this fountain memorializes the man whose philanthropy enriched the city's cultural heritage. The fountain, erected in 1952, was designed by Otto Eggers, and features a decidedly cosmic slant: Look closely behind the fountain's overflowing waters and you'll see the signs of the zodiac, placed there by sculptor Sidney Waugh.

National Aquarium. *See* Commerce Department Building

---

56 | Open to the Public | ## National Archives (Constitution Avenue at 8th Street, NW; 202/523–3000)

Once upon a time, this site was the home to the Center Market, the major market-place of downtown Washington. Around this thriving marketplace (especially during the Civil War), clustered the city's largest collection of undertakers and embalmers.

John Russell Pope designed the archives building, which was completed in 1935 as a central and safe repository for the ever-growing stacks of documents, papers, diaries, letters, and other ephemera generated by the nation and its people.

The archives are used by many serious historians and scholars, but their true draw, as evidenced by the millions of visitors who pass through the main hall of the building's Rotunda each year, are the original copies of the *Declaration of Independence*, the *U.S. Constitution* and the *Bill of Rights*, all displayed in cases vacuum sealed with inert helium to best preserve the delicate documents. At the end of every day, the precious documents are mechanically lowered into a bombproof vault for safekeeping.

The trio of America's most historic declarations was first united at the Archives in 1952. That year, the *Bill of Rights*, already in residence since 1938 (it had previously been on display at the old Department of State), was joined by the other two works, which had been on display at the Library of Congress. For years, these three pieces had been shuffled around Washington, on display or in storage at various locations. The *Declaration of Independence* spent much of the nineteenth century exhibited on a wall (in direct sunlight, no less!) at the old Patent Office Building; it then went back to its birthplace, Philadelphia, for the 1876 Centennial Exposition. Upon its return, the Declaration did some time at the State Department before being moved along with the *Constitution* to the Library of Congress in 1921. During World War II, the documents were stored at Fort Knox (proof that they're considered good as gold).

But these famed historic papers are the tiniest and most visible tip of the archives' vast store of materials. From newsreels to newspapers, ship logs to prairie schooner journals, love letters to divorce decrees, family photographs to sheet music, the trivial and triumphant life and history of America is laid out within the vaults and drawers and shelves of the National Archives.

The variety of materials stored at the archives, and the ways in which they are used, are countless. Carl Sandburg used the Matthew Brady photographs stored here for research on *Storm Over the Land*; and even diplomatic records can be the basis for a musical, as proven by Margaret Landon, who wrote *Anna and the King of Siam* (better known in its Broadway incarnation as *The King and I*) after pouring over Siamese consular records.

In front of the Archives, facing Constitution Avenue, stands an unimposing monument to Franklin Delano Roosevelt. Roosevelt asked that no memorial be erected in his memory, or if the people insisted, that it be as plain as possible and no larger than the size of his desk. Dedicated in 1965, the monument is indeed plain and small, a mere wedge of marble with a simple inscription.

See Also: Library of Congress (Chapter 3)

---

57 | Open to the Public | **Old Post Office (1100 Pennsylvania Avenue, NW; 202/289–4224)**

Built in 1899 by Willoughby Edbrooke, the building was thought by many to be a monstrosity of Romanesque architecture. When the federal government bought the Triangle area in 1928, a master plan set forth by the McMillan Commission called for a collection of thematically integrated, Beaux Arts buildings—a death knell for the Old Post Office. But the redevelopment of the area stalled again and again, through world wars and depressions, and by the time the destruction of the Post Office became a real possibility, the city's move toward preservation policy had begun to take hold. Scrubbed clean and refurbished with commerce in mind in 1983 by the king of classy redevelopment, Arthur Cotton Moore, the Old Post Office still serves as a federal office building for the postal service, although it also features a shopping and dining complex known as the Pavilion.

Remembrances: The Center Market

"On reaching Seventh Street a procession of heavily laden boarding house keepers will usually be seen coming from Center Market, formerly called the Old Marsh Market, the ground here once having been a marsh or bog. Many famous men have come here in person to do their marketing, among the more notable are mentioned the names of Daniel Webster, Chief Justice Marshall, and William Henry Harrison—but times have changed wonderfully since then. Imagine, if you can, Secretary [Elihu] Root, Marcus Alonzo Hanna, or Chief Justice Fuller wandering through the Market House looking for bargains in scrapple, or sampling choice print butter, or poking a forefinger into a sirloin steak to test its tenderness."

—**Thomas Fleming, *Around the Capitol* (1902)**

A highlight of the Old Post Office building is its clock tower, which offers a wonderful view of downtown Washington and the surrounding city. The National Park Service runs tours to the top throughout the day, although reservations are recommended in advance during the summer months when tourism is at its peak.

See Also: Tariff Commission Building

PLACES: Judiciary Square Area

This section of downtown is composed of district government buildings and federal courts. The newer architecture is of a generally bland, post-modern genre. But there are a few prominent sites:

58 | Open to the Public | **Darlington Fountain (In northeast block of 5th and D Streets, NW)**

Installed in 1923 as a tribute to popular, powerful local lawyer Joseph Darlington, this fountain created quite a stir among the legal set. The statuary group includes a nude nymph and a fawn, but it was the nymph part (or, rather, parts) that got the fountain's sculptor, Carl Jennewin, into hot water among the city's moral guardians. Jennewin is said to have responded that the nymph's form was the work of God, unsullied by the hands of a dressmaker.

59 | Open to the Public | **The D.C. Courthouse (Old City Hall) (4th and D Streets, NW)**

The site of countless trials ranging from the sensational proceedings against Mayor Marion Barry to the mundane everyday business of a city's judicial center, the D.C. Courthouse has been the airing ground for some of the city's dirtiest laundry. Perhaps the most dramatic trial to take place at the courthouse was that of Charles Guiteau, the assassin who struck down President Garfield at the nearby B&P Railroad Station on July 2, 1881. Guiteau, a disgruntled and disturbed office seeker who felt he had been ignored by Garfield and his staff, was at first charged with attempted murder for the presidential shooting; when Garfield died two months later, the charge was changed to murder. Guiteau was found guilty of the crime, and hanged on June 29, 1882, almost a year after the shooting.

The trial got Washington quite riled up, as is evidenced in *Walks About Washington* (1915), by Francis Leupp and Lester Hornby. The authors gave an eyewitness account of the police measures needed to protect Guiteau from the growing lynch-mob mentality of the crowds who gathered daily at the courthouse:

The D.C. Courthouse. (*Picturesque Washington*)

"The popular rancour against Guiteau was so strong that in order to get him safely to the Court House from the 'black Maria' which brought him from the jail every morning, and to reverse the operation at the close of every day's session, the vehicle was backed up within twenty feet of one of the basement doors, and a double file of police, standing shoulder to shoulder with clubs drawn, made a narrow little lane through which he was rushed at a quick step, his face blanched with terror, his furtive eyes fixed on the ground."

This Greek Revival building, which also served as Washington's first City Hall, was designed by George Hadfield, whose best-known work in the area is probably the Lee Mansion at Arlington Cemetery. The central part was constructed in 1820 and the wings added in 1826 (east) and 1849 (west). During the Civil War, the building was called into various forms of service, including use as a temporary fortress in 1861, and a hospital in 1862. Up until 1850, a slave market was sometimes held at the site, which was also used as the U.S. Patent Office for a time. The first statue erected in Washington of President Lincoln stands in front of the courthouse.

See Also: Vista International Hotel; National Gallery of Art (Chapter 4)

---

60 Douglas Row Houses Site (200 block of I Street, NW:

This block was once home to a trio of attached houses which were the residences of some of Washington's once and future powers. Stephen A. Douglas purchased the corner house, 201 I Street, in 1857. Douglas, best known for his famous debates against his Republican presidential opponent, Abraham Lincoln, lived in the house until 1861. During his residency, the genteel social gatherings he hosted earned the home the title of "Mount Julep."

Another Douglas Row house, 205 I Street, became the home of Ulysses S. Grant in 1867; his tenancy was a mere two years (Grant moved into the White House in 1869). But he didn't leave his Civil War roots behind when he left—in fact, he sold the house to friend and fellow Union hero William Tecumseh Sherman, who lived in the house until 1874, when he subdivided the property and finally sold it all together. The row of houses had disappeared from Washington by the mid–1960s as new development encroached.

---

61 George McLellan Home Site (334 H Street, NW)

At this site once stood the home of Union commander General George McLellan. President Lincoln and his chief of staff, General Henry Halleck, arrived at the house on the morning of September 2, 1862 to request that "Little Mac" (as the diminutive, dandified general was sometimes known) take over command of the city's defenses and the Army of the Potomac. McLellan was not liked by Lincoln's cabinet, and the president's decision to give him the post sent shock-waves through the White House; indeed, Lincoln would later rue his selection. But until McLellan was removed from the post (mainly because he drilled and drilled his men but rarely sent them into battle), he had an easy commute between his house on H street and the nearby headquarters of the Army of the Potomac located on Lafayette Square.

See Also: U.S. Court of Claims Complex: Cutts-Madison House (Chapter 1).

---

62 | Open to the Public | ### National Building Museum (Old Pension Building) (F Street between 4th and 5th Streets, NW; 202/272-2448)

One of the grandest buildings in Washington, the Old Pension Building was constructed in 1882, and nearly torn down several times by planners unappreciative of this Victorian pleasure palace. The building was designed by General Montgomery Meigs, President Lincoln's Army Quartermaster and a fine architect in his own right. Until World War II, the building housed the Pension Office, which processed payments to World War I veterans and their families. Following the war, the building was used for spare federal office space, and the occasional presidential inaugural ball—Presidents Cleveland, Harrison, Franklin Roosevelt, Nixon, Carter, Reagan, and Bush all held their inaugural festivities in the massive central courtyard.

In 1980, the building was finally and officially recognized for the masterful work of architecture that it is, by being transformed into the home of the National Building Museum, the first such museum devoted specifically to architecture in this country. Thus, the building itself is the greatest piece in its own collection.

In preparation for its reincarnation as a museum, the Old Pension Building was completely renovated. The central courtyard with its four levels of balconies with ornate iron grillwork has now been restored to its original, dramatic self. Its eight central Corinthian columns—which, at seventy-six feet tall and twenty-five feet around, are the largest in the world—once again preside over the striking courtyard with an air of Victorian authority. The courtyard itself, which is about as long as a football field, is the largest enclosed open space in Washington.

---

63 | Open to the Public | ### National Law Enforcement Officers Memorial (At Judiciary Square Metro stop, between 4th and 5th Streets, facing F Street)

Officially dedicated by President George Bush on October 15, 1991, this memorial honors law enforcement officers who have given their lives in the line of duty. A police department version of the famed Vietnam Veterans Memorial on the Mall, this memorial consists of a long, sad wall carved with the names of the 12,561 officers who have died to preserve the law of the land. The twenty-four hours leading up to the official dedication ceremony were an emotional one for hundreds of onlookers and participants, who joined together at the new memorial to read aloud the names of America's fallen officers.

See Also: Vietnam Veteran's Memorial (Chapter 4)

---

64 | Open to the Public | ### Lillian and Albert Small Jewish Museum/Adas Israel Synagogue (701 3rd Street, NW; 202/798-0900)

Constructed between 1873 and 1876, the Adas Israel Synagogue is the oldest building in Washington built specifically as a synagogue. Its congregation was formed in 1870, when it splintered off—as a more conservative congregation—from the **Washington Hebrew Congregation.** President U.S. Grant presided over the ground-breaking ceremonies for this site in 1873.

Adas Israel also has a Hollywood claim to fame: The synagogue's own Rabbi Morris Yoelson was the father of Mammy's boy Al Jolson, who, along with his brother, sang in the synagogue choir when they were growing up in Washington. Years later, crowds packed the nearby **Metropolitan Theater** to see the hometown boy star in the city's first "Talkie" picture, *The Jazz Singer.*

Now a National Historic Shrine, the site houses the Lillian and Albert Small Jewish Museum and Jewish Historical Center of Greater Washington—an archive of materials on Judaism and the Jewish-American experience, both in the Washington area and on a national scale. The Adas Israel Synagogue is now located in upper Northwest.

See Also: Metropolitan Theater and **Washington Hebrew Congregation**

Chapter 3

THE CAPITOL AND CAPITOL HILL

F ew sites carry as much symbolism and subtext as the U.S. Capitol. Indeed, it is difficult to imagine the Washington skyline devoid of the architectural masterpiece of the Capitol Dome. Yet, the famed silhouette of the dome as we know it is of fairly recent vintage. The modern dome was not completed until 1863. In a way, the Capitol is a reflection of much of Capitol Hill itself: A melange of old and new, the seat of legislative power and its surrounding neighborhood is an immortal changeling, both in architecture and in historical importance. Despite alterations to its form and function, there remains about the area an Old World feel that mingles the halls of privilege with the alleyways of everyday life.

When the decision was finally made to build the nation's capital here at the fork of the Potomac River (for the Anacostia River was then called the Eastern Branch of the Potomac), the next step was to determine where the actual Capitol Building would be situated. Alexandria, Virginia, a part of the District at the time, featured a prominent hill that was considered for this purpose. With the majority of the district land located across the Potomac, however, the Capitol needed a more central and accessible site. Thomas Jefferson favored locating the Capitol on a hillside in the neighborhood known as Funkstown (also called Hamburgh, and now known as Foggy Bottom). This site would have placed the building just west of the White House. But both Pierre L'Enfant and George Washington preferred the somewhat less-malarial area then known as Jenkins Hill, which L'Enfant described in a letter to Thomas Jefferson as "a pedestal waiting for a monument." These heights were renamed Capitol Hill, and construction on the capitol commenced in 1793. Meanwhile, the surrounding area was quickly developed into a working-class neighborhood of boarding houses, pubs, and public markets.

During most of the nineteenth century, the Canal of Tiber Creek flowed virtually to the doorstep of Congress, tracing the route that modern-day Constitution Avenue covers, then turning south at the Capitol before flowing into the Potomac. Constructed between 1810 and 1815, the canal was both a blight and a blessing for the area. It allowed the easy transport of building materials brought in by ship up the Potomac, but the canal was far from the clean-cut waterway diagrammed on maps of the time. It more closely resembled a long, muddy ditch, and its wretched stench and sludge acted as more of a moat than a route, isolating the waterfront neighborhood of Southwest, which the canal bisected on its way to the river, from the rest of the city.

Thomas Law, a real estate speculator who invested heavily in Southwest, (and who raised the funds to build the canal), soon found himself partially to blame by other investors in the neighborhood, for the canal helped keep that area a desolate, crime-racked spot when the rest of the area near the Capitol had developed into pleasant middle-class com-

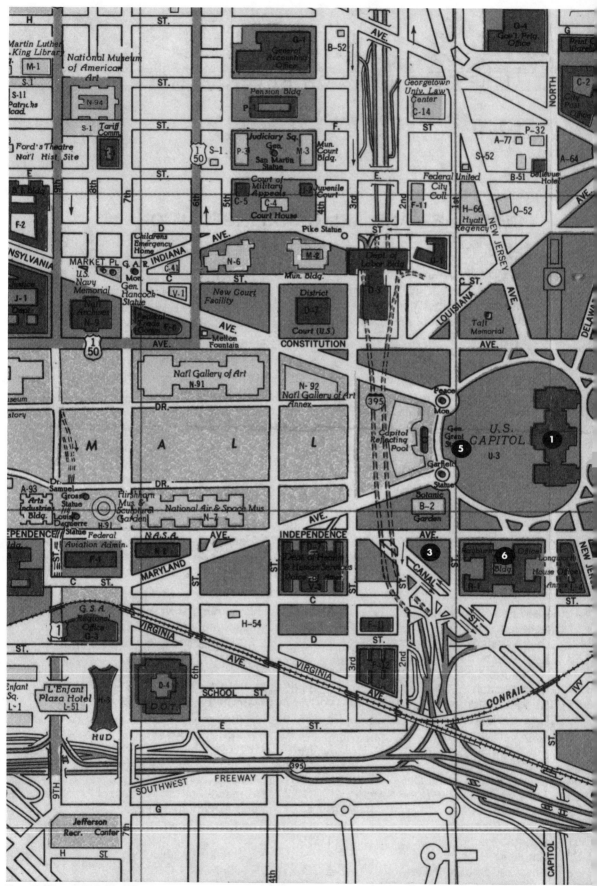

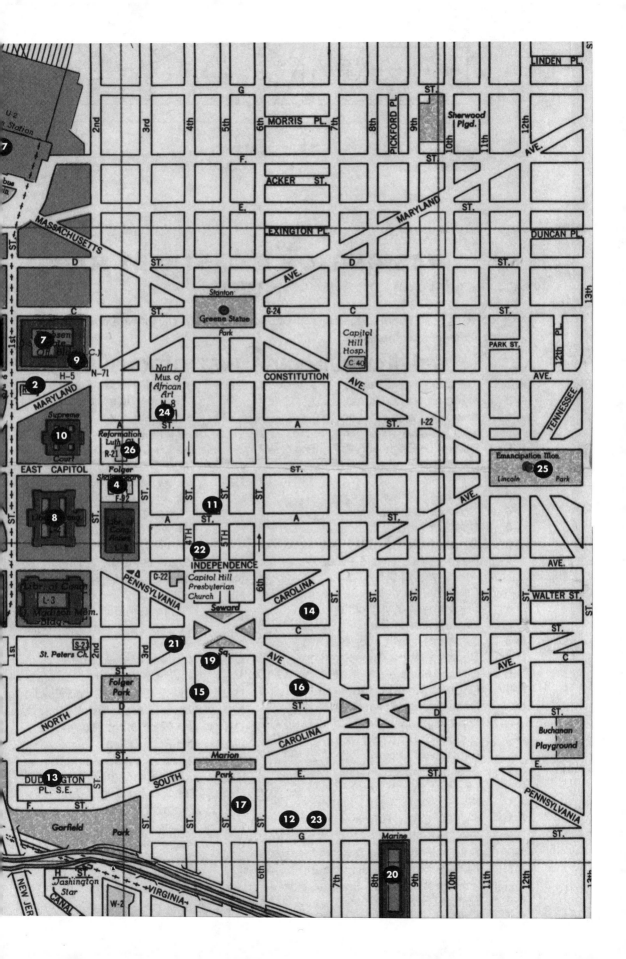

A balloon view of Washington, May, 1861. (Harper's Pictorial History of the Civil War.)

munities. The canal was finally covered over during Boss Shepherd's improvements programs of the 1870s.

Although the entire area became known as Capitol Hill, individual sections took on some odd and amusing names over the years. The area to the south of the Capitol is identified on late-nineteenth-century ward maps as "Bloody Hill," because, some say, of the presence of Providence Hospital, one of the Hill's many overworked facilities during the Civil War. The area further south, around Garfield Park (near the waterfront) was identified by the equally sanguine moniker of "Blood Field." Violence in those days was almost as common as it is today, although the modern death toll in Washington would have shocked even the most jaded citizen of that time.

During the Civil War, Capitol Hill was transformed into one big, well-armed hospital and prison ward. Temporary wooden structures housing infirmaries cropped up everywhere, and makeshift medical facilities were set up in every spare building, including churches and private homes. After the war, when most of the temporary hospital buildings were torn down, many Capitol Hillers took advantage of the cheap lumber left over to build new or additional houses.

Capitol Hill has been actively preserved and protected by its citizenry, for many of whom the neighborhood is as much a crusade as it is a community. Most of the original boarding houses and hotels that once catered to members of Congress and their steady streams of visitors are long gone (having been razed in the 19th century to make way for new government buildings). But many historic townhouses still stand, as do historic churches, including **Christ Church** (thought by many to be the oldest extant church in Washington) and **Ebenezer United Methodist Church.**

Today, the formal buildings of the **Folger Shakespeare Library, Library of Congress,** and the **Supreme Court** that surround the Capitol look as if they have been standing for centuries. It is difficult to fathom that both the Supreme Court and the Folger Library were built in the 1930s. Likewise, the Congressional office buildings and the Library of Congress's Jefferson and Madison buildings are all recent additions to the area around the Capitol. Outside of this charmed circle of federal buildings, within the true Capitol Hill neighborhood that wraps around the Capitol on three sides, it is easy to sense the communal history of this area. The colorful, sturdy rows of townhouses and storefronts jutting out in all directions along Independence Avenue, Pennsylvania Avenue, North Carolina Avenue, Virginia Avenue, East Capitol Street, and all their side-streets are representative of the buildings that were replaced during the past century with the large federal structures that now surround the Capitol.

One element of Capitol Hill that has changed little is that it remains a neighborhood of taverns and bistros. The 100 block of Independence Avenue, with its long stretch of pubs and eateries, was so crammed with restaurants by the middle of the twentieth century that local residents affectionately dubbed the block "Ptomaine Row." Some prominent places are gone now—Tunnicliffe's Tavern,

A Poem of Home From Richard Oulahan's "Capitol Hill" (1879)

Overlooking the river and city
  Nature's exquisite garden spot still
Is the plateau where Liberty's goddess
  Watch and ward keep o'er Capitol Hill.
On the western slope vast and peerless
  Stands the great marble palace of law
With its dome looming up in the heavens
  Fount of pride, admiration and awe!
Far away to the east from the plaza
  Round by brilliant "Olivia's" ville*
To the Ormondie castle of Butler
  Countless beauties grace Capitol Hill. . . .
To be sure there are mansard gilt mansions
  Fancy parking and concreted roads
At the "west end"—where Folly and Fashion
  Dine and pine o'er the swamps of the toads.
While up here in this health-giving region
  Evermore free from ague and chill
Where the old people die when they're ready
  Twins and triplets bless Capitol Hill.
When our patriot pilgrims of freedom
  To our National mecca repair
From the Capitol front they'll look over
  Parks and promenades passingly fair.
For the star of her destiny's rising
  Every long-cherished hope to fulfill
And she'll stand in her beauty unrivalled
  When the sun shines on Capitol Hill.
    —Oulahan, a Capitol Hill resident,
        lived at 614 A Street, SE

* His description of "Brilliant 'Olivia's' ville" refers to The Maples, which was then home to muckraking journalist Emily Edson Briggs, more widely known by her pen name, "Olivia."

Left, a delegation of Sioux chiefs and U.S. Commissioners pose on the Capitol steps (Sitting Bull on end of third row). Right, movie stars Charlie Chaplin and Mary Pickford sell Liberty Bonds at Capitol in 1917. (Library of Congress)

Capitol Hill's most renowned gathering place, which once stood at the southwest corner of Pennsylvania Avenue and Ninth Street, S.E., was razed in 1932 to make way for a gas station. But the feel of the old taverns can still be found in establishments like the Tune-Inn, where Hill staffers and Hill residents alike gather for after-work drinks.

Capitol Hill residents have long been proud of their neighborhood, boasting of its middle-class superiority over the upper-class "West End" neighborhoods. During the nineteenth century, the neighborhood was touted by its citizens as being far from the swamp fever and other zymotic diseases that plagued the rest of the city. One fellow named Richard Oulahan—a local booster but a lousy poet—harped on this difference in a little poem he wrote in 1879, titled "Capitol Hill." In this poem, he describes the fashionable "West End" as being a place "where Folly and Fashion/Dine and pine o'er the swamps of the toads," and then goes on to compare this pretty pestilence to his beloved Capitol Hill, which he describes as ". . . this health-giving region/Evermore free from ague and chill. . . ."

PLACES: U.S. Capitol and Grounds

❶ Open to the Public **U.S. Capitol Building (First Street, between Constitution and Pennsylvania Avenues; 202/224–3121)**

The first session of Congress in the new Capitol was called to order on November 22, 1800. Construction was still underway on the building when John Adams, the first president to live in the White House, insisted Congress make the final move to Washington. He did so in spite of the Capitol's unfinished state, and the doubts of many members about whether the city itself was yet livable. But what the stark two-story building lacked in comfort, it made up for in aura—executed as the central point of Pierre L'Enfant's plan for the City of Washington, the Capitol was the center of Washington in a very real way. Even the city's four quadrants converged here, radiating outward in broad avenues that defined the divisions of northwest, northeast, southwest, and southeast.

The original design for the U.S. Capitol, selected during a competition, was submitted by Dr. William Thornton. Like the original architect of the White House, James Hoban, Thornton lacked professional training as an architect, but his innate eye for form and almost spiritual sense of structure won him the design competition. Thornton envisioned this center of legislative power as a simple sandstone building, constructed of stone from George Washington's own quarries at Aquia Creek, Maryland, and topped with a low, wide dome.

The cornerstone for the building was laid in 1793 by George Washington. In 1803, Benjamin Latrobe took over as architect of the Capitol, erecting a second wing that provided the House with its own building to match the original, which the Senate maintained as its home. The Capitol was a house divided for four years until the two branches of the legislature were

The Great Debate

The so-called "Great Debate" over states' rights in 1830 between Senators Daniel Webster of Massachusetts and Robert Hayne of South Carolina laid the oratorical cornerstone for the rift that spawned the Civil War. The discourse began during debate over a fairly simple resolution on the sale of some public land, placed before the Senate at the end of the 1829 session. The true "Battle of the Giants," as the debate was later dubbed, arose in the midst of a typical North versus South exchange, during which Senator Hayne commenced a brutal, well-versed, and damning attack on the State of Massachusetts in general, and on Senator Webster in particular. Hayne also attacked the constitutional framework upon which the states' supposed subservience to the Union was based. He literally declared a one-man war on the North, stating that he would carry the battle all the way to Africa if need be, to establish the rights of the Southern states to rule their own destiny.

Hayne raged on for two full days. The timing seemed to be designed to catch Webster, the great defender of the North, off his guard—which it did, as he was deeply involved as lead counsel in trying an important case before the Supreme Court at the time. Webster requested the debate be postponed until he could prepare a rebuttal, but Hayne refused. The Senator from Massachusetts, who may well have been the finest orator ever to walk the corridors of Congress, dug in to prepare a rebuttal to the monumental attack he had just endured.

On January 26, 1830, Daniel Webster took the floor before a full Senate and a gallery (and lobby, and even stairwells) packed with spectators, many of whom had travelled great distances to witness the North's response. The entire House of Representatives skipped work to crowd into the Senate chambers as well. Many feared that if Webster did not effectively answer Hayne's attack, the Union would soon lie in splinters. But the throng was not disappointed, for Daniel Webster delivered a speech so emphatic, so driven by reason and the luster of language, so brilliantly argued as to transfix the multitudes. After his speech, the silence was as thick as the crowd, and not a soul spoke for several minutes. Daniel Webster had effectively staunched the flow of impending rebellion, or at least reduced it to a trickle that would take another three decades to regain its full power. Months later, Webster reputedly asked Hayne to join him in a drink, toasting him with the statement, "General Hayne, I drink to your health, and I hope that you may live a thousand years," to which the Southern gentleman responded, "I shall not live more than one hundred if you make another such speech."

Inaugural Moments

The Capitol's East Terrace has been the traditional site for inaugural events. Highlights include President John F. Kennedy's 1961 inaugural call to public service, "Ask not what your country can do for you, but what you can do for your country," and President Franklin Roosevelt's admonition to a depressed nation, "We have nothing to fear but fear itself," offered during his second inaugural address. President Ronald Reagan inaugurated a new tradition in 1981 by being sworn in on the steps of the West Terrace.

The Capitol's outdoor inaugurals date back to March of 1817, when Congress (still residing in the Old Brick Capitol), bickered incessantly over whether the House or Senate Chambers should host the inauguration of president-elect James Monroe. Monroe took matters into his own hands, opting to take his oath of office outside in the open air, which neither the House or the Senate could claim as its own realm.

Perhaps Monroe would not have inaugurated this outdoor tradition had he known it would contribute to the death of a successor. On March 4, 1841, when William Henry Harrison took to the inaugural podium on the east portico of the Capitol, it was icy cold and drizzling rain. But he withstood the elements, bareheaded, for an hour and a half as he delivered the longest (and some said dullest) inaugural address in American history. President Harrison barely had the chance to attend his inaugural balls before falling deathly ill with fever and chill. Full-blown pneumonia developed, and exactly one month after the ill-winds had blown on his long-winded speech, the new president was dead. Harrison's successor, John Tyler, took the oath of office (at his temporary residence, Brown's Silver Queen Hotel on Pennsylvania Avenue) on April 6th, 1841, becoming the first vice-president to ascend to the highest office of the country by

connected via a simple wooden walkway. Latrobe also altered Thornton's original, low dome, raising it up to a more commanding position.

Congress had been operating out of its bicameral building complex for only seven years when the British invaded the city in 1814 and set a torch to the Capitol. The books of the Library of Congress, then located in a chamber of the Capitol, were used as kindling to fuel the flames. The building was destroyed beyond repair, and might have been burned to ashes had not a violent thunderstorm swept into the city that night, dampening the British flames. The city's luck did not hold out, however, as a tornado whipped through the Washington the very next day, destroying what remained of a number of damaged buildings.

At this point, many members of Congress—having lived in Washington, slept with its mosquitoes, trudged through its mud, and breathed its sometimes fetid canal breath—began voicing their long-held second thoughts about the city. When the issue was brought to a vote in early 1815, a full third of the Congress was in favor of moving the capital and the Capitol to a new location rather than rebuilding the city on the Potomac. Nevertheless, Congress finally voted money to reconstruct the federal buildings destroyed by the British, including the Capitol, on their original sites.

While waiting for the new Capitol to rise again, Congress met first at Blodgett's Hotel in Downtown, and then in a hastily constructed temporary capitol financed by a group of

(Continued)

succession. Not that Washingtonians were happy with this first test of Constitutional transfer of power; some bitter presidential hopefuls even began calling President Tyler "His Accidency."

Perhaps the rowdiest inaugural on record was that of Andrew Jackson. Jackson's hurly-burly Ol' Hickory image endeared him to the common man to the point where his constituency nearly mobbed him as he made his way to the Capitol for the ceremony. Jackson was forced to sneak in behind the building, climb a wall, and duck through the basement of the Capitol to avoid the raucous crowds who had arrived on the grounds to witness his swearing-in. These same crowds poured into the White House later that day and did the most damage to the mansion since the British had gutted the house in 1814.

More threatening still were the rumors of an assassination plot that swirled around the first inaugural of Abraham Lincoln in 1861. With the country on the verge of war, and Lincoln's election considered the final straw cast in favor of rebellion, the president-elect was forced to sneak into the city and then hide out at the Willard Hotel until the ceremonies. Great precautions were made to protect Lincoln at the Capitol swearing-in; although his inaugural was held in the open on the East Front, a special wooden inaugural stand was erected to help separate the podium from the crowds below. At Lincoln's second inaugural, a photograph taken at the ceremony later revealed that John Wilkes Booth and several other conspirators in the assassination plot were actually within shouting distance of the president during his address.

The outdoor tradition of official inaugurals was broken only once—by Ronald Reagan, at his second inaugural (on January 21, 1985), when a snowstorm and arctic air forced the ceremonies to move indoors to the warmth of the Great Rotunda.

prominent citizens and built behind the destroyed original (at the site where the **Supreme Court** stands today). Congress occupied the Old Brick Capitol, as it was called, for five years while the Capitol was rebuilt.

Latrobe remained the Capitol architect during the first half of the rebuilding process. In 1817, he passed the baton off to Charles Bulfinch, who rebuilt the Capitol on a grander scale. The old dome having been demolished by the British, Bulfinch installed a new, more stately version made from wood and surfaced with copper to give the building a Byzantine glow in the sunlight. He also added a number of ornamental and functional touches to the Capitol grounds, including a pair of sturdy but elegant gatehouses (which now stand on the Ellipse).

In 1819, Congress moved back into a Capitol that, once again, was unfinished but inhabitable. It would be another fifty years before the building would take on the appearance modern Americans recognize today. In 1851, Congress authorized architect Thomas Walter to greatly enlarge the building through the extension of elongated new wings for the House and Senate. Bulfinch's dome, though pretty, was too small for the new proportions of the Capitol. A new cap (engineered by Walter, in conjunction with Lincoln's Army Quartermaster General, Montgomery Meigs) was also planned, although the nine-ton iron dome would not be completed until after the Civil War. The story of its construction and decoration is a remarkable tale of engineering skill and political compromise. (See "**A Dome for the Capitol**.") The Capitol has been the stage upon which some of the greatest debaters in the history of the country have performed. From Henry Clay and Daniel Webster, to James G. Blaine (ever the Republican

Naughty Nuggets from *Washington Confidential*

Jack Lait and Lee Mortimer made more public enemies and private friends than just about any other tag team of journalists in the twentieth century when they wrote such trashy exposes as *Chicago Confidential, New York Confidential,* and, of course *Washington Confidential. Washington Confidential* was published in 1951, and became an instant bedside companion for those wanting to know about the seamy side of capital life. The book's Appendix E is perhaps the best distillation of the spirit of Lait and Mortimer's *Washington Confidential.* The brief contents of Appendix E are as follows:

"*LUPO'S LOG BOOK:* Being some notes to file away where your wife won't look.
Backstage Phone No: The Capitol Theater, RE-7193. Star's dressing room call RE-1000 and ask for extension 305.
Boy Meets Girl Dance: Every Saturday, Victory Room, Hotel Roosevelt.
District Age of Consent: 16
Lipstick Stains Removed (No Odor): Texas, phone MI-9301
Lonesome Gals: Friday and Saturday Nights at the Officer's Service Club, 1624 21st St.
Florist, All Night: Charles Chisley, 603 4th St., ME-8709
Tourist Courts: On the Baltimore Highway"

—Jack Lait and Lee Mortimer, *Washington Confidential* (1951)

presidential hopeful), to "Uncle Joe" Cannon, the halls and chambers of the Capitol rang with brilliant oratory and foolish filibuster. The famous "Great Debate" of 1833 over states' rights, between Daniel Webster of Massachusetts and John Hayne of South Carolina, stirred the legislative fire as perhaps no other argument ever had, or has since. (See "The Great Debate.")

Through the years, the powerful blend of political prowess and money that has characterized many Congressmen has led to some fairly flagrant scandals. One of the most gossiped about in recent years involved the confession that former Congressional wife and future Playboy model Rita Jenrette made in *Playboy* Magazine's April, 1981 issue. Ms. Jenrette claimed that she and her (soon-to-be ex-) husband, John, had made love on the steps of the Capitol. According to Jenrette, the pair coupled away amidst the comings and goings of members and staffers, rushing about during a major House vote. (John Jenrette had also made headlines the previous year when he took a bribe from federal agents posing as wealthy Arabs seeking Congressional favors and became embroiled in the Abscam scandal.)

Other legends say that more than a few children were conceived in the Capitol. President Harding, while Senate Majority Leader, reportedly fathered a child with long-time paramour Nan Britton in his office. Britton later wrote a book about her affair with Harding, *The President's Daughter*, published in 1927, in which she described the day of the conception thus:

"The first part of January, 1919 I went over to Washington. . . . We went over to the Senate Office in the evening. We stayed quite a while there that evening, longer, he said, than was wise for us to do, because the rules governing guests in the Senate Offices are rather strict. It was here, we both decided afterward, that our baby girl was conceived. Mr. Harding told me he liked to have me be with him in his office, for the place held precious memories and he could visualize me there during the hours he worked alone. Mr. Harding was more or less careless of consequences, feeling sure he was not now going to become a father. 'No such luck!' he said. But he was mistaken; and of course the Senate Offices do not provide prevention facilities for use in such emergencies."

One of the nastiest scandals to hit the Capitol involved Bobby Baker, a legislative assistant to then-Senate Majority leader Lyndon Johnson. Baker was hired as a secretary by Johnson in 1955, and wasted little time assembling the gears of a well-oiled influence-peddling machine. Working out of Johnson's offices, Baker wheeled and dealt with Senators and Congressmen to obtain defense department contracts for the Serv-U Corporation (a vending machine company owned by Baker). Baker also allegedly used his influence to help Lyndon Johnson sell air time on a radio station owned by Ladybird Johnson. He was a part-owner of a naughty little establishment called the Quorum Club, where Congressmen and staffers could unwind with girls in skimpy outfits. In 1963, the owner of a rival vending machine company blew the whistle on Baker. After his friends on the Hill deserted him during a grueling Senate Rules Committee investigation, Baker resigned his position as vice presidential aide. In 1967, Baker was indicted on charges that included tax evasion and theft, and eventually spent seventeen months in prison.

Another popular scandal was the tale of the two-fingered typist, Elizabeth Ray, and the Democratic Congressman from Ohio, Wayne Hays, who hired her to work in his office. Despite her obvious lack of secretarial skills (Ray admitted she could barely work the phones), she was a kept woman—kept on the payroll, that is. The two carried on a torrid affair until Ray blew her cover and the freshly-married Hays's career when she cooperated in a front-page exposé by Washington *Post* reporters Rudy Maxa and Marion Clark that appeared on May 23, 1976.

Not only has the Capitol seen its share of scandal, it has also seen its share of violence. The first major attempt on the life of the president occurred there in 1835, with Andrew Jackson as the intended victim. In attendance at the Capitol funeral of South Carolina Senator Warren R. Davis, President Jackson was descending the steps of the eastern portico when a disgruntled painter named Richard Lawrence stepped into his path. Raising a pistol at the president, he attempted to fire a shot, only to have the weapon misfire. He aimed another pistol, clutched in his left hand, and again tried to fire, but failed again. Enraged, Jackson leapt at his assailant and might well have caned Lawrence to death if his friends hadn't physically restrained him.

Lawrence initially claimed he had tried to kill the president because Jackson

President Jackson narrowly escapes assassination.
(*Our First Century*)

had killed his father. This story was discounted, however, by the would-be assassin's behavior at his trial, during which he insistently proclaimed himself to be the King of England—and therefore not subject to American law. Not surprisingly, the jury found Lawrence not guilty by reason of insanity, and he passed the remaining thirty or so years of his life in an asylum.

Jackson's life may have been spared, but the country seemed to have lost its innocence that day. As described in *Our First Century*, a Centennial volume published in 1876, the nation's reaction to the attempted assassination was instant and prophetic:

> "Like wildfire on the flowing prairie, did the announcement of the attempted assassination of President Andrew Jackson, on the thirtieth of January, 1835, spread over the country, to its furthermost limits. Consternation filled the public mind, at the thought that the tragical mode of dealing with the crowned heads of kingdoms and empires, had at last been tried—though fortunately with abortive result—upon the person of the popularly elected ruler of a free republic!"

Despite such melodrama, the Capitol remains most remarkable and memorable as the proving ground for the American system of government. Every chamber, cloakroom, and corridor has witnessed some great debate or fight, deal or deadlock that occurred within the confines of this magnificent marble structure.

Places in the Capitol
Great Rotunda:

The first room that most visitors to the Capitol see is the magnificent Rotunda, with its dome mural and friezes. Here, in the center of the floor, a colored tile marks the spot where great leaders have lain in state. When President Kennedy lay in state here in 1963, so many mourners lined up to pay their respects that the Capitol was kept open all night to accommodate the sobbing throngs. The catafalque upon which the slain president's coffin lay is on view in the basement crypt.

The magnificent dome mural, "The Apotheosis of Washington," by Italian immigrant and Capitol Hill resident Constantino Brumidi, caused a bit of a scandal when it was unveiled. Those in the know snickered when they saw that the abundant and angelic "maidens" fluttering about George Washington bore a striking resemblance to certain ladies of the evening with whom Brumidi was known to keep company. Brumidi was also responsible for the frieze-like fresco that wraps around the room. An artistic triumph, it proved ultimately fatal to the gifted painter, who died shortly after a near fall from the scaffolding beneath the fresco.

Of the eight giant oil paintings hung around the room, half (those depicting George Washington) were created by John Trumbull, Washington's aide, who painted the scenes from his eyewitness memory of the great moments. The most famous of the Trumbull paintings on display, which depicts the signing of the Declaration of Independence, required a bit of fast tinkering by the artist. Having finished the work, he discovered he had painted all the crossed legs of the seated men facing in the same direction. The resulting chorus line of calves led Trumbull to cover a few up with painted-in tables.

During the Civil War, Union soldiers were bivouacked in the Rotunda, their boots and sabers clattering against the polished floor as they came and went for drills on the Mall. The soldiers covered up the famous paintings hanging in the Rotunda to help preserve them from the rigors of camp life.

House and Senate Chambers:

The chambers where the House and the Senate conduct their business have witnessed some of American history's greatest moments. The debate over secession of the states (and the "Great Debate" in the House chambers that preceded it by nearly a decade), the battles over everything from prohibition to universal suffrage, the verbally violent disputes over civil rights—all have taken place upon the stages of the House and Senate Chambers.

In May of 1868, Andrew Johnson became the only president impeached by the House of Representatives. The Senate, which required a two-thirds majority to carry out the ouster, missed its goal by a single vote, and so it was by the narrowest of margins that Johnson was spared the most ignominious of fates. The impeachment proceedings came as no great surprise to insiders, as Johnson had doomed any friendship he might had developed with Congress on the day he became vice president. Sick with a bad cold that day, he begged that he be allowed to take the oath of office at his quarters, but was informed he must appear in the Senate Chambers for his swearing in, sick or not. So Johnson, a teetotaler, fortified himself with a liberal medicinal dose of whiskey before appearing for his inaugural, and in his subsequent address to Congress delivered a drunken, rude diatribe. It was thus with some glee that Congress proceeded to bring impeachment proceedings against Johnson three years later—a process during which Johnson's drunken inaugural was often mentioned. (Searching for the proper charges to bring for impeachment, Thaddeus Stephens had even suggested "insanity or whiskey" as being a possible crime worthy of impeachment.)

Not all the action in the chambers has taken place amidst the casting of votes. One of the most infamous episodes in the Senate (in the Old Senate Chambers), was the near-fatal caning of Senator Charles Sumner by a fellow senator on May 22, 1856. The House got a similar, if more high-tech dose of violence on March 1, 1954, when a gunfire attack on the floor of the House of Representatives by a group Puerto Rican Nationalists left five Congressmen wounded.

Statuary Hall (Old House of Representatives Chamber):

The old chamber of the House of Representatives (where the House met until 1857) was also known as the Whispering Hall because of an odd acoustical effect that allows those standing on one side of the hall to easily hear the whispers of those across the room. There are only a few spots in the hall where this phenomenon occurs, and one can imagine how eagerly members of Congress must have fought for a seat near these natural "bugs." The hall is now encircled with the statues representing great Americans, requested from every state. But the most intriguing memorial is a gold star on the floor of the room, which marks the spot where John Quincy Adams fell to the floor after suffering a fatal stroke in 1848. (He died in an adjoining room.)

Old Senate Chamber:

Like the Old Supreme Court Chamber, the Old Senate Chamber (which was also home to the Supreme Court) has been transformed into a historical exhibit. It was here that the Senate met upon its return to the Capitol in 1819, until it moved to the new Senate wing shortly before the Civil War.

Old Supreme Court Chambers:

Another highlight of the Capitol is the Old Supreme Court Chambers, now preserved as a museum. The Supreme Court held forth in this little basement room until 1860. It then moved over to the Old Senate Chamber—which was vacated by that body upon completion of the new Senate wing—before finally getting a building of its own in 1934. In contrast to today's Supreme Court, which must try to interpret a 200–year-old Constitution, the Supreme Court of

Blood in the Chambers

Charles Sumner was an erudite, cool, and dedicated senator from Massachusetts who, from the day he took office, fought for the abolition of slavery. This was a position that could make a man enemies in the South—and in Sumner's case, it nearly got him killed. On May 22, 1856, Sumner concluded a well-reasoned, two-day-long argument in favor of admitting Kansas—which had just passed a state constitution barring slavery—to the Union. In the course of this speech, he had made particular attacks on the legislators from South Carolina.

Preston Brooks caning Charles Sumner.
(Our First Century)

After Sumner's speech, the Senate shut up shop early upon the announcement that a colleague from Missouri had died. Sumner stayed on in the Senate Chamber to work, alone but for a member of the House of Representatives, the Honorable Preston S. Brooks of South Carolina. Brooks approached Sumner where he sat at his desk and castigated Sumner for his attack on South Carolina and its representatives, Brooks then, without warning, commenced whacking the sitting Senator on the back of his head with a "heavy gutta percha cane," as the instrument of violence was later described. Sumner tried to rise, but was blinded by pain and blood, and fell back as Brooks continued to beat him senseless, landing anywhere from twelve to twenty blows on his head and shoulders. Two senators from New York who were in the ante-chamber overheard the commotion. They rushed in and pulled off the madly swinging Brooks, whose cane was by now a splintered twig from the force of the beating. The desks nearby, as well as Sumner's own, were badly splattered with the senator's blood.

the nineteenth century was more directly involved with the immediate evolution of that sacred document. For the first hundred years, the Court was accorded so little respect for this work that it was thus stuffed into the Capitol basement. Another reason for the lack of a separate courthouse may have been the legendary enmity between city planner Pierre L'Enfant and John Jay, the first Chief Justice of the Supreme Court. Their relationship was so sour that it has been said that L'Enfant deliberately left out the letter "J" from the otherwise flawlessly alphabetized city streets. To this day, there is no J Street in Washington.

(Continued)

Sumner's injuries were grievous indeed, and, although the Senator lived to return to the Capitol, his recuperation took several years. His attacker, Preston Brooks, was censured by the House for his attempted murder of Sumner. Upon hearing of the vote, Brooks delivered one of the most amazing defenses in the history of violent crime: "If I had desired to kill the senator from Massachusetts," Brooks told the House, "why did I not do it? You all admit that I had it in my power. Let me tell you, that, expressly to prevent taking life, I used an ordinary cane presented by a friend in Baltimore. I went to the senate deliberately. I hesitated whether I should use a horsewhip or a cowhide, but knowing that the strength of the senator from Massachusetts was superior to mine, I thought he might wrest it from me. If he had, I might have done what I should have regretted for the rest of my life. . . ." At this point, the minutes record a voice in the House calling out, "He would have killed him!" Brooks then resigned from Congress. He returned to South Carolina, where he was treated as a hero and quickly re-elected to the same seat he had just resigned. Brooks returned to the House on January 8, 1857, only to die that same month, on the 27th of January, from a violent throat infection. He was thirty-eight years old.

Charles Sumner was not well enough to return to his Senate seat until 1859. He bore the wounds inflicted against his words throughout the rest of his life and died while still in office in 1874, one of Washington's most unforgettable freedom fighters.

For all the Congressional in-fighting, it seems amazing that so little violence has reached the legislature from the outside world. On one occasion, however, Congress's luck ran out. On March 1, 1954, four Puerto Rican Nationalists—three men (Rafael Cancel-Miranda, Irving Flores-Rodriguez, and Andres Figuero-Cordero), and one woman (Lolita Lebron)—entered the House of Representatives's House Gallery 11 (for visitors). Others in the gallery dove for cover and ran in terror as the attackers—infuriated over America's treatment of their island nation—pulled out guns that they had smuggled in through the then-lax security of the Capitol. They opened fire on Congress. Five congressmen were wounded, but no one was killed. The four gunmen were sentenced to lengthy prison terms, and maintained throughout the process that they were being made political prisoners. Since that time, security at the Capitol has been a priority of national importance.

Aside from serving as the meeting place for many a great judicial mind, the cramped basement courtroom also played a role in telecommunications history. On May 24, 1844, after more than a year spent building a telegraph line between Washington and Baltimore (funded by a grudging but curious Congress), Samuel F. B. Morse sat down at the transmitter he had installed in the courtroom. In short order he typed in the Biblical message, "What hath God wrought!" Almost instantly, the words were received, via telegraph, by an operator waiting in Baltimore. The woman who chose those first tapped words (from the twenty-third verse of the twenty-third chapter of the Book of Numbers) was Miss Annie Ellsworth, the daughter of the Commissioner of Patents. Miss Ellsworth had delivered to Morse the news that he had indeed been granted the Congressional funding he did not expect to receive. So shocked and elated was Morse that he offered the lady the honor of selecting the first words to be telegraphed.

A Dome for the Capitol

Charles Bulfinch's lovely little dome was too tiny to top the newly sprawling Capitol in 1851, and so it was decided that a new dome would be placed atop the building. The architect of the latest version of the Capitol, Charles Walter, worked with Lincoln's Army Quartermaster General, Montgomery Meigs (a skillful architect who also designed the Smithsonian's Arts and Industries Building and the Pension Building), to design the new dome. It was a radical engineering task the two set forth to accomplish: The new dome was to be constructed entirely of iron, so as to make it fireproof, a characteristic sadly lacking in the original dome torched by the British. (Montgomery Meigs was known to be a fan of fireproofed construction, much to the dismay of those who hated his Pension Building and dreamed of it reduced to ashes.)

But designing the dome was an easy task compared to getting it installed and deciding what should go on top of it. Fights broke out in Congress over the design of the statue that was to top the dome, for the original figure was shown sporting a liberty cap, worn by the freed slaves of Rome. In this time of bitter discussion over the abolition of slavery in America, such headgear did not sit well with the Southern representatives—nor for that matter with Jefferson Davis, who was then the Secretary of War. Davis insisted that the artist, Thomas Crawford, change the headpiece of the statue. ("Freedom" now bears a feather-bedecked helmet—often mistaken for a Native American headdress.) After the statue headgear issue was resolved, the completion of the dome was slowed down by a far greater dispute: the Civil War. As thousands of wounded soldiers poured into Washington, most public (and quite a few private) buildings were transformed into makeshift hospitals. The Capitol was no exception, and it was soon a-scurry not only with legislators, but also with doctors, nurses, and patients. At times, this overcrowding slowed progress on the replacement of the dome to a crawl. Yet it never ceased, for President Lincoln had ordered the engineers to press on with the dome's completion as a symbol of the Union's endurance. Thus, despite the frantic pace of life at the wartime Capitol, despite the shortage of iron needed to construct the nine-million-pound dome, the once-controversial Freedom was raised into place atop the finished dome in late 1863. Guns from a battery on Capitol Hill and those at the dozen forts that surrounded the city fired an exchange of salutes as the nineteen-foot-tall statue was hoisted into place that December day.

Below the Great Rotunda

As historic sites go, one worth seeing is important not because of what happened there, but because of what did not happen there: Namely, the crypt in which George was to have been interred, until his family insisted his remains remain at Mount Vernon. The catafalque upon which Presidents Lincoln and Kennedy laid in state in the Rotunda is on view here.

The supports for the nine-million-pound iron dome can also be seen in the chamber of the Capitol beneath the Rotunda; the graceful barrel vaulting which provides the structural fortitude to uphold the weighty dome was designed by Montgomery Meigs, one of the chief architects of the dome itself. Also in the basement is one of the Capitol's most delightful and

The Hidden Capitol

In 1859, when the new Senate and House wings were completed, the Congress had enormous marble bathtubs installed in the basement so that members could refresh themselves during long sessions. (Bathtubs were scarce in Washington, so this was the only place in the city where many members could bathe.) The baths no longer exist, save for one unused bathtub. But a ghost story about a towel-wrapped VIP continues to circulate. President Grant's vice-president, Henry Wilson, supposedly caught a bad chill after being called away from his bath for an emergency, and he died a few days later. Legend has it that his ghost, clad in a towel and wheezing from the cold, has been seen drifting aimlessly through the old basement bathing area.

During the Civil War, the basement of the Capitol was also called into service as a bakery. Giant ovens were installed, and bakers worked day and night to make bread and biscuits for the thousands of soldiers crowded into every public and private building, park, and garden of the city. Meanwhile, wounded men were being treated in makeshift hospital wards throughout the Capitol building.

In the late nineteenth century, the Capitol harbored a bar. "The hole in the wall," as it was known, was a closet-sized drinking room just off the House cloakroom, where members could duck in between votes and quaff a drink before returning to the nation's business.

The tunnels through which the Congress and their staffers escaped during the Death March of the Bonus Army in July of 1932 are still in use beneath the Capitol. (The Death March was a macabre parade staged by thousands of desperate World War I veterans who had descended on Washington to demand that Congress pay them a promised cash bonus.) It has been said that one could walk for miles underground, popping into and out of most of the official buildings around the Capitol without ever seeing the light of day. A mini-tram runs through some of these tunnels between the Capitol and the legislators' office buildings. A similar, if smaller, circuit of tunnels connects the White House to the Treasury Building and its annex.

The bread ovens under the Capitol.

See Also: "The Armies of the Mall" (Chapter 4)

**Schoolchildren viewing the Washington Statue on the Capitol Grounds in 1899.
(Library of Congress)**

little-known visual treats, the Brumidi Hallways. Painted by dome artist Constantino Brumidi, these fancifully decorated vaulted hallways look like a page from a brightly colored Victorian scrapbook. Brumidi painted a series of cameos of historic events, and left a number blank for future artists to insert appropriate depictions. One of the most moving additions is a portrait of the crew of the Challenger Space Shuttle that exploded over Florida in January of 1986.

See Also: Brumidi House, The Supreme Court, and **The Library of Congress;** The White House (Chapter 1); Blodgett's Hotel Site (Chapter 2); "The Burning of Washington" (Chapter 10)

The Capitol Grounds

During the 1870s, the landscaping of the Capitol Grounds became a major priority. Frederick Law Olmsted, the designer of New York's Central Park, was hired to transform the grounds into a garden of democracy. He set his Victorian sensibilities to the task with remarkable results, and the reserved, rounded, intricate patterns of the walkways and greenery remain one of the best formal landscapes in Washington. The Capitol grounds also feature a variety of monumental and ornamental landmarks, including the Grant Memorial, added in 1937, and the Capitol Reflecting Pool.

Gone from the grounds are the Bulfinch Gatehouses, as well as the oil lamps Bulfinch had installed on the Capitol steps. The "Tripoli" statue now on display at the Naval Academy in Annapolis, Maryland, also once stood on the steps. Another famous—or rather, infamous—statue that once graced the grounds was the Washington Statue, which had for years rested on the back lawn of the Capitol, more a pedestal for pigeons and parade-watchers than a treasured monument. Originally commissioned for the Rotunda, the statue, oversized and overweight but underdressed, arrived in Washington in 1841. The city was scandalized by the image of Washington wearing a loosely draped toga and little else, but the statue was installed in its intended place anyway. The weight of the piece was too great for the Rotunda floor, however, which began buckling under the massive bulk of the statue. The statue was then placed outside on the Capitol grounds, where it remained until given to the Smithsonian in 1908. It is now displayed in a seldom visited hall in the west wing of the Museum of American History.

See Also: Museum of American History (Chapter 4)

PLACES: Around the Capitol

❷ American Civil Liberties Union (ACLU) Headquarters (122 Maryland Avenue, NE)

This Federal-style house was home to Theodore Roosevelt's Bull Moose Party running mate, Senator Hiram Johnson from 1930 to 1945. In 1947, the house became the Headquarters for the General Commission on Chaplain and Armed Forces Personnel. It now serves as the headquarters for the American Civil Liberties Union, which moved into the historic building in the mid–1980s.

❸ Open to the Public | Bartholdi Fountains (Independence Avenue, at 1st Street and Canal Avenue)

This giant cast-iron fountain won a major award at Philadelphia's Centennial Exhibition before being transported here after the fair. The sculptor, Frederic Bartholdi, incorporated electric lights into the basin of the fountain (which is held up by three large iron ladies), one of the first public displays of the new technology.

❹ Open to the Public | Folger Shakespeare Library (201 East Capitol Street, SE; 202/544–4600)

Oil magnate and bard-lover Henry Clay Folger put up the funds and the original collection with which the Folger Shakespeare Library was established. The Library opened to the public in 1932 with a fine collection of Shakespearean literature and related items, and has grown in stature to become the world's largest library of Shakespearian manuscripts and artifacts.

While on a state visit in the spring of 1991, Queen Elizabeth II made a point of visiting the library, much to the joy of Washington's ogling Anglophiles.

Grounds of the Folger Shakespeare Library. (Jack Looney)

Even before the Folger Library opened, it already had an intimate connection to an English Queen named Elizabeth, as noted by Olive Ewing Clapper (wife of prominent Washington journalist Raymond Clapper), in her 1946 memoir, *Washington Tapestry*:

"One day in November, 1931, [the library opened officially in early 1932] my husband asked me to go to the exquisite new Folger Shakespearean Library on Capitol

Hill and find out if they had Queen Elizabeth's [the First] corsets there. Ex-President Calvin Coolidge had asked Ray to find out, but Ray felt too shy to ask—so he made me do it. I went. "Yes," they told me, "her corsets are here, but they are so old and fragile we keep them from public display in order to preserve them."

In early 1991, the Folger Shakespeare theater company that performed on the Elizabethan stage here moved to a larger theater in Downtown, located at the redeveloped Lansburgh's Building on 7th Street, NW.

See Also: Lansburgh Building (Chapter 2)

---

❺ Grant Memorial (In front of the Capitol, on the East Mall at 1st Street)

It was said that this statue killed its sculptor, Henry Merwin Shrady, who devoted twenty years of his life to creating the magnificent marble and bronze memorial to Union general and U.S. President Ulysses S. Grant. Shrady died two weeks before the unveiling of his masterpiece, which in its time was the most expensive memorial ever funded by Congress.

---

❻ ❼ House Office Buildings (South of the Capitol, along Independence Avenue) and Senate Office Buildings (North of the Capitol, along Constitution Avenue)

Despite the massive size of the Capitol, by the turn of the twentieth century there just wasn't enough space for all the members of Congress and the Senate to work. Hence the construction of office buildings to the south (on the House side) and to the north (on the Senate side) began shortly thereafter. The people of Capitol Hill were hardly overjoyed to witness this latest flurry of federal construction which meant mounds of dirt and clouds of dust everywhere. Nevertheless, the office space was sorely needed, as noted in the journal of Ellen Maury Slayden, the wife of a congressman (who, like many legislators, often had to work at home for lack of office space). Here, she describes the ceremony surrounding construction start-up of the Cannon Office Building:

> "(April 15, 1906) The cornerstone of the new House Office Building, Uncle Joe Cannon's great conception, was laid yesterday to the sound of rolling drums and much oratory. The Marine Band and the Engineers' tried to drown one another out, and Teddy [Roosevelt] laid down the law more emphatically than ever. It will be a magnificent addition to the plaza, and most of the congressmen expect to facilitate their work, but...habit compels them to make vocal protest against 'that awful squandering of the people's money.'" —Ellen Maury Slayden, *Washington Wife* (1962).

Now both the House and the Senate side of the Capitol feature clusters of buildings that provide office space for the legislators and their support staffs. The congressional offices on the House side of the Capitol are the Cannon, the Rayburn (where Wayne Hays played with Liz Ray in his office, Suite 2264), and the Longworth Buildings. South of the Capitol stand the Senate Office Buildings—the Hart, Dirksen, and Russell buildings. The Russell Senate Office Building in particular has seen more than its share of historic events. It has been the site of some of Washington's most dramatic Senatorial hearings, including the 1954 Army-McCarthy investigations, the 1973 Watergate hearings, the 1987 Iran-Contra Hearings, and the 1991 Judge Clarence Thomas Confirmation Hearings, which transfixed the nation when law professor and former Thomas aide Anita Hill charged the Supreme Court nominee with sexual harassment. The Thomas hearings will likely go down in history as the most sexually graphic and soul-searching confirmation hearings ever to take place on Capitol Hill.

The House and Senate office buildings were erected, like other recent-vintage Capitol Hill structures, on sites that had previously held taverns and boarding houses. Many of the now lost boarding houses served as homes for members of the Congress and the Senate. Among the most renowned of these boarding houses was Mrs. Conrad's, which was Thomas Jefferson's home in 1800–1801 during his tenure as vice president under John Adams. Jefferson remained at Mrs. Conrad's even after his election to president, strolling from here to the Capitol to be sworn in as the third president of the United States. Jefferson stayed on another dozen days at the boarding house after his inaugural to give the Adams family a chance to move out of the White House. Mrs. Conrad's Boarding House later became the Varnum Hotel, which continued to serve legislators on the Hill until it was torn down in 1929 to make way for the Longworth Office Building.

See Also: The U.S. Capitol

---

8 Open to the Public **The Library of Congress (Main Building: 1st Street, SE; 202/707-5000)**

In 1800, Congress allotted a sum of $5000 for the procurement and management of a reference library. The library, which took up a single room in the Capitol building, was a working library where Senators and Congressmen turned to settle everything from legislative disputes to personal bets. That first collection of the Library of Congress was lost, along with the rest of the building, when the British burned Washington in 1814. Indeed, the British were out for literary revenge, as the Americans had just recently torched a major British library in Canada during the escalating nastiness of the War of 1812. So the British took apparent pleasure in using the books of the fledgling Library of Congress as kindling to stoke the fires in the burning building.

Fortunately, the federal government was able to replace the substance of the collection in a single transaction. Thomas Jefferson, who needed money at the time, sold his personal but substantial collection to the government soon after the library's burning. Until the library's new quarters were completed in the new capitol, it moved temporarily into the Old Brick Capitol along with Congress.

For the next century, the Library of Congress was often referred to as "Mr. Jefferson's Library." Indeed when the collection had finally grown too large for the capitol and the library was honored with its own building, this new home was named the Jefferson Building. Unfortunately, only a sampling of Jefferson's library is still in existence, as a second fire at the Library on Christmas Eve of 1951 destroyed most of the rare collection. Luckily, Jefferson's handwritten log of the library, in which he documented every volume in the collection, was preserved. Replicas of this fascinating document are on sale to the public.

The Library of Congress moved to the Jefferson Building in 1897 amidst great fanfare. In the intervening years, the collection has grown to include nearly every book published in the U.S. and many worldwide. Today, the collection numbers some 27 million volumes of books, bound reports, and early manuscripts, along with millions of periodicals, photographs, maps, charts, and other ephemera.

The famed Main Reading Room of the main (Jefferson) building, with its high-domed ceiling, feels more like a church than a library. This reverential aura seems wholly appropriate for the room where seven scholars worked through the night on the eve of President John F. Kennedy's funeral to research the funerary ceremonies for another slain president, Abraham Lincoln. They worked at the request of Jacqueline Kennedy, who wanted to use the precedents set by Lincoln's funerary events as the guidelines for her husband's funeral. The result of this long night of sad scholarship was a funeral procession through the streets of Washington in 1963 that was an evocative reminder of that other mournful day in 1865, even down to the riderless horse with riding boots reversed in the stirrup—a symbol of a fallen hero—that followed Kennedy's casket.

The Main Reading Room was closed for renovation for several years beginning in the late 1980s, despite the protests of outraged scholars and researchers who staged all-night read-ins (to no avail, as they were eventually forced out to make way for the workmen). But the room reopened in 1991, with newly installed computer technology and other research tools offering library users a dizzying array of high-tech information resources.

The library also has two annex buildings: the Adams Building (at the northeast corner of 2nd Street and Independence Avenue), built in 1939, which houses administrative offices and storage facilities; and the Madison Building (across Independence Avenue from the Main Building), an airy, light-infused building built in 1980 to house the library's ever-growing collections of photographs and prints, maps and architectural drawings, as well as films (this is the site of the Pickford Theater) and other materials.

The main Library of Congress building was constructed at the site of a row of historic houses called Carroll Row, which stood at 1st and A Streets. Built by Daniel Carroll (of **Duddington Manor**) in the early 1800s, the five houses of Carroll Row served a variety of uses before being torn down in 1887. The city's first inaugural ball, held for James Madison in 1809, was held in a Carroll Row hotel that was among the city's first elegant hostelries. Boarding houses were another Carroll Row specialty, and among the most notable was Mrs. Sprigg's, home to a young Congressman named Abraham Lincoln from 1847 to 1849. During the siege of Washington in 1814, the British commandeered the Carroll Row house of local physician Dr. Charles Ewing, transforming his home into a hospital for enemy wounded. Later, during the Civil War, the entire row of houses became Carroll Prison, where political prisoners were interred, often without the benefit of a trial.

Another residence that stood on this site—at what was then 279 B Street (now Independence Avenue), SE—was the home of Congressman Thaddeus Stevens from 1859 to 1868. Stevens shared the shabby brick rental home with his mistress, Lydia Smith. Had the Confederate Army ever made it to Capitol Hill, Stevens's home would have been among the first set ablaze, for he was a rabid abolitionist with a deep-seated hatred of all things Southern.

See Also: U.S. Capitol; "The Burning of Washington" (Chapter 10)

 Open to the Public **Sewall-Belmont House (144 Constitution Avenue, NE; 202/546-3989)**

This historic Federal-style townhouse nearly bit the dust in 1974 to make way for a Senate parking lot, but an act of Congress saved it. Built in 1800 by local powerplayer Robert Sewall, the house was rented to a variety of Washington movers and shakers—most notably Treasury Secretary Albert Gallatin, who lived here from 1801 to 1813. While living here, Gallatin worked at home for want of an office; and thus it was at this house in 1803 that he arranged the best land deal since Manhattan was bought for a pittance: the Louisiana Purchase. For a mere $15 million, Gallatin purchased from Napoleon Bonaparte the land that was to become the American West.

When the British invaded Washington in 1814, Sewall House (as it was then known) was the site of the only vigorous opposition. Someone within fired at the soldiers as they rode by, shooting the horse out from under General Ross, who had been leading the attack on Washington. The British promptly burned the house to the ground.

The house was rebuilt, and eventually came into the hands of suffragette Alva Belmont, who gave the house to the National Women's Party in 1929. The National Women's Party was founded by Alice Paul, who also authored the Equal Rights Amendment (in 1923), and who lived in the Sewall-Belmont House. The party headquarters had previously been located just

National Women's Party Headquarters, 1920. (Library of Congress)

down the street at the Old Brick Capitol (where the **Supreme Court** now stands). Today the house displays a variety of artifacts from various female leaders, including a desk that belonged to Susan B. Anthony.

See Also: Belva Lockwood's House Site (Chapter 2)

 Open to the Public **The Supreme Court (First Street, between Maryland Avenue and North Capitol Street, NE; 202/479–3211)**

For a full century after it first officially convened in 1790, the Supreme Court was considered the lowliest of the three branches of government. From 1801, when it moved to Washington from Philadelphia, until 1860, the court held forth in a basement chamber of the Capitol. After the new Senate and House chambers were added to the Capitol, the court got nicer quarters (in the Old Senate Chamber). But it was not until 1934 that the highest court in the land finally moved to its own grand, brand-new home across the street.

During its tenure in the Capitol, the Supreme Court decided the fundamental issues of the nineteenth century (many of which, as in this century, dealt with the rights of individuals). Among the cases heard and decided at the Capitol were many that had direct bearing on the issues of slavery and civil rights in America—most notably Dred Scott v. Sandford (1857), in which the court found that slaves had no rights as citizens and that Congress held no powers to prohibit slavery in U.S. territories; and Plessy v. Ferguson (1896), which established the "separate but equal" doctrine which legalized segregation in America until 1954, when Brown v. Board of Education of Topeka led the way to school desegregation. The many other landmark decisions handed down during the Supreme Court's tenure in the Capitol include McCullough v. Maryland (1819), which decreed that the powers of the federal government overrode those of the states; and the first major anti-trust ruling (in 1904), which ordered the dissolution of the Northern Securities Company.

The twentieth century has seen the courthouse rocked by social causes and civil rights, most notably the dissolution of legalized segregation. This century's Supreme Court probably will be remembered most for the progressive decisions handed down during the years of Chief Justice Earl Warren, and by the reversal or slow chipping away of many of these decisions as the court swung solidly to the right during the Reagan/Bush administrations. The issues of reproductive rights have transfixed the court and the American public during the 1980s and '90s much as the battle for civil rights polarized the nation during the 1950s and '60s. The stage has been set for a showdown over whether the Supreme Court will overturn the 1971 Roe v. Wade decision, which found that the Constitutional right to privacy applies to a woman's personal reproductive freedoms, including the right to choose to terminate an unwanted pregnancy.

If the Democrats regain the White House soon, they will be faced with a potentially hostile Supreme Court. But history shows that there is little a president can do to alter the make-up of the court beyond the appointment of new justices to fill the vacancies caused by the natural attrition of aging and ill-health. Franklin Roosevelt learned this lesson the hard way when his New Deal legislation came up against the "nine old men" (as FDR sneeringly called the members of the court) who again and again ruled his programs unconstitutional. Shortly after his second inauguration in 1937, Roosevelt met with the leaders of Congress and requested the authority to appoint an additional justice for each sitting justice over the age of seventy who had served for a decade or more on the Supreme Court. This would have allowed Roosevelt to appoint six new judges, enough to counteract the anti-New Deal rulings that were killing his programs. The Senate Judiciary Committee voted down the president's plan by a margin of 10 to 8, but the court of public opinion and historical judgment has passed an even harsher judgement against FDR's court-packing ploy. No president has since attempted such a flagrant alteration of the Supreme Court's bench.

Of course, not all Supreme Court cases have been of monumental importance, especially during the nineteenth century, when the highest court was often called upon to deliver opinions on simple matters of taste and substance. A case in point is described in a 1915 guide to the city, *Walks about Washington*, by Francis Leupp and Lester Hornby:

"One such instance [of a light-weight case] was in the case of an imported delicacy which might have been classed either as a preparation of fish or as a flavoring sauce. The customs officer had levied duties on it as a sauce, and an importer had appealed. The Justices, when they came to compare notes, confessed

The Old Brick Capitol. (*Walks about Washington*)

themselves sorely puzzled, and one of them suggested that, since technical arguments were so well balanced, it might be wise to fall back upon common sense. That evening he carried a sample of the disputed substance home to his wife, who was an expert in culinary matters.

"'There my dear,' said he, 'is a sauce for you to try.'

"With one look at the contents of the package, which she evidently recognized, she exclaimed: 'Pshaw! That's no sauce, that's fish. Didn't you know it?'

"The next day the Court met again for consultation, and on the following Monday handed down a decision overruling the customs officers and sustaining the importer's appeal."

The building in which the court now reigns supreme was completed in 1935, and designed in the Neo-Classical style by Cass Gilbert. Gilbert did a splendid job in creating a courthouse that exhibits the marble formality of a timeless landmark. Onlookers, however, might be warmed to know that the architect and some of his buddies were themselves the models for the frieze of robed justices that decorates the main pediment of the building. The Supreme Court is open to spectators, although most visitors to Washington don't realize they can sit in on the proceedings and watch the judgements of history.

On the site of today's Supreme Court Building once stood the Old Brick Capitol. When the British burned the Capitol in 1814, a group of prominent citizens formed an investment group, the Capitol Hotel Company, and began building a temporary Capitol here at the site of a former tavern and hotel. In the interim, Congress met at Blodgett's Hotel (in Downtown). In December of 1815, the temporary Capitol was ready for occupancy, and Congress met here for five years—with the House of Representatives adjourning to the second floor of the three-story building, and the Senate to the ground floor. The cramped quarters led the displaced legislators to jockey for political positioning, and it was one such argument (about which floor should host President Monroe's swearing) that led the new president to stage his inaugural ceremony out in front of the building on March 4, 1817.

At the end of 1819, Congress moved back home to the (still unfinished) new Capitol, and their temporary quarters commenced a long and colorful career—first as a private school, then as a boarding house, followed by a war-time tenure as a notorious federal prison, and at last as the home to a women's rights organization. During its early incarnation as Hill's Boarding House, Senator and statesman John C. Calhoun lived and died in one of the units. An

Remembrances of the Supreme Court

"The Supreme Court, having finally moved out of its dingy room in the Capitol Building into its fabulous eleven-million-dollar marble temple across Capitol Plaza, in 1934, was a noble sight for visitors to behold. . . . When they moved to their new palace, Justice Brandeis expressed regret and said he would rather the Court continued to use the little room off the corridor which connected the House and Senate Chambers, because 'our little courtroom kept us humble.'

"Justice Stone commented to [an acquaintance] as he showed him through the new building with its grandeur, pink marble pillars and red plush curtains, 'We'll look like nine black cockroaches when we get into that room.'"

—Olive Ewing Clapper, *Washington Tapestry* (1946)

opinionated southerner who claimed psychic powers, Calhoun startled his friends by insisting that President Washington had appeared to him in a vision, warning of imminent secession and the likely dissolution of the Union. After his death in 1850, Calhoun was said to have continued his residency as a ghost at the Old Brick Capitol. When the building was transformed into the Old Capitol Prison during the Civil War, tales of Calhoun's specter increased amid rumors that his spirit was checking the progress of his premonition.

Anne Royall, famed in the mid-nineteenth century for her shocking journalistic exposés (published in her newspaper, *Paul Pry*), was another resident of the Old Brick Capitol. Royall is often alleged to have sat on President John Quincy Adams's clothes one day when he was taking a dip in the Potomac, and refused to give them back until he gave her an interview on the spot. (The story is probably untrue, as Ms. Royall did not arrive in Washington until after Adams had left the White House.)

During its prison term, the building housed several renowned war criminals, including two wily female agents of the Confederacy, Belle Boyd and Rose Greenhow. Mrs. Greenhow, who was transferred to the prison from her home-turned-prison on Lafayette Square (it stood at the site of the modern-day Hay-Adams Hotel), was incarcerated in the very same room where she had nursed her husband's dying friend, John C. Calhoun.

But perhaps the most infamous inmate of all was Henry Wirz, the vicious commandant of the Confederacy's Andersonville Prison, where thousands of Union soldiers were said to have died in captivity. As punishment for his war crimes, Wirz was hanged on November 10, 1865 in the yard behind the Old Capitol Prison.

The legend of Calhoun's ghost was soon joined by tales of a female specter (thought to be Belle Boyd, come back to haunt the site of her humiliating imprisonment), as well as rumors of the wandering wraiths of Confederate soldiers and Union guards.

Following the Civil War, the capitol-turned-prison was sold to the Senate's sergeant-at-arms, George T. Brown, who transformed the building into a block of elegant townhouses. These in turn were sold in 1922 to the National Women's Party, for use as its headquarters and dormitory space. The suffragette organization, instrumental in leading the continuing battle for women's rights, resided in the building until 1929, when it moved to the **Sewall-Belmont House** on Constitution Avenue.

See Also: The U.S. Capitol and **Sewall-Belmont House;** Hay-Adams Hotel (Chapter 1); Blodgett's Hotel Site (Chapter 2); Dumbarton Oaks (Chapter 6)

PLACES: Capitol Hill—Southeast

⑪ Brumidi House (326 A Street, SE)

Once the home of Capitol Dome artist Constantino Brumidi, this house was erected around 1850. Brumidi, an Italian immigrant who came to America as a political refugee, devoted much of his life's work (a full twenty-five years) to painting the Capitol's interior murals and frescos. Brumidi felt a great debt to his adoptive country, and he often told those who asked about his decades of dedicated painting that he felt this was a way to pay tribute to America.

Brumidi eventually gave his life while working on the fresco that rings the Rotunda. According to *Milestones into Headstones* by Peter Exton and Dorsey Kleitz, Brumidi had designed sliding scaffolding that allowed him to move smoothly around the room. On October 1, 1879, Brumidi's painting chair slipped from the scaffolding, leaving the 72–year-old painter dangling 60 feet above the ground. Terrified, Brumidi hung there for a quarter hour before being rescued. The shock he suffered was too much for him, and he died at home five months later. He is buried at the Glenwood Cemetery in Northeast Washington.

See Also: The U.S. Capitol; Glenwood Cemetery (Chapter 10)

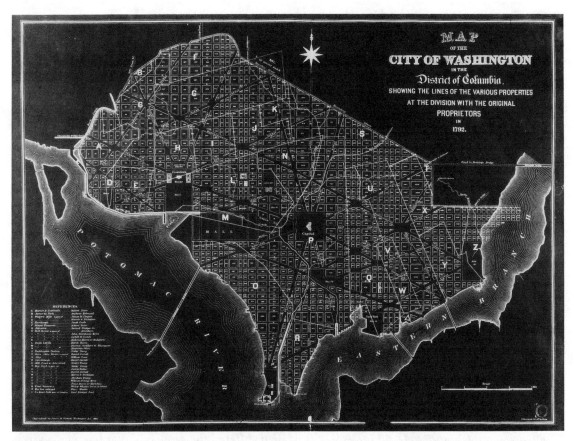

Daniel Carroll owned parcels P, R, and V, as shown on this map of the holdings of the original Washington landowners; David Burnes owned parcel L. (National Archives)

---

12 | Open to the Public | **Christ Episcopal Church (620 G Street, SE)**

Christ Church is the oldest church within the original city limits of Washington. (St. Paul's Church in upper Northwest is older, but was technically in the suburbs until 1890.) The church congregation was originally established in 1794, and its first quarters were in Daniel Carroll's tobacco barn. The congregation then moved on to another temporary site on New Jersey Avenue, before moving into its permanent (and current) residence, designed by Benjamin Latrobe and built in 1807.

In 1808, the church was the site of the wedding between Latrobe's nubile daughter, Lydia, and Nicholas Roosevelt (whose great-nephew, Teddy Roosevelt, would make his own historical mark). As Lydia had fallen in love at age thirteen, her mother and father disapproved of the young love, but allowed the wedding to take place nevertheless. March king John Philip Sousa was also married at the church. (Sousa was, in fact, born just down the street, and is buried in Congressional Cemetery, Christ Church's burial grounds.) Christ Church was also a popular presidential parish in its early days: James Madison, Thomas Jefferson, and John Quincy Adams all attended the church.

See Also: John Philip Sousa Birthplace; St. Paul's Church (Chapter 9); Congressional Cemetery (Chapter 11)

⑬ Duddington Manor Site (Between 1st and 2nd Streets, SE, at Duddington Place)

Duddington Manor was built by Daniel Carroll, the young land-owner who had inherited much of the land needed for the capital city. Carroll wanted to build a home nearer the power center, and so set about constructing an estate on Capitol Hill in August of 1791. The problem was that Pierre L'Enfant had just completed his plan of the city streets, which included placing New Jersey Avenue at precisely the spot where Carroll was laying down the foundation for his new house. An indignant L'Enfant ordered the construction of Duddington Manor halted and even had the foundations destroyed. The ensuing fight was solved by George Washington and three local commissioners, who convinced Carroll to situate his new house a bit farther east (and offered an indemnity of $4,000 to make up for his losses). L'Enfant did not fair as well. The Carroll house fiasco had raised the ire of the Congress once too often, and L'Enfant was soon dismissed as city planner. He then commenced a journey down the straight and narrow avenue toward destitution and ridicule.

One odd footnote to this tale of two enemies: In the last years of his life, L'Enfant was taken in by the prominent Digges family, and lived at their estate, Green Hill, until his death. He was even buried at Green Hill until his later re-interment with honors at Arlington Cemetery. This would not be such a strange occurrence, were it not that the matron of the family, Mrs. Digges, was none other than Eleanor Carroll, the daughter of Daniel Carroll.

In 1796, Capitol architect Benjamin Latrobe put the finishing touches on Duddington Manor. The regal in-town estate, which featured a spring house for Carroll Spring, took up approximately six acres of land, which were entirely enclosed by a high brick wall. Carroll's home became famous for the lavish entertainments held there, and for the powerful visitors—including Presidents Washington, Adams, Jefferson, Madison, and Jackson—who were frequent callers.

Daniel Carroll died in 1849, but his daughter continued to live at Duddington until the late 1880s, when the house was sold for $60,000. It then suffered the same fate that had cursed its birth: A street (this time called Heckman) was cut through the estate. Soon the house was dismantled, the branch of the spring that had served the house buried into a sewer, and the land subdivided into new housing developments.

See Also: Supreme Court

⑭ Open to the Public Eastern Market (7th Street and North Carolina Avenue, SE)

Established at this site in 1802, Eastern Market is one of the oldest surviving marketplaces in Washington. Like Center Market, which was established in 1801 at the present site of the National Archives, Eastern Market served as a major source for staples and over-the-counter gossip. Currently housed in a drafty, stable-esque brick building erected in 1873, Eastern Market serves as a kind of catch-all farmer's market and open-air boutique, with everything from fresh produce and meats to hand-made jewelry and t-shirts on sale at a pot-pourri of indoor and outdoor vending stalls and carts.

The building itself was designed by Adolph Cluss, who drew up the plans for many buildings during the construction boom of the late nineteenth century. Cluss, a German who immigrated to America

Eastern Market. (Jack Looney)

around 1850, spent his early years in Washington promoting and translating the work of his friend Karl Marx before turning to architecture. In the early 1870s, Alexander "Boss" Shepherd hired Cluss to design an elegant row of townhouses, known as Shepherd's Row along Farragut Square, in which they both lived. The relationship quickly fizzled, however, after Cluss testified against Shepherd, likening him to New York's infamously corrupt Boss Tweed in Congressional hearings that were investigating Shepherd's fiscal misconduct.

See Also: Farragut Square (Chapter 7)

---

15 Ebenezer United Methodist Church (4th and D Streets, SE)

Originally built in 1838 and rebuilt in 1897, Ebenezer United Methodist Church is the oldest black church on Capitol Hill. But it holds an even greater distinction: The church, originally known as Little Ebenezer Church, also served as the first schoolhouse for blacks in Washington. For a little more than a year, from March of 1864 to May of 1865, Little Ebenezer offered the first educational facility for blacks in the city.

---

16 Friendship House (The Maples) (619 D Street, SE)

When General George Washington visited The Maples (as it was then known), he pronounced it a fine house in the woods. The house, built in 1795 for Captain William Mayne Duncanson, is believed to have been erected on the site of an even earlier estate. A newspaper history account from 1908 described the estate as dating back to the reign of Queen Anne, which would have placed it here just after the turn of the eighteenth century.

Captain Duncanson, a land speculator who built the house in expectation of living a life of luxury in the new nation's capital, saw his investments falter and was forced to sell the property. The estate went through a variety of owners and managers over the years, including Francis Scott Key, who purchased the property in 1815 but moved on shortly thereafter. In 1814, when the British attacked Washington during the War of 1812, they turned The Maples into a field hospital to treat their wounded from the Battle of Bladensburg.

In the 1840s, Major and Mrs. A. A. Nicholson, a prominent Capitol Hill couple, moved into The Maples. But the house's citywide fame only served to spotlight the couple's sad life and troubled marriage. Mrs. Nicholson, clearly unhappy in the house (and increasingly suspicious about her husband's neighborly attentions to Daniel Carroll's daughter Sallie), fell into a deep depression. She committed suicide at the house, much to the shock of Capitol Hill society, and her husband later married Sallie Carroll, proving his doomed wife's suspicions.

In 1856, Senator John Clayton bought the house, and added on a ballroom that he had decorated by his neighbor, Constantino Brumidi, the painter of the Capitol interiors. Various other owners held the deed to The Maples until 1871, when it came into the hands of its most controversial and famous resident, Emily Edison Briggs, who wrote scathing commentary and investigative stories under the pen name of "Olivia."

In 1937, the estate was transformed into a community social services and cultural center, a role that it still carries out today, in its guise as Friendship House, a settlement house (a center of social services for the needy), which was first begun by a group of local citizens in 1904.

See Also: "A Poem of Home"; "The Burning of Washington" (Chapter 10)

---

17 Gary Hart's Townhouse (517 6th Street, SE)

Now a popular stop on the Washington "Scandal Tour" led by a local comedy troupe, this notorious townhouse was the home to former Democratic Senator Gary Hart of Colorado. In 1987, Senator Hart looked like he might just grab the brass ring of the Democratic presidential nomination. Instead, he made the mistake of grabbing something else. Questions had long circulated about the married Hart's womanizing ways, and, in an apparent bluff to stop the rumors from dominating his campaign for the Democratic nomination, Hart unwisely dared the press to put a tail on him, insisting they would find his clean. In April, when *Miami Herald* reporters got wind that Hart had been seen in Florida with Miami model Donna Rice, they decided to take Hart up on the offer.

The *Herald* didn't have to wait long: Rice showed up in Washington on May 1, and, while reporters staked out the front of Hart's townhouse, the senator and the model cozied up for a quiet weekend at home, or so it seemed. But the otherwise savvy scoop snoops had failed to stake out Hart's back door, and the Senator later claimed that he and Rice came and went through that rear entrance and spent little time in the townhouse alone together. The reporters couldn't prove otherwise. But they did have a juicy photo of Hart cuddling Rice in his lap during a Florida pleasure cruise on a rented yacht (appropriately named the "Monkey Business"). The *Herald* printed the story of the Capitol Hill weekend, and then published the Monkey Business snapshot. And Gary Hart was suddenly in drydock.

18 Joseph Holt's House Site (NE corner of New Jersey Avenue and C Street, SE)

This site was once the home of Judge Joseph Holt, who was the presiding judge at the trial of the Lincoln Assassination conspirator Mary Surratt. Holt sentenced Surratt to death for her part in the plot to murder the president. Joseph Holt had previously held the post of Secretary of War under President James Buchanan. The site is now occupied by the Cannon House Office Building.

See Also: Fort McNair (Chapter 12)

19 J. Edgar Hoover's Home Site (413 Seward Square, SE)

Here on the present-day site of the Capitol Hill United Methodist Church once stood the birthplace and long-time home of J. Edgar Hoover, who forged the FBI into a fighting force of gangster-hunters and then used his powerful agency to gather dark secrets about the country's most powerful men. Hoover was born in this house in 1895, and he lived here with his mother, to whom he was extremely close, until her death in 1938. He then moved to a home in Forest Hills, Maryland, with his longtime FBI companion Clyde Tolson, where he lived until his death in 1972.

See Also: FBI Building (Chapter 2)

20 Marine Corps Barracks (8th Street between G and Eye Streets, SE; call 202/433–6060 for parade reservations)

Installed at the turn of the nineteenth century, this is the oldest Marine post in the country, and it has the added distinction of having been situated here at the behest of President Thomas Jefferson. A few days after his inauguration in 1801, Jefferson rode his horse through Washington, taking the lay of the land and searching for perfect fortification posts. He chose this site for the Marine Barracks because of its strategic location between the Navy Yard and the Capitol. The street address became so well-known that Marines stationed here are known as the "Eighth and Eye Marines." Today, the "Eighth and Eye Marines" serve mainly as a ceremonial force whose duties include guarding the president when he is away at Camp David.

The Marine Barracks served as the official headquarters for the Marine Corps until 1901, and is still home to the Marine Corps Band and the Drum and Bugle Corps. The post underwent a nearly total reconstruction in the early 1900s, leaving the famous bay-windowed

Commandant's House (built in 1805) as the only original building on the base. The house has been the home of every Marine Corps Commandant since it was built.

One of Washington's great spectacles continues to take place every Friday afternoon during the summer here, when the Marines go through the paces of their Evening Parade. Colored banners fly, the Drum and Bugle Corps play, and the marines march in dress blues before the gathered crowd of civilians and officers. Although a three-week advance reservation is required to be admitted to see the parade, it is well worth the wait.

The Maples. *See* **Friendship House**

㉑ Joseph McCarthy's Apartment (3335 C Street, NE)

Senator Joe McCarthy lived in an apartment at this site while he was masterminding the Red Scare of the early 1950s with his inquisition-style hunt for Communists in the government and in the arts (via the House Un-American Activities Committee, aka HUAC). It was later revealed that, despite McCarthy's claims that he had a long list of names of "known Communists" employed by the federal government, not a single Communist was ferreted out during the damning hearings. McCarthy later lived in a duplex on 3rd Street, NE.
See Also: U.S. Capitol and **Joseph McCarthy's House**

㉒ Open to the Public **St. Mark's Episcopal Church (3rd and A Streets, SE)**

Built in 1888, St. Mark's is a Hill landmark, not only for its lovely architecture and garden, but also because it has served as the house of worship for many of Washington's most powerful people, including President Lyndon Johnson.

㉓ John Philip Sousa Birthplace (636 G Street, SE)

The "March King," John Philip Sousa, was born John Philip So, at this house on Capitol Hill in 1854. Legend has it that he later added the letters USA to his Polish surname as a tribute to his homeland. Sousa spent much of his life on the Hill, and was married and buried in this Washington enclave as well.
See Also: Christ Episcopal Church; Congressional Cemetery (Chapter 11)

PLACES: Capitol Hill—Northeast

㉔ Open to the Public **Frederick Douglass Home (316 A Street, NE; 202/287–3490)**

This house has served as a beacon of black history and culture on Capitol Hill for more than a century—first as home to abolitionist leader Frederick Douglass, then as the original site of the Museum of African Art. Douglass bought this house in 1872, upon settling in Washington as the editor of *The New National Era.* He shared the home with his first wife, Anna Murray, until 1878, when he purchased his famous estate, Cedar Hill, across the Eastern Branch of the Potomac (now called the Anacostia River). Douglass's Capitol Hill home was later transformed into a historic house museum, and it was here and in the adjoining rowhouses that the Museum of African Art first opened its doors in 1964. In 1979 the museum was officially absorbed into the Smithsonian Institution, and in 1988 the museum moved to new quarters on the Mall. (It is one of the two underground museums.) An amazing bit of irony is that the new museum is located near the approximate site where two of the city's most notorious slave pens (the Williams and the Robey) plied their human trade during the first half of the nineteenth century.

See Also: U.S. Treasury Annex (Chapter 1); Museum of African Art (Chapter 5); Cedar Hill (Chapter 11); "Slavery in Washington" (Chapter 12)

---

25 Open to the Public **Lincoln Park (Intersection of East Capitol Street, North Carolina Avenue, Tennessee Avenue, Kentucky Avenue, and 11th through 13th Streets)**

The Bethune statue at Lincoln Park. (Jack Looney)

Lincoln Park is a lovely green park and traffic rectangle with monuments to black history, including one financed by former slaves. The Emancipation Monument depicts a newly freed slave, broken chains dangling as he gazes up at a life-sized Abraham Lincoln who holds a copy of the Emancipation Proclamation. Legend has it that the sculptor, Thomas Ball, used a photograph of Archer Alexander, the last man seized under the aegis of the *Fugitive Slave Act*, as the model for the statuary freedman's face. Former slaves raised the money ($17,000) to commission and install the statue, and Frederick Douglass was the keynote speaker at its unveiling in 1876.

The park's other monument, the Mary McLeod Bethune statue, memorializes the famous educator and civil rights activist in her guise as a teacher, imparting wisdom to two rapt children. And, as most Washington photographers know, another notable sight at the park is the fine view looking toward the Capitol and the Washington Monument beyond, especially during the winter months when the trees that line East Capitol Street are bare and L'Enfant's vision is clear.

---

26 **Joseph McCarthy's House (20 3rd Street, NE)**

This was McCarthy's last Washington residence. The congressman and his family lived here, in a duplex whose other occupant was his wife's mother, from 1953. He died in 1957.

See Also: **U.S. Capitol** and **Joseph McCarthy's Apartment**

---

27 Open to the Public **Union Station (Massachusetts Avenue between 1st & 2nd Streets, NE; 202/371-9441)**

Now restored to its former glory, Union Station is one of Washington's most glamorous and delightful public buildings. Still the central railroad terminal for the city, Union Station was designed by architect Daniel Burnham and completed in 1908. It was built to replace and consolidate the city's two major railroad stations: The B&P Railroad Station, which stood where the National Gallery of Art is now located, and the B&O Railroad Station, which stood where the new Union Station was constructed. (It was at the B&O Station that Abraham Lincoln arrived incognito for his first inaugural in 1861—and from which his funeral train departed for Springfield, Illinois, in 1865.)

The area in which Union Station was built was once an infamous place in Washington—Swampoodle, a neighborhood aswarm with pick-pockets, cut-throats, and prostitutes. And by the second half of this century, it looked as though Union Station was reverting back into the primordial urban swamp from which it rose. But the station was saved from its sad and sordid state of disrepair by a splendid, $160 million restoration, completed in 1988, that returned it to a 1980s version of its original self. The new rendition of the old station left out some of the original features—the mortuary, ice-house, swimming pool, bowling alley, and nursery. In their place is a sophisticated shopping mall, complete with a food court in the basement, and a multiplex cinema that features classic movie palace entrances for each of the theaters. But most of the old favorites remain, including the spectacular Main Hall with its gold leaf decoration and Augustus Saint-Gaudens's statues of Roman Legionnaires (whose original nudity caused a scandal when the station was first built—hence the hastily added shields that still cover up the appropriate appendages).

Adirondacks, one of the restaurants at the newly refurbished station, is of special historic interest. The elegant rooms it now occupies were once the Presidential Suite, designed for the private use of the president and other important guests. Had such a suite been available to President Garfield at the old B&P train station, he might well have avoided his assassin altogether. The first president to avail himself of the suite was the overstuffed William Howard Taft, while the list of the many royals who have taken a load off at this once-private sanctum includes Queen Elizabeth II, Queen Marie of Romania, and King Hassam of Morocco. When the Emperor of Ethiopia, Haile Selassie, arrived at Union Station on October 1, 1963, President Kennedy met him at the train (after Selassie had implied that the greatest way to honor a guest was to travel a great distance to greet him).

Union Station has also been the arrival or departure site for the funeral trains of fallen leaders. Franklin Roosevelt's casket was transferred at the station on April 14, 1945, en route to Hyde Park, New York, for burial; and Robert Kennedy's body arrived at the station with great ceremony on June 8, 1968, the last stop on a Memorial Train tour to Washington for burial at Arlington Cemetery.

Happier occasions at Union Station have included the inaugural balls of Presidents Carter (in 1977) and Bush (in 1989), held in the truly grand Grand Concourse. And over the years, the chambers of the station have echoed with the cheers of crowds who gathered to greet such conquering heros as British Prime Minister Winston Churchill and General Dwight Eisenhower on June 18, 1945; and the Washington Senators Baseball Team, arriving home with a 9–1 record on their first major road trip in 1949. The Washington Redskins arrived to an equally raucous welcome when they returned home the NFC East champions on December 5, 1937 after a 49–14 victory over the New York Giants at New York City's Polo Field. The 10,000 fans awaiting the team's Union Station homecoming at 11 p.m. so inspired the Redskin's flamboyant owner, George Preston Marshall, that he decided on the spot to stage a victory parade from the station up Pennsylvania Avenue. The local police informed Marshall that, without a permit, his celebration was a no-go. Undeterred, Marshall staged a sneak parade with a small number of band members, only to have the team's drum major placed under arrest (as a symbolic gesture in lieu of arresting the entire band). Marshall bailed the drum major out of jail and grumbled about the incident for years afterward.

Even the royalty of rock have passed through the vaulted rooms of Union Station. On their first U.S. tour, the Beatles arrived by train from New York for their first public U.S. concert, held at the old Washington Coliseum on February 11, 1964. Just as in the famous news footage of the mop-topped band's arrival at Kennedy Airport, the Beatles's arrival at Union Station elicited squeals of joy from throngs of teeny-boppers waiting for a glimpse of the Liverpool lads.

Rock stars and royalty weren't the only ones to get special treatment at Union Station. At the outset of America's involvement in World War II, the "Servicemen's Canteen" opened at the terminal, offering twenty-four-hour food service and a nickel price-tag limit on all victuals. The canteen stayed open for five years, serving millions of five-cent foodstuffs to the throngs of soldiers who passed through the station. (During the first World War, temporary dormitories

Interior of Union Station. (Washington Convention & Visitors Association)

were erected on the grand plaza in front of the station to house the flood of new female government employees who descended on Washington to work for the war effort.)

On January 15, 1953, Union Station suddenly looked like a war zone itself, after the Pennsylvania Railroad's runaway "Federal Express," en route from Boston, slammed full-force into a concourse of the main terminal. The train's brakes had failed, but it was hoped that the Federal Express would be slowed down by the incline it would face on the approach to the station's upper concourse. (All other tracks were occupied with trains at the time.) Union Station was packed that day with travelers arriving in Washington for the pending inaugural of Dwight Eisenhower, and the Federal Express was bringing even more inaugural celebrants. When the Federal Express—featuring a 200–ton locomotive and 16 rail cars—made its unscheduled stop inside Union Station, it caused a million dollars in damages, destroyed a news stand, and sent some of its cars plummeting onto the lower level. But there were no severe injuries in the terminal, and none of the forty passengers injured on the train was killed. The 1976 Gene Wilder/Richard Pryor film *Silver Streak*, in which a runaway train slams into a station, was based in part on this incident.

There were a few precedents for Union Station's role as a celluloid muse. The opening scenes of the aptly named 1951 thriller *Strangers on a Train*, directed by Alfred Hitchcock, were filmed in Union Station. And the very first commercial film to use a Washington setting, *Filial Love* (1912), featured scenes shot at the Columbus Fountain, which graces the traffic circle in front of the station. (The Columbus Fountain was also the scene for another dramatic event—this one political, not cinematic—on Columbus Day, 1991, when demonstrators doused the fountain's statue of Christopher Columbus with red paint to protest the continued hero-worship of Columbus).

By the 1970s, the terminal had fallen on its hardest times yet—a thin layer of dirt and a pervasive stench filled the corridors and clung to the once-glorious vaulted ceilings. In 1976, a misguided attempt at adding a visitor information center in the Main Hall only made matters worse, for the public information pit installed drew more derelicts and petty thieves than it did eager tourists. There was talk of tearing the place down altogether, but with money raised through private donations, the station was renovated instead.

Today, Union Station continues to evolve into a public treasure with a social conscience; in 1990, a memorial statue honoring A. Philip Randolph, the founding leader of the Brotherhood of Sleeping Car Porters that fought hard for the rights of (mostly black) train porters, was added to the train concourse near the baggage claim area.

See Also: National Gallery of Art (Chapter 4); Howard University Hospital (Griffith Stadium Site) (Chapter 9); Old Washington (Uline) Coliseum (Chapter 10)

Chapter 4

THE MALL

To Washingtonians, the Mall is the city's playground, a swath of lawn and graveled walkways interjected with marble monuments and museums; to tourists, it is a collection of museums and landmarks connected by a cohesive parkland that does double duty as a parade ground and stomping ground. For both locals and visitors, and even for those who have only seen Washington on the front of postcards or from the back row of a movie theater, the Mall is a symbolic Garden of Eden for the nation's collected (and collective) culture and memory.

The history of the Mall as a gathering place is one of pomp and circumstances, of parades and protests and military maneuvers. Much as Pennsylvania Avenue has played the role of America's Main Street—complete with inaugural parades and funeral processions—so the Mall has taken on the duty of America's fair grounds, witnessing countless celebrations, festivals, rallies, and demonstrations. With the U.S. Capitol at one end zone and the White House at the fifty-yard line, the Mall is an arena for activists with a message for the nation and its leaders.

From suffragettes to Klansmen, practically every group with a cause or a master plan has rallied on the Mall. When Marian Anderson, the famous black contralto, sang on the steps of the Lincoln Memorial on Easter Sunday in 1939, she set the stage for the monument's future use as a pedestal for civil rights causes. For it was on these same steps that the Rev. Dr. Martin Luther King, Jr. delivered his "I Have a Dream" speech before hundreds of thousands of civil rights marchers in 1963. In 1968, after King's assassina-

The Grand Army of the Republic (GAR) encampment on the Mall in 1892. (Library of Congress)

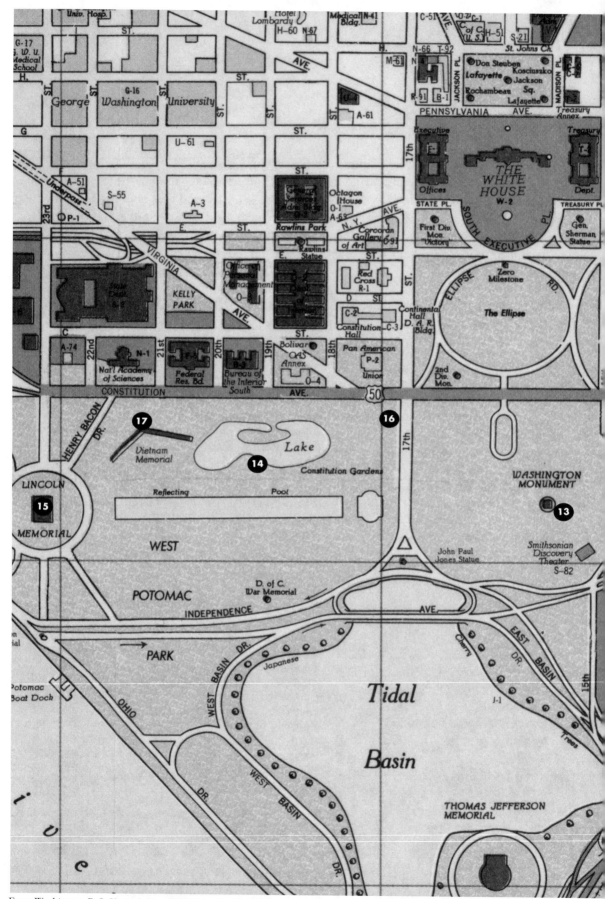

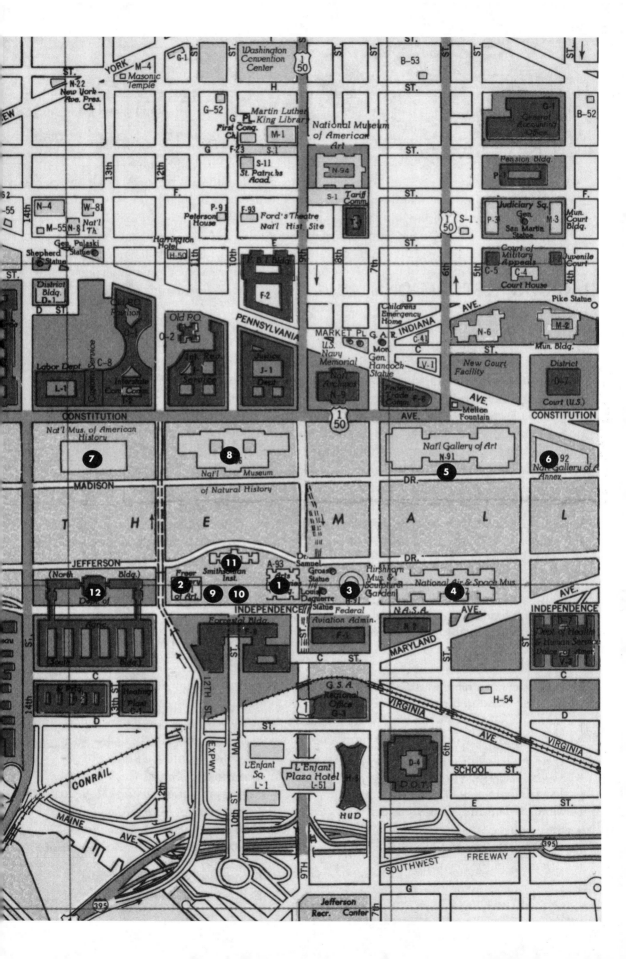

tion, the Poor People's March participants descended on the Mall, encamping and protesting the problems of poverty.

The 1970s, despite the early years rampant with anti-War demonstrations, faded to bland as the decade of the disco wore on and the idealists of the 1960s entered the workforce. But by the late 1980s, the Mall once again bloomed with placards and banners. Arguably the most powerful and widespread (literally) gesture of the decade was the unfurling of the Names Project Quilt on the Mall for several years in a row in the late 1980s. Sewn by longtime companions, parents, siblings, children, and friends, the quilt documented the individual lives and deaths that made up the growing mortality statistics of the AIDS epidemic. Eventually, the quilt grew too large to exhibit even on the vast expanse of the Mall—perhaps the ultimate symbol of its silent plea for understanding and research dollars.

The early 1990s saw a continuation of the issues of the 1980s. There were also flash-fire rallies against the war with Iraq in early 1991, and on June 8, 1991, a Victory Celebration that filled the Mall with Stealth Bombers and Patriot Missile Launchers installed for the largest military parade in the city's history. This was not the first time the Mall was home to the military—in fact, during the Civil War, the Mall became the campsite for hundreds of soldiers of the Army of the Potomac, who ate, slept, and drilled here. A half-century later, the Bonus Army of World War I veterans called the Mall (and much of the surrounding city) home, staging a bitter protest for a much-needed lump-sum payment of the veterans' bonus promised by Congress, which they had been receiving only in small increments. (See **"The Armies of the Mall."**)

To Washingtonians, the spurts of protest and pomp along the Mall are blips on the long-range calendar of events that is always highlighted by such annual festivities as the Fourth of July celebrations. For a few years in the late 1970s and early 1980s, the July 4th concert on the Mall was performed by the Beach Boys. That tradition ended abruptly and controversially when President Reagan's Secretary of the Interior, James Watt, vowed to ban the band due to what he considered the unruly and undesirable kinds of audiences attracted to rock and roll. Since that time, the Beach Boys have been replaced by country and western, jazz, and classical music stars. Other annual Mall events include the Festival of American Folklife and the Smithsonian Kite Festival.

Tradition is ingrained in the Mall. From the beginning, when L'Enfant laid out the plans for the city, the Mall (or at least its eastern half) was diagrammed much as it exists today. The only difference was that L'Enfant envisioned the central core as a broad ceremonial boulevard surrounded by a park-like setting, along which grand mansions would be built, rather than the museums and galleries for which it is now known. Other master planners have placed their imprint on the Mall as well—prominent among these was Andrew Jackson Downing, whose 1850 plans for the beautification of Washington's parks included much of the ornamental planting and landscaping of the central Mall park. Downing died at the age of 37 in an 1852 steamboat accident and never lived to see his work completed. His partner, Calvert Vaux, commissioned a memorial urn statue commemorating Downing's life and love of classical forms, which still stands on the grounds of the original Smithsonian Building.

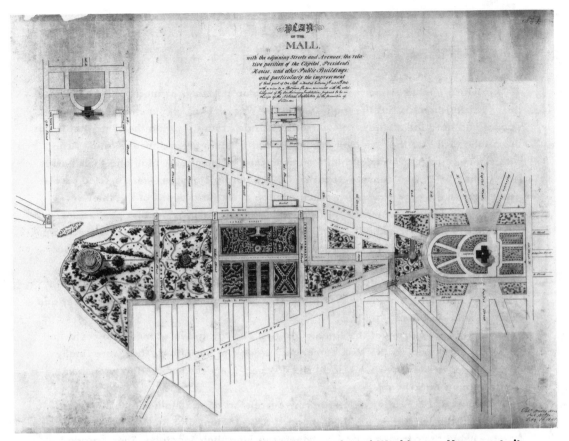

Plan of the Mall, dated 1841, showing Canal of Tiber Creek and Washington Monument site. (National Archives)

During his 1870s crusade to turn the muddy town of Washington into a modern city, Governor Alexander "Boss" Shepherd of Washington set his sights on clearing the Mall of the scars of the Civil War. The most obvious evidence of the war could be found in the ugly railroad tracks that dug into the soft earth of the parkland. Shepherd knew he would have a long, drawn-out fight with the railroad company (Baltimore and Pacific) that owned the old rails if he initiated a discussion about their removal. And if there was one thing that Boss Shepherd hated, it was lengthy planning procedures. (Within two years, he paved the streets, laid the sewers, and basically accomplished more than all city planners had in the whole history of Washington). Thus Shepherd instructed his workers to begin disassembling the tracks under cover of darkness. By the next morning, many of the tracks still remained, but the president of the rail company was so amazed at Shepherd's gall that he offered the Boss a job. The Boss refused, however, as his crusade to transform the city was still in progress.

The McMillan Plan was also instrumental in creating the Mall as it is today. The blueprint of this 1901 commission (whose work was later carried out under the authority of the Fine Arts Commission appointed by Congress in 1910) set in motion the creation of the Lincoln Memorial, the Monument Reflecting Pool, and most of the other formal touches on the Mall itself. The McMillan Commission's suggestions about beautifying the

The Armies of the Mall

Perhaps no other civilian section of Washington has seen as much military action (and inaction) as has the Mall. During the War of 1812, the enemy burned the Capitol and used the Mall as their personal parade grounds during the siege. But it was during the Civil War that the Mall became a true training ground for the Union Army, with regiments of the Army of the Potomac encamped across the Mall and their horses stabled nearby at the Treasury Department. Temporary structures were erected as office space for the over-crowded wartime capital. Even the grounds of the then-unfinished Washington Monument went to war, transformed into grazing pasture for thousands of heads of cattle destined to become meat for the men of the northern army.

The Union Army returned to the Mall for one long, last fling in 1892, when 80,000 members of the Grand Army of the Republic (Union veterans of the Civil War) encamped on the Mall, reminiscing and parading up a storm to celebrate their deeds of thirty years earlier. (A monument to the G.A.R. and its founder stands at 7th Street and Pennsylvania Avenue.)

In 1894, Coxey's Army of the Unemployed—a rag-tag group of men who could find no work—encamped on the Mall demanding work and social aid. They were finally coaxed to leave the city when a local shopkeeper provided money to pay for their transportation back home.

On August 8, 1925, a far different army descended on the Mall: the Ku Klux Klan. So empowered did this group of 50,000 hooded KKK-ers feel that they marched barefaced, without their trademark white sheets masking their identities. They paraded gaudily down Pennsylvania Avenue before assembling for a "patriotic" rally on the grounds of the Washington Monument. In years since, Klan rallies have been far less well-received, sometimes causing near riots as protestors try to break through police barriers to confront the white supremacists. But in 1925, the hate mongers drew mainly curious throngs who came to enjoy the parade.

The most famous Washington encampment was that of the 1932 Bonus Army—a group of thousands of World War I veterans hoping for payment of a long-promised cash bonus. As it did with Coxey's Army, Congress tried the ticket-home tactic. The buy-off offer backfired, however, when the angry marchers dug in their heels. In July, General Douglas MacArthur's troops were called in to rout them from the city in an ugly battle that helped to doom President Hoover's re-election bid that year. (A smaller contingency of desperate men known as the Hunger Marchers had already "invaded" the capital in 1931, but had quickly lost interest in their cause and wandered back home, so the determination of the Bonus Army to hang on until they got their bonus pay shocked the city.)

During the Vietnam War, the Mall was the site of countless protests for peace by demonstrators who borrowed a page from the non-violent tactics of the Civil Rights Marchers by passively resisting arrest. Such protests were seen once again on the Mall during the Gulf War in 1991, although the short-lived conflict left a far greater mark on the Mall area (in the form of tank ruts on Constitution Avenue) during the Victory Celebration later that year.

city were responsible for the removal of some of Downing's Victorian greenery to achieve again the more formal, boulevard-like Mall area originally planned by L'Enfant, a renovation accomplished in 1930.

The western half of the Mall (from the **Washington Monument** to the **Lincoln Memorial**) was originally the docking area and canal entry port for the Potomac, the waters of which lapped all the way up to modern-day Constitution Avenue. The land for the Mall area west of the Washington Monument, along with the Tidal Basin and East and West Potomac Parks, was created through the Army Corps of Engineers river dredging project that began in the 1880s. Around the same time, the Canal of Tiber Creek was also filled in. This stinking waterway had traversed the same route as modern-day Constitution Avenue before cutting in front of the Capitol and then spilling its sludgy issue out into the Potomac at the waterfront.

Despite its history of protest and planning, the Mall is probably best known as a national treasure—a home to the **Smithsonian Institution** museums and the **National Gallery of Art,** and a patriotic pathway leading to the city's most moving monuments. The Smithsonian was first established here, in James Renwick's Gothic Revival castle building, in 1855.

But the Smithsonian Institution that Americans know and love today as "America's Attic" was not established for the purposes of collecting American bric-a-brac and Archie Bunker's Chair—it was created as a serious institute for the study and advancement of scientific matters. It was only when the nations of the world donated their Centennial Exposition exhibits from the Philadelphia 1876 fair to the federal government that the Smithsonian's collection of everything under the sun began. That collection was housed in what for many years was called the "New National Museum," and is now known as the Arts and Industries Building. Other buildings soon followed, and today the Mall is lined with such fantastic collections as the **Museum of American History, The Museum of Science and Technology, The Arthur M. Sackler Gallery, The National Museum of African Art**, and the **Hirshhorn Gallery.**

Another Smithsonian institution, the National Zoo, got its start on the Mall, at the site of the present-day Enid Haupt Garden. In the 1880s, the taxidermists of the Smithsonian who were busily mounting animal specimens, arranged for the installation of live "models" on the Mall. The miniature zoo that was established for the taxidermists to study soon attracted a following among tourists and locals alike, and a Washington tradition was born. Among the species displayed on the Mall was a small herd of buffalo. As visitors came and saw these noble beasts of the plains nibbling on the grass of the Mall, they began to realize the importance of saving the majestic species. This epiphany resulted in the creation of federal regulations that banned the further slaughter of the dwindling buffalo herds in the west. In 1889, the zoo moved to a large plot of land on the edge of Rock Creek Park.

Also along the Mall is the gracious John Russell Pope-designed National Gallery of Art, and the East Wing of the National Gallery of Art, added in 1978 in the post-modern design of architect I.M. Pei to hold much of the gallery's modern art collection. The site where the National Gallery of Art now stands was once home to the Baltimore and Potomac Railroad Station where President Garfield was shot by assassin Charles Guiteau in 1881.

The Mall's monuments, of course, are the true symbolic landmarks of the city. The Washington Memorial was planned from the beginning, as early maps can attest, but work did not begin on the city's tallest official structure until 1848 and did not end until 1885. From the changes in plans to the long, drawn-out building process, the Washington monument beat out even the Capitol's long-term improvements for a record in tardy construction. (The only building in the city to take longer to complete is the Washington National Cathedral.) The Lincoln Memorial underwent similar planning changes, although it didn't take nearly as long to finish. The **Vietnam Veterans Memorial,** a still controversial black wedge of a wall inscribed with the names of the soldiers killed during the Vietnam War, is the most visited monument on the Mall, and seems to invoke the most emotional response, as evidenced by the tokens of grief and love still left along its pathway every day of the year by visitors.

PLACES: The East Mall

B&P Railroad Station. *See* **National Gallery of Art**

1 | Open to the Public | **Arts and Industries Building (900 Jefferson Drive, SW; 202/357–1481)**

Like so many lavish federal buildings, the Arts and Industries Building was, early in its life, called on to serve double duty as a ceremonial site. Indeed, its first official function was as a ballroom: President Garfield's 1881 inaugural ball was held at the museum a few days before it was opened to the public as a museum.

Today, the Arts and Industries main exhibit hall offers a permanent display of items from the 1876 Centennial Exhibition. It is a fitting exhibit indeed, given that the National Museum (as it was first known) was originally built to house several tons of exhibits and displays left over from that spectacular 1876 Centennial Exhibition held in Philadelphia. Most of the foreign governments donated their exhibits to the American government instead of paying to transport them back home. The end result was that in a single year, the federal government was given an entire museum full of mechanical wonders and cultural icons. The problem was where to put it all, as the Smithsonian Institution—although a repository of historical artifacts—was housed in a single building, and its philosophy was devoted to pure science rather than to base culture. But a U.S. National Museum collection had already been established in 1858 to accept a collection of models from the U.S. Patent Office, and the collection had subsequently become the catch-all for bits and pieces of Americana given to the federal government. The obvious answer was to finally give the U.S. National Museum its own home—and as fast as possible, as trainloads of World Expo booty were steaming their way rapidly into Washington. Congress voted money to build a National Museum to house the largesse, and set wheels in motion for the eventual transformation of the Smithsonian Institution into "The Nation's Attic," as it has come to be called.

The second of the Smithsonian museums built, the Arts and Industries Building was created in 1881 by the team of Adolph Cluss and Paul Schulze. The design was based on plans by the Army Corps of Engineers' General Montgomery Meigs, who also designed the spectacular Pension Building (now the National Building Museum).

2 Open to the Public ## Freer Gallery (12th Street at Jefferson Drive, SW; 202/357–2700)

The Smithsonian's first museum devoted exclusively to the collection and display of works of art, the Freer was built in 1923 to house the Oriental art collection donated to the federal government by Charles Freer. Freer was a tycoon who made his millions manufacturing railway cars, and spent them amassing one of the most important privately owned Oriental art collections in the western world. Freer also collected the works of Western painters whom he admired, concentrating particularly on those of James Abbott McNeill Whistler, whom Freer counted among his closest friends. Freer's extensive collection of Whistlers is also on display at the gallery, and, although he missed out on the artist's most renowned work of all—"Arrangement in Black and White" (a.k.a "Whistler's Mother"—he did at least manage to acquire "Whistler's Father."

3 Open to the Public ## Hirshhorn Museum of Modern Art (7th St. and Independence Avenue, SW; 202/357–3235)

The Hirshhorn was Washington's official answer to long-held gripes that the city was a haven for classic art but a desert for modern work. Designed by Gordon Bunschaft in a decidedly twentieth-century mode, the museum opened in 1974. It was named for Joseph Hirshhorn, the Latvian-born, self-made millionaire who acquired some six thousand modern paintings and sculptures, then offered to give them away on the condition that a museum be devoted to their display. The Smithsonian was one of a dozen art institutions around the country vying to receive the artwork. It won the honor when federal funds were voted to build the Hirshhorn Museum and Sculpture Garden. A deal was struck in 1966, and the doughnut-shaped gallery was built in eight years, opening in October of 1974.

A decidedly old-fashioned museum once stood where this modern doughnut of a building now reigns. The Army Medical Museum, home to some of the U.S. military's weirdest specimens and battlefield samplings, was moved here in 1897 from its previous home at Ford's Theater. This museum displayed such Lincoln assassination artifacts as the bullet that was removed from the president's brain, and the surgical probe that was used to remove it. The museum also exhibited the gunshot vertebrae of the next president to be assassinated, James Garfield. (The curators had performed the autopsy on the slain president in 1881.) But perhaps the most popular exhibit of all was General Daniel Sickle's leg, which the Union general lost at the Battle of Gettysburg and donated, along with the cannon ball that removed the limb, to the museum. Sickles, already famous as the man who murdered District Attorney Philip Barton Key, added to his legend by visiting his lost leg, and drinking a toast to it, on each anniversary of its amputation.

When the historic building was razed in 1968 to make way for the Hirshhorn, the collection of the Army Medical Museum was moved to Walter Reed Army Medical Center in upper Northwest.

See Also: Jackson Place Houses: 730 Jackson Place (Chapter 1); Ford's Theater (Chapter 2); Walter Reed Army Medical Center (Chapter 9)

4 Open to the Public ## National Air and Space Museum (7th Street and Independence Avenue, SW; 202/357–1400)

As befits such an all-American museum, the Air and Space Museum opened officially to worldwide applause on July 4, 1976, and it has continued to draw record-breaking crowds ever since. The most widely visited museum in the world, the Air and Space Museum spotlights the history of aviation and space exploration with a variety of permanent and changing exhibits.

The collection of the Air and Space museum was previously displayed in an earlier museum on the Mall, called the National Air Museum, until America entered the space age, at which point it became the Air and Space Museum. Housed in a World War I-era structure that resembled a hangar (originally built as a wartime aircraft testing facility), the first Air and Space Museum was located on the present-day site of the **National Museum of African Art** and the **Arthur M. Sackler Gallery**. The earlier Air and Space Museum was a much smaller museum than its successor, but it did have its attractions—including outdoor walkways lined with rockets such as a 75–foot Atlas and a 28–foot Polaris.

According to Howard K. Smith's lively 1967 book, *Washington, D.C.: The Story of Our Nation's Capital*, one of the most famous exhibits at the Air and Space Museum, the Wright Brother's famous first airplane, was installed in the earlier Air and Space Museum in 1948 only after the Smithsonian had embarrassed itself in a strange scheme to deny the Wright Brothers their claim to being first in flight.

The Smithsonian had had its nose out of joint ever since one of its most famous directors, Samuel P. Langley, was beaten by the Wright Brothers in the race to build mankind's wings. Although Langley, an avid engineer, had come close to building a working airplane, none of his vehicles had made it off the ground long enough to fly; in the meantime, the Wright Brothers made the first successful powered flight at Kill Devil Hill, North Carolina on December 17, 1903. Although Langley was devastated when the Wright Brothers succeeded where he had failed, he accepted the brothers' accomplishment with grace and poise.

The Smithsonian Institution was a bit less gracious about its director's failure. After Langley's death, the Institution asked the Wright Brothers to donate one of their later planes for exhibition at the Smithsonian. The museum displayed the plane along with one of Langley's early (non-working) models, leaving visitors with the impression that Langley's was the original flying machine. Adding to the insult, Smith notes that under the auspices of the Smithsonian, one of the Wright Brothers' competitors secretly altered Langley's model based on the Wright Brothers' successful design, and then had the gall to fly the new-and-improved Langley version to establish it as the true original. The plot was foiled by damning before-and-after photographs that clearly showed evidence of tinkering.

This site was formerly home to the Washington Armory, which stood at 6th and B (now Independence) Streets from 1855 until 1964, when it was razed to make way for construction on the Air and Space Museum. The old Armory served a variety of purposes during its existence. When it first opened, the Armory was used to store the weapons of local volunteer militia; it also housed a small museum of Revolutionary War artifacts and weapons. When John Brown raided Harper's Ferry in 1859, militia assembled at the Armory and readied themselves to defend Washington in case a similar attack was planned on the capital.

During the Civil War, the Armory became the central receiving building for the Armory Square Hospital, a massive complex of wooden hospital wards that spanned the Mall between 7th and 5th Streets. Steamships bearing badly wounded soldiers would unload them at the nearby landing for transfer to this hospital complex. Funeral services were held on the grounds for the many who died here. Poet Walt Whitman was among the hundreds of volunteer nurses who gave aid and comfort to wounded Union soldiers here.

After the Civil War, the Armory was left empty (and some said haunted by all the death and misery it had witnessed), until 1878. It then became a storage facility for the objects donated by the various nations who had exhibited at the 1876 Centennial Exposition in Philadelphia. The Centennial donations became the foundation of the Arts and Industries building collection. The Armory was later used as the site for the United States Fish Commission (now the Fish and Wildlife Service), which bred fish and then shipped them around the country to restock public recreational waters.

See Also: Quadrangle Museums; Walt Whitman's Boarding House(s) (Chapter 2)

⑤ Open to the Public **National Gallery of Art (Constitution and 4th Avenues, NW; 202/842–6246)**

The National Gallery of Art opened here in 1941. The bulk of the original collection and the initial funds for the gallery were a gift to the nation from millionaire industrialist Andrew Mellon (who was hooked into buying much of the collection through the brilliant machinations of art dealer Baron Joseph Duveen while a resident at the McCormick House, now the home to the National Trust of Historic Preservation).

Among the masterpieces displayed here are the works of the Old Masters that were the focus of Mellon's collecting. Rembrandt, El Greco, Raphael, and Renoir all share gallery space here, as do Monet and Titian. And this is the only gallery in America that owns a Leonardo da Vinci (the Ginevra de Benci); all of the Italian master's other works are owned by European galleries or collectors. Until 1904, this site had been occupied by the B&P Railroad Station, the city's main terminal until it was supplanted by Union Station. Built between 1873 and 1878, the station was a Victorian Gothic of the highest order, but within three years of its completion, the B&P became a tragic landmark to rival Ford's Theater.

On July 2, 1881, President William Garfield, en route to the commencement of his alma mater (Williams College), was making his way through the train station with his entourage. As they passed the Ladies Waiting Room, he was suddenly confronted by a pistol-toting former civil service employee, Charles Guiteau, who had been incessantly hounding White House staffers for a government appointment. Rebuffed once too often, Guiteau had decided to kill the man he felt had denied him a well-deserved bureaucratic post. Guiteau fired two shots at the president, mortally wounding him.

Two months passed between the shooting and Garfield's death, during which time his doctors did all they could, including the requisite move to the seashore for fresh air. Garfield died at the family's seaside summer home in Elberon, New Jersey on September 19, 1881. Medical historians who have studied the president's treatment

In 1881, the B&P Railroad station was draped in mourning after Garfield's assassination there. (Library of Congress)

agree that simple techniques developed in the early twentieth century would have saved his life. His life might also have been prolonged were it not for the bungling of his doctors: Alexander Graham Bell invented a metal detector to aid in locating the bullets still embedded in the president's body. But the doctors failed to removed the steel springs on the patient's bed during the use of Bell's contraption, rendering it useless.

The B&P Railroad station was draped in mourning after the president's death, and a memorial plaque was installed at the site of the shooting.

Guiteau was arrested and held for the attempted murder of the president, a charge that was changed to murder upon Garfield's death. Despite questions about his sanity, Guiteau was judged fit to stand trial. Convicted of the president's murder, he was hanged on June 29, 1882.

In 1901, when the McMillan Commission recommended that all Victorian architecture in the Mall area be replaced by a unified Beaux-Arts complexion, it dealt a death blow to the B&P Station. It was soon torn down to make way for the new tracks being laid for Union Station, completed in 1904.

The area where the gallery now stands was also home to numerous row houses, many of them boarding houses. The most renowned boarding house here was an elegant establishment that became known as Tyler House after Vice President John Tyler lived there during the year of 1841. Although many of the row houses were taken down to make way for the B&P Station, Tyler House and a few others were left standing until 1931, when they were demolished.

During the 1930s, the land where the National Gallery now stands was a wood yard, where wood for New Deal construction projects was cut and stacked. Plans for the site had long included the George Washington Memorial Building, an auditorium and civic center honoring World War I vets. Although the cornerstone was laid for the building in 1921, and the foundation and ceremonial stairs were built, the project was scrapped in the late 1930s after funds ran dry and the site was needed for the National Gallery.

See Also: National Trust for Historic Preservation (Chapter 6); Old Courthouse (Chapter 2); Union Station (Chapter 3)

---

6 | Open to the Public | **National Gallery of Art/East Wing (4th Street and Constitution Avenue, NW; 202/737–4215)**

The East Wing of the National Gallery of Art often overshadows its older sister, drawing larger crowds and longer attendance than the quieter collection next door. It is in fact the most visited art museum in America. Designed by I.M. Pei and completed in 1978, the East Wing was not without its critics, many of whom argued that the modern, sharply angled building would stand in shrieking contrast to its elegantly domed neighbor. The notion of glass pyramids in the courtyard also raised eyebrows. Yet, although Pei's subsequent modernization of the Louvre has scandalized Parisians, critics have come to admire this quirky, angular building, and tourists have always loved it. In fact, a visit to Washington is not complete for many without a pilgrimage to rub a hand along the surface of the most sharply angled wing (to right of the main entrance). So many tourist hands have pressed against the smooth marble that the stone has darkened there from the years of oily contact.

See Also: National Gallery of Art

---

7 | Open to the Public | **National Museum of American History (Constitution Avenue at 14th Street, NW; 202/357–1481)**

The Museum of American History—originally called the National Museum of History and Technology—is probably the most famous of the Smithsonian museums. It displays such classic exhibits as the First Ladies' Gowns and the Fort McHenry flag that inspired Francis Scott Key to write the "Star Spangled Banner." Much of the collection here was originally part of the U.S.

National Museum collection, created in 1850, which was housed for a time at the Arts and Industries building. The present building, in Beaux Arts style, was completed in 1964.

One of the museum's least-known pieces (tucked away in a hallway of the west wing) was perhaps the greatest folly of Washington memorial statuary: Horatio Greenough's classical depiction of a regally seated George Washington, wearing a tastefully draped toga from the waist down—and nothing else. Congress commissioned Greenough to sculpt a statue noble enough to be placed in the Rotunda of the Capitol, giving him full rein over the style and form of the statue (although the head was to be based on a statue of Washington in Richmond, Virginia). Greenough took his task quite seriously, working on the marble piece for eight years in his Florence studio, slowly crafting a Washington of truly mythic proportions based on such works as Pithias' mammoth Zeus. But when the statue finally arrived in Washington in 1841, a doorway had to be partially cut away to make way for the statue's placement in the Rotunda. Next it developed that the statue was too heavy—almost as soon as it was installed, the Rotunda floor beneath the statue began to buckle. Congress quickly relegated the statue to the Capitol grounds, where it was a popular tourist attraction until 1908, when it was taken in from the cold by the Smithsonian.

During World War II, the land where this museum now stands played host to "tempos"—temporary war buildings constructed to house an Army Air Force detachment of intelligence officers. Home to many of the code-breakers during the war, the buildings were finally razed to make way for the National Museum of History and Technology.

The temporary intelligence buildings had replaced another forgotten Mall wonder—a collection of thirty-five greenhouses, open to the public, housing U.S. Department of Agriculture plant exhibits of flowers, ornamental plants, fruit trees, and other colorful specimens of flora. (The original Adolph Cluss-designed Agriculture Building was just across the Mall from this site, where the newer building now stands.)

See Also: Arts and Industries Building and **U.S. Department of Agriculture Complex (Jefferson Drive Building);** U.S. Capitol (Chapter 3)

---

8 | Open to the Public | **National Museum of Natural History (Constitution Avenue and 10th Street, NW; 202/357–2747)**

While schoolchildren never forget the elephant in the entrance hall of the Museum of Natural History, there is another museum piece here that has a far more direct and dark link to the heritage of Washington, D.C.: The famed (and many say, cursed) Hope Diamond. The largest marquis diamond in the world, the Hope once hung around perhaps history's unluckiest neck of all—that of Marie Antoinette. But the diamond's last private owner was Washington society queen Evalyn Walsh McLean. Shortly upon acquiring the diamond, Mrs. McLean's mother-in-law died unexpectedly (she had only recently handled the diamond), and her small son was hit by a car and killed soon after. Her husband, Edward, who had inherited the *Washington Post* from his father, became embroiled in the Teapot Dome scandal, went bankrupt, was declared insane, and eventually died in an asylum. The newspaper was sold at auction to Eugene Meyer, whose daughter Katherine Graham still heads the company today. Mrs. McLean, who wore the gem everywhere (except to bed), had always warned others not to come near it for fear they would be injured. She finally sold the Hope Diamond to famed jeweler Harry Winston, who donated it to the Smithsonian to start its jewelry collection.

See Also: Washington Post Building (Chapter 2); Walsh-McLean House (Chapter 7); McLean Gardens (Chapter 8)

Quadrangle Museums (Underground)

 Open to the Public **The Arthur Sackler Gallery** (1050 Independence Avenue, SW; 202/357–2104)

 Open to the Public **National Museum of African Art** (950 Independence Avenue, SW; 202/357–4860)

These galleries—a collection of Oriental art (the Sackler Gallery) and African art (the National Museum of African Art)—became the newest museums on the Mall when they opened in 1988. But they also hold a far greater distinction: With Mall real estate at a premium, the Smithsonian developed a down-under plan for building its newest dynamic duo. As the first underground museums in Washington, the pair have been a remarkable success. Entrances at the ground level are classically whimsical constructions (the peaked roof of the Sackler in delightful contrast to the rounded dome of the African museum) that barely hint at the wealth of historic artwork and folk craft pieces to be found below ground. More than 95 percent of the gallery space is below ground.

This was once the site of the National Air Museum, which was housed in an old World War I building originally used for aircraft experiments. The pathways around the museum were dotted with rockets. The **National Air and Space Museum** replaced this earlier museum.

One note of historic irony is that not far from the National Museum of African Art (which had originally occupied the Frederick Douglass row houses on Capitol Hill) stood a pair of Washington's most notorious slave pens. The Robey and the Williams slave pens, were located within a block of this site along B Street (now Independence Avenue) at 6th and 7th Streets. If the ground here was once haunted by the memory of these heinous institutions, perhaps it is now hallowed instead by being hollowed out to hold this collection honoring the finest works of African artists.

See Also: National Air and Space Museum; "Slavery in Washington" (Chapter 12)

 Open to the Public **Smithsonian Institution Building (Castle) (1000 Jefferson Drive, SW; 202/357–2700)**

The actual and symbolic architectural star of the Mall museum collection, the so-called "Smithsonian Castle" serves as the headquarters for the Smithsonian museum family. This Gothic Revival masterpiece designed by James Renwick and completed

This sketch of the burning of the Smithsonian Castle appeared in *Harper's Weekly*, Feb. 11, 1865. (Library of Congress)

in 1855 was the first of the Smithsonian buildings.

The Smithsonian as an institution owes its existence to British Amero-phile James Smithson. Had Smithson's family procreated with a bit more determination, however, America's finest museum system would never have been born: Smithson's 1826 will called for his estate to be passed on to the offspring of his only kin, a nephew; if the nephew didn't produce an heir, however, then the United States was to inherit the estate. The will stated that the money was to be used ". . . to found at Washington, under the name of the Smithsonian Institution, an establishment for the increase and diffusion of knowledge among men." Smithson was himself the bastard son of nobility, and his tainted blue-bloodline haunted him throughout his life. Perhaps he, more than anyone, knew the true value of having his name legitimately passed on to future generations.

In 1835, Smithson's nephew died, heirless, and the money did indeed pass into the coffers of the federal government. Joseph Henry, a trusted and respected scientist at the time, was appointed by Congress to become the first Secretary of the Smithsonian, and it was Henry who refined the rather amorphous goals laid out in Smithson's will, creating an institution of scientific inquiry and exploration. Henry got so involved in creating the Smithsonian that he actually lived in rooms in the east wing of Renwick's castle building from 1847 until his death in 1878.

Although James Smithson never managed to make it to America in his lifetime, the Smithsonian brought him home to the institution which bore his name, first locating his body in Scotland, then shipping it to Washington for an honorable entombment at the Renwick Building. Smithson's crypt is still on display in the ceremonial room created to hold his tomb.

Over the years, the institution expanded beyond its original boundaries of scientific exploration. Gradually, it developed into "America's Attic," as it acquired more and more unusual collections and built museums around them (which were themselves built around the Castle). One of the great Washington disasters of the nineteenth century occurred in January of 1865, when the original sandstone Castle was gutted in a severe fire. Almost everything the institution had collected in its thirty years of existence was lost, although the building and its interior were restored. After a major renovation, Renwick's Castle was re-opened to the public.

See Also: Arts and Industries Building

---

⑫ U.S. Department of Agriculture Complex (Jefferson Drive building) (Jefferson Drive between 14th and 12th Street, SW)

This multi-block complex, built between 1904–1908, eventually took the place of the old Agriculture Building, which stood on the Jefferson Drive side of the present-day building from 1868 to 1930. Designed by Adolph Cluss, the first Agriculture Department Building was an elegant Second Empire building with formal gardens, a Victorian greenhouse, and grounds that spread all the way across the mall to Constitution Avenue. The first floor of the building housed

Stereographic view of the General Noble Tree House. (Library of Congress)

a museum of seeds, plants, produce, and other agriculture goods, displayed in shining glass and walnut cases.

According to James M. Goode's exhaustive 1979 book on now-gone Washington sites, *Capital Losses*, during the 1920s the grounds of the old Agriculture building—which once stretched all the way across the Mall to the modern-day Constitution Avenue—held a collection of tiny demonstration buildings. These were used to educate the visiting public in everything from ice-cream making to meat-packing. Until 1932, the grounds also held another very popular tourist attraction: The General Noble Tree House.

The giant sequoia-turned-tree house was named for John Noble, secretary of the interior from 1889 to 1893, who championed legislation to preserve America's forest lands. The tree house lived up to its majestic billing, for it was created from a 2,000–year-old tree that had stood 300 feet high, with a diameter of 26 feet. Harvested in the General Grant National Park in Tulare, California in 1892, the tree was removed in small pieces so it could easily be reassembled—although legend has it that when the twenty-three wood cutters finally felled the tree, the thunderous crash felled the cutters as well, for they could not stand up for several minutes afterward.

The tree was re-assembled at the World's Columbian Exposition that year, with its trunk hollowed out, a gabled roof plunked on top, and a circular staircase installed inside. Two years later, the General Noble Redwood Treehouse arrived in Washington, where it stood on the Agriculture grounds until being put into storage in 1932. Its remains were destroyed in 1940, hardly a noble end for such a noble tree.

See Also: National Museum of American History; Department of Agriculture Building (Chapter 12)

---

13 Open to the Public   **Washington Monument (On the Mall between 15th and 17th Streets; 202/426–6841)**

No other monument in Washington has the actual or symbolic presence that the Washington Monument has—and for good reason: There is even a federal law that states that no building in Washington may be taller than the Washington Monument. It now dominates the Mall and most of downtown D.C. with a timeless presence that belies its relative youth and difficult birth. From Washington's earliest days, when L'Enfant's plans were the blueprints for an as-yet invisible federal community, there were plans (made against Washington's own wishes) to include a statue honoring the first president. The original plans called for a classic equestrian statue of Washington, astride a noble mount. L'Enfant himself selected a mathematically precise site suitable for a memorial honoring the surveyor president. The memorial was to complete a perfect isosceles triangle, situated as it was at the intersection of the southern axis of the White House and the western axis of the Capitol building. But precision was soon abandoned for engineering when it became apparent that the chosen site was too swampy to hold such a noble venture (but in 1804 Thomas Jefferson placed a memorial stone at the place just the same). The site for the planned statue was moved to a higher and dryer location some 260 feet south and 320 feet east.

Having chosen the perfect place, planners decided a mere equestrian statue was too simple a memorial for the Father of the Country. Accordingly, the Washington National Monument Society (founded in 1833 to raise money for the monument) sponsored a competition to find a more fitting memorial for Washington. The winning submission, by Robert Mills, was selected in 1845. It was a fanciful, Greco-Roman rotunda of a memorial tomb designed to hold the graves of Revolutionary War heros, topped with an obelisk. And to truly honor Washington above all others, the memorial was to include a statuary group featuring the first president at the helm of a chariot drawn by four horses.

The plan for this grandiose monument, though hailed by politicians and patriots, soon proved itself a fundraiser's nightmare. Proposed elements of the memorial, from the statuary group to the heroic tombs, were slowly peeled away from the monumental undertaking, leaving only the simple obelisk behind.

Work on the modified monument began in 1848. The final cap stone was not put in place until 1885. The lagtime between beginning and end was due in part to a twenty-year halt of construction precipitated by the Civil War, and dragged out by lack of public interest and funding. Several different planning committees over the years led fund-raising and promotional drives, but the thing seemed jinxed by the excessive passage of time between its conception and its birth. There was talk of using the land for other purposes, and indeed, during the Civil War the federal government fenced off the grounds as a grazing area for thousands of head of cattle slated for Union provisions. Local wags dubbed the unfinished memorial "Beef Depot Monument" in response to this land-use scheme.

The Washington Monument on Armistice Day, 1921.
(Library of Congress)

Work finally began again on the monument in 1876, with the Army Corps of Engineers getting into the act to finish the construction. A variation in color between the monument's lower and upper half is still visible, for by the time work had begun anew, the quarry from which the earlier stone had been taken was depleted and a different quarry had to be used to finish the project.

Minor scandals abounded throughout the monument's building, but probably the most outrageous first surfaced when a stone for the monument, donated by the Pope, disappeared from the work-site in 1853. Fingers were immediately pointed at members of the "Know Nothing" Party, who were famous for their anti-papal sentiments (and who later sabotaged efforts to raise funds for the monument). But the Know Nothings claimed they knew nothing about the missing Catholic stone. In 1892, divers working under the Long Bridge discovered an unusual-looking stone on the riverbed of the Potomac and hauled it up onto the bridge; sure enough, it matched the descriptions of the missing monumental stone (which was made of African marble and inscribed "Rome to America").

The Pope Stone, as it was called, drew great attention from curious old-timers, who swarmed to the bridge to see the recovered artifact. The engineers working on the diving project were unsure of what to do until it could be certified as the actual missing piece, so the stone was placed in a locked shanty nearby. That day, they kept a close watch on it, and then went out for dinner that evening, after first making sure the stone was securely locked. But upon their return (and they insisted the site had been left alone for no more than an hour and a half, and in the middle of the night, at that), they discovered the stone was missing once again, never to be seen again. A *Washington Post* account dated June 21, 1892, describes the scene when a reporter and a lapidary expert showed up the next day to see the stone, unaware that it was gone again:

> "Capt. Williams was found seated on the pump barge, with a forlorn look on his usually good-humored face.
> "'Where's your wonderful stone, Captain?,' inquired the reporter.
> "'Gone,' was the laconic reply.
> "'Well, where's it gone?'
> "'That's what I'd give a good deal to know,'" said the captain, adding with considerable emphasis, "Some blank [%$&*] thief made a sneak on it last night, and it's gone clean."

The Washington Monument was dedicated (without the papal stone) in 1885 at a memorable ceremony on the Mall. But even after it was up and running, the monument was not without its problems—one of the most notable being its elevator, a steam-operated contraption installed soon after the monument was finished that was considered so dangerous that women and children were banned from using it. Today, a high-tech elevator whizzes visitors up the monument in about ninety seconds. Those who still prefer to climb can take guided Park Service Tours that tell the history of the 188 stones donated by states, organizations, and individuals during the building of the monument.

PLACES: The West Mall

14 | Open to the Public | **Constitution Gardens (East of the Vietnam Veterans Memorial)**

A recent addition to the Mall is the mini-park within a park of Constitution Gardens. The little lake and its surrounding landscaped gardens (built to commemorate the signers of the Constitution) were placed here in 1976. The park was originally envisioned as a tourist attraction along the lines of Copenhagen's Tivoli Gardens, but the full-scale concessions extravaganza was squelched by intimidating costs. Today there are often more mallard ducks in the lake than visitors on its banks.

Construction of temporary War Relief Buildings in 1942. (Library of Congress)

Constitution Gardens made local headlines in the late 1980s when ducklings began disappearing from the lake at an alarming rate. At first, police suspected a duck-napper was snatching the little darlings in the dead of night, but then the true culprit was discovered: Giant catfish were swallowing the ducklings whole. The lake had to be drained and the dastardly duck-eaters removed, so that the waters could once again be made safe for all fowl inhabitants.

The site of Constitution Gardens was once the home to the Main Navy and Munitions Buildings complex, otherwise known as the "Main Navy." This temporary office space was hastily erected in 1918 for use during World War I, but continued standing, in altered form, until 1971. The complex was occupied by the Bonus Marchers in 1932, and enlarged during World War II to provide further working room. The sprawling three-story concrete complex of buildings provided 1.8 million square feet of office space, but looked like a row of railcars from above. The land on which the "temporary" buildings was built had to be reinforced with thousands of thirty- to fifty-foot piles driven into the still-soggy Potomac River Bed land that had been dredged and filled in during the late nineteenth century. Other temporary buildings were erected nearby during World War II, but these were the grand-old temps that lasted until 1971.

See Also: "The Armies of the Mall"

---

15 | Open to the Public | **Lincoln Memorial (Western end of the Mall, at 23rd Street NW;   202/426–6841)**

Built in 1922, this temple of hope was designed by Henry Bacon; the statue of Lincoln was the work of Daniel Chester French. Time and legend have created the aura that hangs about the place like a ghost of the great man himself. Indeed, Lincoln's spirit is all about the memorial, from the words of his Gettysburg Address and his Second Inaugural Address that flank him on either side, to the role the monument itself has played in the history of Civil Rights protest—a history that would have pleased Old Abe to no end.

The event which marked the Lincoln Memorial's inauguration as a Civil Rights platform took place on Easter Sunday, 1939, when the great contralto Marian Anderson stood upon its steps and sang to a crowd of more than 30,000. Anderson gave the performance at the invitation of the White House after being denied the opportunity to sing on the stage of the nearby DAR Constitution Hall because she was black. Eleanor Roosevelt had been particularly appalled at the actions of the Daughters of the American Revolution (DAR), as were most of the New Dealers. In protest, Mrs. Roosevelt resigned her membership in the DAR and requested that Secretary of the Interior, Harold Ickes, make arrangements with the National Park Service to provide the Lincoln Memorial as an alternative stage for the famous singer. Anderson's performance set the stage for future rallies and civil rights protests to come, making the steps of the Lincoln Memorial a symbolic monument in and of themselves to the power of free speech—and song.

It was a legacy solidified on August 28th, 1963, when 250,000 Freedom Marchers gathered at the foot of the Lincoln Memorial for a historic rally that served as the grand finale to the March on Washington. The Rev. Dr. Martin Luther King, Jr. took the podium on the steps of the Lincoln Memorial that day, and delivered one of the most famous oratories in American history, his ringing call for racial equality that became known as the "I Have a Dream" speech. And Marian Anderson returned to sing once again on the steps of the Lincoln Memorial for the Civil Rights marchers that day.

This was not Anderson's first return to sing at the memorial. On April 21, 1952, she had performed on the steps again before a crowd of 10,000, in a memorial concert honoring Harold Ickes, who had died the previous February.

Despite its peaceful purpose and legacy, the Lincoln Memorial also has the distinction of being the only building in Washington to be fired upon (albeit by friendly fire) during World War II. The incident occurred when a soldier manning one of the big guns atop the Department of the Interior Building (at 18th and C Streets) accidentally spun the gun in the direction of

Canal of Tiber Creek

The area surrounding the Mall would hardly be recognizable to a time traveler from the twentieth century going back to the mid-nineteenth century—and not only because only half of the Mall as we know it was then solid land. Perhaps the most jarring surprise would be the swampy Canal of Tiber Creek. But for more than half of Washington's existence, that canal was a major landmark (and eye- and nose-sore) of the Mall area and Southwest Washington.

L'Enfant's plans called for a "Canal of Tiber Creek," (often identified on early maps as the "Tiber Canal," and sometimes referred to as the "Washington City Canal"), as a useful and ceremonial waterway to bring supplies and materials to the public markets, the Mall, and the Capitol. The canal was constructed between 1810 and 1815, with funds raised by local real-estate speculator Thomas Law.

The canal flowed from the Potomac River, which then, depending on tidal conditions, sometimes flowed all the way up to the Ellipse, covering the area we know as the west Mall, West Potomac Park, the Tidal Basin, and the place where the Jefferson Memorial stands. At the point where the Lock Keeper's House still stands (at the southwest corner of 17th Street and Constitution Avenue), the waterway was fairly wide. It narrowed as it flowed east along the modern-day Constitution Avenue route, past the marketplaces that once filled present-day Federal Triangle, and then on to the Capitol, where it turned south and flowed back out to the river.

The canal was not the pretty thing that L'Enfant envisioned, however. By the mid-nineteenth century it had turned into a muddy open sewer that spread a toxic scent wherever it flowed. The canal by then had become an obsolete means of transportation; the railroads brought in materials more quickly and efficiently over land than could be shipped up the Potomac. By the 1870s, the canal had deteriorated into such a smarmy little stream that it was covered over as part of Boss Shepherd's capital improvements.

Lincoln and then fired off a round at the unsuspecting memorial. The attack blew off a good bit of marble along the roofline where the state seals are etched. Maryland was badly damaged, and both Connecticut and Texas received minor injuries as well. The wounds were patched, but are still slightly visible to eagle-eyed visitors.

Another little-known point of interest is the cave beneath the memorial, which can be seen from a basement viewing window (in the hallway where the restrooms are located), or during one of the tours conducted by the National Park Service during the warm months. (See **"Tunneling Under Washington."**)

See Also: DAR Constitution Hall and Department of the Interior Building (Chapter 5)

16 Lock Keeper's House (Southwest corner of Constitution and 17th Streets)

An anachronism amid the monuments, this little fieldstone house still stands despite its long-lost usefulness. The house, a lock keeper's cottage built in the mid–1830s, is still marked as the "Weighing Station for the Washington Canal." It was here that barges stopped for inspection and transfer between the C&O Canal and the Canal of Tiber Creek. The National Park Service now stores landscaping equipment in the little building.

See Also: "The Canal of Tiber Creek"

---

17 | Open to the Public | **Vietnam Veterans Memorial (Constitution Avenue at 21st Street, NW; 202/634–1568)**

This stark black marble monument to the dead and missing of the Vietnam War will likely go down in Washington history as the most controversial memorial ever erected in the city. Maya Lin, a Chinese-American Yale student, won the design contest sponsored by the Vietnam Veterans' Memorial Fund, a group of veterans and their supporters who raised money for the memorial. Lin's design angered many—unlike typical white marble monuments that soared above the land with statuary and inspiring inscriptions, Lin's memorial was a stark V-shaped wedge slicing out of the earth like black marble shrapnel, engraved with the names of every man and woman killed in the Vietnam War. Despite protests that the memorial was too dark and dolorous, the Fine Arts Commission okayed the plans, and the Wall, as it has become known, was dedicated in 1982. To temper criticism that the memorial lacked traditional values, a statue designed by Frederick Hart and featuring three war-weary soldiers (two white, one black, but all male) was installed in 1984 just to the south of the wall.

Since its dedication, the Vietnam Memorial has become the most heavily visited of all Washington monuments, with friends and family and just plain tourists moving solemnly past the 50,000 etched names (listed chronologically in the order of their death). The memorial has become a healing ground, a place to come to terms with the harshest of lessons in grieving. Tokens of love and longing are often left behind on the grass at the foot of the black panel bearing the name of the lost loved one: flowers on birthdays and holidays, letters from widowed wives, teddy bears from bereaved parents, photographs of children never seen by their fathers.

Chapter 5

FOGGY BOTTOM

A diverse residential and academic enclave wedged between the federal city of Washington and the social scene of Georgetown, Foggy Bottom has played varied roles in the history of the nation's capitol. From the signing of the Treaty of Ghent at the **Octagon House,** to the banning of Marian Anderson from **DAR Constitution Hall,** events that reverberate through history have taken place up and down these mid-town streets. The bungled break-in at the Democratic National Headquarters offices at the **Watergate** complex set in motion the nation's most far-reaching political scandal. And the touch-and-go emergency surgery performed on President Reagan after his shooting brought the eyes of the world to the **George Washington University Emergency Medical Center**.

An ordinary area into which extraordinary events are sometimes implanted, Foggy Bottom is actually a melange of several neighborhoods. The original Foggy Bottom area was a place of working-class German and Irish immigrants, many of whom toiled at nearby waterfront factories. This area forms the western part of today's neighborhood, bounded by the Potomac River and Rock Creek Park, Pennsylvania Avenue and 23rd Street. The neighborhood that now forms central Foggy Bottom (where George Washington University resides) was actually an upper-middle-class enclave on the eastern fringes of early Foggy Bottom. To many, the area was an extension of the posh Lafayette Square neighborhood; indeed, the **Octagon House Museum,** and **Corcoran Gallery,** though built nearly a century apart, harken back to the time when high society still nestled around the fringes of the White House grounds. The Federal Rectangle area (between E Street and the Mall) started out as waterfront property—moist, vaporous bottomland, which gave Foggy Bottom its name. Then in the 1880s, the Army Corps of Engineers dredged the Potomac, filling in the West Mall and making this section more habitable. It is now dominated by modern federal offices and organizational headquarters.

The original Foggy Bottom neighborhood was founded in 1765 when Jacob Funk, a German immigrant who had settled in nearby Frederick, Maryland, purchased a plot of land that sprawled west from around 24th Street down to the riverfront. He subdivided the land into 234 lots, which he thought would sell easily because of their proximity to Georgetown (then beginning to establish itself as an important tobacco shipping port). But few lots sold, and the area went undeveloped until plans to build the capital city emerged in 1791. The plots then sold quickly, and Funkstown (or Hamburgh, as it was sometimes called by the large population of German immigrants) soon developed into a lower-class neighborhood of laborers.

Pierre L'Enfant included the neighborhood in his plans, placing Washington Circle at the top of a hill near the northeast corner of Funkstown. This hill, which the neighborhood clung to on its descent toward the river, became known as Camp Hill in honor of the military fort that was planned there to fortify the new city. Thomas Jefferson even thought Camp Hill an ideal location for the situation of the Capitol building itself, but L'Enfant and George Washington selected Jenkin's Hill (now Capitol Hill) instead, in part because Foggy Bottom was known to become a soupy, malarial steambath during the summer

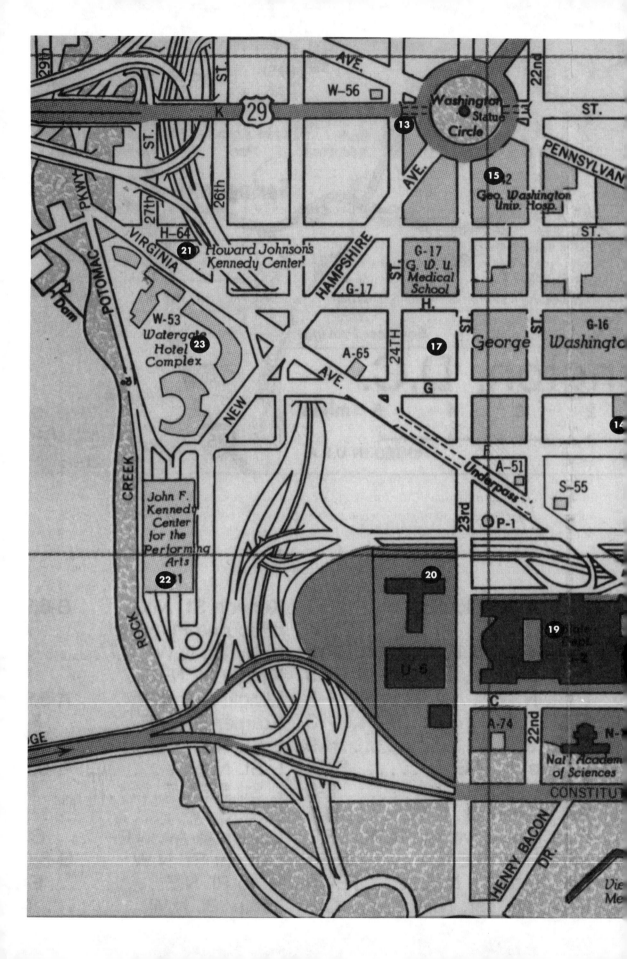

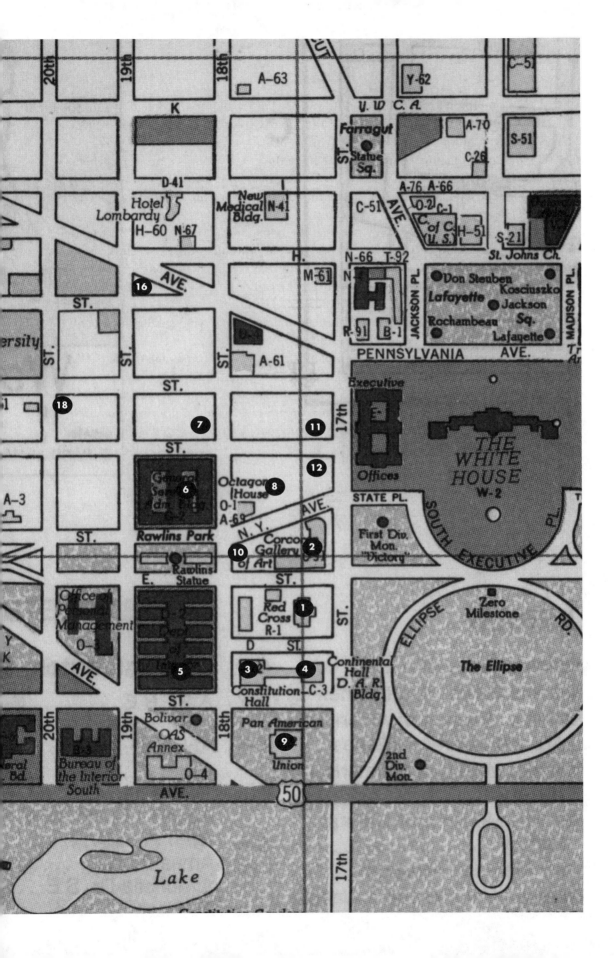

months. During the War of 1812, the hill was used as a lookout and defense post. And the hill later served as the original location of the Naval Observatory, which was erected in 1844 at the spot now occupied by the Naval Medical Command.

The first major factory that sprang up along the riverfront was a brewery, which opened in 1796 (thus inaugurating the area's long history of waterfront breweries). The Glass House opened nearby in 1807 to manufacture glass for the building of the city, and other factories soon followed.

K Street became a dividing line between the upper and lower classes, with wealthier Washingtonians building their homes along this main thoroughfare between the new city and the old port of Georgetown. Nearer the White House, fine homes sprang up in all directions (particularly around Lafayette Square). The rest of Foggy Bottom, though bordered by these upper-class neighborhoods, was inhabited by a mix of working-class laborers and middle-class merchants, and the neighborhood remained a diverse mix of classes and professions for most of the nineteenth century.

The Washington Gas and Light Company's gas storage facility, constructed in 1856 at Virginia and New Hampshire Avenues, became an ugly landmark that stood out on the Washington skyline. It served as a beacon to draw the eye toward the waterfront factories that belched beer and churned concrete until the middle of the twentieth century, when the area was re-developed under the aegis of the National Capital Planning Commission.

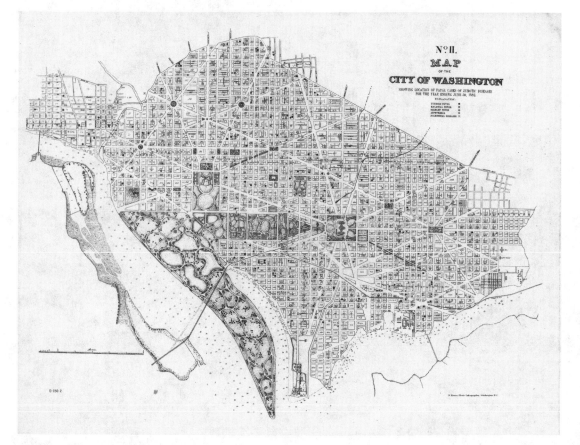

(National Archives)

The Civil War transformed lower Foggy Bottom into a miniature military encampment: Camp Fry—home to the Veteran Volunteer Corps which guarded the federal buildings—was established along the Potomac between 21st and 22nd Streets (where the National Academy of Sciences now stands). Around the area where the **State Department** now stands, the Army also built Camp Fuller, a massive complex of stables and corrals that housed some 30,000 horses and livestock.

Following the war, a wave of southern blacks swept into the city. Many settled in the Foggy Bottom neighborhood because of its class structure and proximity to factory jobs and work on the Georgetown canal. So many black families settled in the neighborhood that they soon overwhelmed the two mainstream churches in the area—St. John's of Lafayette Square and the Church of the Epiphany, Downtown—which allowed blacks to join the congregation. The white church members—who permitted the blacks to join them but still enforced segregation and preferential treatment for whites—banded together and raised money to build a church in Foggy Bottom for the growing black community. James Renwick was commissioned to build the church, **St. Mary's Episcopal Church,** in 1887.

The turn of the century found Foggy Bottom in sinking spirits. The nearby C&O Canal was fading fast as a waterway, taking many canal-related jobs with it. Meanwhile, the area's attraction as a community bridging Georgetown to Downtown weakened as Georgetown's influence in Washington's commercial and residential life began to pale. Block after block of Foggy Bottom's working-class homes were deserted as even long-time residents began migrating to other neighborhoods.

In 1912, **George Washington University** relocated from its Downtown location to property south of Washington Circle, transforming part of Foggy Bottom. Mansions and townhouses were converted into student dorms, taverns into classrooms, and churches into auditoriums. The school eventually took over some twenty blocks of the neighborhood, which distressed some of the locals who had stuck out the bad times in Foggy Bottom only to witness their landmarks being made into a college campus. To assuage fears and help save the neighborhood, the University took special care to relocate or otherwise preserve some of the historic buildings endangered by the school's development. However, a number of older sites were lost as the University demolished neighborhood blocks to build modern administration buildings and study centers.

While the core of upper Foggy Bottom is now basically an urban campus for George Washington University, the older sections to the east and south fringes of the neighborhood remain historic and culturally diverse areas. The neighborhood near the White House and Ellipse is still a delightful mix of galleries, organizations, parks and memorials, and historic buildings. The federal structures in the area that was once the foggiest bottomland in the city continue to age gracefully, displaying the same solid grace of much of Washington's official settlement.

To the west of the heart of George Washington University, along the Potomac waterfront once lined with breweries and factories, stand two relatively recent additions that changed the face and history of Washington forever: The elegant **Kennedy Center for the Performing Arts** and the infamous **Watergate** Apartment and Hotel complex. Now a center of high culture for many Washingtonians, with the concerts, plays and performances at the "Ken Cen" (as insiders call it) and such fine restaurants nearby as the

Watergate's Jean-Louis, the area has been transformed into an elegant corner of the city. While the class structure may have changed and the soot and fog faded from the landscape, in many ways—at least in spirit—Foggy Bottom remains what it was in the early days of Washington: A crossroads where the city's diverse elements meet and mingle.

PLACES: East Foggy Bottom (17th and 18th Streets)

This section of Foggy Bottom is so close to the goings-on in and around the White House that it's a toss-up whether to call it part of the White House neighborhood or part of Foggy Bottom. The block of 17th Street facing the Ellipse was once lined with houses as historic and well-bred as any Lafayette Park residence. Indeed, what was considered by many to be the finest home in Washington, Van Ness House, was located in the block now occupied by the headquarters of the **Organization of American States** and the **Daughters of the American Revolution.** Until 1899, the Van Ness lot also held the cottage of David Burnes, the Scotsman who originally owned much of the land upon which official Washington was built. The oldest building remaining in this area is the famous **Octagon House**, now a museum, where James and Dolley Madison resided after the British burned the White House to the ground in 1814.

---

❶ Open to the Public **American Red Cross National Headquarters (430 17th Street, NW; 202/737–8300)&&:**

This complex of three buildings is the spiritual home base and bureaucratic headquarters for the Red Cross. The most elegant of the three is the neo-classic marble building that faces 17th Street (with its giant Red Cross on the facade), constructed in 1917 by A.B. Trowbridge and Goodhue Livingston. The building itself serves as a living memorial to the nurses who offered aid and comfort during the Civil War (epitomized in the work of Clara Barton, who founded the American Red Cross in 1881). On view in the lobby are relics and artifacts of the Red Cross, including early uniforms, public information materials, and exhibits on the organization's work in times of emergency and conflict.
See Also: Clara Barton's Boarding House Site (Chapter 2); Clara Barton's House (Chapter 9)

Art Museum of the Americas. *See* Organization of American States Building

---

❷ Open to the Public **Corcoran Gallery of Art (17th Street and New York Avenue, NW; 202/638–3211)**

This wonderful gallery was built to handle the overflow from the original Corcoran collection, which was first housed just around the corner at the Renwick Gallery on Pennsylvania Avenue. Built in 1897 by Ernest Flagg (the Clark Wing was added in 1927 by Charles Platt), the gallery still holds many of art collector William Wilson Corcoran's greatest acquisitions. It has also added a variety of both modern and classic paintings, sculptures, and multi-media works. The Corcoran is the home of one of the country's finest small art schools, the Corcoran School of Art. Located in the gallery building, with its entrance on New York Avenue, the art school was founded by William Corcoran when the new gallery was first established.
See Also: Renwick Gallery (Chapter 1)

3 | Open to the Public | ## DAR Constitution Hall (18th and D Streets, NW; 202/638–2661)

DAR Constitution Hall, while famous as one of the city's greatest concert halls, is most infamously renowned for a concert that did not take place here. In 1939, the great African-American contralto Marian Anderson was denied the opportunity to sing at Constitution Hall because the Daughters of the American Revolution staunchly insisted the theater was for Whites Only. Urged on by First Lady Eleanor Roosevelt, Interior Secretary Harold Ickes then authorized the Park Service to give Anderson the Lincoln Memorial as a stage, and on Easter Sunday, Anderson gave a free concert there for a crowd of 75,000.

Constitution Hall recovered its composure after the racist incident, and is still one of Washington's most popular venues for concerts, graduations, and fund-raising performances. Built in 1930 by John Russell Pope, the hall is renowned for its magnificent decorative ceiling, as well as the other ornamental elements throughout the building.

See Also: DAR Memorial Continental Hall; Lincoln Memorial (Chapter 4)

4 | Open to the Public | ## DAR Memorial Continental Hall (1776 D Street, NW; 202/628–1776)

The museum and headquarters of the Daughters of the American Revolution, Continental Hall was built in 1910 by Edward Pearce Casey as the home for this historical and genealogical organization that proudly traces its well-guarded roots to those who served in the Revolutionary War. Continental Hall was the site of the 1921 Washington Conference for Limitation of Armament. The conference, which opened session in the hall on November 12, 1921, was called by Congress to thwart an escalating naval arms race in the Pacific among the U.S., Great Britain, and Japan. The representatives from the nine greatest naval powers who attended the conference agreed on limitations on the construction of new naval ships and restrictions on the use of already available military apparatus (including submarines and chemical weapons), as well as the delineation of spheres of influence in the Pacific region. On February 6, 1922, the nine separate treaties that emerged from the Washington Conference were signed; these helped stave off international hostilities until the outbreak of World War II.

At this site once stood the home of Thomas Carbery, a prominent Washingtonian whose civic involvements included heading up the Washington Monument Society. He also served as the city's mayor in the early 1820s, and operated Carbery's Wharf at what today is the intersection of 17th and Constitution Avenue. This wharf served the Canal of Tiber Creek and the Potomac River and

DAR Memorial Continental Hall. (Jack Looney)

provided dock space for shipments of materials used in the construction of the President's House and other nearby federal buildings. His simple brick townhouse was one of several in the block owned by prominent citizens. (His next-door neighbors were the Van Nesses.)

See Also: DAR Constitution Hall

⑤ Open to the Public **Department of the Interior Building (18th and C Streets, NW; Museum: 202/343-2743)**

The main headquarters of the Department of the Interior, which encompasses many of the recreational departments (Park Service, Forest Service) that Americans come into contact with during their camping trips, was the site of a breathtaking debacle during World War II. The Interior Building, like many federal edifices in Washington, had anti-aircraft weaponry mounted on its roof, although this armament was more for show than for actual defense. (A later examination of the weaponry even found that most were stocked with the wrong kind of ammunition.) Nevertheless, there was one episode in which the federal guns were fired, and it occurred atop this building with embarrassing results. A soldier manning an anti-aircraft gun on the roof leaned on his gun, swinging it around until it was in alignment with the Lincoln Memorial, then accidentally fired off a blast. He hit the Lincoln Memorial square in the roof, damaging the state seals of Maryland, Connecticut, and Texas. The monument was repaired, although the injuries can still be seen by keen-eyed visitors.

See Also: Lincoln Memorial (Chapter 4)

⑥ General Services Administration Building (18th and F Streets)

Until the Department of the Interior moved to its new quarters at 18th and C Streets, this was its home-base. And it was in this building that one of the most flagrant political scandals was engineered—the Teapot Dome Scandal. In 1922, President Harding's Interior Secretary, Albert Fall, secretly leased government-owned lands in Teapot Dome, Wyoming, to wealthy oil interests (who gratefully gave Fall money and gifts worth nearly half-a-million dollars). The deal allegedly was done in the fifth-floor dining room of this building, which, until the site was destroyed in a fire in August of 1991, was listed on the Register of Historic Places for the infamous act that unfolded there. Fall eventually fell (he got a year in prison), as did many of Harding's other corrupt government officials. Harding himself died suddenly while traveling out West, just before the scandal broke and before he could be implicated.

See Also: Department of the Interior Building; Teapot Dome Scandal House Site (Chapter 7)

⑦ John Marshall House (1801 F Street, NW)

Built in 1825, this house—often referred to as the Ringgold-Carroll House—has been home to a number of Washington greats. Famed Supreme Court Chief Justice John Marshall lived here when the building was a rooming house. Presidents Madison and Monroe also lived here for a time, as did Civil War general George McLellan.

See Also: Cutts-Madison House and U.S. Treasury Annex (Chapter 1); McLellan House (Chapter 2)

⑧ Open to the Public **The Octagon House (1799 New York Avenue, NW; 202/538-3105)**

One of the most historic homes in Washington, the Octagon House has witnessed the comings, goings, and doings of great leaders and their followers. The house was designed in 1798 by William Thornton, first architect of the U.S. Capitol building, for Col. John Tayloe (whose Tayloe House on Lafayette Square also saw its share of history).

When the British attacked and sacked Washington on August 24, 1814, the most savage act of the War of 1812, they left the city in a shambles. The White House was in ruins and uninhabitable, but the Octagon House was undamaged. One theory as to why the mansion went unscathed is that the French Minister was in residence at the Octagon House when the British attacked, so the French flag was flying over the residence. Though long-time enemies of the French, the British were not then at war with the Gallic nation, and spared the building that flew the French flag. While the White House was repaired, the Octagon House became the first temporary Presidential Mansion. Shortly after James Madison and his family moved in, the

War of 1812 took a decided downturn for the British. On February 4, 1815, word reached Washington that Andrew Jackson had won a decisive victory over the British at the Battle of New Orleans. Two weeks later, President James Madison sat down at a desk in the drawing room of the Octagon House and signed the *Treaty of Ghent*, which officially ended the War of 1812. A celebration unequalled since the sack of the city followed the signing of the treaty, hosted by that irrepressible socialite, Dolley Madison.

In late 1815, the Madisons moved on to one of the renowned but now-gone rowhouses known collectively as the Seven Buildings (which were located nearby at the northwest corner of Pennsylvania and 19th Street, NW). President Madison finished out his term at this second temporary residence, as the White House was not ready for occupancy again until Madison's successor, James Monroe, officially re-opened the Executive Mansion in 1818.

Octagon House, about 1915.
(Walks about Washington)

The Octagon House residency may have been a special time in the life of Dolley Madison, for, as legend has it, the house is haunted by the ghost of the vivacious first lady. Her specter seems to get around quite a bit, as she has also been seen at Lafayette Square's Cutts-Madison House and at the White House. By the turn of the twentieth century, the house had become somewhat run-down, with as many as ten families living there in a kind of communal squalor. Then in 1899, the American Institute of Architects (AIA) officially took possession of the house, making it their home in 1910. Eventually, the AIA was able to restore the historic home to its previous splendor. In 1971, however, the AIA tore down the Octagon House stables, along with the Lemon Building (constructed in 1890 to house a printer's shop), to make way for an expansion of their headquarters, which now wraps around the back of the Octagon House.

See Also: Cutts-Madison House, Tayloe House, and The White House (Chapter 1); Dumbarton House (Chapter 6); Seven Buildings Site (Chapter 7); "The Burning of Washington" (Chapter 10)

---

9 | Open to the Public | ### Organization of American States Building (17th Street at Constitution Avenue; 202/458-3000)

The home of the Organization of American States (OAS), originally known as the Pan-American Union, was heralded at the time it was built as one of the finest Beaux-Arts buildings in Washington. It stands on the site of two of Washington's most famous early buildings—the home to David Burnes, original land-owner of much of official Washington's real estate, and the renowned Van Ness House.

When "Crusty Davey Burnes" established his tobacco plantation here, the land was waterfront property. (The Potomac came up to this point until the 1880s, when the Army Corps of Engineers dredged the river.) His simple wooden-frame farm house, often known as the Burnes Cottage, was built in 1750. He continued to live at this house after he sold much of the property to the federal government in 1792. While in residence, Burnes played host to a number of influential people. One guest at the cottage, the poet Tom Moore, penned a rhyme that gives a wicked sense of what the slow-to-develop city was like in the late eighteenth century:

> "This fam'd metropolis where Fancy sees
> Squares in morasses, obelisks in trees;
> Which second-sighted seers, ev'n now, adorn
> with shrines unbuilt and heroes yet unborn."

Burnes's only child, his daughter, Marcia Burnes, married Peter Van Ness, and the couple settled in Van Ness House, built behind her father's house on the same lot. Mrs. Van Ness's 600–acre inheritance was worth about 1.5 million dollars at the time the couple moved to their handsome Greek Revival mansion, built by Benjamin Henry Latrobe between 1813 and 1816.

Peter Van Ness had an illustrious career of public service that culminated in his becoming Mayor of Washington in 1830. Following his death in 1846, the house was owned by Virginia newspaperman Thomas Green. Legend has it that in the original plan of the Lincoln Conspirators, which called for kidnapping rather than murdering President Lincoln, the kidnapped president was to be hidden in the Van Ness House wine cellar. In any event, the house certainly went downhill after the Civil War. No longer a private residence, it became the site of a German beer garden, a botanical nursery, and finally the Columbia Athletic Club.

The Burnes cottage as it appeared several years before it was razed. (*Picturesque Washington*)

The Burnes House was torn down in 1894, despite the preservation fight—one of the city's first and fiercest—led by prominent citizens. The Van Ness House was demolished in 1907.

After the newly relocated George Washington University bought the land and decided the plot was too small for its needs, the site was sold to the federal government, which completed the Pan American Union Building (now the OAS Building) at the site in 1910.

When the Pan-American Building was dedicated in 1910, the ceremonies surrounding its establishment made headlines throughout the Western World. The building was opened with much fanfare and political jockeying, with President Taft and the leaders of other continental American countries posing for a multitude of photo-op shots.

The organization, formed as a Latin American, Caribbean, and American alliance under its current title in 1948, is the oldest multi-nation political alliance with which the United States has maintained solid ties (counting the previous incarnation as the Pan-American Union). In its role as a cultural beacon for the Latin American community, the OAS maintains the Art Museum of the Americas (201 18th Street, NW; 202/458–6016&&), the first museum in the world devoted exclusively to recent works of Latin American and Caribbean artists. A historical highlight of the museum can be found in the wonderful Aztec Gardens, where an artifact of the 1910 grand opening still grows. With much ceremony (and press coverage), President Taft planted the "Peace Tree" here as a symbol of unity. A horticultural oddity, the Peace Tree was grafted from a fig plant and a rubber tree, a marriage meant to embody the joining of seemingly disparate cultures.

See Also: Mary Surratt House (Chapter 2)

---

10 United Unions Building (Girl Scout Little House Site) (1750 New York Avenue, NW)

The United Unions Building was constructed here at the site of the "Girl Scout Little House," a 7–room house used by the Girl Scout National Council as a training and demonstration center for home economics. The Little House was originally built on the Ellipse in 1923. Constructed of the finest building materials then available, it was originally intended as a showplace of American workmanship. According to James M. Goode's *Capital Losses*, President Harding even presided at the official opening of the model home. The house, sponsored by the National Federation of Women's Clubs, was exhibited on the Ellipse for six months, and then offered to the Girl Scouts.

Mrs. Herbert Hoover helped raise the funds to move the house to a new home, and it was soon transported to this site, owned by the Phillips family (of the Phillips Gallery). Subsequently, thousands of Girl Scouts learned how to cook economical meals and keep a tidy home at this cozy, perfect little cottage. To show off their homemaking skills, the Girl Scouts often had company over—in the form of VIPs. In fact, Queen Elizabeth II (then Princess Elizabeth) dined at the house in 1939. Presidents were invited often, and the Coolidges even ate their Thanksgiving turkey here in 1925.

After transforming the house into office space during World War II, the Girl Scouts moved out in 1955. The Phillips family took possession of the property again and demolished the Girl Scout Little House to make way for the United Unions Building.

See Also: Phillips Gallery (Chapter 7)

---

11 The Winder Building (604 17th Street, NW)

Built in 1848, the Winder Building, some said, brought Washington into the modern world. It was the first "high-rise" office building, soaring an impressive five stories upwards. (Of course, due to the height restrictions requiring that no building in Washington be taller than the Washington Monument, "high rise" has a limited meaning in Washington.) It was also the first building in Washington constructed with steel beams, and warmed by a central hot water heating system.

The building was named for General William Winder, who commanded the losing American forces against the British invaders at the Battle of Bladensburg in 1814. But far more victorious military strategies were undertaken at Winder's namesake high-rise during the Civil War—the building served as office space for some of the greatest Union commanders, from General Winfield Scott to General Ulysses S. Grant. President Lincoln was a daily visitor to the offices, strolling over from the White House for dispatches and news of the war.

As the war first loomed in the early spring of 1861, General Winfield Scott met with one of his favorite commanders, Robert E. Lee, at the Winder Building offices, and asked Lee to consider taking command of the Union forces should war break out. In April 1861, Lee returned to the neighborhood for another, more famous meeting, across the street at Blair House, during which Francis P. Blair more forcefully requested that Lee take the Union command. But neither Scott nor Blair could persuade Lee to lead an army against his beloved Virginia, and Lee returned home to the south to head the Confederate Army instead.

According to Richard M. Lee's *Mr. Lincoln's Washington*, the building was also the site of a roof-top signal corps base. From here, flag-waving signalmen exchanged messages with the ring of forts that surrounded Washington, even into the captured territory of Northern Virginia. The fifth floor of the Winder Building was turned into a hospital in 1862, and it was rumored that Confederate prisoners were used as workers on that floor.

At the end of the Civil War, three important federal justice offices moved into the Winder Building—those of the Judge Advocate General, the Commissioner for the Exchange, and the Bureau of Military Justice. With these tenants, the Winder became the command post for the efforts to capture and put on trial the Lincoln conspirators. Today the Winder is still used by the executive branch as office space.

See Also: Blair House (Chapter 1); Fort McNair (Chapter 12)

12 YMCA Site (FDIC) (1736 G Street, NW)

The offices of the Federal Deposit and Insurance Corporation now stand at the site of a Washington recreational institution that was the setting for a sex scandal during the 1960s. The "G Street Y," as this public facility of the Young Men's Christian Association was known, was a popular sports and recreation facility for those working in and around the White House and other executive offices. It was also known as a gathering place for gay men, a fact which led the local police to place the YMCA under surveillance in the early 1960s.

On the evening of October 7, 1964, Walter Jenkins, President Lyndon Johnson's chief White House aide and close friend, went over to the G Street Y. Within the hour, Jenkins and another man were arrested in the men's room. The charge was disorderly conduct in the form of "indecent gestures." Those who read between the lines knew that Jenkins's actual "crime" was engaging in homosexual activity.

The timing couldn't have been worse—less than a month remained before the presidential election. Within two days, the story was leaked to the Republican National Committee, which quickly spread the word to the media. Once the news broke on the UPI wire, the local and national press went into a feeding frenzy, and it was soon revealed that Jenkins had previously been arrested in 1959 and charged as a "pervert."

While all the president's men were desperately trying to perform damage control, Jenkins was hospitalized for a breakdown (although there were rumors he was simply trying to avoid the press). On October 15, President Johnson released a statement saying that he had accepted his top aide's resignation. Johnson was re-elected with a 61 percent share of the popular vote. Jenkins's career was over.

PLACES: George Washington University and Environs

George Washington University moved to its present location from the Downtown area in 1912, eventually buying up some twenty blocks of Foggy Bottom—an acquisition that has made the university second only to the federal government as the city's biggest landowner.

The school's birth was a long and laborious one. George Washington himself had left provisions in his will (in the form of Washington Canal stock) for the founding of a national university. But Congress bickered over the issue for so long that eventually the funding was dissolved. Despite the efforts of James Madison, the establishment of Washington's oldest non-sectarian university was left unaccomplished until the Baptist Church took over the project and raised the funds to create the school.

Originally known as Columbian College when it was founded in 1821, the university was first located in Columbia Heights (then known as Columbia Hill). The first graduation commencement, held in 1824, was attended by a plethora of personalities, including the touring Marquis de Lafayette, as well as President James Monroe, Henry Clay, and John C. Calhoun.

In 1909, after merging with the George Washington Memorial Association, the school at last took the name of its founding father, becoming George Washington University. The school had relocated by that time to downtown Washington, but soon outgrew its quarters, and began casting an eye about the city for a larger plot of land. The economically depressed neighborhood of Foggy Bottom, with its empty houses and central location, seemed ideal for the school's planned urban sprawl.

In 1912, George Washington University began purchasing sections of upper Foggy Bottom, eventually expanding its reach a full twenty blocks into the neighborhood. The school bought up private homes and public buildings, allowing some tenants to stay but also taking down a number of historic homes and buildings to make way for new school buildings. Nevertheless, the school became sensitive to the history of the neighborhood, and eventually made efforts to preserve some important social and cultural landmarks in Foggy Bottom.

🔳 Fox Home Site (2300 K Street, NW)

British Minister Henry Fox, who lived in this house just southeast of Washington Circle during his diplomatic appointment in the 1840s, was an eccentric fellow whose appearance frightened small children. (He was quite tall and kept his head tilted to one side.) According to Suzanne Sherwood Unger's essay on Foggy Bottom in *Washington at Home* (1988), Fox slept all day, appearing only at night to fulfill diplomatic duties, although he was hardly the life of the party when he did attend soirees and other functions. He refused to shake hands with women, and supposedly refused to hold parties at his house for fear of having to receive female guests. Fox died at home in 1846; the cause of death was thought to be an overdose of opium. A strange death for a strange man.

This was later the site of the St. Ann's Infant Asylum, which opened here in the 1870s under the auspices of the Roman Catholic Church. One of the only institutions that took in black children, St. Ann's is still in operation as the St. Ann's Infant and Maternity Home, now located in Hyattsville, Maryland. Today the Fox Home site is occupied by George Washington University's Helen L. and Mary E. Warwick Memorial Building.

🔳 Lenthall Houses (606–610 21st St., NW)

This pair of red brick Federal townhouses, dating back to 1800, were originally located at 612–614 19th Street. The houses each measure a mere twenty feet wide and were designed to be used as a unit. Their first owner, Joseph Lenthall, served as the chief assistant to Benjamin Latrobe in the construction of the U.S. Capitol. Much later, one of the houses (originally at 614 19th Street) was owned by the locally renowned artist Bertha Noyes, and it was in this house in 1916 that the Arts Club of Washington was founded.

In 1978 to 1979, the houses were moved to their present location by George Washington University, which has made efforts in the past few decades to preserve some of the early architecture residing within the school's holdings.

See Also: Arts Club of Washington (Chapter 7)

15 | Open to the Public | **George Washington University Emergency Medical Center (901 23rd Street, NW)**

March 30, 1981 was a day that shook the nation to its core, as the city (and the world) got the news that President Reagan had been shot. As Reagan left the Washington Hilton Hotel following a speech, John Hinckley, Jr., stepped out of a crowd and fired a cheap handgun at the presidential party, wounding Reagan, Press Secretary Jim Brady, and two others. Reagan's limousine raced downtown to the George Washington University Emergency Medical Center immediately after the shooting.

Upon his arrival at the hospital, the president was rushed into surgery, where a team of hastily assembled trauma specialists (always on call for just such a national emergency) worked for several hours to save his life. Although initial press reports indicated that Reagan's wounds were not life-threatening, harrowing accounts later revealed the brilliance of the surgical team's efforts, without which the president would almost certainly have died on the operating table.

While the press was releasing overly optimistic reports of the president's condition, the media erred in the opposite direction when it came to the health of James Brady. Television anchors pronounced Brady dead less than two hours after the shooting. They were, happily, wrong again. Brady had survived the shooting. But his brain was so badly damaged that he has spent the intervening years in intensive and often painful physical therapy.

Reagan eventually recovered fully from his wounds, and in 1991 was honored by the university during a ceremony marking the tenth anniversary of the shooting. During the festivities, the school announced the creation of the "The Ronald Reagan Institute of Emergency Medicine" at the site of his treatment, as an educational and research center for the development of emergency medical treatments. The family waiting room where Nancy Reagan nervously awaited news of her husband's condition has been remodeled and now displays a plaque honoring Mrs. Reagan.

Reagan himself made headlines at the ceremony with the surprising announcement that he supported the "Brady Bill," legislation that James Brady and his wife Sarah had tirelessly been promoting to Congress to require a seven-day waiting period for the purchase of handguns. The support that Reagan (a card-carrying member of the NRA) voiced at the anniversary ceremonies gave the Brady Bill an almost instant impact. In early May of 1991, the legislation passed the House for the first time in its embattled history.

See Also: Washington Hilton Hotel (Chapter 8)

16 | Open to the Public | **Red Lion Row (Pennsylvania Avenue between 20th and 21st Streets)**

This row of modern shops ensconced in an antique facade was once the site of a popular nineteenth-century neighborhood saloon called the Red Lion Tavern. That even the exterior of the historic tavern block was preserved is a tribute to the abilities of preservationists and developers to work together. Red Lion Row was saved—at least for appearance's sake—by the fill-in architecture approach taken by the mini-mall developers who put in a row of eateries, boutiques, and a giant record store in 1983 at the site where the tavern once stood.

17 | Open to the Public | **St. Mary's Episcopal Church (728–730 23rd Street)**

James Renwick designed this stunning church, completed in 1886, for a congregation of black Foggy Bottom residents. This congregation had previously attended St. John's in Lafayette Square, where blacks were relegated to the balcony, and the Church of the Epiphany, at 13th and G Streets, where blacks had to wait to take Holy Communion until after all white worshippers had done so. The black congregations had been swelling since the Civil War, as a steady stream of poor southern blacks flowed into Washington, the city of freedom.

White churchgoers were unwilling to share their own churches equally with black members, but the idea of setting aside a special church for them seemed the perfect solution to the awkward problem. Land for the church was donated, and an interim church—a wooden chapel—was imported to the site until a worthy house of worship could be build. This chapel was left over from the grounds of the Kalorama Hospital—one of the city's many Civil War medical facilities, this one located on the grounds of the Kalorama Estate. (That first chapel still stands on the grounds, albeit hidden behind a brick facade). Parishioners from St. John's and the Church of the Epiphany raised funds to pay for the services of Renwick, who designed a fine Victorian Gothic rendition of an English country church.

See Also: Kalorama (Chapter8)

---

18 | Open to the Public | **United Church (1920 G Street, NW; 202/331–1495)**

The United Church is one of the few remaining links to the community of German immigrants that once filled Foggy Bottom. The church, which has congregations of both Methodist and German Lutheran persuasions, still performs services in German as well as in English. It is located at the site of the Concordia Lutheran Evangelical Church (built here in 1833), which later merged with the 1845 Methodist Church.

PLACES: Lower Foggy Bottom (along Constitution Avenue)

It is hard to imagine what this area looked like a century ago, but this was once waterfront property. The Potomac lapped up to the shores where Constitution Avenue now presides.

During the Civil War, Camp Fry was located here, housing the soldiers of the Veteran Volunteer Corps, a group of invalid military men who could no longer fight on the battlefield but who chose to continue their service by guarding federal buildings.

American University (now located in upper Northwest) operated out of buildings near the State Department until moving to its own campus in Upper Northwest in the 1920s. During the first and second World Wars, this area and the section of the Mall across Constitution Avenue (near Constitution Gardens) was prime real estate for the temporary wartime offices erected by the federal government. The last of these structures didn't come down until the early 1970s.

This area is now the core of an official quadrant that includes such federal departments as State and Interior, along with a variety of quasi-governmental agencies and organizations, among them the Federal Reserve and the National Academy of Sciences.

---

19 | Open to the Public | **Department of State (2201 C Street, NW; 202/647–3241)**

Heavily fortified during times of war, the Department of State can actually be toured when security risks are down. The department was formed as the first Cabinet-level post, in 1789. The State Department moved here from its site at the State, War and Navy Building (now called the Old Executive Office Building) in 1947. The building itself is a simple, uncomplicated modern work; but the collection of historic artifacts and furnishings (including the desk that Thomas Jefferson reputedly used to write the *Declaration of Independence*) is a compelling enough reason to take the tour.

During the Civil War, this was the site of Camp Fuller, the Army Remount Depot that stabled more than 30,000 horses. On December 26, 1861, an unexplained fire at the stables killed 200 horses instantly. A thousand more, wild with fear, set out on a tumultuous stampede through the city streets. The recapture of the horse took several days.
See Also: Old Executive Office Building (Chapter 1)

---

20 Old Naval Observatory (23rd and E Streets, NW)

Now the site of the Navy Medical Command, Building 2 of this complex was originally the site of the Naval Observatory. Built here in 1844, the observatory gained international renown under the guidance of Matthew Fontaine Maury (who was nicknamed "The Pathfinder of the Seas"), for its advances in navigational charts and instruments. It was here in 1877 that Asaph Hall discovered the moons of Mars, using the observatory's 26–inch telescope. The discovery was considered the most important astronomic find since the 1846 discovery of Neptune.

The Old Naval Observatory.
(*Picturesque Washington*)

In 1893, the observatory moved to its present location in upper Northwest. The original observatory site is listed on the National Register of Historic Places.
See Also: Naval Observatory (Chapter 8)

PLACES: Waterfront Area

"Watergate" is a name so redolent with political intrigue and the bad morning-after-taste of the "long national nightmare" endured by the city and the nation in the early 1970s that the original name and meaning have been forgotten. The actual Watergate is the ceremonial sweep of steps that rise from Rock Creek Parkway upwards to the Lincoln Memorial. Once used as a ceremonial gateway (hence the name) at which important visitors arriving by ship were met, today the Watergate seems an incongruous hillside stairway. But even after its ceremonial purpose had ended, there was a time when the warmth of the sun against the cool white steps drew summertime crowds to National Symphony Orchestra concerts at a floating bandshell.

This whole waterfront area takes its name from these steps, although the Watergate complex of apartments, offices, restaurants, and a hotel is the only namesake site. Factories and breweries once ruled the waterfront along this curving stretch of riverbank. The Christian Heurich Brewery stood at approximately the site where the Kennedy Center now presides, and a variety of other manufacturing facilities creating bricks, glass, and other materials also lined the banks here. Until 1946, the most visible landmark of the old waterfront was the Washington Gas and Light Company's gas storage facility, a hideous smokestack of a building that was finally torn down to make way for a redevelopment project overseen by the National Capital Planning Commission. By 1966, the area was also cleared of the Heurich Brewery and a group of temporary buildings erected during World War II that had housed CIA offices.

It took some twenty years to fully transform the area from a factory wasteland to a cultural wonderland. Today, the clear, crisp lines of the **Kennedy Center for the Performing Arts** and the semi-circular **Watergate** complex buildings give an altogether pleasing view of the Washington waterfront from across the river. It is a vision that was further extended in the 1980s with the controversial construction of Arthur Cotton Moore's witty Washington Harbour complex along the Georgetown waterfront, creating a visual riverfront continuum of smooth, serpentine architecture.

The John F. Kennedy Center. (Washington Convention and Visitors Association)

㉑ Open to the Public **Howard Johnson Motor Lodge (2605 Virginia Avenue, NW; 202/965–2700)**

This particular branch of the classic American roadside restaurant and hotel has a far greater claim to fame than most of its pit-stop brethren: On June 17, 1972, the Watergate "Plumbers" (the code name used by the break-in perpetrators), posted scouts here to keep watch while they broke in to the Democratic National Headquarters across the street at the Watergate Hotel complex. When the Ho-Jo look-outs on the seventh floor spotted a hotel guard on the floor where the break-in was taking place, they radioed over to warn their partners. But they were too late. Within moments, the guard had discovered the taped-up lock on the door and burst in upon the intruders. The curtain had risen on the first act of the scandal that would lead to President Nixon's resignation.

See Also: Watergate Complex and **John F. Kennedy Center for the Performing Arts**

The Christian Heurich Brewery stood on the present-day site of the Kennedy Center from 1894 to 1966. (Library of Congress)

---

22 | Open to the Public | ## John F. Kennedy Center for the Performing Arts (2700 F Street, NW; 202/254–3600)

Long before the Kennedy Center ever graced the waterfront, this was the site of Washington's famed Christian Heurich Brewery, built here in 1894 after a fire destroyed the original Heurich Brewery in Georgetown on 29th Street (which had previously been the Schnell Brewery). The brewery and its equally famous and flamboyant owner, Christian Heurich, were Washington institutions for more than half a century. Even during prohibition, when the brewery had to stop making beer, it managed to eke out a living selling ice. When prohibition was repealed, the kettles were cooking once again.

During its last years, Heurich brewed up one of the city's favorite beers: Senate Beer, which the company continued to produce until the brewery closed in 1956. Christian Heurich, founder and brewmaster, had died in 1945, at the age of 102. The city condemned the brewery in 1961, buying up the land and renting out the buildings until it demolished what remained of the brewery in 1966 to make way for the Theodore Roosevelt Bridge and the Kennedy Center. But before the brewery was torn down, for a time it was inhabited by the Arena Theater (which now has its own Arena Stage near the waterfront in Southwest).

Since the 1930s, various plans had circulated to build a cultural center in the capital city. In 1954, Congress gave the go-ahead for the building of what was then called the "National Cultural Center," but the project eroded as disputes over design and placement turned the issue into a political albatross for lawmakers and city planners. In 1959, Edward Durrell Stone was chosen to design the center, because planners envisioned a John Russell Pope-esque building. Even after the decision was made to build the new cultural center in the waterfront redevelopment area where the new Watergate complex already stood, the apathetic public was slow to support the expensive project. But when President Kennedy was killed in 1963 and the center was renamed in his honor, it suddenly became a national memorial, and moral as well as financial support poured in from around the world.

When the Kennedy Center opened in 1971, tourists shocked the management by stealing for souvenirs every piece of ornament that wasn't nailed down or screwed up (the marble bathroom fixtures were favorites among pocket-fillers). Things have calmed down considerably since then, and tightly installed hardware and eagle-eyed security guards have cut down on pilfering.

During the summer and fall of 1972, the Kennedy Center's underground parking lot may have played a role in the Watergate scandal. According to some rumors, the mysterious Watergate informant "Deep Throat" met here with Washington Post investigative reporters Bob Woodward and Carl Bernstein. Whether Woodward and Bernstein actually did rendezvous here with the mystery man (or woman) remains known only to those immediately involved.

Today, the Kennedy Center is Washington's jewel in its once-Spartan crown of culture, a performing arts mecca akin to New York's Lincoln Center. With six theaters, including an Opera House, a Concert Hall, the Eisenhower Theater, the Terrace Theater, the Theater Lab, and the American Film Institute (AFI) movie theater, the Ken Cen offers venues for every kind of performing arts.

See Also: Howard Johnson's Motor Lodge and **Watergate Complex;** Heurich Brewery Site (Chapter 6); Heurich Mansion (Chapter 7)

---

23 | Open to the Public | **The Watergate Complex (2650 Virginia Avenue, NW)**

One of Washington's ritziest addresses will go down in history for an infamy that brought the downfall of the president. On June 17, 1972, the spark that lit the fuse that blew the lid off the most explosive White House scandal in American history was ignited here.

At 2:30 a.m. on the morning of June 17th, a security guard at the Watergate noticed tape on the lock of the door to the Democratic National Committee's campaign headquarters for George McGovern. Entering the offices, he confronted five men frantically packing up to beat a hasty retreat. The men, who later came to be known as the "White House Plumbers," were Bernard Barker, James McCord, Virgilio Gonzalez, Eugenio Martinez, and Frank Sturgis. They had been hired to wire-tap McGovern's campaign headquarters and photograph sensitive documents in the office of DNC Chairman Lawrence O'Brien. The men were arrested, and their surveillance equipment and cameras were confiscated—along with a supply of sequenced $100 bills that had been part of their pay-off.

The burglars had checked into the Watergate Hotel the day before, in preparation for the attempted break-in. After several aborted attempts in the previous month, they had managed to enter the DNC Headquarters on May 28 to plant listening devices and photograph Lawrence O'Brien's correspondence. But the bugging equipment was badly placed, and the Plumbers were ordered to break back into the DNC to fix the bad leaks. Attorney General John Mitchell (and Director of the Committee to Re-Elect the President, aka CREEP), who lived in an apartment at the Watergate, gave the order to attempt the fateful June 17 break-in.

Despite the apparent enjoyment and facility with which they played the espionage game, Mitchell and his cohorts had left behind a subtle but damning trail of evidence (ranging from incriminating briefcases to traceable phone bills). The arrest of the Watergate Burglars put an ingenious pair of *Washington Post* reporters, Bob Woodward and Carl Bernstein, on the scent. The rest of the story is a long, involved *danse macabre*, played out in headlines and courtrooms, on tape (both magnetic and red), and eventually in the history books. On August 9, 1974, Richard Nixon became the first president to resign from office, although he had little choice: Impeachment was imminent.

The *Washington Post* won the Pulitzer prize for Woodward and Bernstein's investigative journalism. The riveting story of how the reporters tracked the trail of the Watergate break-in all the way to the oval office was told in their bestselling account, *All the President's Men* (1975), which was later made into a motion picture starring Robert Redford as Bob Woodward and Dustin Hoffman as Carl Bernstein. Journalism schools around the country reported a 75 percent increase in applications after the superstardom of the *Post* pair.

Long before the Plumbers immortalized the name of the complex—indeed, even before it was built—the Watergate had already seen its share of scandal. It was originally planned as "Watergate Towne," by its developers, Societa Generale Immobiliare (SGI), a Rome-based real estate investment company. The Vatican was a partial share-holder in SGI, a connection that led syndicated columnist Drew Pearson to write a column in 1962 describing how the Catholic Church was planning to build a major development on the Washington waterfront. Protests from around the country poured in to Congress, and religious groups from non-Catholic sects set up an organization to fight the Vatican's American "headquarters," as many people mistakenly perceived the project. The Vatican had only a minority interest in the large investment company (SGI had other projects pending worldwide as well), and later withdrew its holdings in the SGI all together. The rumor was finally quelled before it destroyed the Watergate project, which was completed in 1971.

The Watergate is probably the city's most prestigious apartment address, with such current occupants as Senator Robert Dole and his wife, Elizabeth, the head of Red Cross. The hotel's proximity to the Kennedy Center also makes it popular with the actors, dancers, and musicians appearing on stage across the street. Likewise, the Watergate is a watering (and eating) hole for much of Washington's power elite, who come to dine at Jean-Louis, which has been hailed by restaurant critics as one of the country's best.

See Also: Howard Johnson's Motor Lodge and **Kennedy Center for the Performing Arts;** Washington *Post* Building (Chapter 2)

Chapter Six

GEORGETOWN

A tobacco port town turned Washington neighborhood, Georgetown has an illustrious history that pre-dates Washington's by nearly a half-century. In fact, it was here that George Washington and a newly anointed board of commissioners met in 1794 with local landowners to hammer out an agreement for the purchase of property on which to build the city of Washington. The site of their meeting was Suter's Tavern, the same tavern later used by Pierre L'Enfant and Andrew Ellicott as a headquarters while they were laying out the plans for the city. These plans called for the inclusion of Georgetown (or the Town of George, as it was then known) within the boundaries of Washington, although it was agreed that the older port city would retain its independence as a separate township.

The Town of George had been authorized as a township by the Maryland Assembly in 1751, and prior to that, had already served for almost a decade as a warehouse district for tobacco shipments from Maryland growers. But even before it was established as a tobacco trading port, the Town of George (named in honor of King George II), had long been a site for settlement. This fact was documented in 1632 by a British fur trader and adventurer by the name of Henry Fleet, who sailed up the Potomac before anchoring "two leagues short of the falls." Assuming Fleet was referring to Great Falls, he would have set foot near the site of present-day Georgetown. He found there a well-established Native American settlement, which he identified in his writings as "Tohoga." He clearly liked the environment and stayed a while to set up a trading practice with the villagers. "This place is without question the most pleasant and healthful place in all this country," Fleet wrote as he settled in, "and most convenient for habitation, the air temperate in summer and not violent in winter." After being captured by the friendly natives, he ended up staying in Tohoga for two years. Tohoga may have been the oldest Native American settlement in the area. The Natcotchank village to the east, noted by Captain John Smith in 1608 (at present-day Anacostia), is thought to have been established later than the village of Tohoga.

The land upon which most of the Town of George was later built was deeded by Lord Baltimore to a Scotsman, Colonel Ninian Beall, in 1703. Beall called his 795–acre plot of land the "Rock of Dunbarton," after a landmark castle in his homeland. In 1751, the General Assembly of Maryland officially recognized the Town of George as covering some 60 acres of land, and the port city was plat mapped according to the boundaries set forth by Maryland legislators.

From Members of Congress to officers and gentlemen, the powerful and the hopeful migrated back to Georgetown along the country lanes of Washington as soon as their workday was done. As commutes went in those days, it wasn't a long one, but the conditions (dirty, rutted roads; few street lamps) made it a somewhat miserable trek. Townhouse living, much the vogue in London, was genially adapted to the cobblestone streets of Georgetown. In many ways, Georgetown resembled the port city of Alexandria, Virginia, just across the Potomac. Both had a brisk shipping trade, and each could claim rich and powerful citizens among its denizens. But Alexandria was an older and larger

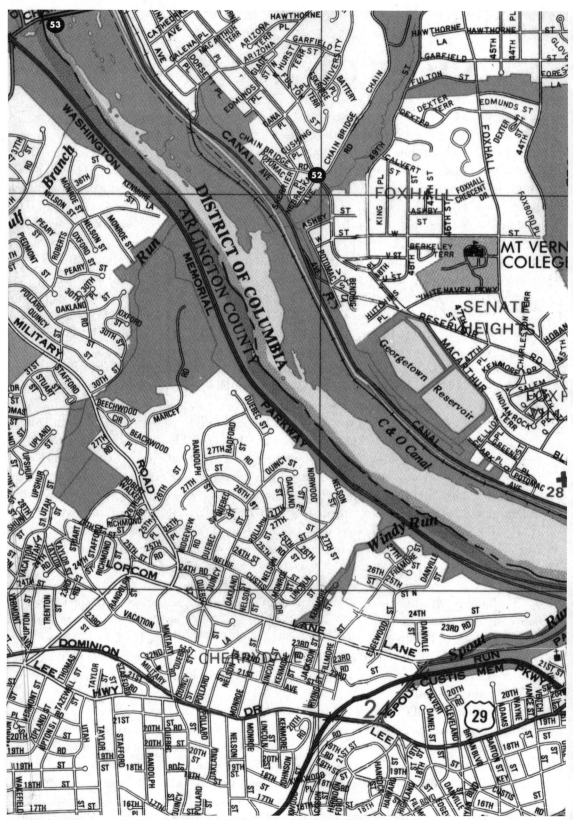

From the D.C. Transportation Map prepared by the D.C. Department of Public Works

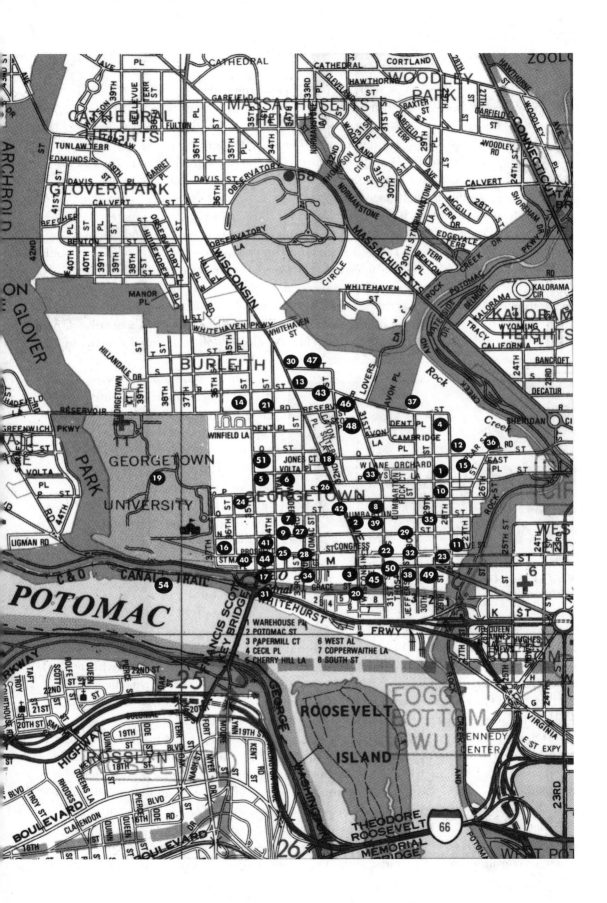

port, and, situated more closely to the South, became the truer point of entry into the lower and western states. Nevertheless, Georgetown's land proximity to the capital made it a desirable suburb for the housing needs of local statesmen (with the exception of such Virginia gentlemen as George Washington and Thomas Jefferson).

As a port city, Georgetown's major export was tobacco from Maryland farms. Within twenty years of the capital's founding, however, Georgetown's influence as a river port city began to fade. As steamships started to replace the classic sailing vessels of the eighteenth century, deeper ports to the South were sought by shippers. By the mid-nineteenth century, even this patina of glamor had begun to dull. Other fashionable neighborhoods—Lafayette Square, Kalorama, LeDroit Park, and Dupont Circle—were siphoning off would-be Georgetowners by the 1870s. Indeed, by the time Georgetown officially joined Washington in 1871, its status as the prime residential district in the area had been supplanted by the upstart city neighborhoods that mimicked its chic streets and townhomes. Although it lost many a millionaire resident to these newer areas, Georgetown still retained a solidly upper-middle-class stature, and its taverns and saloons continued to attract a mix of lower-class workers and upper-class tipplers.

View of the wharves at Georgetown, circa 1886.
(*Picturesque Washington*)

During the Civil War, white Georgetown was a staunchly Confederate city, despite its proximity to the Union capital. It swarmed with Southern spies, and when the federal government took over the **Union Hotel** for use as a hospital, the local outcry was loud and raucous. Even after the war, the rift continued; southerners like Robert E. Lee who were no longer welcome in most Washington homes were still treated as honored guests at Georgetown estates such as **Tudor Place.**

The main black neighborhood in Georgetown, Herring Hill, was said to be named for the most frequently caught fish in Rock Creek. It was bounded by the area between Rock Creek Park and 29th Street, north of P Street, and was a popular neighborhood for laborers, farmers, and those who worked as servants in the nearby Georgetown mansions. The strong presence of this black community made Georgetown an important stop on the Underground Railroad—most notably at **Mount Zion United Methodist Church** and at **Halcyon House.**

Herring Hill remained a mainly black neighborhood until the late nineteenth century, when more well-to-do black families began trickling down into the now less-fashionable Georgetown homes being vacated as other neighborhoods became more popular for whites. In the meantime, poorer whites moved into the Herring Hill houses, and the upshot was that Georgetown became an ethnically diverse area in a kind of black gentrification.

Georgetown regained its cachet among white, white-collar Washingtonians during FDR's administration, when New Dealers who wanted to avoid the appearance of conspicuous consumption in the midst of the Depression began buying up the townhouses in

Georgetown that were now occupied by black families. This effectively re-gentrified Georgetown, pushing back out the same lower-class citizens the New Dealers were attempting to help.

In the late 1950s, Georgetown was a favorite neighborhood for the rambunctious Kennedy clan: Pre-presidency, John F. Kennedy and his wife lived just around the block from Bobby Kennedy and his brood. After her husband's assassination, the widowed first lady returned to another Georgetown house, only to find herself living in a fishbowl watered by tears of a nation. She moved to New York City—for privacy!

The cachet of having a Georgetown address has reached as far west as Hollywood: A number of movie stars, including Merle Oberon, Myrna Loy, and Elizabeth Taylor (as the wife of Virginia Senator John Warner) maintained houses here. And literary legends ranging from Walter Lippmann (who bought the **Alexander Melville Bell House**) to Louisa May Alcott (who served as a nurse at the Union Army hospital set up in old **Union Hotel** on M Street) lived here as well. The quiet elegant streets of Georgetown still hold sway over those who live here, and those who wish they could. The powerful still flock to the townhouses and mini-mansions of Georgetown. Among the many rich and powerful who maintain homes in Georgetown are former Washington *Post* Executive Editor Ben Bradlee, unauthorized biographer Kitty Kelley, novelist Herman Wouk, make-up magnate Donald Lauder, ABC News correspondent Sander Vanocur, former HEW secretary Joseph Califano, social doyenne Pamela Harriman, former Senator Eugene McCarthy, and Washington *Post* Publisher Katherine Graham.

PLACES: Georgetown

❶ Dean Acheson House (2805 P Street, NW)

This house was purchased in 1922 by Dean Acheson, who went on to become President Truman's secretary of state. Acheson lived here the rest of his life, enlarging the nineteenth-century house to make it more conducive to the elaborate entertaining for which he became known. The Trumans attended their final Washington dinner party here in 1953, just before they left Washington to return to the Midwest.

❷ | Open to the Public | Au Pied de Cochon (1335 Wisconsin Avenue, NW; 202/333–5440)

This popular little French bistro was the site of perhaps the only known instance of a spy going back out into the cold war again. It happened here on November 2, 1985, when Vitaly Yerchenko, a top KGB official who had defected to the United States in July, got fed up with his CIA handlers. After finishing a meal at Au Pied de Cochon in the company of his keepers, Yerchenko slipped the spooks while they were paying the check and hot-footed it back to the Soviet compound to re-defect. By November 6, Yerchenko was back in the USSR.

One of the reasons Yerchenko gave for returning to his motherland was his contention that the CIA agents had forced him to dine on lousy french food at Au Pied de Cochon (although restaurant regulars hotly contested the charge that the food was no good here). To commemorate the strange incident, the restaurant has placed a plaque at the booth where the pig-headed Yerchenko dined on the day he re-defected.

Remembering the *Maine*

On February 17, 1898, the battleship USS *Maine* exploded under mysterious circumstances in Havana harbor, killing 260 sailors. The American public quickly jumped to the conclusion that the deed had been perpetrated by Spain, which was then tyrannizing the Cuban people. The bodies of the martyred sailors were shipped back to the mainland to be buried in Arlington National Cemetery. Soon afterwards, thousands of people lined M Street to watch the solemn parade of black-decked horses pulling the caissons that bore the sailors' flag-draped coffins.

Funeral cortege for those killed in the explosion of the *Maine* passes the Key Mansion en route to Arlington Cemetery. (Library of Congress)

③ Bank of Columbia Building (3210 M Street, NW)

Erected in 1796, this building was originally home to the Bank of Columbia, the second oldest bank established within the District limits. After the bank moved on to another location in 1806, the building became home to a succession of important public services. The Bureau of Indian Trade occupied the building from 1807 until 1822; and in 1823, the building became the Georgetown's Town Hall and Mayor's Office. In 1883, the building was remodeled into a fire station, and so it remained until 1940. In 1981, the building was auctioned off (despite efforts to have it transformed into a firefighting museum), and the proud site is now home to a Burger King franchise.

(Continued)

The following journal entries about the commencement of the Spanish-American War, written in 1898 by Ellen Maury Slayden (and later published as *Washington Wife* in 1962) are a reminder of just how little America has changed from war to war—many of these words could have been written today, although they are nearly a century old. . . .

"(February 17, 1898) [My husband] came running upstairs with the *Times* and read me the brief telegram: 'The battleship Maine blown up in Havana harbor.' It was some time before I realized that one of the high notes of history had been sounded and that it would be long before we heard the last of it. We thought it meant immediate war with Spain. . . . I believe I have a prenatal terror of war—a child of the sixties—and my knees trembled and I felt sick all day.

"(April 20, 1898) The President signed the [war] resolutions at 11:24 this morning, and Polo de Bernabe, the Spanish Minister, may leave at any moment. Society holds its breath . . . Shop windows are full of pictures of military and naval heroes, and of battles long ago, even to the Spanish Armada. Everyone wears a little American flag—they are peddled at five cents—and street boys whistle "The Star Spangled Banner." The rest of us sing it as far as we know the words—first and last two lines of the first stanza."

❹ Beall-Washington House (2920 R Street, NW)

This is one of the earliest remaining mansions in Georgetown, although its original appearance has been greatly altered. It was built in 1784 for Thomas Beall, who was a descendant of Ninian Beall (the original landowner of the "Rock of Dunbarton" tract of land that encompassed much of modern-day Georgetown). Beall passed the house on to his daughter, Elizabeth, upon her marriage to Colonel George Corbin Washington, a great-nephew of the first president. Other notable occupants through the years include "Wild Bill" Donovan, the World War II head of the Office of Strategic Services (O.S.S.), the agency that later became the CIA), and *Washington Post* doyenne Katharine Graham, who still resides in the historic home.

See Also: The Washington *Post* Building and Old Washington *Post* Building Site (Chapter 2)

❺ Alexander Melville Bell House (1525 35th Street, NW)

Alexander Graham Bell bought this house for his parents in 1891, and it was here, in the property's carriage house, that he set up his laboratory. While working here, Bell perfected his disk-graphophone technology, which later became the basis for the creation of phonograph records. The house was later subdivided and sold off in bits and pieces (including the laboratory, which now is a separate, private house at 3414 Volta Place).

In 1938, journalist and political pundit Walter Lippmann bought the house. He lived here until 1946, when he moved to a magnificent house that had been the deanery of the Washington National Cathedral.

The house remains in private hands and is not open to the public.

See Also: Alexander Graham Bell Laboratory and **Volta Bureau;** Alexander Graham Bell House Site, Bell Experimental School, Bell-Morton House, and Frankfurter-Lippmann House (Chapter 7); Walter Lippman House (Chapter 8)

6 Alexander Graham Bell Laboratory (3414 Volta Place, NW)

This building, once the carriage house to the **Alexander Melville Bell House,** became the famous inventor's laboratory when he moved his parents to the nearby house in 1891. Besides working on his disk-graphophone here, Bell also continued his work on technologies to aid the hearing impaired (his wife, Mabel, was deaf). The laboratory was also known as the Volta Bureau (named for the French prize for research he received). This name is now applied to a building at the corner, which Bell helped found.

See Also: Alexander Melville Bell House and **Volta Bureau;** Alexander Graham Bell House Site, Bell Experimental School Site, and Bell-Morton House (Chapter 7)

7 Bodisco House (3322 O Street, NW)

The home of Russian Minister Baron de Bodisco, who arrived in 1838, served as the Russian Legation during his tenure in that post. Bodisco married an American woman, and ended up spending eternity in Georgetown, for he is buried in **Oak Hill Cemetery**. The house was built around 1815.

See Also: Oak Hill Cemetery

8 Open to the Public Christ Church (31st and O Streets, NW)

Henry Laws designed this charming little Gothic church, which was built in 1886. Among the church's prominent members was Francis Scott Key.

See Also: Key Bridge

9 Cox's Row (3327–3339 N Street, NW)

This block of five Federal rowhouses was built by Colonel John Cox, the first Mayor of Georgetown, around 1790. General Lafayette is said to have been entertained at 3337 N Street during his 1824 visit to Washington. A similar row of townhouses in the next block (3255 to 3263 N Street) known as Smith's Row was built in 1817. Both Cox's and Smith's Rows are fine examples of typical Georgetown residential streets as they appeared over a century ago. With the exception of some renovations that transformed a few of the homes from Federal style to Victorian, the blocks retain their original early nineteenth-century aura.

10 Open to the Public Daw's Musket Fence (2803–2811 P Street):

This war monument, sometimes known as "Reuben Daw's Fence" (for the eccentric who erected it in the 1860s), consists of musket barrels from the Mexican-American War of 1848. Daw, a locksmith, got the guns the easy way: He bought them from a pawnshop.

11 Susan Decatur House (2812 N Street, NW)

Susan Wheeler Decatur moved to this quiet home after her husband, Commodore Stephen Decatur, was killed in a

Daw's Musket Fence. (Jack Looney)

duel with a fellow naval officer in 1820. The house, built in 1813, was an elegant yet less costly residence for Mrs. Decatur, who could no longer afford to maintain the Decatur House mansion on Lafayette Square.

See Also: Decatur House (Chapter 1)

---

12 | Open to the Public | **Dumbarton House (2715 Q Street, NW; 202/337–2288)**

Originally known as "Bellevue," this house, not to be confused with Dumbarton Oaks, is another of Georgetown's beautiful Georgian mansions. Legends abound about the house, including the tale that President James Madison and his wife rendezvoused at Bellevue in 1814 to plan their escape route out of the city as the British burned the White House. If the story is true, the Madisons arrived at a slightly different location than the site of present-day Dumbarton House, for, until 1915, the house occupied the land across which Q Street now passes. Plans to build the "Buffalo Bridge" connecting Q Street to Downtown called for the house to make way, so Congress passed an act that ordered Bellevue to move over, which it did. Originally built between 1800 and 1810, Bellevue was purchased in 1928 by the National Society of Colonial Dames of America, which continues to maintain the site as a house museum.

See Also: Octagon House (Chapter 5)

---

13 | Open to the Public | **Dumbarton Oaks (1703 32nd Street, NW; 202/338–8278)**

Built in 1801, Dumbarton Oaks remains one of the city's loveliest estates—as famous for its gardens and collection of pre-Columbian art as it is for the historic events that have taken place here. Most notably, the estate was the scene for the Dumbarton Oaks Conference that led to the United Nations Charter. In late summer 1944, Franklin Roosevelt initiated a series of meetings with representatives from the four major world powers, as called for in the Atlantic Charter he had just signed with Winston Churchill. The diplomats in attendance were: Lord Halifax (representing Great Britain), Dr. Wellington Koo (representing China), Andrei Gromyko (representing the Soviet Union), and Edward Stettinius (representing the United States). They met in the Music Room of the main house, a site selected for the calming effect it seemed to have on most visitors. The press was denied access to the conference and its attendees, thus allowing the diplomats to work without worrying about public reactions to anything they might say or do in private. The outcome of the conference was the agreement to create a United Nations that would be organized along the lines of a General Assembly with a Secretariat leadership, with various sub-assemblies, including Security, Social, and Economic Councils. A year later, the United Nations Organization was officially ratified in San Francisco, based on the groundwork laid at the Dumbarton Oaks Conference.

Dumbarton Oaks was not always the scene of such civilized diplomacy. In fact, during the early 1800s, the house was in the spotlight for the decidedly undiplomatic tack of its residents: South Carolina Senator John C. Calhoun and his wife. The Calhouns were renowned entertainers at Oakly (as they called the estate), having hosted the Marquis de Lafayette there during the French hero's farewell tour of America in 1824. Ironically, however, after Calhoun became Andrew Jackson's vice president, they became better known for who they chose *not* to entertain.

The scandal erupted when Senator John Henry Eaton married the lovely (and some said loose-moraled) widow Margaret "Peggy" O'Neale, a local tavern-keeper's daughter, on January 1, 1829. The couple were said to have coupled long before their marriage. Snickers turned to jeers when Senator Eaton was named Secretary of War by his good friend, the newly elected president, Andrew Jackson. Mrs. Eaton's swift elevation to the level of a cabinet wife gave more than a few genteel ladies the bends.

Both Eatons were ostracized by Washington society, with the snub-warfare being led by Vice President Calhoun's wife, who refused to entertain or otherwise socialize with the new secretary of war and his bride. Other cabinet wives followed suit, as did the rest of the city's political and financial power base. Jackson's entire administration was soon embroiled in the social tiff, which quickly escalated to political warfare as sides were taken and allegiances broken. Aside from her own husband, Peggy Eaton's staunchest defender had become President Jackson. (Jackson's wife, who died shortly before he took office, had suffered from a similar social castigation.) Among Jackson's cabinet, only Martin Van Buren (then secretary of state) sided with Jackson.

The Eaton Affair climaxed in 1831, with implosion of the cabinet. The first to go were Van Buren and Eaton, who left so Jackson could regain control of his cabinet. Three pro-Calhoun cabinet members—Treasury Secretary Samuel Ingham, Attorney General John Berrien, and Navy Secretary John Branch—were then ousted from the cabinet as well.

The cabinet shake-up and its causes made headlines around the country. Most Americans, a generally sympathetic lot when it comes to romance, took the Eatons' side, and later elected the couple's champion, Martin Van Buren, to the presidency. John C. Calhoun, on the other hand, lost political favor as a result of the struggle. He never attained the White House, although he had been considered an almost sure-shot for the presidency before the Eaton Affair.

Haunted Georgetown

Apparitions are apparently more at home in Georgetown than they are anywhere else except the White House. One of the more popular tales of Washington hauntings involves Georgetown itself—not a particular house, mind you, but the actual town itself. In 1755, during the French and Indian War, the British sent in a crackerjack commander, General Edward Braddock, to engage a French force at Fort Duquesne. General Braddock's forces docked at Alexandria, then, a thousand strong, they crossed the Potomac on the Georgetown Ferry. Braddock and his men marched up the hill of Georgetown, heading out toward what they assumed would be a terrible defeat for the enemy. But the French surprised them with a full-force attack at the fork of the Ohio River. The General and some 700 of his men were killed, and those who survived (including a young George Washington) learned well the lesson of the surprise attack.

Soon after this bloody battle, legends began to grow that Georgetown was now a ghost town. For more than a hundred years, citizens reported hearing the mysterious marching of men at midnight as they climbed up the hill to meet their fate. The hauntings were said to escalate to a feverish pitch around the anniversary of the battle. The story was further elaborated upon during the Civil War, when a Union scout swore he heard a troop of soldiers marching across the bridge, but when he looked, none could be seen. The legends began to fade as the construction and noise of Georgetown increased over the years.

Not so hard to see or hear, according to those who claim to have experienced their presence, are the ghosts of the Old Stone House. Volunteer staffers at the house claim that one ghost in particular (whom they have named "George") is a misogynist who has attempted to murder several women at the house. Claims of sexual assault have

One thing that Dumbarton Oaks was *not* known for (or rather, by) until the twentieth century was its name. The place went through a handful of name changes before acquiring its well-known moniker. The name "Dumbarton" dates back to the tenancy of the house's first owner, Ninian Beall, who owned virtually all of what is known as Georgetown today. Beall named the estate after the Rock of Dunbarton, a landmark castle near his Scottish homestead (for which **Dumbarton House** was also slightly mis-named). In 1805, the house passed into the hands of Robert Beverley, a romantic who planted an orangery on the estate, and renamed the place "Acropholos" in honor of the hilltop orange grove. When Beverley's son sold it to the Calhouns of South Carolina, the estate became "Oakly."

The next name attached to the place was "Monterey." It was so-named after a military victory in Mexico by its next owner, Edward Linthicum, who rebuilt the house in 1860. In 1891, Henry Fitch Blount, a Midwesterner with a farm tool fortune, purchased the estate, and renamed it "The Oaks." Blount—who had a taste for the dramatic—had a tiny attic theater built and filled the yard with peacocks. The Oaks rapidly deteriorated until 1920, when the estate was purchased by Robert Woods Bliss and his wife Mildred. Harkening back to the estate's original name, they added a "Dumbarton" to "Oaks," and thus was born Dumbarton Oaks.

The Blisses themselves had an unusual history: Their own parents (his father and her mother) had married in 1894, when Robert was eighteen and Mildred four years younger. In

---

(Continued)

also been mentioned, although how a ghost could engage in such activity is hard to imagine. Volunteers also say that they have seen figures dressed in clothes from various eras passing silently through the house, and visiting children have often reported similar sightings.

Another reputedly haunted house in Georgetown is Halcyon House (now known as Stoddert House), which once served as a stop on the underground railroad. But its dank basement sometimes became a chamber of death; runaway slaves seeking refuge there after swimming the Potomac and crawling through a tunnel to get to the house would sometimes die from exposure and exhaustion. The spirits of those who died here have supposedly haunted the house ever since.

Now but a ghost itself, Georgetown's Key Mansion was supposedly a haunted house in its own right. The home of "Star-Spangled Banner" composer Francis Scott Key was sold upon his death in 1843 and turned into a combination rental property and tourist trap. The new owners painted "KEY MANSION" in bold letters on the side of the building, to advertise its historic heritage. Reports soon surfaced of horrific moaning, blood-curdling screams, and similar eerie sounds, and, upon going to investigate the source of this racket, one of the tenants discovered a frightful stain of dried blood on the attic ceiling. Although there was no record of murder or other violence in the house, ghost experts implied that whoever was so badly injured as to stain the attic ceiling with his or her blood would probably be a good candidate for ambivalent ghosthood. The hauntings apparently stopped when the house was renovated in 1912. The house was torn down in 1948 to make way for the Whitehurst Freeway connection to the Key Bridge. One can't help but wonder whether drivers exiting off the Key Bridge ever think they see the shadowy form of an old mansion looming in front of them as they drive into Georgetown.

1908, the junior couple became marital Blisses as well, and twelve years later they bought the estate. Over the next decade, Robert Bliss (a former ambassador to Argentina) and his wife transformed the somewhat run-down Georgian manor house and grounds into a true showplace, filling the mansion with rare pieces of European artworks, including many from the Byzantine period. They filled their social calendar with glittering events, with some of the world's greatest musicians and composers often on the guest list. Polish pianist Ignace Jan Paderewski was a favorite, as was Russian composer Igor Stravinsky. A frequent guest and performer in the Blisses' Music Room, Stravinsky was so fond of the Blisses that he composed "The Dumbarton Oaks Concerto" (also known as Concerto in E Flat) for their 30th wedding anniversary.

In 1941, the Blisses gave the estate and its valuable holdings to Harvard University, so that, as the historic plaque at the estate reads, "the continuity of scholarship in the Byzantine and Mediaeval Humanities may remain unbroken to clarify an ever changing present and to inform the future with wisdom." When the United States entered the Second World War, Harvard allotted half of the estate for the use of the National Defense Research Committee, but reclaimed the full estate after the war.

In 1963, renowned architect Philip Johnson designed a controversially modern gallery, attached to the Main House, to exhibit the collection of Pre-Columbian works acquired by the estate. The Main House is still filled with the Blisses' remarkable collection of European furnishings and artworks, among the most famous of which is *The Visitation* by El Greco, which hangs in the Music Room. Harvard University continues to operate the estate, portions of which are open to the public.

See Also: Oak Hill Cemetery

⑭ Duke Ellington School of the Arts at Western (35th and R Streets, NW)

This institution claims a remarkable number of successful alumni, including Margaret Gorman Cahill, the first Miss America (she won the title in 1921, although she didn't graduate from Western until 1923), feminist and *Ms.* founder Gloria Steinem (Class of '52, she was a transfer student from the Midwest), D.C. Council chairman David Clarke (Class of '61), and television writer Thad Mumford (graduating in 1968, he has gone on to work on shows ranging from "A Different World" to "ALF.") The first black president of the student council, Clegg L. Watson (Class of '62), went on to become a powerful executive at the Xerox Corporation.

Previously known as Western High School, the school was founded in 1890 as a sister school to Eastern High School in Northeast. It was a prestigious public institution with an all-white student body for the first half of the twentieth century. Then enforced desegregation led to a slow but steady enrollment of black students as well. Today, the school is likened to the School of the Performing Arts in Manhattan (which gained fame through the film *Fame*), for the Ellington School is a breeding ground for talented singers, musicians, and actors.

⑮ Evermay (1623 28th Street, NW)

Evermay was built in 1801 for Samuel Davidson, who was part-owner of the land on which the White House and its surrounding neighborhood was built. Davidson was famed for his obsession with privacy, a reputation gained at least in part by a spectacularly off-putting warning he had published as a newspaper advertisement in 1810. The announcement warned that anyone who approached his home without a proper invitation or other acceptable business would face the wrath of a servant named Edward, who was under Davidson's orders to guard Evermay with a variety of means and weapons, including (as listed in the advertisement) ". . . a good cudgel, tomahawk, cutlass, gun and blunderbuss, with powder, shot and bullets, steel traps and grass snakes." The advertisement concluded on the pleasant note, "Therefore, I beg and pray of all my neighbors to avoid Evermay as they would a den of evils, or rattlesnakes, and thereby save themselves and me much vexation and trouble."

Despite the frightful reputation of its first owner, Evermay remains one of the finest homes in Georgetown. Recent occupants of the house—still a private residence—have included the du-Pont family. The classic Georgian mansion was designed by Nicholas King, and remains a highlight on the annual Georgetown Garden Tour. In fact, the traditional tea party that takes place at the end of the event is usually held here. Samuel Davidson no doubt spins in his grave at this annual invasion of his once-private sanctum.

🌐 *The Exorcist* Steps (3600 Prospect Street, NW)

The property of Georgetown University, these steps were the setting for the gruesome finale to the 1973 movie *The Exorcist*. The steep downhill set of steps has since become a mecca for horror fans who visit and photograph the so-called "Exorcist Steps," where Jason Miller fell to his death, carrying the spirit of the devil with him.

See Also: Georgetown University

The "Exorcist Steps."
(Jack Looney)

🌐 Forrest-Marbury House (3350 M Street, NW)

Offered for sale in early 1992 as part of a complex called "Forrest Marbury Court," the historic house nestled in amidst the modern retail-office complex dates back to 1788. Washington history was made at this home on March 29, 1791, when George Washington met with local land-owners at the home of Uriah Forrest (the Mayor of the Town of George at the time) to pitch the federal government's purchase offer for the land needed to build the new capital city. The meeting was a success, and the agreement was sealed shortly thereafter.

The next resident, real estate investor William Marbury, moved into the mansion in 1800 while he was buying up large amounts of land in the Anacostia area. He is most renowned for the indelible mark he left on the the federal judiciary: His (lost) battle with President James Madison over promised federal appointments landed in the Supreme Court, and the outcome of *Marbury v. Madison* (1803) established the crucial precedent of the judicial review. The house remained in Marbury's family for most of the nineteenth century, and in subsequent years has been used as both a residential and commercial property.

🌐 | Open to the Public | Georgetown Lutheran Church (Wisconsin Avenue and Volta Place, NW)

This church stands at the site of a much earlier version, built of logs. George Washington reportedly worshipped at that log cabin of a church when in Georgetown.

🌐 | Open to the Public | Georgetown University (37th Street from Prospect Avenue to Reservoir Road, NW; 202/687–3600)

Established in 1789, Georgetown University is not only Washington's oldest university—it's also the oldest Roman Catholic university in America. The university still uses some of the original buildings that were constructed for the school when it was founded by John Carroll, whose family owned much of the land in the eastern part of the Washington area. The spired, gothic Healy Building (named for the first black man to earn a Ph.D. in America, Reverend Patrick Healy) which was built between 1877 and 1879, is listed on the National Register of Historic Places. The Old North Building, completed in 1792, was the original main building of the university, and is still a central part of the school's campus.

The social issues of modern society are coming into increasing conflict with Georgetown's religious foundations. The most onerous social debate of the 1980s involved a gay organization that requested funding as a campus group from the school. The university denied the group's application for aid on the grounds that it went against the fundamental teachings of the Roman Catholic church, which the university is required to uphold. The ensuing publicity and law suits have kept the school embroiled in controversy. In 1991, an article published in the campus paper accused the school of lowering its standards for black applicants to the Law School; the ensuing backlash against the author of the article (who had based his story on confidential admissions applications to which he had access at a campus job) and against the university system opened yet another wound in the ongoing social struggle to match the needs of the community with the deeds of the school.

See Also: The *Exorcist* Steps

---

20 | Open to the Public | **Grace Episcopal Church (1041 Wisconsin Avenue, NW)**

One of Washington's loveliest Gothic Revival churches, Grace Episcopal was built in 1866 and quickly established itself as a social and religious center of Georgetown. The Church also served as a mission to help C&O Canal boatmen keep on the moral high ground despite the temptations of waterway life.

See Also: "The C&O Canal"

---

21 Haldeman Home (3402 R Street, NW)

This house was the object of communal derision during the Watergate scandal, as it was then the home of key player H.R. Haldeman (Nixon's aide who took one of the biggest falls). Urban legend has it that a neighbor across the street hung out a sign declaring "Impeach Nixon" to taunt Haldeman.

See Also: The Watergate Complex (Chapter 5)

---

22 Harriman House (3038 N Street, NW)

This house remains the home of Pamela Harriman, famed hostess and political activist, whose husband, Averell Harriman, was a long-time presidential advisor and statesman. The Harrimans were good friends of the Kennedys, and it was to this home that Jacqueline Kennedy first came upon leaving the White House after her husband's assassination in 1963.

See Also: Kennedy Houses

---

23 Heurich Brewery Site (1229 29th Street)

In 1872, Christian Heurich, a German immigrant, bought an interest in the Schnell Brewery at this site. Within a year he owned the whole place, and had begun the beer dynasty of the Christian Heurich Brewery. The 1870s saw Heurich expanding (although he continued to wear most of the hats in the organization, from brewmaster and kettleman to clerk and collector). By the end of the decade, his beer could be found in the best taverns in the city.

In 1881, Heurich built a larger brewery at the same 29th Street site. When the factory was destroyed in an 1892 fire, he moved the brewery to the Foggy Bottom waterfront, at the site where the Kennedy Center now stands.

See Also: John F. Kennedy Center for Performing Arts (Chapter 5); Washington Historical Society/Heurich Mansion (Chapter 7)

---

24 | Open to the Public | ## Holy Trinity Church (36th and O Streets, NW)

This church is a newer version of the oldest Catholic church in Washington. (The original Holy Trinity Church stands a block away, between 35th and 36th Streets on the north side of N Street.) The old Holy Trinity Church was the site of the first public Catholic mass held in Washington, in 1794. Until that time, Catholics were required to worship in the privacy of their own homes.

The new Holy Trinity was built in 1849. One church legend tells of a funeral held here in 1862 which President Lincoln was expected to attend. The church sexton had been instructed to keep the aisle clear to make way for the president's arrival. But when Lincoln showed up, the sexton failed to recognize him and wouldn't let him pass, explaining that the president was expected shortly.

---

25 ## Harry Hopkins House (3340 N Street, NW)

This 1830s private residence was one of the many regentrified by the New Dealers during the 1940s. Harry Hopkins, an advisor to Franklin Roosevelt who was active in promoting social change, lived in this house from 1943 to 1945. Previously, from 1940 to 1943, FDR had allowed Hopkins to live at the White House and use the Lincoln Bedroom as a room of his own.

Kennedy Houses

John F. Kennedy and his family were the life's blood of Georgetown for many years; they brought the same sparkle and vitality to the streets of this somewhat staid enclave as they would later bring to the White House. And Georgetown mourned Kennedy, perhaps as no other neighborhood in Washington did, for it was here that the young Senator had brought his bride after their marriage, here that he had lived while running for president, and here that his young widow returned after his death. Robert Kennedy and his family lived in Georgetown as well. In happier days, the Kennedy family, famed for its rambunctious athletics, often turned their block of N Street into their own impromptu playground. William Walton, a friend of the Kennedys who later wrote a historical and social profile of the nation's capital entitled *The Evidence of Washington* (1966), recalled the spirit of N Street during the Kennedy residency:

The Kennedy House at 3307 N St., NW. (Jack Looney)

"The young Senator, lithe and vigorous, organized touch football games that surged up and down the block between Thirty-third and Thirty-fourth. His brother Robert came from his house around the corner on O Street, and sometimes passing students joined the fray. Caroline ran in or out with Miss Shaw, her nurse, bound for the park or a friend's house nearby."

The Houses:

All of the houses listed here are private residences; they are not open to the public.

26 **The First JFK House** (3271 P Street, NW): This was the first Washington home for John and Jacqueline Kennedy after their marriage. They lived here from 1953 to 1954.

27 **The Last JFK House** (3307 N Street, NW): This was the home of JFK and his wife during the 1960 presidential campaign. They bought the house in 1957. Built in 1812, the red brick house became well-known to Americans as reporters gathered to record the president-elect's announcements of his cabinet appointments, at press conferences that were usually held in front of the house.

28 **The Press Plaque House** (3302 N Street, NW): Mounted on the side wall of this house is a plaque, placed here by members of the press corps who tirelessly covered the election and life of President Kennedy, in thanks for the kindness and hospitality accorded the journalists by the future president and his entourage.

29 **Jacqueline Kennedy's House** (3017 N Street, NW): This was the home of President Kennedy's widow, Jacqueline Bouvier Kennedy, after her husband's death. Mrs. Kennedy purchased this townhouse after a brief stay at the nearby house of her friends, Averell and Pamela Harriman. Although she had hoped to find peace and quiet at her new Georgetown home, Jackie Kennedy and her children soon found they had become a living monument, trapped in the house by gawking tourists and zealous paparazzi. The public's incessant fascination with the family's grieving process eventually led Mrs. Kennedy to relocate to a New York City apartment.

30 **Robert F. Kennedy's House Site** (3214 S Street, NW): Robert "Bobby" Kennedy, his wife, Ethel, and their growing brood of children lived in a house at this site (now gone) from 1951 to 1957. During these years, RFK became known on Capitol Hill as a shrewd lawyer, through his work as counsel for a number of Senate committees and sub-committees. Kennedy and his family also lived in a nearby house on O street.

See Also: Harriman House and **"The C&O Canal";** The White House (Chapter 1); U.S. Capitol and the Library of Congress (Chapter 3); John F. Kennedy Center for the Performing Arts (Chapter 5); Saint Matthew's Cathedral (Chapter 7)

31 **Key Bridge (Key Mansion Site) (Linking Georgetown with Rosslyn, Virginia)**

The 1923 construction of Key Bridge forced the demolition of an important landmark that had once stood near the Georgetown entrance to the bridge at 3518 M Street—the Key Mansion, the former home of Francis Scott Key. After the house left the Key family, it was converted into a tourist attraction and reputedly became a magnet for especially ghoulish ghosts.
See Also: "Haunted Georgetown" and **"The C&O Canal";** Friendship House (The Maples) (Chapter 3)

32 **Laird-Dunlop House (3014 N Street, NW)**

Built in 1799 for prominent Georgetown tobacco merchant John Laird, this house was the home of Abraham Lincoln's son Robert Todd Lincoln, who lived at this house until his death in 1926. Ironically, a former owner, Judge Dunlop, had been removed by Abraham Lincoln as

Chief Justice of the Circuit Court of the District of Columbia because of his southern sympathies.

Robert Todd Lincoln's life was filled with irony—or perhaps just very bad timing—for he managed to be at or near the three presidential assassinations during his lifetime. The first must have been the most painful for the younger Lincoln, for it was his own father's murder. Arriving late to join his parents at Ford's Theater on the night of April 14, 1865, he discovered his father being borne away, mortally wounded, to the house across the street. Then on July 2, 1888, while Robert Todd Lincoln was serving as the secretary of war, he came upon a frighteningly similar scene, at the Baltimore and Potomac Railroad Station (where the National Gallery of Art now stands). President James Garfield had just been shot and was being carried off to the White House. And on September 6, 1901, Lincoln was *also* on hand at the Pan-American Exposition in Buffalo, New York, during which President William McKinley was assassinated by Leon Czolgogz.

See Also: Ford's Theater and Petersen House (Chapter 2); National Gallery of Art (Chapter 4)

33 Lanman House Site (3035 P Street, NW)

Now occupied by new townhouses, this site once held the residence of Charles Lanman, secretary to Daniel Webster. Lanman was famed for his ability to draw top-notch guests to his soirees and dinner parties, and entertained such literary figures of his day as Washington Irving and Charles Dickens. Perhaps all those writers inspired Lanman, who eventually penned a biography of Daniel Webster.

34 | Open to the Public | Market House (M Street at Potomac Street)

The red-brick Market House is a small but typical example of the public markets that served as the commercial and social anchors for many Washington neighborhoods. In the days before general stores and Mom and Pop groceries, merchants, farmers, butchers, and fishermen set up stalls and peddled their goods in public markets such as this warehouse. Larger marketplaces, such as the still-standing Eastern Market (on Capitol Hill) and the now-gone Center Market (which once stood where the National Archives is now located), took up entire city blocks and were the social centers where all the classes met, if not mingled.

Completed in 1865, the Market House was used as a local marketplace until 1945. It then served as warehouse space and as an auto parts shop. In 1966, the market was declared a landmark, and in the 1970s, it was restored to a replica of its former self (in the form of a collection of food stalls).

See Also: National Archives (Chapter 2)

35 | Open to the Public | Mount Zion United Methodist Church (1334 29th Street, NW)

Mount Zion United Methodist Church is Washington's oldest known church started by and for blacks, dating back to 1816. In Civil War days, the church served as a local stop on the underground railroad.

See Also: Mount Zion Cemetery

36 | Open to the Public | Mt. Zion Cemetery (Q Street, between 27th Street and the Buffalo Bridge)

This historic black burial ground, established on the edge of the Dumbarton Cemetery, was leased in 1879 by the **Mount Zion Methodist Episcopal Church.** Already interred there at the time were German mercenary soldiers who had died when the British attacked Washington in 1814. The last burial here took place in the 1950s, by which time the cemetery had fallen into disrepair.

Activists eventually managed to get the cemetery designated as a Historic Landmark, thereby protecting it from future attempts to develop the land.

See Also: Mount Zion United Methodist Church

---

37 | Open to the Public | **Oak Hill Cemetery (30th and R Streets; 202/337–2835)**

Oak Hill Cemetery is the final resting place of such capital legends as Truman's Secretary of State, Dean Acheson; nineteenth-century Republican legislator and cabinet member James G. Blaine; Lincoln's Secretary of War, Edwin M. Stanton; the Russian Minister Baron de Bodisco; Peggy O'Neale Eaton (of the infamous "Eaton Affair" that brought down Andrew Jackson's cabinet), and quite recently, the beloved Washington television sportscaster Glen Brenner.

Also buried here is John Howard Payne, the playwright who was best known as the lyricist of the popular song "Home, Sweet Home." Payne was originally buried in Tunis, but thirty-one years after his death in 1852, his body was disinterred and brought here for burial. His is probably the only memorial in history (or at least in Washington) to have undergone a shave—for when Payne's friends saw the heavily bearded bust that topped the grave, they objected that Payne had never worn such a face of hair. The sculptor then chipped away the beard, leaving only the moustache in place. Later, a Matthew Brady photograph of Payne was examined and discovered to reveal that the songwriter had indeed sported just such a beard. But as far as the embittered sculptor was concerned, the tablet could grow the hair back itself if it wanted another face job, for he wasn't about to try and replace the lost beard.

Aside from the gravesites of the great, the cemetery also features a lovely little chapel designed by James Renwick and built in 1850, as well as the famous Gatehouse, built in 1839 by George la Roche. The cemetery was given to the city by William Wilson Corcoran (after whom the art gallery is named).

See Also: Dumbarton Oaks and **Daw's Gun Barrel Fence**

---

38 | Open to the Public | **Old Stone House (3051 M Street, NW; 202/426–6851)**

The Old Stone House is believed to be the oldest standing house in Washington (and the only homegrown one that pre-dates the Revolutionary War). It was built in 1765 by a cabinet maker named Christopher Layman, and its uses have been remarkably varied. It has been a private home, a boarding house, a tavern, a house of prostitution, a craftsman's studio, and home to several shops as well.

The house owes its preservation not to its age so much as to its murky heritage. During the 1950s, locals saved the site from destruction because it was mistakenly thought to have been the site of historic **Suter's Tavern.** In 1972, the house was officially designated a historic site and placed in the care of the National Park Service. To this day, stories still circulate that the building was possibly the headquarters for Pierre L'Enfant while he was planning the city.

The Old Stone House is believed to be one of the city's most haunted sites—ghosts from virtually every period dating back to before the Revolutionary War have supposedly been seen throughout the building by caretakers and visitors (especially children).

See Also: Suter's Tavern Site; The Lindens (Chapter 8)

---

39 **Drew Pearson's House (2820 Dumbarton Avenue, NW)**

During the residency of journalist Drew Pearson, this mansion was one of the city's most feared institutions—for it was here that Pearson cranked out his intimidating daily column (later taken over by Jack Anderson) called "Washington Merry-Go-Round."

A Ride on Drew Pearson's "Washington Merry-Go-Round"

It may have been his long experience among subject peoples in the Far East, where size of retinue is the mark of rank, that gave him the taste, but throughout his public service, Herbert Hoover has always surrounded himself with a small army of personal servitors. . . .

"This body of assistants has been a never-ending source of wonder, confusion and despair to politicians and newspapermen. Its purpose was apparently to facilitate and improve the dispatch of Presidential business. As it has functioned in actual practise the exact opposite has been the case."

—From "The Vestal Virgins," in the original book,
Washington Merry-Go-Round (1931)

"The speak-easies [of Washington] with few exceptions are foul joints. Those in the downtown districts are harassed in particular by the police vice squad. Nearly all are operated behind heavy oak doors with steel trappings. Close at hand is a waiting cesspool into which the liquor stocks are dumped in case of a raid."

—From "The Capital Underground," reprinted in the
book *More Merry-Go-Round* (1932)

"Several clerks and attendants of the Supreme Court once got into an argument as to who was the stupidest justice on the bench. The debate narrowed down to [Pierce] Butler and [James C.] McReynolds. Finally it was decided in favor of the latter, although one point never definitely was determined, namely, whether McReynolds is chiefly stupid or lazy.

"Apparently, however, he is both."

—From "Nine Old Men," reprinted in the book *More Merry-Go-Round* (1932)

The column was a spin-off from a book with the same title, *Washington Merry-Go-Round* (1931), co-authored by Drew Pearson and Robert S. Allen. It made its first appearance on December 12, 1932; by the end of the 1933, the column was being carried in some 225 papers nationwide. Locally, the column appeared first in the Washington *Herald* (under the editorship of Cissy Patterson), and then in Patterson's combined *Times-Herald*. When the Washington *Post* bought out the *Times-Herald* in 1954, "Washington Merry-Go-Round" moved over to that paper, where Jack Anderson's column continues to appear.

Taking few prisoners, "Washington Merry-Go-Round" dissected the Washington political, social, diplomatic, and media scene, skewering the high and mighty (even of the Washington underworld) to the delight of many Americans (but few Washingtonians). Pearson often received death threats for his unmasking of the rollercoaster ride of life in the Nation's Capital.
See Also: "A Ride on Drew Pearson's 'Washington Merry-Go-Round'"

⓵ Prospect House (3508 Prospect Street, NW)

Built in 1788, this is one of Georgetown's oldest and most illustrious residences. During the 1940s when a wave of New Dealers moved in to Georgetown, the first Secretary of Defense,

James E. Forrestal, called Prospect House home. During the early 1950s, Prospect House was used as the federal government's guest house for visiting dignitaries—a role usually played by Blair House, which was occupied at the time by President Truman and his family while the White House was being renovated. The stunning view, or "prospect," of the Potomac and outlying areas from the hill atop which the house is perched gave the house and the street their names.

See Also: Blair House (Chapter 1)

41 Quality Hill (3425 Prospect Street, NW)

Another house with a spectacular view, Quality Hill was built in 1798, and still bears the name that was once the nickname of this entire exclusive enclave of hill-side townhouses. The house was built by John Thomson Mason, the nephew of Bill of Rights author George Mason. Most of its original interior has been exceptionally well maintained, and the house is listed on the National Register of Historic Places. The house remains in private hands.

See Also: Stoddert House (Halcyon House)

42 Open to the Public St. John's Episcopal Church/Georgetown Parish: (3240 O Street, NW)

Affiliated with the famed St. John's on Lafayette Square, the Georgetown Parish, built in 1809, was designed by Capitol architect William Thornton, although renovations have greatly changed the original design over the years.

See Also: Saint John's Church (Chapter 1)

43 Scott-Grant House (3238 R Street, NW)

President Ulysses S. Grant used this home as his in-town "Summer White House" during his presidency. (Other presidents had similar in-town retreats, notably Grover Cleveland's Upper Northwest estate, and Abraham Lincoln's cottage at the Old Soldier's Home.) Built in 1858 by A. V. Scott of Alabama, the house was rented during the Civil War to Lt. General Henry Hallick, and it was to this house that President Lincoln sometimes rode to consult with Hallick.

44 Stoddert House (Halcyon House) (3400 Prospect Street, NW)

Once known as "Halcyon House," this big old townhouse was built in 1787 by Benjamin Stoddert. Stoddert, who became the first Secretary of the Navy in 1796, followed up that accomplishment by becoming the Secretary of the War in 1800. Stoddert was also one of the

original landowners with whom the real estate agreement was made to build the capital city.

At one time, a tunnel into the basement of the house served as a haven for escaped slaves traveling from south to north on the Underground Railroad. Sadly, some slaves were said to have died in the dank basement from exhaustion and exposure after swimming the Potomac to reach a tunnel into the basement of the house.

A later owner of the house, Albert Adsit Clemon, was an eccentric character

Stoddert House. (Jack Looney)

who had little appreciation for the beautiful design of the original house. Afflicted with a strange fear that he would die if he did not continue to build onto or into the house, he spent a lifetime tacking on additions and changes willy nilly. The result is a house filled with maze-like corridors and many useless rooms. As luck would have it, he tampered very little with the historic garden in the back. The garden has a magnificent view of the Potomac, and once must have looked out upon a harbor filled with tall ships and military vessels. The garden was designed for Stoddert by his friend Pierre L'Enfant, a frequent visitor to the house.

See Also: Quality Hill

---

45 | Open to the Public | **Suter's Tavern Site (Probably in the 1000 block of Wisconsin Avenue, NW)**

According to recent evidence uncovered by Washington historians, this is the most likely site of the famous tavern run by John Suter in the days when Georgetown was still the Town of George. On May 29, 1791, Suter happily provided the tavern (officially called the Fountain Inn) as a meeting place for George Washington and the three new city commissioners (among them Daniel Carroll)—locals appointed to oversee the building of the capital. The four met with the area's main landowners and convinced them to sell to the federal government any property it would need to establish the city. The going rate was about $66.66 an acre. The next day, the landowners signed an agreement that gave Washington and his planners the go-ahead to create the nation's capital at their chosen location. (The Settler's Memorial on the Ellipse honors those original landowners).

Suter's tavern was also used as the base-camp for Pierre L'Enfant and Andrew Ellicott when they began laying out the plans of the city. And in 1800, the tavern was called into federal service once again, this time as a makeshift meeting place of the House of Representatives, who were trying to sort out the tight battle for the presidency between John Adams and Thomas Jefferson. (Jefferson won out over the incumbent Adams.) After Suter's Tavern was torn down sometime in the mid- to late-nineteenth century, the records of its exact location were lost.

See Also: Old Stone House; U.S. Capitol (Chapter 3)

---

46 Robert A. Taft House (1688 31st Street, NW)

The son of President William Howard Taft, Robert A. Taft served as a senator from Ohio. He became renowned in his own right as a staunch carrier of the GOP banner and was even known as "Mr. Republican." Taft first rented this property in 1941, then bought it four years later. He used the house as his residence until his death in 1953. The house remains privately owned.

---

47 Elizabeth Taylor's House (3230 S Street, NW)

In late 1976, the much-married movie queen Elizabeth Taylor walked down the aisle yet again, this time with Virginia gentlemen John Warner (whom she helped get elected to the Senate shortly after their marriages). Taylor and her new husband lived at this townhouse during much of their life together. The couple also kept a home in the Virginia Hunt country. They separated in late 1981, and were divorced the following year.

---

48 | Open to the Public | **Tudor Place (1644 31st Street, NW; 202/965–0400)**

Considered one of the classic Georgetown mansions, Tudor Place was built in 1794 by Dr. William Thornton, who went on to design the U.S. Capitol. The Marquis de Lafayette was a guest here during his 1824 visit to Washington; and another general (one who was far from feted upon his return to Washington), Robert E. Lee, was said to have been a welcome guest at the house following the Civil War. The lovingly maintained house remained in the family of the original occupants—Martha Parke Custis (Martha Washington's granddaughter) and her husband Thomas Peter—until 1983, when it was opened to the public as a historic house museum.

Tudor Place as it appeared circa 1915.
(Walks about Washington)

49 Union Hotel Site/Crestar Bank (Northeast corner of 30th and M Streets)

The old Union Hotel once stood at this site now occupied by a Crestar bank. It is probably best known for its service as a hectic Union Army hospital during the Civil War. It was at this hotel/hospital that Louisa May Alcott briefly served as a nurse. Alcott nicknamed the hospital the "Hurly Burly Hotel," after the manic pace set by the constant flow of wounded soldiers she treated. The gruesome work took its toll on Alcott, who arrived in Georgetown to work at the hospital on December 13, 1862, only to be stricken down by a near-fatal case of typhoid fever barely a month into her work at the hospital. Her vivid descriptions of her experiences as a nurse in the Union Hotel Hospital were serialized in 1863 (and later published in book form) as *Hospital Sketches*.

See Also: "A Few Pen Strokes from Louisa May Alcott's *Hospital Sketches*"

50 Open to the Public U.S. Post Office (Old Custom House) (1221 31st Street, NW)

One of Georgetown's most beautiful public buildings, this post office was originally completed in 1858 as a customs house. As shipping traffic to the once-active port slowly declined, the need for the Customs House all but disappeared as well. Nevertheless, the customs house offices remained on the second floor until 1967.

51 Open to the Public Volta Bureau (1357 35th Street, NW)

This exotic edifice facing the gates to Georgetown University was built and maintained with money provided by Alexander Graham Bell. Bell invested some of the money he made from his patent on the telephone to support the institution—and twelve-year-old Helen Keller turned the first shovel of dirt at the groundbreaking ceremonies in 1893. To this day, the building houses the American Association for the Teaching of Speech to the Deaf. Inside the building stands the Alexander Graham Bell Monument, a token of thanks from the bureau, dedicated to Bell's life and work.

See Also: Alexander Melville Bell House and **Alexander Graham Bell Laboratory;** Alexander Graham Bell House Site, Bell-Morton House, and Bell Experimental School (Chapter 7); Washington National Cathedral (Chapter 8)

A Few Pen Strokes from Louisa May Alcott's *Hospital Sketches*

I n August of 1863, Louisa May Alcott's *Hospital Sketches* was published in book form. The work had first been serialized in the Boston *Commonwealth* from May 22 to June 26, 1863. The following excerpt was written about the influx of wounded she treated at the Old Union Hotel just after the Battle of Fredericksburg, in December of 1862:

"In they came, some in stretchers, some in men's arms, some feebly staggering along propped on rude crutches, and one lay stark and still as a covered face as a comrade gave his name to be recorded before they carried him away to the dead house. . . .

"The sight of several stretchers, each with its legless, armless or desperately wounded occupant entering my ward, admonished me that I was there to work, not to wonder or weep. . . . The house had been a hotel before hospitals were needed, and many of the doors still bore their old names; some not so inappropriate as might be imagined, for my ward was in truth a *ball-room,* if gun-shot wounds could christen it. Forty beds were prepared, many already tenanted by tired men who fell down anywhere and drowsed till the smell of food rowsed them."

—From Louisa May Alcott's *Hospital Sketches* (1863)

PLACES: West of Georgetown

The area west of Georgetown often falls between the cracks of Washington's experience. It is mainly a place for recreation along the C&O Canal (Fletcher's Boathouse, 3 miles west of the Georgetown section of the canal, is a historic boathouse that still rents bikes and canoes to Towpath athletes) and a place of quiet neighborhoods and wealthy enclaves along and surrounding Foxhall Road. Among the important sites in this area:

52 `Open to the Public` **Battery Kemble Park (Chain Bridge Road at MacArthur Boulevard)**

A small but well-preserved Civil War landmark is the centerpiece of this park: A battery of cannons installed to defend the city from Confederate forces still points out toward the Potomac from its position here, preserved and protected by the National Park Service.
See Also: "The Civil War Forts of Washington" (Chapter 10)

53 **Chain Bridge (Off Chain Bridge Road crossing into Virginia)**

This is the city's oldest remaining bridge, still serving commuters between Virginia and Washington. During the Civil War, the bridge was a common route for Union Troops. Originally built in 1797, it was destroyed in 1804 and twice rebuilt, the second time using chains as reinforcement—hence its name. Even so, it still needed to be rebuilt twice more; although it has undergone extensive renovation since that time, its last total overhaul was in 1874. A fellow named Albert Davis must have liked that last reconstruction a lot, because a dozen years later, on New Years Day, 1886, Davis tried to steal the Chain Bridge. It would not, however, fit under his coat, and he was arrested.

Union soldiers defending Chain Bridge (*Harper's Pictorial History of the Civil War*)

54 Foxall Foundry Site (just north of the Key Bridge, between the Potomac River and the C&O Canal)

For more than half a century, Henry Foxall's famed foundry (founded in 1800) stood at this site, churning out finely honed cannons. The foundry gained notoriety during the War of 1812, for it was said to be a major British target (the guns were renowned as the best America could make). When the enemy attacked Washington in 1814, Foxall vowed he would build a church if his foundry were spared. Someone must have heard his pleas, for a vicious thunderstorm struck the city before the British could strike the gun factory. In thanks, Foxall funded the construction of the Foundry Methodist Church (the congregation of which still worships in upper northwest). Foxall sold his foundry a year after the British attack. The new owners operated the foundry until the 1860s. But Foxall's name lives on in the slightly altered monniker of Foxhall Road nearby.

See Also: Glover-Archbold Park (Chapter 8); Washington Foundry Methodist Church Site (Chapter 9); "The Burning of Washington" (Chapter 10)

Coxey's Army of the Unemployed sails up the C&O Canal in 1894. (Library of Congress)

The C&O Canal

Now considered a quaint little waterway that lends charm to Georgetown's shopping district and ambience to one of the best bikepaths in the area, the Chesapeake & Ohio Canal was once a major transportation artery for the eastern states. John Quincy Adams presided over the groundbreaking ceremonies for the C&O near the Maryland end of the Chain Bridge during the Independence Day festivities of 1828. The canal did not reach its final destination—its terminus in Georgetown—until 1840. Along the way, the canal builders accomplished some of the great engineering feats of the century, including the Paw Paw Tunnel in Paw Paw, West Virginia, which carves a 7100-foot route through mountains to make way for the canal. The canal utilized seventy-four locks to move its traffic along the nearly 185-mile length of the waterway, although little of the original canal is still accessible as such today. But the Towpath (so-named because mules would walk on this path along the canal to tow the barges) remains visible along most of the old route. The last section of the canal completed—the twenty-two miles from Seneca, Maryland, to Georgetown—remains the best preserved.

For a short time, the canal was the nineteenth-century equivalent of today's modern highways. Traffic, however, moved at a slower pace—the average speed of the mule-drawn "canal clippers" was four miles per hour. Until the late nineteenth century, the C&O and similar canals served as the fastest and most reliable transport method for shipping whiskey, tobacco, building materials, food staples, and other essentials. Then railroads effectively sidetracked the canal system for good. Visitors today can get a tame but genuine taste of what barge life was like by taking a ride on the authentic "Georgetown," a mule-drawn tourist barge that plies the waters of the canal, leaving from a dock at 30th and M Streets.

In the 1950s, the canal was nearly paved over to make way for the Whitehurst Freeway. But Supreme Court Justice William O. Douglas successfully led the fight to save the canal, and the freeway was built on an overpass instead.

The Towpath on which the mules walked has become a popular route for bikers, hikers, and joggers, and is relatively safe. It was a deadly route, however, for a young woman named Mary Pinchot Meyer. On October 13, 1964, Meyer was apparently out for a noontime stroll when she was attacked, for no known reason, and shot to death. A suspect was later acquitted on lack of evidence, and the case has never been solved.

Meyer's murder would have been just one more shocker for the police blotter (and at first it was), except that she had a secret that soon got out. According to friends, she had been having an affair with President Kennedy from 1961 until his death in November of 1963. She had allegedly kept a diary detailing the story of the affair (about which her sister Tony and Tony's then-husband, Ben Bradlee, a *Washington Post* editor, may have already known). Although the legendary journal was disposed of (probably by the CIA) before it could be published, some of its most salacious details were scooped by the press.

(Continued)

One shocking revelation in the alleged diary was a description of an assignation with JFK (while his wife was away), during which Meyer and the president supposedly smoked three joints of marijuana she had smuggled into the White House. She wrote that Kennedy turned down another three joints, saying, "Suppose the Russians did something now."

Chapter 7

DUPONT CIRCLE
AND ENVIRONS

An eclectic mix of residential brownstones, boxy glass office buildings, Old-World mansions, and Third-World storefronts, the neighborhoods spiralling off in every direction from Dupont Circle reflect the diversity that is Washington at its hometown best. Here, around Dupont Circle, the city's wealthiest citizens built grand mansions, which today have been converted into embassies or offices. And here, in New Downtown, where once stood the fine nineteenth-century residences of Washington's most powerful players, there now stand twentieth-century office buildings, crowded with lawyers and lobbyists who brown bag their lunch in the elegant parks nearby.

Long a cultural and social magnet for the city's most creative and powerful figures, Dupont Circle has managed to maintain its historic allure despite the redevelopment of the K Street corridor and its neighboring areas. But the elegant, eclectic image that Dupont Circle now projects is a far cry from the marshy wasteland that once filled this land. When Washington was first being developed, this section of town was known as "The Slashes," after the Slash Run (aka Slash Creek) that ran through the area. It was wet, mushy countryside populated with a few shacks here and there, but for the most part both uninhabited and uninhabitable. That all changed with the brief (1871–1874) reign of "Boss" Shepherd, the irrepressible head of the Board of Public Works (and short-termed Territorial Governor of Washington). Shepherd almost single-handedly civilized the city by ordering the grating of its streets, the laying of sewer lines, and other measures necessary to bring Washington up to par with other cities of its size and prestige. Shepherd owned some of the land in the area that would one day become Dupont Circle—and it was a given that this area would top the list of neighborhoods in line for the city-wide fix-it he was implementing. The news spread fast among land speculators that what was then countryside would very soon be citified.

In no time, a land buy-out of the Slashes area was instigated by a gang of developers who came to be known as The California Syndicate. This coalition of westerners included Nevada Senator William Stewart, who built the once-famous Stewart's Castle on Dupont Circle; Curtis Hillyer, who had made his money through mines; and Thomas Sunderland, another mining baron. These men saw gold where the rest of the city saw mud; they snatched up the area for a mere 60 cents a foot. All three built houses on or near the circle, and "Boss" Shepherd lived up to his reputation. Soon the streets were graded and paved and the area had become an affluent downtown enclave. Slash Run was covered over, and Pacific Circle, an intersection circle that may have been so named in deference to the California Syndicate, was created.

In 1882, Pacific Circle was renamed Dupont Circle to honor Admiral Samuel Francis duPont, who had distinguished himself in naval battles during the Civil War. Two years after the circle was renamed for duPont, a bronze statue of the Admiral by Launt

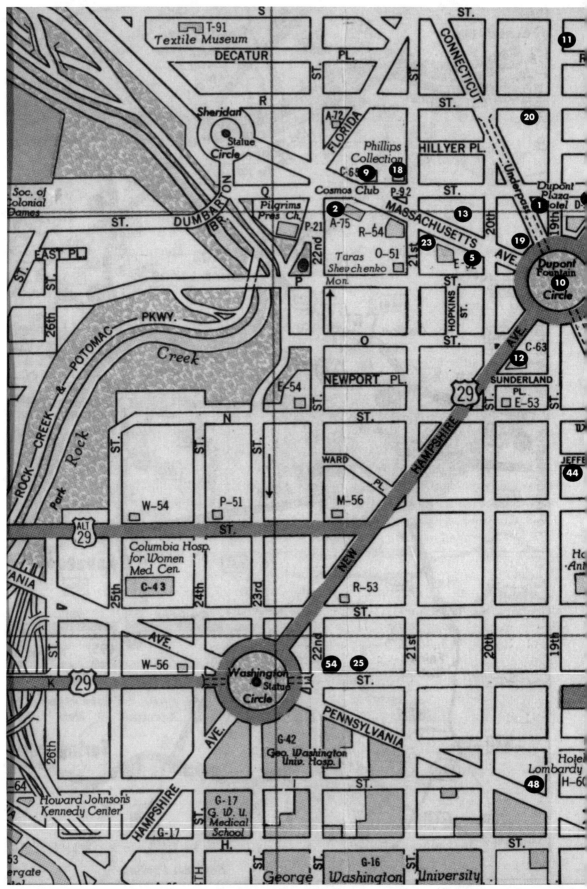

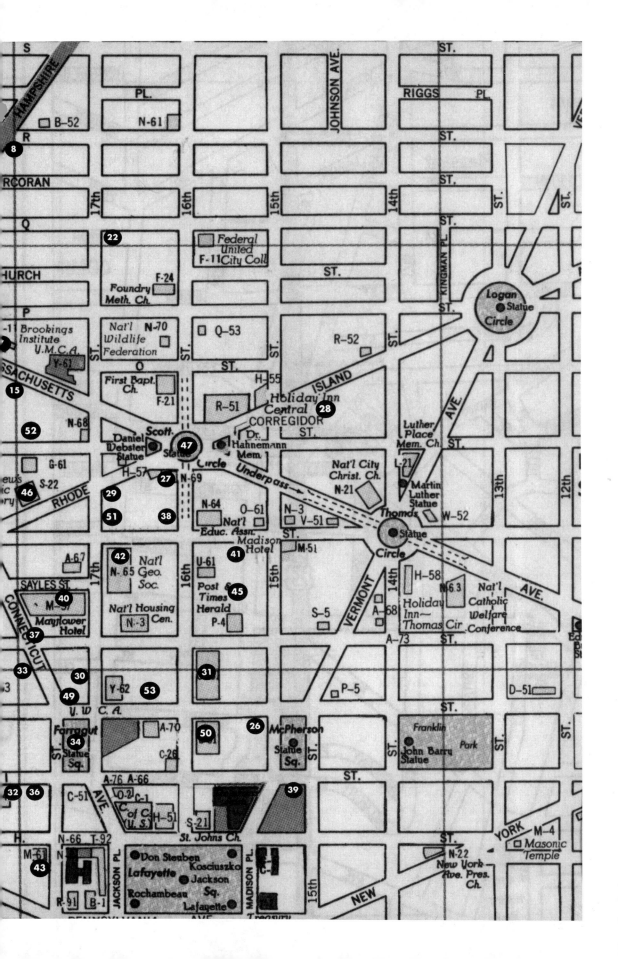

Thompson was installed in the park within the circle. In the 1920s, the duPont family transplanted the statue to a park in their hometown of Wilmington, Delaware. It was replaced by a marble memorial fountain created for the circle by Daniel Chester French, the pre-eminent sculptor in Washington at the time, who was also working on his master-piece, the seated statue of Lincoln for the Lincoln Memorial.

Dupont Circle. (Washington Convention and Visitors Association)

The neighborhood around the circle has ridden a social rollercoaster in the twentieth century. Though it entered the century as a fashionable, elite sector of town the equal of today's Georgetown, by the late 1960s it was blighted by vandalism and urban decay. But a renaissance in the 1970s and 1980s renewed the neighborhood's earlier spirit, blending into the mix a healthy dose of funky cafe society and college-kid verve. Former mansions are now embassies, and the elegant rowhouses are now group homes for young professionals working in the liberal non-profit organizations whose offices are located throughout the area.

East of Dupont Circle is Scott Circle, surrounded by a variety of new and old apartment buildings, embassies, and office complexes. It seems to be an architectural melting pot—the posh old brownstones-and-cafes area of the Dupont Circle neighborhood mingling here with the modern offices and carry-out eateries of New Downtown, situated just south of Dupont Circle.

New Downtown is both the nemesis and breadbasket of Northwest Washington. Lawyers and lobbyists ply their trade along the glitter-box corridors of Connecticut and K Streets where fantastic mansions once stood in proud proximity to the White House. The history of this small wedge of offices and shops can be defined more by what used to be here than by what remains (although such restaurants as **Harvey's** and **Duke Zeibert's** can claim fame in modern times). Yet, tucked away amidst these modern city blocks are a few remaining historical sites—the **Sumner School** and the **St. Matthew's Cathedral**, for instance—as well as such renowned institutions as the **National Geographic Society Building** and **The Mayflower Hotel**.

Dupont Circle in the 1880s

In 1884, *Century Magazine* published an article entitled "The New Washington," which described the changes throughout the capital city. Among changes discussed were the neighborhoods growing up around the circles and squares of Washington:

> "The new buildings have clustered about Scott Square and Dupont Circle, and the other little squares and circles, forming small settlements, separated from each other by long distances of vacant fields, unbroken except by the asphalt roads and the lines of trees. This scattering of the new building forces has given a very incongruous and ludicrous appearance to some of the most handsome avenues. Everywhere there are superb residences looking out upon fields of red clay and weeds, and flanked on either side by such shanties as perch on the rocks in the upper part of New York.
>
> ". . . This is naturally to be expected in a place which was first planned, and subsequently improved, out of all proportion to the requirements of the moment. It grows in spots, which, like the settlements in the Far West, form each a little center of development, radiating and extending toward its neighbor, until finally they will all join together and form a civilized whole. When this process is completed in Washington, it will be, among cities, the wonder of the world."

PLACES: Dupont Circle

❶ Open to the Public | Anchorage Building (1900 Q Street, NW)

Now an office building featuring such ground-floor neighborhood standards as The Daiquiri Factory and Kramer Books and Afterwords Cafe, this once-famous apartment building was home to numerous legislators and celebrities. The most famous (and long-term) resident was Speaker of the House Sam Rayburn, who lived at the Anchorage from 1929 to 1961. Rayburn, a Texan to the core, found his two-room apartment on the third floor was too small, so he persuaded the management to let him expand his terrain by knocking down some adjoining walls. The apartment never had a kitchen, however, as Rayburn preferred to eat his meals out. Among the other renowned residents of the Anchorage were Robert Kennedy, novelist Frances Parkinson Keyes, Charles Lindbergh, and Tallulah Bankhead.

The Anchorage Apartments (as they were originally known) were built in 1924, with Jules de Sibour as the architect. The building's owner, Marie "Ma" Williams, was one of Dupont Circle's major socialites, hosting dinner parties and sponsoring charity events. She was also one of the founders of the **Sulgrave Club.** After her death in 1945, her estate managed the property until 1962, when the Anchorage was sold. Within two years, the building was transformed from apartments into offices, and so it remains to this day.

See Also: The Sulgrave Club

2 | Open to the Public | ## Anderson House (Society of the Cincinnati) (2118 Massachusetts Avenue, NW; 202/785-2040)

Anderson House. (Jack Looney)

The Anderson House is one of those lesser-known gems that seem to echo out in every direction from the core of Dupont Circle. The house was completed in 1902 for Larz Anderson, a diplomat with a taste for the grandeur that abounds throughout this masterpiece of elaborate Beaux Arts architecture. As a career diplomat, Anderson had plenty of opportunity to entertain foreign dignitaries, and one of the house's most memorable occasions was a ball held for the King and Queen of Siam.

The Society of the Cincinnati took over the house in 1937. Formed in 1783 by a fraternal group of officers who had served in the Revolutionary War, the Society of the Cincinnati is named for the famed Roman general Lucius Quinctius Cincinnatus, with whom George Washington was often favorably compared. Membership in the society is limited to direct male descendants of the original members—and usually further limited to the first-born at that. While it is difficult to join the society, it is easy to see its headquarters: The Anderson House is open to the public, and has been beautifully preserved with vintage furnishing and artworks, including portraits of society members by such eminent painters as John Trumbull and Gilbert Stuart. Revolutionary War artifacts are also in evidence throughout the house, and an excellent reference library with materials on the war is open to the public as well.

3 ## Alexander Graham Bell House Site (1355 Connecticut Avenue, NW)

The grand mansion built here by Alexander Graham Bell in 1891 was destroyed in 1930. Bell spared no expenses when building his home just below Dupont Circle—he was by then a wealthy man, thanks to his invention of the telephone. Bell lived at the three-story mansion until his death in 1922; but he worked out of the laboratory he had set up in a carriage house adjacent to his father's Georgetown house on Volta Place.

See Also: Bell Experimental School Site and **Bell-Morton House;** Alexander Melville Bell House, Alexander Graham Bell Laboratory, and Volta Bureau (Chapter 6)

4 ## Belmont House (Order of the Eastern Star) (1618 New Hampshire Avenue, NW)

This spectacular mansion was built in 1909 for the then staggering sum of $1.5 million. The home was constructed for the Belmont family, whose name can be found on everything from horse races to Adams Morgan roadways. The family also played an influential role in Washington politics—Perry Belmont, for whom the house was built, was a Congressman from New York who also served as the U.S. Ambassador to Spain. Despite the lavishness of this manor, it was a mere home-away-from-home for the Belmonts, who still maintained "The Elms," a sprawling mansion in Newport, Rhode Island. After the Belmonts finally closed up their Washington residence for good in 1926, the place was virtually abandoned until 1935, when it was sold to the Order of the Eastern Star, a masonic organization.

5 | Open to the Public | **Blaine House (2000 Massachusetts Avenue, NW)**

Blaine House was built in 1881 as the residence for Republican party stalwart James G. Blaine. Despite several runs at the presidency, Blaine never managed to secure the job. Instead, he had to settle for such roles as Speaker of the House and Senator from the State of Maine. Blaine and his family lived at the house that still bears their name for less than three years before moving on. The house then became a rental property until it was purchased in 1901 by George Westinghouse. Westinghouse, the inventor of the air brake and the founder of the company that bears his name, had rented the house for three years before he bought it; he lived there until his death in 1914. The house was broken up into rental apartments in the early 1920s, and, in 1948, was transformed into office space.

The Blaine House, circa 1886.
(Picturesque Washington)

See Also: Jackson Place Houses: 736 Jackson Place and Rodgers House/Belasco Theater Site (Chapter 1)

6 Boardman House (Embassy of Iraq) (1801 P Street, NW)

During the 1991 Persian Gulf War, the Iraqi Embassy was under constant surveillance by U.S. government agents keeping a watchful eye out for spy activities, and the D.C. Police, who were attempting to protect the embassy from angry protestors and overzealous patriots. The Iraqi Ambassador, Mohamed Sadiq Al-Mashat, and most of his diplomatic staff were ordered out of the U.S. when the war began, leaving behind a skeleton crew to hold down the proverbial fort in the midst of enemy territory until the Persian Gulf War was over.

A brick mansion built in 1893 by Hornblower and Marshall for the influential Boardman family of Cleveland, Ohio, the house is a rare remaining example of the once-popular Richardsonian Romanesque style. Mabel Boardman, one of the founding incorporators of the Red Cross, as well as one of Dupont Circle's great hostesses, was also one of the hardest working preservationists of her day. When she died in 1946, Mabel Boardman left the mansion to the National Cathedral, which promptly put it on the market. The house remained empty until 1950, when it was purchased by the Hungarian Reformed Federation of America. Twelve years later, Iraq purchased the house for use as its embassy.

See Also: Sulgrave Club

7 | Open to the Public | Brookings Institution (1775 Massachusetts Avenue, NW; 202/797–6000)

One of Washington's most venerable centrist think-tanks, the Brookings Institution moved here in 1960. The institution had evolved in 1927 from an organization called the Institute for Government Research, founded in 1917. Like the Brookings, that organization was run by private funding and had a mission of leading the way to federal fiscal responsibility through the study of the social sciences, notably economics. The institute became the Brookings when, a decade after its founding, a young Missouri businessman named Robert Brookings stepped in and raised the funds to bale it out of financial difficulties.

The Brookings and its grounds were constructed on the site of some important homes—including the house of Henry Cabot Lodge at 1765 Massachusetts Avenue. Lodge was a powerful Massachusetts Republican who served in both the House and the Senate in the late nineteenth through the early twentieth centuries. He also served as President Harding's appointed delegate and ambassador to the 1921 Washington Conference on the Limitation of Armaments, held at the DAR Memorial Continental Hall.

Another house that was destroyed to make way for the Brookings Institution was the elegant mansion, located at 1770 Massachusetts Avenue, that was built by local literary star Frances Hodgson Burnett in 1890. Burnett lived there until her death in 1924, and her years in the house were the most productive of her life. According to David Cutler's *Literary Washington* (1989), Burnett wrote more than fifty novels and plays while living here, including *The Secret Garden* (1909), and the play *The Little Princess* (1905). (The work for which Burnett is probably best remembered, *Little Lord Fauntleroy* (1886), was written when she lived in an earlier house at 12th and I Streets.)

See Also: Frances Hodgson Burnett's Second House Site and **McCormick Apartment Building;** Frances Hodgson Burnett's First House Site (Chapter 2); DAR Memorial Continental Hall (Chapter 5)

---

8 Butler House (1744 R Street, NW)

The Butler House was built in 1912 for A.B. Butler, who paid for this elegant Italianate mansion with millions gained from Texas oil wells. Germany purchased the home in 1933 and used it as the German Chancery until World War II. Then, no longer welcome in Washington, the Germans closed up shop for a few years. They re-opened the Chancery after the war, maintaining the property until they sold it to a local law firm as office space in 1963.

---

9 Cosmos Club (Townshend House) (2121 Massachusetts Avenue, NW)

Now the home to an elite power clique, the Cosmos Club, the Townshend House has an illustrious and curious history of its own that pre-dates the Cosmos occupancy. The house was built in 1900 at the outset of the early twentieth-century Dupont Circle building boom that also produced such neighboring mansions as the Anderson House and Woodrow Wilson House. It was built by Peter Townshend, who had headed the Erie and Pittsburgh Railroad before retiring to his new Washington mansion. The house was constructed on the site—indeed, on the actual foundations—of the Hillyer Mansion, built in 1873 by one of the original "California Syndicate" group, Curtis Hillyer. That house was a magnificent three-story mansion built in the Second Empire style. The Townshend House that replaced it is an even more stately (some say too fussy) Beaux Arts home that was designed by the same architects responsible for the House and Senate office buildings, Carrere and Hastings. The Hillyer Mansion was razed in 1899, but its foundations were preserved and used for the new house because Townshend's wife had been warned by a soothsayer that evil would visit her home unless some evidence of the earlier house was incorporated into its replacement.

The Townshends reigned in their mansion until the 1930s, becoming famous for their lavish dinner parties and social soirees. Later occupants were equally socially adept—especially Franklin Roosevelt, who lived at the house briefly before moving to even more elegant quarters at 1700 Pennsylvania Avenue.

The Cosmos Club purchased the site in 1950, moving from its previous home in the Cutts-Madison house on Lafayette Square. A social club where men (and men *only*) of wealth, power, and fame gathered, the Cosmos has long been a favorite among presidents and millionaires. But in the late 1980s, with its sexist membership policy attracting threats of law-suits and federal action, the Cosmos Club had a sudden change of heart and gender, allowing female members to join for the first time in its history. More than a hundred women are now on the Cosmos roll call.

See Also: Cutts-Madison House (Chapter 1)

---

⑩ Dupont Circle Tunnels (blocked-off entrance visible at northeast side of the circle at 19th Street)

Beneath Dupont Circle lie the tunnels that once served as streetcar routes. The only underpass that remains open is the one which routes Connecticut Avenue auto traffic beneath the circle.

The earliest, horse-drawn streetcars in Washington began running on a very limited basis between federal buildings during the Civil War. Within two decades, more than a hundred miles of streetcar lines ran to and from the city's most popular residential and business districts. In 1888, electric streetcar service began in the city, although Congress quickly outlawed the unsightly overhead wires within the city limits (but not beyond the Florida Avenue boundaries). Over the next few decades, a variety of streetcar methods were tried, including a cable car system (the tracks can still be seen in Georgetown). In 1902, most of the disparate lines were merged to form the Washington Railway and Electric Company—although one exception, the Capital Traction Company, continued to operate independently.

The automobile eventually took its toll on Washington's streetcar system, which had all but died out by 1950. Today, the evidence of the streetcar culture can still be seen in the old car barns throughout the city that have been converted into elegant condominiums or retail centers. And the National Capital Trolley Museum in Silver Spring, Maryland (301/384–6088) lovingly recalls the history of Washington's early transit lines, and even offers a mile-and-a-half trolley ride.

Over the years, the abandoned streetcar tunnels have been used as storage facilities for government supplies. They almost got a new lease on life in the 1970s, when local architect Arthur Cotton Moore (known for such merry modern innovations as Washington Harbor in Georgetown) dreamt of turning the tunnels into an underground pedestrian mall and retail area. The project never got off—or rather, under—the ground, however, due to citizens' concerns about construction hassles that would have transformed the already chaotic circle into a motorist's nightmare. So the tunnels remain, underground and under-used.

See Also: "Tunneling Under Washington" (Chapter 4)

---

⑪ Frankfurter-Lippmann House (1727 19th Street, NW)

Two great men lived in this house at different times. Felix Frankfurter, who would later become a Supreme Court justice, lived here from 1912 to 1914. At the time, the home was what we now refer to as a "group house," shared by friends all struggling in their careers as young professionals. Following in Frankfurter's footsteps was journalist Walter Lippmann. Lippmann and his wife lived here from 1917 until 1938, when they moved to Georgetown to live in the house Alexander Graham Bell had originally purchased for his parents.

See Also: Alexander Melville Bell House (Chapter 6); Walter Lippmann House (Chapter 8)

12 Open to the Public **Heurich Mansion (1307 New Hampshire Avenue, NW; 202/785–2068)**

Once the home to D.C. beer baron Christian Heurich, this glorious Beaux Arts mansion now houses The Historical Society of Washington (formerly known as the Columbia Historical Society). Heurich was Washington's beermeister from the time he arrived in the city in 1888 to invest in the Schnell Brewery. Within a year, he owned it, and was soon selling beer under his own name label. Heurich had more luck in beer-making than he did in life—his first wife was killed in a tragic automobile accident. He married his dead wife's very young niece, and they had a long and relatively happy life together, producing several children. Heurich died at the age of 104 in 1945, having seen his brewery through three wars—two world ones, and one called Prohibition (during which his waterfront plant manufactured ice to stay in business).

His palatial Romanesque Revival mansion was built in 1880, and featured such extraordinary (for the time) elements as an elevator and private bathrooms. The house has been

The Heurich Mansion. (Jack Looney)

The Turf Wars of Alice Longworth

Alice Roosevelt Longworth, wife of House Speaker Nicholas Longworth, was renowned in Washington as a powerful political ally and dangerous social enemy. During her reign, she became embroiled in two of the most public social feuds the city had seen in years. One of these involved Dolly Curtis Gann, the half-sister of Herbert Hoover's vice president, Charles Curtis. And it was alleged that Dolly Gann "started it."

Her husband, Edward Everett Gann, was a little-known Washington lawyer; but when her half-brother became vice-president (and made Dolly his hostess), the Ganns moved from their quiet Cleveland Park home to a suite at the Mayflower Hotel. Through the lavish entertainments Dolly held at the Vice President's home and in her own suite, she began pushing herself and her husband into the social limelight—while pushing the reigning society queen and king, Alice and Nicholas Longworth, off the social pages.

Thus commenced the battle of two strong-willed wives determined to prove themselves Washington's top hostess. Not that the feud was fueled solely by the animosity between Alice Longworth and Dolly Gann. On the contrary, as Drew Pearson noted in his "Washington Merry-Go-Round" column (reprinted as "Boiled Bosoms" in the 1931 collection *Washington Merry-Go Round*), the two warring wives were aided and abetted by their husbands:

"Mr. Gann may be shorter and less prepossessing than his wife . . . but he never flinched at the major social war whirling disturbingly around his head. On the contrary, he loved it. He set his jaw and egged his wife into the fray. He subscribed to clipping bureaus. He read with avidity everything written about his wife. If he did lovingly preserved as a living historical monument to a long-lost age of glorious excess and un-compromising style.

See Also: Kennedy Center for the Performing Arts (Chapter 5); Heurich Brewery Site (Chapter 6)

⓭ Longworth House (2009 Massachusetts Avenue, NW)

This was home to House Speaker Nicholas Longworth and his vivacious wife (and daughter of Theodore Roosevelt), Alice Roosevelt Longworth. Nicholas Longworth served in the House of Representatives from 1909 to 1913 and from 1915 to 1931; he was Speaker of the House from 1925 to 1931.

Alice Roosevelt Longworth was long considered one of Washington's great social doyennes. She outlived her husband by forty-nine years, and continued to entertain even in her old age. (She died in 1980). She was equally famous for protecting her social turf with the tenacity of a pit-bull, notably in longstanding feuds she had with two other Washington hostesses and neighbors, Eleanor "Cissy" Patterson and Dolly Gann.

See Also: "The Turf Wars of Alice Longworth" and **Patterson House**; House and Senate Office Buildings (Chapter 3)

(Continued)

not like it, he complained to the editors. Most especially, he complained about the adjectives 'meek' and 'mild' when prefixed to his own name. . . .

"Mr. Longworth . . . took the controversy just as seriously. He considered his wife's war his war, a war to uphold the dignity of the Speaker of the House."

The bitter battle for custody of Washington society raged on until Mrs. Longworth was distracted from the cause by a renewal of a long-held rivalry with her neighbor, Cissy Patterson.

The Longworth-Patterson feud (which supposedly dated back to their debutante days), was renewed after Cissy Patterson became the publisher of the Hearst-owned Washington *Herald.* The paper was soon printing attacks aimed at Mrs. Longworth's refusal to grant press interviews. Alice Longworth responded with her customary media silence, but managed to get back at Cissy by hosting ever more elaborate parties in an escalating high society battle.

One of the most famous stories about the pair's tug-of-war (one which pre-dated the second-heat of the feud) involved a dinner party held at the Longworth house, during which Alice flirted with a charming young nobleman who was sitting to her right. After the dinner, Cissy Patterson (also a guest) allegedly led the young man off for an intimate encounter in an upstairs library. While the story may be apocryphal, it was often repeated with pride by Cissy Patterson. As Drew Pearson retold it in the "Washington Merry-Go-Round" piece "Boiled Bosoms," Alice Longworth supposedly sent a note the day after the party to Cissy Patterson, which read:

"Dear Cissie [sic]—Upon sweeping the library this morning, the maid found several hair-pins which I thought you might need and which I am returning.—Alice."

To which Cissy Patterson responded, according to Pearson, "Dear Alice—Many thanks for the hair-pins. If you had looked on the chandelier, you might have also sent back my shoes and chewing gum. Love, Cissie."

14 Open to the Public   **McCormick Apartment Building (National Trust for Historic Preservation) (1785 Massachusetts Avenue, NW; 202/673–4000)**

The McCormick House was built on the site of another historic building, the Beldon Noble House, a soaring red brick Romanesque Revival mansion. In 1906, it was ostensibly purchased and remodeled by Stanley McCormick, the son of the reaper inventor (and founder of International Harvester). Several years later, McCormick—or somebody using his name and money— tore the house down and built the apartment house that still stands on the site today.

Stanley McCormick fell mentally ill, and was declared legally incompetent by California courts the same year he bought the Noble House. Until his death in 1947, he was locked away at a Santa Barbara estate which had been converted into his own private asylum. His estate, however, ordered the remodeling, demolition, and new construction at the site, and hired noted Beaux Arts architect Jules Henri de Sibour, (who designed several other buildings in the neighborhood) to design the apartment building.

When it was completed in 1917, the McCormick House immediately excited the interest of wealthy Washingtonians, for the entire building was divided up into only six apartments. Each unit featured luxuries both grand (the apartments averaged six bedrooms and six fireplaces each) and small (gold and silver-plated doorknobs were the rule). Over the years, tenants included Perle Mesta (the Ambassador to Luxembourg who inspired the Broadway musical *Call Me Madam*), Robert Woods Bliss (owner of Georgetown's Dumbarton Oaks estate), and Alanson B. Houghton (ex-president of the Corning Glass Company who later served as Ambassador to Great Britain and Germany).

Perhaps the most famous tenant was millionaire industrialist Andrew Mellon, who leased the top-floor apartment from 1921 until his death in 1937. The exquisite apartment included a skylight—the better for looking at fine art, one of Mellon's costlier predilections. Indeed, the National Gallery of Art is said to have been born here—thanks to a scheme by the brilliant and conniving art dealer Baron Joseph Duveen of Millbank.

Baron Duveen saw in Andrew Mellon the perfect client—an American with a taste for art and the money to feed that taste. (In the early 1930s, Mellon had purchased millions of dollars worth of art when the Hermitage Museum in Leningrad began selling off its collection.) Duveen made his first move in 1936, the year Mellon returned to Washington after serving a stint as Ambassador to the Court of Saint James in London. Duveen convinced the family leasing the apartment below Mellon's to turn over their lease, then filled the apartment with an exquisite collection of art—and gave Mellon the key. Mellon spent hours appreciating Duveen's collection, then offered to buy the lot—eighteen sculptures and twenty-four paintings in all, with a price-tag of $21 million. These works, when added to his already burgeoning collection (mainly of Old Masters), became the foundation for the National Gallery of Art, which was Mellon's gift to the nation.

During World War II, when office space was even more precious than living space in Washington, the McCormick House was handed over to the British, who turned it into the Washington headquarters of the British Purchasing Commission and the British Commonwealth Scientific Office. After the war, the American Council on Education took over the building for two decades, until it was bought by the **Brookings Institute** (located next door). The Brookings Institute rented the building out to various organizations until 1977, when it was tendered to the loving care of the National Trust for Historic Preservation. If ever a building deserved such a tenant, it is this delightful place where art and finance once shared fine quarters.

See Also: Brookings Institution; National Gallery of Art (Chapter 4)

15 Moore House (1746 Massachusetts Avenue, NW)

When the *Titanic* went down in 1912, it took with it a prominent Dupont Circle land-owner—Clarence Moore. Moore, a coal and oil magnate known for his horsemanship, was returning home after a European shopping spree that had netted him a dozen Welsh ponies. Just a few years before his fateful journey, Moore had had this Beaux Arts house built for him. The house was designed by noted French architect Jules Henri de Sibour, and finished in 1909. The architect, who claimed Louis XVI as an ancestor, had studied at the Ecole Beaux Arts in Paris at the turn of the century, and became one of the most sought-after architects upon his arrival in Washington. Other examples of de Sibour's work are visible throughout the Dupont Circle neighborhood, including the house at 1607 New Hampshire Avenue, built in 1911 for Woodbury Blair, son of Lincoln's Postmaster General. De Sibour's later work can be seen just up the street from the Moore House, at 1780 Massachusetts Avenue, the house which was finished in 1922 for the Ingalls family (and now serves as the Yater Clinic). But his most famous building is probably the **McCormick Apartment Building** at 1785 Massachusetts Avenue, now home to the National Trust for Historic Preservation.

See Also: McCormick Apartment Building; Titanic Memorial (Chapter 12)

16 Open to the Public National Women's Democratic Club (Whittemore House) (1526 New Hampshire Avenue, NW)

The National Women's Democratic Club was only five years old when it moved into this building in 1927. Founded in 1922, the organization was created by former suffragettes who wanted to ensure that women would be sufficiently savvy about politics to effectively wield their newly won right to vote. At the gala ceremonies to inaugurate the club's new head-quarters, First Lady Edith Galt Wilson reportedly leaned out an upstairs window and unfurled the American flag with a flourish, only to discover she had released the Stars and Stripes in an ignominiously upside-down manner.

The house was originally built in 1892 for Sarah Adams Whittemore, a prominent and imaginative Washington hostess descended from the powerful Adams family. Whittemore commissioned noted architect Harvey Page to build the house according to her eclectic taste, and the result is a charmingly different home featuring a rare reddish brown brick that came from a New Jersey clay deposit.

17 Thomas Nelson Page House (1759 R Street, NW)

The home of popular (and now all-but-forgotten) Virginia writer Thomas Nelson Page is only one of two in Washington designed by New York architect Stanford White. (The other is the **Washington Club.**) The Page house was built in 1896, designed for its occupant in a style that well suited Page's literary legacy: Southern and genteel. Page, a Southern sympathizer during the Civil War, authored a variety of fiction and non-fiction works, many for youngsters, with titles that included *Old Dominion: Her Making and Her Manners* and *Two Little Confederates.* Page's book *Washington and Its Romance* (1923) is a history of the city that also reveals the author's admiration for his adopted hometown. The following excerpt, which describes a conversation between travelers as they cross into Washington, reflects this admiration:

> "Crossing the Potomac in a railway train, not long ago, as it reached the Washington side, with its broad green park along the river, bathed in sunshine, with the White House beyond on one side, and the noble dome of the capitol on the other, while above the whole, towered the noble shaft of Washington—a splendid bar of

snowy marble reaching to the heavens—a traveller exclaimed to the strangers about him, 'What a wonderful city this will be fifty years from now. Think what the people who come here then will see!'

"'What a wonderful city it is now!' replied another."

See Also: Washington Club (Patterson House)

Patterson House. *See* Washington Club (Patterson House)

---

18 `Open to the Public` **Phillips Gallery (1600 21st Street, NW; 202/387-2151)**

The Phillips Gallery, which was considered the first gallery of modern art in America, opened to the public in 1923 in the lovely townhouse residence of Duncan Phillips, one of the city's great art collectors. Phillips and his wife, Marjorie, spent much of their lives transforming their home into a showplace for great artists and promising talents alike. And then, having achieved the ultimate private collection, they generously opened their doors and turned their art-filled home into a bona fide gallery. The house itself was built in 1897, and has been frequently refurbished over the years to improve its quality as a gallery. Most notable of these architectural reconfigurations was the 1988 addition of the Goh Annex, which gave the museum the room it so sorely needed to grow and show all its treasures. The most famous work on display here is Augustus Renoir's "The Boating Party"; also on display are works by Pablo Picasso, Vincent Van Gogh, Georgia O'Keefe, Mark Rothko, Paul Klee, Claude Monet, Paul Gauguin, and other artists.

See Also: Girl Scout Little House Site (Chapter 5)

---

19 `Open to the Public` **Riggs Bank Building (Site of Stewart's Castle) (1 Dupont Circle)**

On this site once stood the first building erected at Dupont Circle—a mansion designed by Adolph Cluss for William Stewart, a Senator from Nevada. Built in 1873, the house came to be known as Stewart's Castle because of its ornate, pointed tower. Stewart's Castle also became the first building to be destroyed at the circle, when it was razed in 1901.

---

20 **Adlai E. Stevenson House (1904 R Street, NW)**

This house, now used as apartments and professional offices, was the rental home of Adlai E. Stevenson from 1941 to 1943. Stevenson is best known as the "egghead" governor of Illinois who ran as the unsuccessful Democratic presidential candidate against Dwight Eisenhower in 1952 and again in 1956. He also served as the U.S. Ambassador to the United Nations. While living at this address, Stevenson was working as an assistant to Naval Secretary Frank Knox.

---

21 **Sulgrave Club (Wadsworth House) (1801 Massachusetts Avenue, NW)**

The Wadsworth House was built in 1903 as the home of Herbert Wadsworth and his wife, Martha. The Wadsworths were famed for their elaborate entertaining, and the house became well-known for its social scene. Built on the site of the Holy Cross Episcopal Church, the house was willed to the Red Cross upon the death of Herbert Wadsworth in 1918. Neighboring preservationist and Red Cross member Mabel Boardman saved the house from being sold and turned into a church when she and twenty-two friends formed the Sulgrave Club, and bought the Wadsworth House as their headquarters in 1932. A ladies club where gentlemen were welcome (Arthur Rubinstein performed here on occasion), the club established itself as an eminent social, literary, and cultural salon, which it remains to this day. The house is listed on the National Register of Historic Places.

See Also: Boardman House (Embassy of Iraq) and **Washington Club (Patterson House)**

Townshend House. *See* Cosmos Club (Townshend House)

22 | Open to the Public | **Trio Restaurant (1537 17th Street, NW; 202/232–6305)**

Truly one of Washington's classic diners, the cheap and lively Trio Restaurant (and its sister Trio in Adams Morgan) is famed as much for its surly waitresses and fly-specked ambience as for its all-day breakfasts. Waylon Flowers, the ventriloquist whose "Madame" puppet went on to television fame in the 1960s and 1970s, is said to have created the cantankerous prima donna in the likeness of his favorite bee-hived waitresses from the restaurant.

23 Walsh-McLean House (Embassy of Indonesia) (2020 Massachusetts Avenue, NW)

This was once the home of a family that may well have been cursed by the infamous Hope Diamond. Thomas Walsh, who made his millions from Colorado gold mines, built the home at the turn of the century, lavishly incorporating chunks of real gold into the house's design. (The front entrance includes a pediment that allegedly includes a piece of gold.) When the mansion was completed in 1903, it was said to be the most expensive house in the area, beating out such neighboring mansions as the **Anderson House** and the **Townshend Mansion,** with cost estimates ranging upwards of $800,000.

Sadly, tragedy haunted the Walshes for decades. Within two years of moving into their new home, the Walshes' son was killed in a traffic accident, a loss that sapped Walsh of his own will to live. He died five years later. The family misfortune was apparently passed on to Walsh's daughter Evalyn Walsh—who may not have helped matters any by acquiring the allegedly cursed Hope Diamond. Her marriage with newspaper magnate Edward Beale McLean (of the Washington *Post* family) was fraught with bitter tragedy, ranging from the death of their son in a fluke traffic accident to the ruin of McLean's name (as well as his sanity and marriage) in the Teapot Dome scandal.

During World War II, the Red Cross used the house for much-needed war-time offices, and the building now serves as the Indonesian Embassy.

See Also: McLean House Site; Washington *Post* Building (Chapter 2); National Museum of American History (Chapter 5); McLean Gardens (Chapter 8)

24 The Washington Club (Patterson House) (15 Dupont Circle, NW)

One of two private homes in Washington designed by Stanford White, the Patterson House was completed in 1903 for Mrs. Robert Wilson Patterson, heiress of Chicago *Tribune* owner/editor Joseph Medill, and a socialite renowned in Washington for her elaborate parties and dinners. Her daughter, Eleanor "Cissy" Patterson, became the editor of the Washington *Herald* in 1933, and hence one of Washington's most powerful women. She further strengthened her powers of the press when she purchased the *Herald* and the Washington *Tribune* (both owned by the Hearst organization) and merged the two papers into the Washington *Times-Herald*, a morning paper that gave its competition, the Washington *Post*, fits. The *Post* finally did in the *Times-Herald* by purchasing its rival in 1954, swallowing the Patterson paper up whole.

Cissy Patterson was a bit on the wild side, wearing slacks in public (unheard of at the time), taking numerous lovers, and marrying three times. But while Washington looked askance on Cissy's famous lifestyle (which included public feuding with social rival Alice Roosevelt Longworth), this did not stop local society from flocking to her famous parties.

Charles Lindbergh caused mob scenes at Dupont Circle when he stayed with the Pattersons after his history-making solo flight across the Atlantic in 1927. Even White House occupants felt at home here—Calvin Coolidge and his wife were house guests of the Pattersons during the 1927 renovation of the Executive Mansion.

The house ceased to be a home after Cissy Patterson's death in 1948. It was sold to the Red Cross, which owned the house for only three years before selling it to the Washington Club—an elite social club for women, founded in 1891. The Sulgrave Club, younger by more than a quarter century, is the only other women's social club that even comes close to the cachet of the Washington Club.

See Also: Longworth House, "The Turf Wars of Alice Longworth," and **Sulgrave Club (Wadsworth House);** Washington *Post* Building and Washington *Times-Herald* Building (Chapter 2)

PLACES: New Downtown

The K Street and Connecticut Avenue Corridors, as two of the more famous sections of modern, work-a-day Washington are known, have been reviled for years as a glut of glitter-box buildings. The neighborhood that once stood where New Downtown now presides was one of brownstone townhouses, elegant mansions, and fashionable shops. The variety and charm of the architecture that once typified this area is still visible on a stroll through some of the side-streets of the Dupont Circle neighborhood where it bumps up against this newer area. Fine examples of what once was can be found along the quaintly preserved, single block of Jefferson

"A cabinet officer's daughter automobiling on Connecticut Avenue," from *Around Washington*, 1902.

Street (between Connecticut Avenue and 19th Street) and the block of N Street between 18th and 17th Streets.

---

25 | Open to the Public | **Arts Club of Washington (Caldwell-Monroe House) (2017 I Street, NW; 202/331–7283)**

Built between 1802 and 1808, the Caldwell-Monroe House is one of the earliest standing houses in this part of Washington and is listed on the National Register of Historic Places.

James Monroe lived here during his tenure as President Madison's Secretary of War, and continued his residency during the first six months of his own presidency in 1817 while the White House was being readied for occupancy again. (The British had gutted the Executive Mansion on August 24, 1814, and the repairs to the house took nearly four years to complete.)

Ironically enough, this home became the British Legation in 1822. During the next century, it was the residence of several VIPs, including Charles Francis Adams (John Quincy Adams's son, who grew up to be a diplomat). It also served as a boarding house, and, later as a girl's school. In 1881, an addition built onto the original two-story house added another story and a half to the building's height.

The Arts Club of Washington, a social organization devoted to the appreciation of the arts, purchased the house in 1916, the same year it was founded in one of the now-lost Seven Buildings (at the corner of 19th and Pennsylvania Avenue). The gallery of the Arts Club is open to the public, displaying an eclectic mix of works of both minor and major nineteenth- and twentieth-century artists, along with fine examples of the decorative arts.

See Also: Seven Buildings Site; Lenthall Houses (Chapter 5); "The Burning of Washington" (Chapter 10)

---

26 | Open to the Public | **Franz Bader Gallery (1500 K Street, NW; 202/393–6111)**

The city's oldest extant private art gallery (in the sense that it shows and sells art, not merely displays it), the Bader Gallery opened in 1953. It has given many (then) unknown artists their big break. Among those whose work first appeared at Bader Gallery are such (now) renowned artists as Grandma Moses, Gene Davis, Peter Milton, and John Winslow.

---

27 **Bell Experimental School Site (1234 16th Street, NW)**

A small townhouse at this address was the home to the first kindergarten for deaf children in America. Founded by Alexander Graham Bell at the rented townhouse in 1883, the school became a testing ground for the then-revolutionary technologies that Bell was developing to aid the hearing impaired. The son of a deaf-mute mother (and later, the husband of a deaf wife), Alexander Graham Bell dedicated much of his life to working with the deaf. His firm commitment to education led him to found the Volta Bureau as an educational facility for the deaf in Georgetown in 1893; it still stands today.

After numerous lawsuits were filed claiming that he had not invented the telephone, Bell had to make many court appearances. Although he successfully fought off the lawsuits, the drain on his time forced him to close the Bell Experimental School in 1886. The school was later recognized as a landmark institution in the early education of the deaf. The building was razed in 1920.

See Also: Alexander Graham Bell House and **Bell-Morton House;** Alexander Melville Bell House, Alexander Graham Bell Laboratory, and Volta Bureau (Chapter 6)

---

28 **Bell-Morton House (National Paint and Coatings Association) (1500 Rhode Island Avenue, NW)**

This Scott Circle house, remodeled by John Russell Pope, was home to a number of important Washingtonians. Alexander Graham Bell and his bride, Mabel Hubbard, were given the house as a wedding present by Bell's father-in-law, Gardiner Greene Hubbard, in 1882. The Bells lived here until they moved to a new home at 1355 Connecticut Avenue in 1891. While living at this residence, Bell worked on the invention of wax disks for recording sound to be played on Edison's Phonograph—a disk technology that would later evolve into phonograph records. In 1883, Bell founded and ran the **Bell Experimental School** nearby, which was the first kindergarten for deaf children in America.

The next owner of the house was Benjamin Harrison's vice president, New Yorker Levi Morton. Morton purchased the property as his residence just days before taking the oath of office in 1889. Harrison chose a different running mate for his next campaign, but Morton held on to his Washington home anyway, renting it to a string of wealthy leaders, including Rep. Charles Sprague of Massachusetts and Elihu Root, who served as secretary of state and then secretary of war under Theodore Roosevelt.

One of Morton's most memorable tenants was Count Arturo Cassini, the last of the Romanov diplomats, who transformed the house into the Imperial Russian Embassy. Cassini raised eyebrows in Washington society by publicly living with his mistress, whom he introduced as his housekeeper (at the same time he was also married to two different women). Cassini fathered a daughter with his mistress, and the young woman grew up to mother a fashion designer named Oleg who took his illegitimate grandfather's name as his professional moniker.

One of the house's last tenants was another inveterate inventor, John Hays Hammond. Known in his day as the "Father of Remote Control," Hammond invented everything from refrigerator door lights to stereo amplifiers. His Hammond Research Corporation (run out of a castle Hammond built in Gloucester, Massachusetts) is credited with some of the great military inventions of the twentieth century, including missile guidance and depth-finding systems. Although Hammond called the Gloucester castle home, he lived at this house from 1941 to 1945 while working for the Office of Scientific Research and Development. While a resident here, Hammond installed the city's first private residential elevator at the house.

The National Paint and Coatings Association purchased the mansion in 1939, and it has lovingly maintained the property (with great paint jobs, too!) as its headquarters ever since.

See Also: Alexander Graham Bell House Site and **Bell Experimental School Site;** Alexander Melville Bell House, Alexander Graham Bell Laboratory, and Volta Bureau (Chapter 6); Old French Embassy (Chapter 7)

㉙ | Open to the Public | **B'nai B'rith Headquarters/Klutznick Museum (1640 Rhode Island Avenue, NW; 202/857–6583)**

On Wednesday, March 12, 1977, the B'nai B'rith headquarters, home to the Klutznick Museum (an outstanding collection of Judaica and related historic artifacts), made a little Washington history of its own. A group of angry, epithet-spewing Hanafi Muslims stormed the headquarters, along with the Islamic Center on Wisconsin Avenue and the District Building downtown. They took over the building and took a number of hostages in a siege that lasted until the following Friday morning. No one was badly injured at this site, although a radio journalist was killed and then-City Council member Marion Barry was wounded at the District Building. The violent dispute was eventually settled through diplomatic channels.

This site also houses the National Jewish Visitors Center, a hospitality and information resource center that provides help for those seeking Jewish sites and sources in Washington.

See Also: District Building (Chapter 2); Islamic Center (Chapter 8)

㉚ Frances Hodgson Burnett's Second House Site (1730 K Street, NW)

Like the rest of the elegant townhouses that once lined K Street, the home that once stood here was long ago replaced by a modern office building. One of Washington's literary queens, Frances Hodgson Burnett, lived and worked at this house between 1886 and 1890. Best known for such works as *Little Lord Fauntleroy* (1886), *Sarah Crewe* (1888), and *The Secret Garden* (1909) Burnett was locally renowned for her lively literary salon. In 1890, she moved to a mansion she had built for herself on Massachusetts Avenue, which has since been replaced by the **Brookings Institution.**

See Also: Brookings Institution; Frances Hodgson Burnett's First House Site (Chapter 2)

31 Open to the Public **Capital Hilton (16th and K Streets, NW; 202/393–1000)**

Originally known as the Statler Hotel, and then the Statler Hilton, this was and remains one of Washington's most elegant hotels, and has often been the site of inaugural galas. One of these, the inaugural ball of John F. Kennedy, has led to whispers over the years, for it has long been alleged that JFK snuck upstairs during the festivities to partake of a little extra-marital merriment with actress Angie Dickinson, who was waiting for him in Frank Sinatra's suite. The story was repeated by C. Frank Heymann in his 1989 unauthorized biography, *A Woman Called Jackie*, although the Kennedy family has consistently denied the rumor. Angie Dickinson has remained silent about the evening's entertainment.

32 **Jefferson Davis House Site (1736 I Street, NW)**

On this spot once stood the home of Jefferson Davis, the Mississippi legislator and Secretary of War under President Franklin Pierce who went on to become president (of the Confederacy, that is). Davis lived here with his wife from 1857 to 1860, until the onset of the Civil War forced him south to Richmond to lead the rebel cause. During their years in the house, Davis's beautiful wife, Varina Howell Davis, was a popular hostess whose parties were often attended by the cream of Washington society. Soon after their departure, that same cream was curdling with cries about betrayal of the Union and the capital city that had once been so entertained by the couple.

33 Open to the Public **Duke Zeibert's Restaurant (1050 Connecticut Avenue, NW; 202/466–3730)**

The city's power deli since FDR's presidency (and at this site since August of 1983), Duke Zeibert's is one of the city's prime star-gazing spots. The restaurant was the scene of the one of the more memorable verbal suicides ever committed by a member of the press. While dining at

Jefferson Davis.
(Harper's Pictorial History of the Civil War)

Duke's on January 15, 1988, oddsmaker and TV sports analyst Jimmy "The Greek" Snyder opened his mouth and inserted his foot while the cameras rolled during a video-taped interview. When he was asked about the contributions of black athletes (in honor of Martin Luther King's birthday), Jimmy made a statement to the effect that black athletes are bred to be better at sports. He then added that "If [black athletes] take over coaching like everybody wants them to, there's not going to be anything left for white people." CBS promptly fired Snyder (who protested loudly and often that he had been joking when he made his racist comments).

Duke Zeibert's is also famous as the home to the three Vince Lombardi Trophies won by the Redskins for their victories in Superbowls XVII (1983), XXII (1988), and XXVI (1992). The trophies are on display in custom-made cases.

See Also: Intersection of Connecticut Avenue and L Streets; RFK Stadium (Chapter 11)

34 Open to the Public **Farragut Square (Between the "two 17th Streets" in the block between K and I Streets)**

Admiral David "Damn the Torpedoes! Full Speed Ahead" Farragut is honored at this favorite lawyers' lunch spot with an elaborate statue sculpted by Vinnie Ream Hoxie, installed in 1881. The material for the statue of the Civil War naval hero was created from the bronze propeller of Farragut's ship, the *U.S.S. Hartford.*

Hoxie, a famed female prodigy sculptor of her time, was fifteen years old at the time she was commissioned to sculpt Farragut's figure. She also created the bust of Lincoln that stands in the Capitol.

35 **Harvey's Restaurant (1001 18th Street, NW; 202/833-1858)**

The phrase on the window still read "The Restaurant of Presidents," when Harvey's was forced to close after going into bankruptcy in 1991. Originally located at Pennsylvania Avenue and 11th Street in a building with an amazing cast-iron facade, Harvey's was established in 1858 and was soon the most popular restaurant in town with presidents and politicians, writers and editors. Harvey's was a popular gathering spot for two of the city's most renowned dining salons—the Tapeworm Club, comprised of the New York Congressional Delegation, and the Canvas Back Duck Club, which included among its members the father of political cartooning, Thomas Nast. The building was taken down during the development of the Federal Triangle in the 1930s. Harvey's then moved to Connecticut Avenue, a door away from the **Mayflower Hotel,** where it stayed until 1970, when it moved to this location.

See Also: Internal Revenue Service Building (Chapter 2)

36 **Oliver Wendell Holmes House Site (1720 I Street, NW)**

Now a retail and office complex, this was once the site of Oliver Wendell Holmes's home. One of America's finest lawyers and judges, Holmes was appointed as an Associate Justice to the Supreme Court in 1902. Known as "The Great Dissenter" for his frequent minority opinions, Holmes remained on the high court until 1932; he died in 1935. He lived in the now-gone I Street house (torn down in the mid-twentieth century), throughout his years on the high court.

See Also: Supreme Court (Chapter 3)

37 Open to the Public **Intersection of Connecticut Avenue and L Street, NW**

While in town for his historic Summit with President Reagan in 1987, Soviet Leader Mikhail Gorbachev threw caution (and heavy security) to the proverbial wind while driving through Washington the afternoon of December 10, 1987. The usual lunchtime crowd was shuffling its way along the sidewalks at Connecticut Avenue and L Street when a black limousine pulled up to the curb in front of **Duke Zeibert's Restaurant** and out stepped Gorbachev. He worked the crowd for a few minutes, shaking hands and waving greetings to the excited crowd before stepping back in his car and being whisked away. With the Cold War just warming up and the anxiety of the Secret Service in full swing, the simple gesture of stepping out of a car and shaking the hands of strangers was an event broadcast around the world. When President Reagan went to Moscow for a similar summit, his handlers made certain the president re-enacted a similar scene at Red Square (although the bewildered Muscovites were far more apprehensive at this display of communal good will than were the lunchtime crowds at Connecticut and L).

See Also: Russian Embassy

38 Open to the Public **Jefferson Hotel (1200 16th Street, NW; 202/347–2200)**

Transformed by Rose Narva, the queen of Washington's hotel scene, from a has-been to an is-again great hotel, the Jefferson is one of those quiet Washington legends about which the rich whisper and the rest of us strain to overhear. Harry Wardman originally built the Jefferson as an elegant apartment building, but it was transformed into a hotel and quickly found a clientele among such visiting luminaries as Vivien Leigh, Carol Channing, and Van Cliburn. In January of 1989, the Jefferson was the homebase for the Bush inaugural party, which stayed at the hotel during the month's festivities.

39 **McLean House Site (1500 I Street, NW)**

Here at the edge of McPherson Square stood a mansion as grand as any in Washington. The house, one of only four residences in the city designed by John Russell Pope, was built in 1907 at the site of another historic house—the former home of Hamilton Fish, President Grant's secretary of state who negotiated a trade agreement with Hawaii which led to its annexation as a territory.

The McLean House took up almost half a city block, and actually incorporated Fish's house into its design. The larger house was inherited by Edward McLean, who lived there with his wife, Evalyn Walsh McLean (when not in residence at her own house in Dupont Circle, **The Walsh-McLean House,** or their estate on upper Wisconsin, Friendship). As Washington *Post* publisher, Edward McLean entertained many a prominent politico, and became good friends with President Harding. This friendship led to disaster when McLean was embroiled in the Teapot Dome Scandal that haunted the remnants of the Harding Administration. In 1931, McLean was declared insane; in 1933, the *Post*, nearly ruined by McLean, was sold at a bankruptcy auction to the Meyer family (which still runs the paper). Edward McLean died in the Maryland institution years later, claiming no knowledge of his identity.

Evalyn Walsh McLean leased the house to the federal government in 1935. The Roosevelt Administration installed three New Deal agencies in the building, including the Works Progress Administration (WPA), which hired writers and artists to document American life and culture. One of the most popular guidebook series of all times was the WPA's American Guide series. (The WPA shared its elegant headquarters with the National Bituminous Coal Commission and the Federal Emergency Relief Commission; one can only imagine the coffee klatch chat!). The building was razed in 1939, and replaced by an office building.

See Also: Walsh-McLean House and **Teapot Dome Scandal House Site;** Old Washington *Post* Building Site and Washington *Post* Building (Chapter 2); McLean Gardens (Chapter 8)

40 Open to the Public **Mayflower Hotel (1127 Connecticut Avenue, NW; 202/347–3000)**

Since its completion in 1924, the Mayflower has seen the comings and goings of movie stars and millionaires, royalty and rock stars, and has long been a favorite with foreign trade representatives involved in wheeling and dealing with the nearby K Street Corridor lawyers.

For years, the Mayflower was a popular residential hotel with powerful Washingtonians. Former residents have included: the loquacious Illinois legislator Everett Dirksen (who lived here during his tenure in Congress, from 1938 to 1948); Louisiana "Kingfish" Huey Long (who lived here from 1932 to 1934); and Mr. and Mrs. Edward Gann. (Dolly Curtis Gann, vice-president Charles Curtis's half-sister, feuded socially with doyenne Alice Roosevelt Longworth during her stay at the Mayflower).

The Mayflower has been the site of numerous historic occasions, including a chance lunch meeting in 1937 that changed U.S. labor relations forever. At the time, a bitter unionization battle was going on at the U.S. Steel Corporation. The surprising breakthrough occurred in the Mayflower's dining room when, while lunching with his wife, U.S. Steel President Myron C. Taylor noticed United Mine Worker's head John L. Lewis at a nearby table. At his wife's urging, Taylor invited his rival to join them. The ice broke that day, and secret talks between Lewis and Taylor soon followed, resulting in U.S. Steel's shocking agreement to allow its workers to unionize.

Every president since Coolidge has held an inaugural party at the hotel, most taking place in the Grand Ballroom, one of Washington's finest formal rooms. Joseph Kennedy, father of John F. Kennedy, threw a family-only luncheon at the Mayflower on his son's inauguration day (January 20, 1960). As legend has it, the Kennedy family's crusty patriarch was infuriated when he arrived at the party to find dozens of people he did not recognize, only to discover to his embarrassment that the throng of well-wishers were all indeed members of the enormous Kennedy/Bouvier clan. He had simply never seen all these relatives together in the same room before.

John F. Kennedy allegedly kept a private suite (for presumably private affairs) at the Mayflower during the late 1950s when he was serving in the Senate. According to Vince Staten's 1990 scandal-fest *Unauthorized America*, the Secret Service referred to Suite 812 of the Mayflower as "JFK's playpen."

The Mayflower was built in 1924 on the site of the Academy of the Visitation, a Catholic school for girls that filled this block from 1847 until 1922, when the area was redeveloped for commercial use. Until it was covered over in the mid-nineteenth century, Slash Run, from which the neighborhood once got its name, "The Slashes," sliced through to Connecticut Avenue at about this point.

From the Pages of *The Mayflower's Log*

"Social Notes" (May, 1932): "Mr. and Mrs. William K. Vanderbilt, of New York, were recent guests at The Mayflower when they were in Washington for a few days shortly after their return from a long cruise in tropical waters when they gathered several rare species of marine life to add to their well-known collection."

"Schedule of Capital Events" (April, 1940): "Music (Presented by Mrs. Dorsey's Bureau at Constitution Hall): April 9: Vladimir Horowitz, 'greatest of younger pianists' according to Paderewski, 8:30 p.m.; Sports: Major League Baseball: Home Games of Washington Nationals in April are with Boston Red Sox, April 16, 17, 18; Philadelphia Athletics, April 25, 26. . . ."

"The Passing Parade" (October, 1942): "Seen in The Mayflower Lounge: Annabella congratulating Husband Tyrone Power with an enthusiastic kiss as he showed her his Marine enlistment papers. . . . Edgar Bergen, recently returned from entertaining soldiers and sailors on the distant Aleutian Islands, explaining that he had left Charlie at home this time. . . ."

"Newsreel" (May, 1945): "Mr. Joseph Pulitzer, publisher of the *St. Louis Post-Dispatch*, spent several days at The Mayflower en route to Germany to view atrocity evidence."

The Mayflower Hotel was sold in early 1991 to the Stouffer Hotel Company (which is owned by a Swiss company), for a reported $100 million dollars. The sellers were a group of business men (including Ulysses "Blackie" Augur, of "Blackie's House of Beef") who had owned the property since 1968.

 Open to the Public **Metropolitan A.M.E. Church (1518 M Street, NW; 202/331–1426)**

A landmark in the history of Washington's black community, the Metropolitan African Methodist Episcopal (A.M.E.) Church was founded in 1854 by two earlier congregations which had broken from their original churches (the Israel Bethel A.M.E. Church and the Union Bethel A.M.E. Church). The church quickly became a main stop on the Underground Railroad, as slaves on the run to freedom found safe haven in an upstairs sanctuary known only to church members. Indeed, it was the church of abolitionist Frederick Douglass, and it was here that Douglass's funeral was held in 1895. Despite the 2,500–seat capacity of the church, many in the crowd of mourners had to stand to hear the eulogies delivered by great orators such as suffragette leader Elizabeth Cady Stanton. The church was renovated and expanded in 1886, with bricks from the historic Bethel Hall—meeting place of one of the earliest and most renowned black cultural and political clubs in Washington, the Bethel Literary and Historical Association. The Association, founded by A.M.E. bishop Daniel Payne in 1881, gained a reputation as a place where the black community could join together and discuss their past and future. In 1882, Frederick Douglass first delivered his famous speech, "The Self-Made Man," before the Association. When the Hall (now the site of the Magruder School) was torn down, the Association relocated to the A.M.E. church.

Throughout its history, the Metropolitan A.M.E. has drawn great political and cultural figures to its pulpit, including at least three presidents and one first lady, Eleanor Roosevelt. Even speeches held elsewhere drew crowds to the church, as was the case when hundreds of furious blacks met at the church to discuss President Woodrow Wilson's statement of support for continuing the policies of segregation.

Today the Metropolitan A.M.E. serves as the national headquarters of the African Methodist Episcopalian Church. Memorial plaques in the church mark the pews of Frederick Douglass, Paul Laurence Dunbar (an early black poet), and Julia West Hamilton (a civic activist who headed the Phyliss Wheatley YWCA).
See Also: Frederick Douglass House (Chapter 3); Cedar Hill (Chapter 11)

---

42 Open to the Public **The National Geographic Society Building/Explorers Hall (17th and M Streets, NW; 202/857–7588)**

The headquarters of America's most famous group of adventurers was constructed in 1964. It was the first building in Washington designed by Edward Durrel Stone, and many consider it his masterpiece. The society itself was founded by Gardiner Greene Hubbard in 1888, and held court in various homes, private clubs, and office spaces around the city before finally settling down for good here.
See Also: Twin Oaks (Chapter 8)

---

43 **Old Sans Souci Site (726 17th Street, NW)**

One of Washington's heavy-hitting power restaurants during the 1960s and 1970s, Sans Souci was the "in" place for reporters and politicians alike. This was the restaurant where *Post* reporters Rudy Maxa and Marion Clark waited fruitlessly for Elizabeth Ray to join them and spill the Senate beans about her affair with her boss Wayne Hays. The Sans Souci has gathered her skirts around her and moved to a quieter, more elegant address: 2445 M Street, NW, near Georgetown (202/331–2150).

See Also: U.S. Capitol (Chapter 3)

---

44 Theodore Roosevelt's House Site (1215 19th Street, NW)

A modern office building stands at the site of Theodore Roosevelt's former home. Roosevelt moved here in 1889, after being appointed to the Civil Service Commission by President Harrison. Roosevelt lived at the house for six years, shortly after which he rough-rode his way into the history books at the Battle of San Juan Hill in the Spanish-American War.

---

45 Russian Embassy (1125 16th Street, NW)

The Russian Legation building as it appeared in the late nineteenth century. (*Picturesque Washington*)

The Soviet flag was lowered for the last time from atop this bastion of Communist diplomacy on Christmas night, 1991. On December 26, 1991, Washingtonians awoke to find that the former Soviet Embassy had reverted back to the Russian Embassy, and that the old Russian standard was flying instead of the standard Soviet hammer and sickle issue.

During Mikhail Gorbachev's state visits, the embassy served as his headquarters (and sometimes his home). This embassy is not to be confused with the sprawling Russian Compound, built for housing Soviet embassy personnel, on Wisconsin Avenue near the Washington Cathedral.

See Also: Intersection of Connecticut Avenue and L Street; Russian Compound (Chapter 8)

---

46 Open to the Public Saint Matthew's Cathedral (1725 Rhode Island Avenue, NW; 202/347–3215)

This lovely cathedral seems sadly out of place amidst the modern development and traffic that swirl around it. Built in 1899, the church has long been the house of worship for the city's most powerful Catholics. During his presidency, John F. Kennedy and his family attended mass here. Following Kennedy's assassination in Dallas, his body lay in state at both the White House and the Capitol, but his funeral mass was held at St. Matthew's.

Cardinal Cushing officiated at the funeral mass, which included a reading from President Kennedy's inaugural address. Luigi Vega reprised his performance of "Ave Maria," which he had sung at John and Jacqueline Kennedy's wedding ceremony. The mass was attended by a diverse group of American leaders ranging from the Rev. Dr. Martin Luther King, Jr., to Alabama Governor George Wallace, as well as the Rockefellers, the Trumans, the Johnsons, and the Nixons. The enormous gathering of world leaders at the mass included Britain's Prince Philip, France's President Charles de Gaulle, Belgium's King Baudouin, Ethiopia's Emperor Haile Selassie, the Netherlands's Crown Princess Beatrix, the USSR's Ambassador Anatoly

Dobrinin, West Germany's Chancellor Ludwig Erhard, Sweden's Cabinet Minister Olaf Palme, South Korea's President Chung Hee Park, Japan's Prime Minister Hayato Ikeda, and Israel's Foreign Minister Golda Meier.

Following the funeral mass, the funeral cortege passed slowly through the streets of Washington and over Memorial Bridge to Arlington National Cemetery, where President Kennedy was laid to rest with great ceremony. The site where Kennedy's coffin rested at the altar of St. Matthew's during the funeral is memorialized with an inscribed tablet.

In 1990, the Kennedy family celebrated a happier event at Saint Matthew's, when Robert Kennedy's daughter Kerri and Andrew Cuomo, son of New York Governor Mario Cuomo, were married at the Cathedral.

See Also: The White House (Chapter 1); U.S. Capitol (Chapter 3); Kennedy Houses (Chapter 6)

---

47 Open to the Public **Scott Circle (intersections of Massachusetts Avenue, Rhode Island Avenue, and 16th Street)**

Scott Circle is named for Mexican-American War hero General Winfield Scott, whose statue presides over his namesake. The General was so frail when he posed for the statue that he needed to sit atop a quiet mare rather than his famed war horse; but the artist's accurate rendering of the model horse's sex caused an outcry from the General's friends and countrymen, who insisted that Scott be remembered atop a stallion, as he had always been seen in battle. The appropriate parts were duly added to the statue, and everyone was thus made happy (except, perhaps, the mare who originally modeled for the statue).

---

48 **Seven Buildings Site (northwest corner of Pennsylvania Avenue and 19th Street, NW)**

This corner was once home to a collection of rowhouses known as the Seven Buildings. They were among the first houses built in Washington, as part of the speculative construction undertaken by two of the major real estate syndicates putting up buildings in the new city. Built around 1796, the Federal townhouses became models for many of the later blocks of houses built in this area and on Capitol Hill.

According to James Goode's 1979 work, *Capital Losses*, the most renowned of the houses was the corner building overlooking Pennsylvania Avenue. It served as the first State Department (beginning in 1800), and, in 1814, became the home of Vice President Elbridge Gerry. Gerry was soon displaced by President Madison and his wife, Dolly, after the British burned the White House and the first couple moved from their temporary quarters at the Octagon House to a temporary White House here. Madison spent the rest of his presidential term here. The house once again served as the vice president's manor for Martin Van Buren in 1834. Other occupants included Major Generals George McLellan and M.D. Hardin, who made this their Civil War headquarters.

Destruction of the Seven Buildings began in 1898. The famed end-house, however, survived until 1959, when it was destroyed to make way for a new office building. In the interim, the house also became the birthplace to the People's Drug Store chain, which opened its first outlet in the end house by the early twentieth century and remained there until the building's demise. Two of the original Seven Buildings still exist. 1909 and 1911 Pennsylvania Avenue have been incorporated into the Mexican Consulate, which wraps around the still-elegant old townhouses.

See Also: "The Burning of Washington" (Chapter 10)

49 Shepherd's Row Site (Northeast corner of Connecticut and K Streets, across from Farragut Square Park)

Alexander "Boss" Shepherd, the head of the Board of Public Works who dragged Washington out of the mud and sewers by grating the streets and otherwise modernizing the metropolis, lived and entertained in the first of three magnificent houses that once wrapped around the corner here. All were built by local architectural star Adolf Cluss (who lived in the center house). During the 1870s, Shepherd frequently entertained the president, as well as visiting dignitaries. Shepherd's house (at 1601 K Street) had a variety of residents after he left the city for Mexico in 1880 (in public disgrace after being stripped by Congress of his short-lived title as Territorial Governor for mis-managing the city's resources and allowing corruption to run rampant). Among the later occupants were the Chinese Legation, the Russian Delegation, and Mrs. Washington McLean (mother of John McLean, who purchased the Washington *Post*)—who lent the house to Admiral Dewey after his return from the Philippines. But perhaps the corner house's finest hour took place in 1917, during the occupancy of William F. Draper, Minister to Italy. Draper's daughter married Prince Boncompagni of Rome at the house in one of the most lavish weddings the city has ever seen. It became known as the "butterfly wedding," for thousands of imported butterflies were let loose among the guests when the ceremony ended.

The house and its two sister buildings (at 1603–1605 K Street) were destroyed in 1922 to make way for new development—a fitting end for a row named after the greatest developer of them all, the "Boss." Today, the site is occupied by the Farragut Square North Metro Station and a modern office building.

50 Open to the Public Sheraton Carlton Hotel (923 16th Street, NW; 202/638–2626)

Another of Washington's great hotels, this palatial place was built by master developer Harry Wardman in 1926 as the Carlton Hotel. Unfortunately, Wardman's luck ran out along with the nation's when the Stock Market crashed in 1929, ruining him and allowing his creditors to seize his property. But with or without Wardman, the hotel drew some true luminaries—from movie stars such as Charlie Chaplin, Katherine Hepburn, Joan Crawford, and Robert Redford, to royalty, including the Duke of Windsor and the King of Siam. Some folks even called the Carlton home for extended stays—one live-in, General John Pershing, flaunted federal law during the 1920s by drinking openly from a private flask in the public dining room.

On October 12, 1939, the messenger of one of the most famous letters ever delivered to the White House spent a sleepless night here at the Carlton after his fruitless meeting that day with President Franklin Roosevelt. Alexander Sachs, a wealthy and respected advisor to the president, had hand-delivered a letter signed by Albert Einstein (but drafted by a pair of then-less famous atomic scientists, Edward Teller and Leo Szilard). The letter described the possibility of creating nuclear weapons, and urged the president to authorize their development for America's military arsenal (the writers feared that Hitler's scientists were already at work on such weapons).

Roosevelt dismissed the letter as little more than science fiction; after all, America was not even at war with Germany. Sachs, frustrated at the president's response, spent a tense night at the Carlton Hotel ruminating about how to convince Roosevelt of the letter's importance. Finally, he had a brainstorm: he would simplify the ideas in the letter and relate them to other turning points in the evolution of weaponry. Roosevelt caught on, and America entered the nuclear age via the Manhattan Project.

In 1959, the Sheraton chain took over the Carlton (as well as the Wardman Park Hotel on upper Connecticut Avenue, which was transformed into the Washington Sheraton). The hotel continues to attract a ritzy if diverse clientele that has run the gamut in recent years from Margaret Thatcher to Mick Jagger.

See Also: Sheraton-Washington (Chapter 8)

---

51 [Open to the Public] ## Sumner School Museum and Archives (17th and M Streets, NW; 202/727–3419)

Erected in 1872, the Sumner School was the first black public high school in the country. The school offices also served as the administrative headquarters of the Colored Public Schools of Washington and Georgetown.

The building was designed by Adolph Cluss as a companion to the all-white Franklin School at Franklin Square, which he had also designed. The Sumner School building was honored at the 1873 Exposition in Vienna, receiving a medal for school architectural design. Charles Sumner, for whom the school was named, was the cool but outspoken abolitionist senator who was nearly killed for his beliefs. (He was brutally beaten by South Carolina Senator Preston Smith Brooks following a heated debate over the morality of slavery.)

The Sumner School has been lovingly restored and is now maintained as a historic site and archival center for the study of Washington's educational and black history.

See Also: Franklin School (Chapter 2); "Blood in the Chambers" (Chapter 3)

---

52 [Open to the Public] ## The Tabard Inn (1739 N Street, NW; 202/785–1277)

One of Washington's only true inns, the Tabard was created by merging together three townhouses in this block in 1920. A bit of literary history occurred on the top floor of one of these buildings in 1860, for it was here that Edward Everett Hale wrote his famous story, "The Man without a Country." Much of the area had once been part of an estate, now long gone, owned by General Nelson Miles. One remnant remains—the stables across the street were transformed into a restaurant, the Iron Gate Inn, one of the city's longest operating and finest Middle Eastern dining establishments.

---

53 ## Teapot Dome Scandal House Site (1625 K Street, NW)

On the spot occupied today by the Commonwealth Office Building once stood an unassuming townhouse often referred to as the "Little Green House on K Street." This house was actually one of Washington's most elite and infamous Prohibition-era (i.e., illicit) clubhouses. During the presidency of Warren G. Harding, the house was rented by a string of low-level Ohio politicians, who kept the house as a kind of speakeasy where the President and his buddies could play poker and drink the night away.

The fun house is thought to be the site where members of the corrupt Harding Administration engaged in the dealings that led to the Teapot Dome Scandal. The scandal's key player was Harding's secretary of the interior, Albert Fall, who lined his pockets by secretly leasing federally owned, oil-rich lands in Wyoming to private oil interests. Although Harding himself died suddenly in 1923 just before the scandal broke, a number of other administration officials and presidential confidantes—from the head of the Veterans Bureau to the Alien Property Custodian—took the fall with Fall. As the scandals came to light, five of the "Little Green House"-mates died in quick succession, some by their own hands (although murder was also rumored).

In the end, the wheelings and dealings that went on at 1625 K Street left the Harding Administration with the dubious distinction of being one of the most corrupt in American history.

See Also: McLean House Site; Washington *Post* Building (Chapter 2); General Services Administration Building (Chapter 5); Warren G. Harding House (Chapter 8)

---

54 **James Thurber House Site (2031 I Street, NW)**

One of the nation's most beloved wits, James Thurber, spent part of his formative years at a house that once stood here. Born in 1894, Thurber lived here as a child during the cooler months of 1901 and 1902. (His mother hated the heat of Washington, so the family summered in a cottage in Falls Church, VA.) During those same years, another literary light, Stephen Vincent Benet, was growing up in the same block, according to David Cutler's *Literary Washington* (1989). Thurber later worked as a code clerk at the State Department during World War I, alongside his one-time neighbor Stephen Vincent Benet.

Chapter Eight

UPPER NORTHWEST
West of 16th Street

Upper Northwest to the west of 16th Street, as defined by the original boundary of Florida Avenue, is a place of fine homes and grand apartment buildings, schools and shopping centers and restaurants (not to mention a fine cathedral). It is a place where great writers such as Katherine Anne Porter and Walter Lippmann lived and worked, and where powerful leaders such as Grover Cleveland and Gardiner Greene Hubbard built their estates. It is also a place of embassies and the hidden intrigue of diplomatic doings, and a place where the ethnically and economically diverse neighborhoods of Mount Pleasant and Adams Morgan rub shoulders with the WASP-ish mansions of former presidents and Supreme Court justices.

Kalorama, the neighborhood of mansions-turned-embassies, got its name from the famed Kalorama Estate that once stood its ground atop the hill above Dupont Circle. The estate was already past its prime in the late nineteenth century, when it was broken up and sold to various developers. Kalorama Heights was one of the first communities established on former Kalorama Estate land. Kalorama has the feel of a gateway to Upper Northwest—perhaps because it was once situated just outside the city's boundary. (Florida Avenue was known as Boundary Road and delineated the city's northern boundary until the borders were extended in 1890.)

East of Kalorama lies Adams Morgan. An ethnic stronghold, Adams Morgan has been struggling in recent years with the upper-middle-class impact of gentrification, which threatens to out-price many of the Central American, African, and Caribbean residents who have called the neighborhood home since the 1960s. Adams Morgan is a fairly recent invention, as city neighborhoods go. By the turn of the century, the area was known as Lanier Heights, and blended almost invisibly into the other swank suburban subdivisions that crowded together at the top of the hill, including Kalorama Heights and Meridian Hill. The intersection of 18th and Columbia Roads was a retail and commercial crossroads on par with Wisconsin Avenue and M Street in Georgetown today.

Rising above Kalorama and Adams Morgan are the neighborhoods of Cleveland Park, Mount Pleasant, Friendship Heights, Glover Park, and Chevy Chase. These areas were once fertile farmland, far removed from the newly developed capital city to the south. Most of the area was owned by a handful of powerful land barons, among them General Uriah Forrest—a friend and host to George Washington and Pierre L'Enfant—whose home, **Rosedale,** still survives in the Cleveland Park neighborhood. The hilly landscape that included Meridian Hill was part of an estate built in the eighteenth century and known as Pleasant Plains (hence the neighborhood name of Mount Pleasant), first owned by Robert Peter, the mayor of Georgetown. These estates comprised the majority of the farmland that would one day evolve into the neighborhoods in the hills above work-a-day Washington.

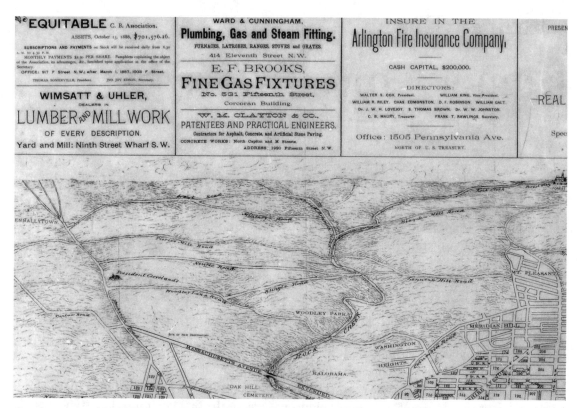

As shown on this 1886 map, Kalorama, Woodley Park, and Mount Pleasant were still very much in the suburbs. Note President Cleveland's house in upper Northwest. (National Archives)

Today, the big, elegant apartment complexes that line the major avenues share the street fronts with shops, restaurants, bars, and offices, while in every direction, serene, shade tree-filled neighborhoods sprawl lazily up and down the side streets. Unlike other parts of Washington, where compact neighborhoods and block-to-block socio-economic changes are more the norm, the residential and commercial areas of this "upper" Upper Northwest are almost uniformly well-spaced neighborhoods of the middle and upper class.

The clue to this heritage may be found in the culture of the country life which Upper Northwest once represented. Until the advent of the trolley car lines in the 1890s, only those who could afford to keep a townhouse in the city for week-night stay-overs, or who had comfortable enough transportation to withstand the daily commute, lived in the outskirts. Having a home in one of these neighborhoods was a symbol of prestige, and, by the late nineteenth century, few self-respecting Washington families of any influence would be without some sort of cottage or mini-manor in the country.

President Grover Cleveland was one of the suburban trendsetters in 1868 when he renovated a humble farmer's home on upper Wisconsin Avenue into the Oak View, his "Summer White House." No sooner had Cleveland and his wife moved into their refurbished rustic retreat than every millionaire and his brother wanted a home just like it, as nearby as possible. Within a few years, quiet farmland was transformed into a landscape dotted with rich, lazy-day mansions offering weekend getaways for the hardworking power-brokers and financiers who called the townhouses of Washington home during the week. These country getaways also provided the perfect excuse for keeping the wife and kids at bay (or at least back at the farm) while still enjoying the part-time pretense of weekday bachelorhood. Upper Northwest—especially the neighborhoods named for President Cleveland (Cleveland Park) and local social heavyweight Charles Glover (Glover Park)—suddenly seemed the perfect solution to the woes of wealthy city-dwellers.

By the 1870s, some of the city's finest estates could be found in Upper Northwest. Many, however, were already being sliced up by developers who saw the potential for rapid residential growth as the city expanded northward. A classic example was Seldon, a vast estate in the Pleasant Plains section near Rock Creek Park, which had been built by U.S. Treasurer William Seldon in 1850. After Seldon (the man) headed South at the onset of the Civil War, Seldon (the estate) was sold at bargain-basement prices to Samuel Brown, a developer from New England, in 1861. Brown expanded the house and bought up much of the surrounding land, developing the area into a neighborhood he named "Mount Pleasant." The northerners who swarmed into the city after the Civil War settled down in Brown's town, transforming it into their own little New England village. And so a neighborhood was born.

Another major estate of Upper Northwest, **Twin Oaks,** is one of the few remaining original Victorians built in the manor manner of Grover Cleveland's Oak View. But perhaps the most famous existing Upper Northwest estate is **Hillwood,** which was built in the 1920s and made famous by its last private owner, social doyenne Marjorie Merriweather Post.

Hillwood was the last of its breed not only because the social order of America was swinging away from the upper crust, but also because the technology of transportation was delivering the lower classes into richer territory. By the 1890s, Washington's streetcar system had made its way up the hills and into the suburbs. No longer merely the access roads to a quiet retreat, the main arteries of Wisconsin, Massachusetts, and Connecticut Avenues and Sixteenth Street had themselves developed a lively cultural character.

The turn of the century saw an apartment building boom, providing housing both elegant and affordable for those without the need or the means for an entire house. This trend attracted its share of powerful figures who found complexes such as the **Kennedy-Warren** and **Wardman Tower** to their taste. But many of the less-elaborate apartment buildings also became home to single professionals and childless couples, who took up residence and then began to transform the cultural and social life of Upper Northwest. To serve the needs of the burgeoning population, the avenues of Upper Northwest sprouted small restaurants and pubs as well as well as milliners, stationers, bakers, and grocers.

If any part of Washington can be seen as more country than city, it is Upper Northwest. Perhaps the serenity of the single-family-home neighborhoods, or the garden paths of apartment complex grounds give the feel of a slower, quieter lifestyle. With fewer offices and more residences in this part of the city, Upper Northwest is indeed one of the last bastions of small-town Washington.

PLACES: Kalorama

Sheridan Circle is the round-about gateway to the Kalorama neighborhood, which stretches upward along Massachusetts Avenue and backs against Rock Creek Park. This was once the site of the thirty-acre Kalorama Estate, so-named for the "Beautiful View" of

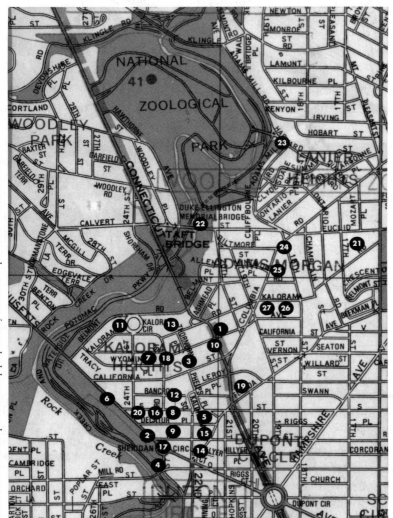

the budding city that it enjoyed from its hillside. One of Washington's finest estates, Kalorama was considered a country home, and was carved from farmland owned by the Holmead Family in the eighteenth century. Sold at first to Major Gustavius Scott, an early city commissioner, it was subsequently owned by such figures as William Augustine Washington (George Washington's nephew); Joel Barlow (a noted diplomat and writer who died of exposure in a snowstorm while traveling to negotiate a trade agreement with Napoleon Bonaparte); and Colonel George Bomford (a noted munitions inventor).

During the Civil War, the estate was used as a Union Army hospital for the isolation and treatment of smallpox. In celebration of the war's end in 1865, doctors threw a party at the hospital that ended in a fire which destroyed much of the main house.

Although the manor house (then owned by a widow named Mrs. Charles Fletcher), was reconstructed after the fire, the estate was doomed: The government planned to cut Massachusetts Avenue through the property, effectively subdividing the estate. In 1887, the family finally sold land to a development company that planned to build a neighborhood, Kalorama Heights, on the site. The last remnant of the estate—its manor house—was torn down to make way for road construction in 1889. The house that stands on the site, at 2300 S Street, became Herbert Hoover's home before and after his presidency.

Kalorama Heights was the first of several fashionable neighborhoods created on the property of the former estate. Their image as close-in country suburbs made them popular with rich and powerful Washingtonians, who erected an eclectic mix of mansions, many of which are now occupied as embassies and consulates. In the early twentieth century, the neighborhood also attracted a number of former and future presidents, including Franklin Roosevelt, Woodrow Wilson, William Howard Taft, and Herbert Hoover.

1 2101 Apartments (2101 Connecticut Avenue, NW)

The 2101 was built in 1928, at the height of the Art Deco apartment building boom sweeping gracefully up Connecticut Avenue. According to James Goode's remarkable 1988 study of Washington's apartment buildings, *Best Addresses*, residents of the building have included FDR's third vice president, Alben Barkley; The "Great Opposer" from Idaho, Republican Senator William Borah; Supreme Court Justice Tom Clark; and local legal legend J. Harry Covington (founding partner of the law firm of Covington and Burling). The building went condo in 1976, but remains one of the most sought-after apartment addresses in Washington.

2 [Open to the Public] Alice Pike Barney Studio House (2306 Massachusetts Avenue, NW; 202/357-3111)

Now operated as a museum under the auspices of the Smithsonian Institution's National Museum of American Art, this charming house once served as the home and studio for Alice Pike Barney, a charismatic painter and playwright. Barney was known as much for her artistic house guests as she was for her artistic endeavors, entertaining such notables as the great tenor Enrico Caruso, the Barrymore acting family, and artist James Whistler. Barney hired architect Waddy Butler Wood (who also designed the nearby Woodrow Wilson House in 1915) to design the house, which was built in 1902.

See Also: Woodrow Wilson House

3 California House (Louis Brandeis Apartment) (2205 California Avenue, NW)

This apartment complex was home to Supreme Court Justice Louis Brandeis during his time in Washington. Nominated to the highest court by President Wilson in January of 1916, Brandeis was confirmed on June 1, 1916, becoming the first Jew to serve on the Supreme Court. Brandeis resigned from the Supreme Court in 1939 and died in 1941.

See Also: Supreme Court (Chapter 3)

4 Everett House (Embassy of Turkey) (1606 23rd Street, NW)

This mansion was once the home of Edward H. Everett, who made most of his millions from his patented bottle cap—the same fluted metal topper still in use today on most glass beer bottles. The house, with its elaborate Beaux Arts embellishments, was designed by noted architect George Oakley Totten, Jr., whose buildings can be found in abundance on 16th Street. It took five years to build and was completed in 1915. Turkey purchased the property for use as an embassy in 1932.

5 [Open to the Public] Friends Meeting House of Washington (2111 Florida Avenue, NW; 202/483-3310)

Built in 1930 in the plain and simple style of the Quakers, the Friends Meeting House was the chosen house of worship for President and Mrs. Herbert Hoover, who lived nearby both before and after Hoover's presidency.

See Also: Herbert Hoover House

⑥ Edith Hamilton House (2448 Massachusetts Avenue, NW)

Classical scholar, author, and teacher Edith Hamilton purchased this house in 1943, and lived here until her death in 1963. Hamilton's lucid re-workings of classical mythologies are still considered among the greatest versions ever written, while her work as an educator and scholar is equally renowned.

⑦ Warren G. Harding House (2314 Wyoming Avenue, NW)

The future President lived in this house from 1917 (while still an Ohio senator) until he moved into the White House four years later.

See Also: McLean Gardens; The White House (Chapter 1); U.S. Capitol (Chapter 2); General Services Administration Building (Chapter 5); Teapot Dome Scandal House Site (Chapter 7)

⑧ Herbert Hoover House (Embassy of Myanmar [Burma]) (2300 S Street, NW)

This was Herbert Hoover's Washington home both before and after his presidency. Hoover first took up residence at the house in 1921 when he came to Washington to serve as the secretary of commerce. Another renowned resident of the house was Washington's "Hostess with the Mostest," Perle Mesta, who moved here in the early 1960s.

The house was built directly behind the site of the Kalorama Estate's manor house, which once straddled S Street at this point. The manor house, the last remnant of this once-grand estate, was torn down in 1889 to make way for the S Street connection to Florida Avenue.

See Also: The Elms

⑨ Charles Evans Hughes House (2223 R Street, NW)

This was once the home of Charles Evans Hughes, the Progressive Movement leader whose illustrious career included the governorship of New York, two separate stints on the Supreme Court, a term as secretary of state, and a run at the Presidency (as the Republican candidate, against Woodrow Wilson) in 1916. Hughes moved here in 1930, the year he was appointed Chief Justice of the Supreme Court. During his eleven years as Chief Justice (he retired at age 79), this townhouse also served as his unofficial chambers. Hughes was still in residence when he died in 1948. The house, built in 1907 and designed by George Oakley Totten, is listed on the National Register of Historic Places.

See Also: Supreme Court (Chapter 3); Charles Evan Hughes First Home (Chapter 9)

⑩ Robert M. La Follette House (Chancery of Senegal) (2112 Wyoming Avenue, NW)

Now the Senegalese Chancery, this was the last home of the famed Progressive leader Robert M. La Follette, who served as Senator from Wisconsin. La Follette moved to this house in 1923, and died here in 1925, a year after his unsuccessful bid (as the Progressive Party candidate) for the presidency.

One of La Follette's earlier homes, a house that he rented from 1910 to 1913, is located at 1864 Wyoming Avenue. Like many formerly private homes in and around the Dupont Circle, it has been broken up into an apartment building.

⓫ The Lindens (Gage House) (2401 Kalorama Road, NW)

In a city where so many residents come from somewhere else, it should be no surprise that there's also a residence from another place (not to mention time!). The Lindens was originally built in Danvers, Massachusetts in 1754, where it resided until being carefully taken apart, brought to Washington, and put back together again at this site in 1936.

The house was built for a merchant named Robert Hooper, and its residency in the Bay Colony was marked by illustrious occupants—notably, it served as the summer house of

The Lindens. (Jack Looney)

Thomas Gage, the last governor of Massachusetts appointed by British royalty before America won its freedom.

The historic home was slated for demolition until George Maurice Morris and his wife, a newly transplanted Washington couple, bought the property and had it moved to its present site. To do the job right, they hired Walter Macomber, the chief architect involved in the restoration and preservation of Williamsburg, Virginia, to oversee the moving process.

While the Old Stone House in Georgetown, built in 1765, is thought to be the oldest extant house in Washington, were it not for the nitpicky detail that the Lindens wasn't actually *in* Washington until the twentieth century, this New England home would be the aged record-holder.

See Also: The Old Stone House (Chapter 6)

⓬ Open to the Public | Mitchell Park (at Kalorama Square development, in the 2200 block of S Street)

E.N. Mitchell and his wife had planned to build a home at this site, but after Mitchell's untimely death, his widow donated the land to the city in 1918 for use as a playground—the only catch was that the grave of Bosque, her pet poodle, be preserved. A chain link fence in the middle of the playground still protects the grave from the games children play.

⓭ Old French Embassy (2221 Kalorama Avenue, NW)

Until the new French Embassy complex at 4101 Reservoir Road was completed in the mid-1980s, this elegant townhouse served as the French Embassy for more than thirty years. But its illustrious history pre-dates this occupancy. The house was built for Joel Barlow, the author-adventurer who was the master of the Kalorama estate from 1807 to 1817. Barlow had purchased much of the surrounding land (for $14,000) at the recommendation of Thomas Jefferson, who foresaw the value of the heights long before it became fashionable to build here.

Nearly a century later, the house was the long-time home of John Hayes Hammond, a wealthy mining executive who entertained such turn-of-the-twentieth-century luminaries as Mark Twain, William Howard Taft, and Andrew Carnegie. Hammond, an inventive sort himself, was drawn into friendships with some of the great creative minds of the day, and his salon was frequented by the likes of Wilbur and Orville Wright, Alexander Graham Bell, Gugliemo Marconi, and Nikola Tesla.

Thomas Alva Edison was a particular favorite in the Hammond household, especially with Hammond's young son, whom the great inventor befriended. The house full of inventors deeply affected John Hayes Hammond, Jr., who grew up to become one of the most prolific inventors

in American history. The younger Hammond made his home in Massachusetts, but returned to Washington during the second World War to work on military inventions.
See Also: Bell-Morton House (Chapter 7)

---

14 Palmer House (2132 R Street, NW)

This lovely rowhouse was once home to A. Mitchell Palmer, a posse leader during the first "red scare" Communist hunt (which swept through Washington after World War I). As President Wilson's attorney general, Palmer led the battle to ferret out possible Communist infiltration in the nation's capital. He made few friends, but lots of enemies: In the summer of 1919, a bomb was thrown at the house, causing minor damage but killing the messenger. Palmer's neighbor, Franklin Delano Roosevelt (then an Assistant Secretary in the Navy), rushed over when he heard the explosion. Palmer and Roosevelt found various human body parts intermingled with debris from the explosion. Palmer immediately launched an all-out hunt for radicals in the nation's capital, Communist or otherwise, making him even more unpopular.
See Also: Franklin Roosevelt House (Embassy of Mali)

---

15 Franklin Roosevelt House (Embassy of Mali) (2131 R Street, NW)

Franklin Delano Roosevelt and his family lived here during his tenure as Assistant Secretary of the Navy (1917 to 1920).
See Also: Palmer House

---

16 [Open to the Public] Textile Museum (2320 S Street, NW; 202/667–0441)

A collection devoted to the textile arts, this museum is a place woven of dreams. Housed in a 1916 mansion designed by John Russell Pope, the home was once the residence of George H. Myer, Director of the Union Trust Company. An avid collector of rugs, tapestry, and other weavings, Myer transformed his home into a public showcase into 1925. The museum collection now includes more than 14,000 piece of textile materials from around the world, and the site also features an extensive research library for the study of textile arts.

17 Sheridan Circle (in Kalorama, at the intersection of Massachusetts Avenue and R and 23rd Streets)

Sheridan Circle gained its place in the annals of Washington tragedy on September 21, 1976, when one of the city's few political assassinations took place here. A remote-controlled bomb, planted in the car of former Chilean Ambassador Orlando Letelier, was triggered as the vehicle rounded Sheridan Circle, killing Letelier as well as his aide, Ronni Karpen Moffitt. Moffitt's husband, who was sitting in the back seat, received only minor injuries.

The bombing was soon linked to the Chilean secret police; Letelier had angered the Chilean government with his outspoken criticism of the Pinochet regime's hard-line rule. One principal suspect in the killing was arrested soon after the bombing. Another was captured in April of 1991, in Florida, after a phone tip put police on his trail. The caller had just seen a segment about the bombing and the missing

The memorial to slain Chilean ambassador Orlando Letelier and his aide. (Jack Looney)

suspects on the television series "America's Most Wanted." Yet another suspect was recently apprehended. A small memorial to the slain diplomats stands behind a tree in front of the Embassy of Ireland, near the spot where the bomb exploded.

Originally known as Decatur Circle after the Washington naval hero, Commodore Stephen Decatur, the circle was constructed in the late 1880s to handle the increased traffic from the development of Kalorama Heights. In 1890, the circle was renamed in honor of Civil War General Philip Sheridan, who had died two years earlier. An equestrian tribute to Sheridan by sculptor Gutzon Borglum—creator of Mount Rushmore—was installed in the center of the circle in 1908, much to the delight of Sheridan's widow. In 1905, she had had a home built at 2211 Massachusetts Avenue just to be within sight of the anticipated tribute.

18 William Howard Taft House (2215 Wyoming Ave., NW)

This was the residence of William Howard Taft from his return to Washington in 1921 until his death in 1930. The former president returned to the capital to serve as Chief Justice of the Supreme Court, buying his new home from Massachusetts representative Alvin Fuller. The mansion, designed in the then-popular Georgian revival style, was built in the early 1900s, and remained in the Taft family until the death of Taft's wife in 1944. It is now a part of the United Arab Republics Embassy Complex.

19 Open to the Public Washington Hilton Hotel (1919 Connecticut Avenue, NW; 202/483–3000)

The Washington Hilton's claim to infamy is barely a decade old, and already it is legendary. On March 30, 1981, President Ronald Reagan was nearly killed in front of the hotel. Reagan had just emerged from the hotel after delivering a speech there when John Hinckley, Jr., fired shots at Reagan and his entourage. Reagan was wounded in the chest and his Press Secretary, James Brady, was shot in the head. A Secret Service Agent and a police officer were also wounded, although not as severely as Reagan and Brady. The President was whisked into his limousine, which tore off downtown to the George Washington University Emergency Medical Center.

Hinckley was apprehended at the scene of the shooting. He subsequently told investigators that he had obtained the weapon (a small-caliber handgun often called a "Saturday Night Special" for its cheap price-tag) with ease after lying about his history of mental illness on the gun purchase application form. Letters found among Hinckley's belongings revealed his motivation—an obsession with actress Jodie Foster. Foster, then a student at Yale University, had starred in the Martin Scorsese film *Taxi Driver* as a young prostitute for whom a crazed cab driver shoots the president as a token of his admiration. Unsuccessful in his attempts to gain Foster's attention through letters and phone calls, Hinckley emulated the film plot, hoping to impress her by shooting Reagan. Hinckley remains incarcerated as a patient in Washington's St. Elizabeth's Hospital.

Until Reagan's shooting, the Hilton had been in the spotlight only at its inception in 1962, when community activists protested the construction of a large hotel complex at the site. Today the Hilton serves as the point of departure for the hilarious "Scandal Tour" bus trip of Washington's shocking landmarks. Before the Hilton was built, this site was known as Oak Lawn in honor of a famous oak tree that had shaded the hillside for several centuries. A National Masonic Memorial designed by Frank Lloyd Wright was planned for the site in the 1920s, but waning funds and interest doomed the project.

See Also: George Washington University Emergency Medical Center (Chapter 5); St. Elizabeth's Hospital (Chapter 11)

20 Open to the Public **Woodrow Wilson House (2340 S Street, NW; 202/673–5517)**

After leaving the White House, President Woodrow Wilson and his wife retired to this house, built in 1915 by Waddy Butler Wood. The Wilsons moved here in 1921, just as their new neighbor, Warren Harding, was moving out of Kalorama to take up residency at the White House. Wilson died here in 1924, and the house is now a museum to the man and his life. The museum honors the efforts Wilson made to promote world peace through the foundation of the League of Nations, as well as other achievements of his presidency, including the creation of the Federal Reserve Board. The House also holds events throughout the year meant to recall the way life was lived during the 1920s. Popular happenings have included tastings of 1920s California vintages from the house wine cellar, as well as an annual 1920s Christmas party.

PLACES: Adams Morgan and Mount Pleasant

Woodrow Wilson's last house. (Jack Looney)

East of Kalorama, and on the other side of Rock Creek Park from the zoo, lie two neighborhoods that share more with each other than they do with the rest of the grand-manored neighborhoods to the north. Situated just above the Florida Avenue (Boundary Road) border until 1890, both Lanier Heights (now Adams Morgan) and Mount Pleasant were close-in suburbs of Washington for government workers who needed more room, for less money, than they could find in Washington.

Back when it was known as Lanier Heights, Adams Morgan was a Dupont Circle-style neighborhood with fashionable shops and townhouses. During the 1950s, it gained its current name from two local elementary schools, one named Adams (attended by whites) and one called Morgan (attended by blacks). In 1955, when Washington became the first major city in the nation to integrate its schools following the Brown v. Board of Education Supreme Court ruling, the neighborhood merged the two school names as a symbol of hope for the future of integrated education.

By the 1960s, the population had begun to shift toward a more ethnic mix, with an influx of South and Central Americans, as well as Caribbeans. In the late 1980s, this multi-ethnic enclave found itself fighting a white-collar tide of gentrification that threatened the area's affordable housing and transformed its longtime ethnic shops and restaurants into suddenly hip haunts of the well-heeled. Then, during the Mount Pleasant riots of early May, 1991, gangs of rampaging youths ransacked shops, making their way into the northern tip of Adams Morgan. In the wake of these brief but violent outbursts, retailers were faced with cleaning up an unearned but nevertheless "bad" neighborhood reputation.

The intersection of Columbia Road at 18th Street was and remains the heart of Adams Morgan. Columbia Road itself has had a far older history than most avenues in the city, for it served as a primary trail for Native American tribes in the region long before Washington was developed. When the city was established, Columbia Road became the most heavily traveled route between Baltimore and Washington. When the Dupont Circle area came into its own, Columbia Road soon became a popular area for developers, who saw a booming construction business in apartment buildings here at the turn of the twentieth century. The street is still lined with fine old apartment buildings like the **Wyoming,** the **Woodley,** and the **Norwood.**

Mount Pleasant is a neighborhood of rowhouses, many built by the influx of New Englanders who settled here after the Civil War. These true northerners had come to work in the booming post-war civil service of the federal government. So many of these new Washingtonians took federal jobs that their neighborhood became known as "Clerksville" for a time.

The area had originally been part of a large estate known as Pleasant Plains that stretched all the way west to Georgetown. Pleasant Plains was later broken up into several smaller (but still substantial) estates, including Ingleside and Meridian Hill, to the east. Another prominent estate, previously owned by U.S. Treasurer William Seldon (who fled the city when the Civil War broke out to return to his beloved, embattled Dixieland), was bought during the Civil War by Maine man Samuel Brown, an army contractor who arrived in Washington in 1861. Brown bought up much of the surrounding area and turned it into a development he dubbed "Mount Pleasant," after another estate just to the east that went by the same name.

The flood of post-war civil servants from the north turned Mount Pleasant into a miniature New England community, complete with town meetings and get-togethers reminiscent of life back north. Then, at the turn of the century, the trolley car line was extended into Mount Pleasant, with the route ending at the intersection of Park Road and Mount Pleasant Street. The arrival of public transit ended Mount Pleasant's isolation as a quiet New England-style village. Many of the original rowhouses, which had been quite large, were broken up into apartments and subdivisions during the World War II housing crunch, and thus there are still a number of "group houses" and house-style apartment buildings in the community.

A large Hispanic community now resides in Mount Pleasant. Sadly, the growing economic depression and mounting crime rates have transformed the community into a rather downtrodden neighborhood. A long-predicted burst of violence consumed part of the neighborhood in early May of 1991 when a police shooting at 17th and Lamont Streets transformed the area around 16th Street into a riot zone. Angry youths burned police vehicles, wounded officers, and looted stores and restaurants along Mount Vernon Avenue. The violence spread to nearby Adams Morgan the following night, with the rioters chanting "Columbia Road, Columbia Road" in defiant announcement of their intended destination. After three days, curfews and a police presence finally put an end to the most graphic bout of mob violence the city had seen since the catastrophic riots of 1968. The city government vowed to find ways to work with the citizens of Mount Pleasant and Adams Morgan to create a better network of community relations. Peace has prevailed ever since, but the neighborhoods remain plagued by a recession that has turned the Great American Dream into a bitter reverie for many of the immigrant citizens of Adams Morgan and Mount Pleasant.

21 | Open to the Public | **Citadel Center/Motion Picture Complex (1649 Kalorama Road, NW)**

Built in 1947 as an Art-Deco roller skating rink and bowling alley, the site also served as the city's first self-service gas station and as a parking lot. Today it is a sound stage and production facility for film and video, catering to the likes of Gene Hackman, Dan Akroyd, James Caan, and Francis Ford Coppola. The Citadel Center, an arena/club at the center, is also a popular concert venue.

22 | Open to the Public | **Duke Ellington Bridge (Calvert Street to Connecticut Avenue)**

This bridge was designed by Paul Cret and built in 1934. It replaced a railway trestle bridge, built at this spot in 1891 by the Rock Creek Railway. It was called the Calvert Street Bridge until it was renamed in honor of home-town musical legend Duke Ellington, who grew up on the other side of 16th Street. The bridge has a deadly reputation as a favorite jumping-off spot for suicidal Washingtonians.

See Also: Duke Ellington Home (Chapter 9)

23 **Harvard Hall Apartments (1650 Harvard Street, NW)**

This apartment complex, which opened in 1929, was the site of one of Washington's weirdest and funniest scandals. The tale, as told by James Goode in *Best Addresses* (1988), started when one of the residents, a widowed magazine writer named Mrs. Pamela Schuyler Young, took an extended trip to South America and asked the building management to sublet her furnished apartment while she was away. In December of 1935, the apartment was sublet to a newly arrived Congressman from Seattle, Marion Zioncheck.

Zioncheck was a party animal: One of his first acts of 1936 was to take over the switchboard at a swank nearby apartment house (he tied up the receptionist), and place Happy New Year's wake-up calls at 3 a.m. to twenty-five residents. In the following months, the Congressman threw numerous all-night parties and was arrested on charges ranging from drunk driving to assaulting a police officer. Upon learning of Zioncheck's behavior, Mrs. Young rushed back to Washington to regain possession of her home in May of 1936. Zioncheck was away on his honeymoon, so Young returned to an empty apartment that had been badly trashed. Many of her antiques were missing or ruined, and she found such anomalies as bedspreads used as rugs, all of the windows open, and a dead herring in a glass in the middle of the floor. She moved back in to her apartment and began to return order to the chaos that had become of her belongings.

When Marion Zioncheck and his bride, Rubye, returned from their trip at the end of May, they fought Mrs. Young's attempts to re-possess her apartment. As the *Evening Star* reported it, Mrs. Young ended up in the hospital, bruised and battered after twice being thrown by the Zionchecks from her own apartment. But Mrs. Young would not give up. She returned to her apartment and had it out with Rubye Zioncheck. When the Congressman returned home, according to the paper, he was at first rather nice to Mrs. Young (reportedly showing her how his pet turtle could dance to the tune "I Can't Give You Anything But Love, Baby.") But when Mrs. Young showed no sign of leaving, she and Mrs. Zioncheck got into a brawl. Eventually Mr. Zioncheck tossed Mrs. Young out of the apartment yet again.

The Zioncheck Affair climaxed in June of 1936 when the Congressman drove the wrong way down Connecticut Avenue (and along the sidewalk) to deliver a bag of empty beer bottles to President Roosevelt as a present. Rubye Zioncheck had her husband committed to a private mental institution in Baltimore, in part to shield him from the arrest warrant against him for his assaults on Mrs. Young. Zioncheck escaped from the institution, however, hitchhiked back to Washington, and hid in his House office for a few hours until being discovered. He was then escorted by the police to Union Station and sent back home to Seattle. Zioncheck ran for re-election in Seattle, but found himself up against seventeen other candidates. Depressed, he committed suicide by jumping from his office window—and landing on the running board of his own car, in which his wife had been waiting for him on the street below.

Mrs. Young finally received compensation for her losses after Zioncheck's property was seized and sold at auction in September of 1936.

24 Knickerbocker/Ambassador Theater Site (Perpetual Savings Bank) (Southwest corner of intersection at Columbia Road and 18th Street, NW)

On this site once stood the popular Knickerbocker Theater, a vaudeville stage and silent movie palace that opened in 1917. Part of local stage magnate Harry Crandall's theatrical chain that also included B.F. Keith's Theater and the Metropolitan Theater downtown, the Knickerbocker had a serenely curved neoclassical facade that whispered of the elegant auditorium within. It seemed a theater for the ages.

But on the evening of January 28, 1922, the Knickerbocker Theater held its final performance. The evening's entertainment was "Get-Rich-Quick Wallingford," a lightweight silent film. A few minutes after 9 p.m., as the organist was playing the finale music, the roof began creaking ominously. Suddenly, it buckled under the weight of tons of snow, dumped by a storm that would eventually blanket the city in twenty-eight inches of snow. The horrified audience rose to flee, but there was no time. Within two minutes, the entire roof had caved in, crushing the patrons where they stood. The dead numbered 96, and another 136 were injured. Rescue equipment had to fight both the snow and the crowds of

The 1922 Knickerbocker Theater disaster. (Library of Congress)

awestruck onlookers to get to the scene of the worst structural disaster in Washington history.

Although the city hauled the architect and theater management into court, the evidence revealed that the building contractor had been negligent in the placement of steel reinforcement rods in the roof. Building codes were strengthened as a result of the tragedy, and a number of theaters and other public gathering places closed down because of poor construction. The young architect of the Knickerbocker, Reginald Wycliffe Geare, saw a promising career in theater design (he had also built Crandall's Metropolitan Theater downtown) crushed by the roof cave-in. Unable to overcome the stigma of the Knickerbocker tragedy, he committed suicide in 1927. Owner Henry Crandall died a decade later, also by his own hand, as his financial empire lay amidst the ruins of the Great Depression.

A new theater, the Ambassador, was built at the site of the ill-fated Knickerbocker. For more than forty years, the Ambassador Theater was a landmark Washington movie palace, but it was torn down in 1969, when the management could no longer afford to maintain the palatial theater. The Perpetual Bank took over the real estate, and still stands at this historic corner.

See Also: Old Ebbitt Grill and Metropolitan Theater Site (Chapter 2); "Washington Disasters" (Chapter 12)

---

25 The Norwood (1868 Columbia Road, NW)

Built in 1917 as a luxury apartment building, the Norwood was once the home of the eminent Bankhead family, which included William Bankhead, a Congressman who later became Speaker of the House, and his teenaged daughter, Tallulah Bankhead, later to become a stage and screen goddess.

---

26 Admiral Peary House (1831 Wyoming Avenue, NW)

This was the home of famed North Pole explorer (or at least attempter—the debate goes on!) Admiral Robert E. Peary, who bought the house in 1914. While living here, Peary wrote *Secrets of Polar Travel* (1917). During World War I, he served as Chairman of the National Aerial Patrol Commission. Peary died in February of 1920.

---

27 The Wyoming (2022 Columbia Road, NW)

One of Washington's most prestigious apartment addresses, the Wyoming, built in 1905, has been home to more than twenty members of Congress as well as to the Eisenhower family—Dwight, Mamie, and the kids lived here from 1927 to 1928 and from 1929 to 1936. Military men seemed particularly at home here, as evidenced by the residency of Battle of the Bulge hero General Anthony C. McAuliffe, as well as Admirals Charles Sigsbee and William S. Benson.

PLACES: Embassy Row/Observatory Hill/Washington National Cathedral

An impressive architectural potpourri of some 150 old and new embassy compounds and diplomatic dwellings, Embassy Row is actually more a state of mind than a definable geographic neighborhood, although it is considered to stretch from Wisconsin Avenue down Massachusetts Avenue all the way to Scott Circle. Many of the embassies in the Kalorama neighborhood were converted from the turn-of-the-century mansions that fill that neighborhood.

As the row creeps up Massachusetts Avenue toward Observatory Hill, original diplomatic compounds begin to appear. Many, like the marvelous **Islamic Center,** reveal quite spectacularly their cultural roots and heritage, while others, including the **Japanese**

Embassy, show a culturally relevant, but more subdued face, to the city. The area just west of Van Ness is being transformed into a similar clustering of embassies, although as yet it lacks the cohesive sense of being a world community that distinguishes Embassy Row.

Observatory Hill, so named for the Naval Observatory that moved here in the 1890s, had

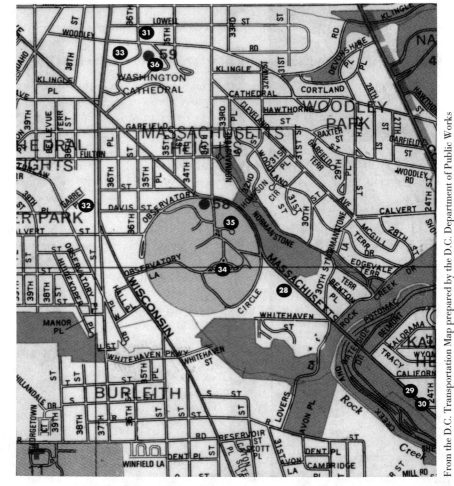

From the D.C. Transportation Map prepared by the D.C. Department of Public Works

its traffic circle added to provide sound insulation for the delicate instruments of the naval facility, threatened by the growing traffic of Massachusetts Avenue. The Chancery Annex of the **British Embassy** climbs up the hill toward the observatory, while the lovely Santa Sophia church presides at the nearby intersection of 36th Street. But the crowning glory of this section of Massachusetts Avenue (and some would say of all of Washington), is the soaring, gothic **Washington National Cathedral,** which sits atop Mount Saint Albans.

28 British Embassy (3100 Massachusetts Avenue, NW)

The only statue in Washington that stands astride the soil of two nations is located at this elegant embassy compound: The statue of a stern and far-seeing Winston Churchill—dressed in a business suit and clutching a cigar—gazes out onto Massachusetts Avenue. The statue's plinth is built upon a mixture of earth imported from Brooklyn, New York (birthplace of Churchill's mum), and from Churchill's own birthplace at Blenheim Palace and his home at Chartwell. And planted firmly beneath both feet is a time capsule to be opened on the hundredth anniversary of Churchill's honorary U.S. citizenship in 2063.

The main embassy was built in 1931 by architect Sir Edward Luytens, the only building in Washington designed by this eminent British architect. Until the USSR built its mammoth embassy in the 1960s, this was the city's largest diplomatic enclave. The young Queen Elizabeth II laid the cornerstone for the Chancery Annex (completed in 1960) during a state visit in 1957. She even used George Washington's Capitol cornerstone trowel to do the honors.

29 [Open to the Public] The Islamic Center (2551 Massachusetts Avenue, NW)

The gorgeously colored minarets of the Islamic Center rise above Massachusetts Avenue like a storybook castle from the Arabian Nights. These towers soar a full 168 feet, exempt through diplomatic immunity from the height restrictions other Washington buildings must follow. Precious metals and semi-precious stones embellish the glossy white marble walls of the Islamic Center building, which was erected as a house of worship and cultural center for the diplomatic corps of Islamic nations maintaining Washington embassies. Construction on the center began in 1955, and President Eisenhower presided over the dedication ceremonies in 1957.

The center found itself the center of attention on March 12, 1977, when a band of Hanafi Muslims stormed the mosque, as well as the B'nai B'rith headquarters on Rhode Island Avenue and the District Building downtown. The siege lasted until diplomatic measures finally convinced the Hanafis to release their hostages.

See Also: District Building (Chapter 2); B'nai B'rith Headquarters (Chapter 7)

30 Japanese Embassy (2520 Massachusetts Avenue, NW)

The first Japanese ambassadors to the United States were received by President Buchanan in May, 1860. (*Our First Century*)

Built in 1931, the Japanese Embassy was one of the first buildings in Washington built specifically to serve as an embassy. Up until this time, most nations had adapted existing mansions and estates to suit the needs of their delegations.

On December 7, 1941, as news of the Japanese attack on Pearl Harbor spread, journalists arrived at the Japanese Embassy only to find Japanese diplomats outside on the grounds hastily burning classified documents in trashbins and makeshift bonfires. The diplomats refused to answer reporters' queries about what they were doing, although they clearly were cleaning house before leaving the (suddenly) enemy capital.

31 Walter Lippmann House (3525 Woodley Road, NW)

Formerly the Deanery of the National Cathedral, this elegant mansion was the last home of Pulitzer Prize-winning journalist Walter Lippmann. Lippmann moved here from Georgetown in 1964, and spent the last decade of his life living and working here. Lippmann is probably best remembered as the author of an incisive column of social and political commentary, "Today and Tomorrow," which he began writing for the New York *Herald-Tribune* in 1931.

See Also: Alexander Melville Bell House (Chapter 6); Frankfurter-Lippmann House (Chapter 7)

32 Russian Compound (2650 Wisconsin Avenue, NW)

After the Carter Administration okayed the location, the Soviets built this enormous, high-security compound for housing its embassy personnel. Intelligence analysts were shocked, realizing that the Soviets had been given one of the highest points in Washington—a perfect place for operating spy cameras, microphones, and other paraphernalia that could pick up information from all over the city. The KGB spy work that began almost immediately at the site has presumably come to a relative halt since the dismantling of the Soviet Union.

The former Soviet Compound played a minor role in one of Washington's weirdest spy cases. It was here that KGB super-spy Vitaly Yerchenko returned to re-defect on November 2, 1985. Yerchenko had defected to the U.S. in July 1985, only to find himself stuck with constant CIA companions. Perhaps yearning for a little privacy, he re-defected by ditching his guards while dining at Au Pied de Cochon in Georgetown, and walking up Wisconsin Avenue to his old compound.

See Also: Au Pied de Cochon (Chapter 6); Russian Embassy (Chapter 7)

33 Saint Albans School for Boys (Massachusetts Avenue and Garfield Street) and National Cathedral School for Girls (Woodley Road and Wisconsin Avenue, NW)

One of Washington's most elite private schools, St. Albans was founded here in 1909 as the National Cathedral School, and was originally intended as an educational facility for the cathedral's choirboys. Over the years, the roster has expanded to include the progeny of Washington's rich and powerful. Among the boys to attend St. Albans have been the sons of Franklin Roosevelt, Robert and Ted Kennedy, George Bush, and Dan Quayle. And the equally impressive alumni list includes television reporter Brit Hume ('61), Washington *Post* publisher Donald Graham ('62), astronauts Michael Collins ('48) and Rick Hauck ('58), and Senator Al Gore ('65).

The school was founded with a $300,000 scholarship fund bequeathed by Harriet Land Johnston, a niece of President Buchanan. Johnston was following in the footsteps of another great lady, Phoebe Hearst, who had founded St. Albans' sister school (which resides on a corner of the campus), in 1900.

The National Cathedral School for Girls opened in Hearst Hall, donated for the use of a girl's school by the wife of California Senator George Hearst, who had made his fortune in mining. Their son, William Randolph Hearst, would become world famous for his publishing empire and colorful life (upon which the cinema classic *Citizen Kane* was largely based).

Much smaller than its brother school (both in size and budget), the National Cathedral School for Girls is located on the other side of the Cathedral. It has had an equally illustrious roster of students, among them the daughters of Jay Rockefeller, Ted Kennedy, and Washington mayor Sharon Pratt Kelly. A 1971 proposal to merge the two schools into a single, co-educational institution led to heated debate from both sides, but was finally shot down the following year by the St. Albans Board of Governors.

34 | Open to the Public | U.S. Naval Observatory (34th Street at Massachusetts Avenue, at Observatory Circle; 202/653–1543)

When the observatory was first established in 1844 atop Camp Hill in Foggy Bottom, its mission was to create and store navigational charts. (In fact, its original moniker was "The Depot of Charts and Instruments.") The Navy became involved in the study of astronomy—the purpose for which the Naval Observatory is now used—in order to test the chronometers of sailing vessels. While at the Foggy Bottom location, the observatory gained world renown after astronomer Asaph Hall discovered the two moons of Mars using the facility's 26–inch telescope.

In 1893, the observatory was moved to this site to isolate it from the shake and shimmy of downtown Washington—which, it was feared, would unbalance the sensitive equipment being used here. All was well at first, as this new site was virtually in the country; but the advent of streetcars and, later, automobiles, brought both development and noisy traffic to the hill. Observatory Circle was installed along Massachusetts Avenue to re-route the bump and grind of traffic away from the Naval Observatory.

Aside from the astronomical observatory itself (which can be toured by visitors), the grounds also feature a Victorian home that once served as a prize residence for senior Admirals. Since 1975, the home has been used as the **Vice President's House** (which cannot be toured).

See Also: Vice President's House; Old Naval Observatory (Chapter 5)

---

35 **Vice President's House (On the grounds of the U.S. Naval Observatory)**

Until the building was taken over as the official residence of the vice president, living in the Victorian manor on the grounds of the Naval Observatory was a perk granted to high-ranking admirals in the U.S. Navy. The mansion became the vice president's home during the presidency of Gerald Ford, when Congress was looking for ways to cut the Executive Branch's expenses. Rather than secure and protect the personal home of the vice president, analysts agreed it would be cheaper to purchase one that was already in a secured environment. So, although Navy brass protested loudly, the house was wrested from their control, and in 1975, Nelson Rockefeller became the first vice president to move in.

Unlike the White House, the vice president's residence is closed to the public. Vice President Dan Quayle made one exception to this rule in 1989 to 1990: On Halloween, trick-or-treaters who lined up at the entrance gate were escorted up to the main house (sans parents) to collect goodies—usually handed out by the VP and his wife, Marilyn, themselves. In 1991, the practice was abandoned.

See Also: U.S. Naval Observatory and **Nelson Rockefeller Home;** The White House and Old Executive Office Building (Chapter 1); Old U.S. Naval Observatory (Chapter 5)

---

36 Open to the Public **Washington National Cathedral (Massachusetts and Wisconsin Avenues; 202/537–6200)**

The Washington National Cathedral was finally completed on September 29, 1990, after more than a century of planning. The sixth-largest cathedral in the world, it looms over Washington with all the majesty of a Gothic church in Paris or London. The cathedral has been the site of numerous state occasions, including the funerals of Presidents Woodrow Wilson and Dwight D. Eisenhower, Generals Douglas MacArthur and Omar Bradley, and various Congressional leaders, including Senator John Heinz (who died in a plane crash outside of Philadelphia in April of 1991). A memorial service for slain Egyptian leader Anwar Sadat was held here, as were services to honor the American soldiers who died in Vietnam. When hostages come home, they are honored here. When wars end, prayers of thanks are given here.

The import of another great event was only realized after a few days had passed: The Rev. Dr. Martin Luther King, Jr., stood at the pulpit and preached what was to be his last Sunday sermon, on March 31, 1968. King was assassinated within the week.

The construction of the Washington National Cathedral (also called the National Cathedral, and officially named the Cathedral Church of St. Peter and St. Paul) commenced in 1907, while a crowd of 200,000 onlookers cheered and jostled for a better view. It was quite an event, with President Theodore Roosevelt dramatically laying the cathedral cornerstone with the same implement used by George Washington to lay the Capitol cornerstone.

From the beginning, when L'Enfant laid out the plans for the capital city, there were plans for the creation of a church for national prayer. But it took another century before a prominent group of Washingtonians (led by Charles Glover, after whom the nearby Glover Park neighborhood was named) set about raising funds to build the Washington National Cathedral. Their job became considerably less taxing when Congress gave its stamp of approval, chartering the Protestant Episcopal Cathedral Foundation in 1893 for the purpose of developing and building a national cathedral. The Foundation selected the site for the church (a hill known as Mount Saint Albans), and hired the renowned British church architect George Frederick Bodley to design the cathedral.

Once the foundation was laid, the construction began in earnest, and the cathedral's first section, Bethlehem Chapel, was put into use in 1912. World War I put a temporary hold on construction, which resumed anew in 1922 under the careful watch of architect Philip Frohman, who served as the supervising architect for the next half-century. Ten years later,

**The Washington National Cathedral.
(Washington Convention and Visitors Association)**

the North Transept, choir, and apse were ready for public use. It would be another thirty years before the South Transept and the carillon bell tower (the Gloria in Excelsis Tower) were opened, and another twenty years after that before the Frederick Hart-sculpted West Front was opened. Today, although no formal congregation calls the cathedral home, the Washington Cathedral is the seat of Washington's Episcopalian Diocese.

Legends abound about the cathedral. One of the most popular is that a bereaved construction worker was refused permission to have his wife's remains entombed at the cathedral, whereupon he mixed her ashes with some concrete used in the cathedral construction—thus ensuring his beloved's eternal interment in the very body of the cathedral itself. Though this legend is likely apocryphal, there *are* some visible and certifiably unique materials incorporated into the Washington National Cathedral: The pulpit is constructed of stones from England's

Canterbury Cathedral, and a moon rock is embedded into a stained glass window commemorating the Apollo 11 Mission.

Other highlights of the Washington National Cathedral include the tombs of notable Americans such as Woodrow and Edith Galt Wilson, as well as Helen Keller and her teacher, Annie Sullivan.

The grounds of the Cathedral are filled with quiet gardens, walkways, and places for contemplation. Here, too, can be found an unusual equestrian statue of George Washington. Intriguingly, the horse upon which the first president sits bears a striking resemblance to the championship racehorse Man O'War. The sculptor, Herbert Hazeltine, had only recently finished a statue of that same horse for another commission before creating this statue of Washington, which was installed in 1959.

PLACES: American University/Spring Valley

American University sits between the Cathedral area and the Spring Valley neighborhood along the Foxhall Road corridor. One of the city's four largest universities (George Washington, Catholic, and Georgetown being the others), A.U. was founded in 1893 and continues to operate on the campus to which it officially moved in the 1920s.

Spring Valley is one of the city's wealthiest sections, crowded with giant mansions and estates that have been home to many Washington notables—Nelson Rockefeller, Perle Mesta, Lyndon Johnson, and the Cafritz family among them. Foxhall Road gets its name from Henry Foxall (the "h" was mistakenly added later by road-sign makers), who was among the first in a now-long established Beltway breed: the defense contractor. He built the Foxall Ordnance Foundry between 1797 and 1800 along a tributary known as Foundry Run Creek (also called the Foundry Branch), just west of Georgetown. Here he manufactured cannon that allegedly were the deciding factor in the Revolutionary War battle of Lake Erie. Understandably, the British were eager to destroy the foundry when they sacked Washington in 1814. They never completed that aspect of their mission, and Foxall was so grateful that his foundry had been spared that he built the Washington Foundry Methodist Church on 16th Street to show his thanks that his prayers had been answered.

---

37 | Open to the Public | **American University (4400 Massachusetts Avenue, NW; 202/885–1000)**

The only university incorporated by the U.S. Congress, American University is one of Washington's largest and most dominant educational institutions. Occupying some eighty acres, the school was originally founded through the efforts of the Methodist Episcopal Church and its Bishop John Fletcher Hurst. The campus site was purchased in 1891, and two years later Congress officially incorporated the school as American University. The first building on campus, Hurst Hall, wasn't erected until 1898, and while awaiting the completion of its campus, the school held classes in Foggy Bottom, near the State Department (at 19th and F Streets, NW).

During World War I, the school donated the campus and its completed buildings to the war effort, and the Army turned the site into a training and testing ground for its "Gas and Flame Division." During this occupancy, the properties of the deadly gas lewisite were discovered by the division. After the war, the campus was returned to American University, which finally moved uptown to its own campus.

Among the American alumni who have gone on to greatness are film director Barry Levinson, writer Ann Beattie, and weatherman Willard Scott. And while no U.S. president has ever graduated from American University, the school has had its share of presidential appearances, most notably President John Kennedy's Commencement Speech on June 10, 1963, in which he stated his plans to seek nuclear test bans in the hopes of curbing the Cold War arms race with the Soviet Union. The closing words of Kennedy's plea for a safer world, free of nuclear dangers, ring as true today as they did then: ". . . is not peace, in the last analysis, basically a matter of human rights—the right to live out our lives without fear of devastation, the right to breathe air as nature provided it, the right of future generations to a healthy existence?"

From Champion's Washington D.C. Street Map © 1991 by Rand McNally, R.L. 91-S-96

The school made headlines that were far from healthy in 1990 when University President Richard Berenzen—known mainly as a tireless academic fundraiser and self-promoter—was arrested for making obscene phone calls about the sexual bondage of children from his private office on campus. Berenzen placed the very wrong number that exposed his problem in the spring of 1990, when he dialed the home of a police officer and began harassing the officer's wife. She listened carefully, taking notes and even encouraging him to call back (so the police could trace the calls).

Publicly exposed and in disgrace, Berenzen checked into a Baltimore clinic for sexual dysfunctions. AU tried to give Berenzen a golden parachute "bail-out," and almost gave in to his request that he be allowed to teach at the school. But student protests led the university to withdraw its purported million-dollar buy out and professorship, and Berenzen was cast adrift, a man who lost his life-line through the phone-line.

38 The Elms (Embassy of Algiers) (4040 52nd Street, NW)

This famous estate buried in the posh Foxhall neighborhood northwest of Georgetown was home to two major Washington powers: Perle Mesta, and later, Lyndon B. Johnson. Mesta, whose talent for entertaining won her the title of "Hostess with the Mostest," gained even greater fame after she was appointed by President Truman as the Minister to Luxembourg. Ethel Merman ended up starring in a broadway musical, "Call Me Madame," based on Mesta's diplomatic career.

Mesta was less than diplomatic with the Kennedys—in fact, her support of Lyndon Johnson in the 1960 Democratic primaries earned her persona-non-grata status at the Kennedy

White House. But LBJ apparently liked Mesta enough to buy The Elms as his vice-presidential mansion; he moved in in 1961, and lived at the estate until his unexpected ascendancy to the presidency in 1963. Mesta, meanwhile, made herself cozy in the S Street home formerly owned by Herbert Hoover. She died in 1975 at the age of 85.

The Elms now serves as the Embassy of Algiers.

See Also: Wardman Tower and **Herbert Hoover House**

---

39 Edward R. Murrow House (5171 Manning Place, NW)

The man behind the voice that pinned America to its radios during World War II, Edward R. Murrow, lived at this Spring Valley home from 1961 to 1963, during his tenure as the head of the U.S. Information Agency (USIA). Murrow was also renowned for his later landmark television and radio broadcasts, "Hear It Now," "See It Now," and "Person to Person."

---

40 Katherine Anne Porter's House (3601 49th Street, NW)

The renowned author Katherine Anne Porter lived in this private home from 1960 to the mid-1970s. While in her early years of residence here, she completed her only (but justly renowned) novel, *Ship of Fools*, which was published in 1962.

---

41 Nelson Rockefeller House (2500 Foxhall Road, NW)

This 1885 mansion was purchased by millionaire politician Nelson Rockefeller in 1941. Rockefeller lived here until 1956, then returned when he was named Gerald Ford's vice president in 1974. During Ford's tenure, the former Admiral's House on the grounds of the **Naval Observatory** was transformed into the **Vice President's House,** and Rockefeller became the first vice president to move into those new quarters, leaving his old house behind in 1975.

See Also: U.S. Naval Observatory and **Vice President's House**

PLACES: Glover Park

This little enclave was named for influential cultural activist and financier Charles Glover, who donated part of the land that became the adjacent **Glover-Archbold Park** to the city. Glover, who became president of Riggs Bank in the late nineteenth century, lived in a Lafayette Square townhouse—but his impact was perhaps greatest in Upper Northwest, for he played instrumental roles in the creation of the **Washington National Cathedral** and in the establishment of **Rock Creek Park.**

Like its sister neighborhood, Cleveland Park, Glover Park was once popular among the summer house set, who built rambling Victorians along the tree-lined streets here. With the advent of streetcar lines, Glover Park was transformed from a suburb of weekend homes to an in-town neighborhood with year-round residents. Most of the old summer houses are gone, replaced by clapboard houses, brick townhomes, and apartment buildings. But the neighborhood remains a calm and old-fashioned (if pricey) alternative to the rush and hustle of closer-in neighborhoods.

---

42 Glover-Archbold Park (Extends north to Massachusetts Avenue and south to the C&O Canal)

This narrow, 100–acre-long strip of nature was donated to the city by Charles Glover and Mrs. Anne Archbold in 1924. The southernmost area of the park, just above the C&O Canal, was once the approximate site of Henry Foxall's foundry, built along the Foundry Branch (also called Foundry Run Creek). The following description, which appeared in the 1937 WPA guidebook, *Washington: City and Capital*, describes the arboreal charm of the park, now, as it was then: "Throughout this area of woodland within the watershed of the Foundry Branch may be found some of the finest trees in the District of Columbia. Tremendous beech groves interspersed with stately elms and oaks as well as with broad stretches of grassland, afford picturesque reminders of the virgin territory on which the early settlers located more than 200 years ago. Their natural beauty makes of the grounds ideal picnic and camping spots."

See Also: Jackson Place Houses: 734 Jackson Place (Chapter 1); Foxall Foundry Site (Chapter 6); Washington Foundry Methodist Church (Chapter 9)

PLACES: Woodley Park

The National Zoological Park (although actually located within **Rock Creek Park**) is a major highlight of the neighborhood to the south and east of Cleveland Park and to the north of Kalorama. Like these nearby areas, Woodley Park is a place of quiet residential streets and magnificent apartment buildings.

43 **Kennedy Warren Apartment Complex (3133 Connecticut Avenue at Devonshire Place)**

One of the city's finest examples of Art Deco architecture, the Kennedy Warren continues to maintain an aura of 1920s glamour through its fine upkeep and ballroom events. Among the prominent Washingtonians to live here, perhaps the most famous was Lyndon Johnson, who shared an apartment with his wife at the complex in the late 1930s. During World War II, the Kennedy Warren swarmed with the wives of high-ranking officers stationed overseas.

The Kennedy Warren. (Jack Looney)

The Kennedy Warren takes its name from its original owners: Edgar Kennedy and Monroe Warren, Sr. The building was designed by Joseph Younger, who integrated aluminum as a decorative element both inside and out. The main section was completed in 1931; the only one of the two planned wings to actually be built was finished in 1935 as demand for apartments grew with the influx of the New Dealers.

44 Open to the Public **National Zoological Park (3000 Connecticut Avenue, NW; 202/673–4800)**

The National Zoo is a Washington landmark as famous for its "star" animals as for its design and layout. The zoo, operated as part of the Smithsonian Institution, opened on this site in 1889. Perhaps the most famous inhabitants of the zoo arrived here in 1972, when the Republic of China gave the United States a pair of rare Giant Pandas named Hsing-Hsing and Ling-Ling during President Nixon's visit to China. The pandas were an instant hit with zoo visitors. The glare of the public eye became ever more intense when the panda pair hit puberty, for zoo officials hoped to breed the rare couple (whose species is endangered), a complicated task in captivity. For more than a decade, pandaphiles breathlessly awaited news of panda

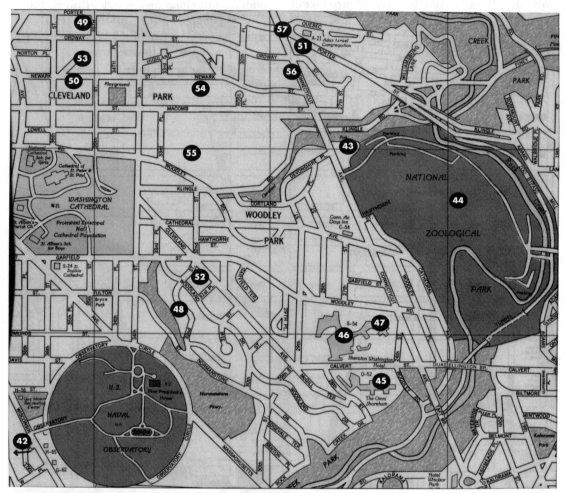

From Washington D.C. Visitor's Map © 1991 by Rand McNally, R.L. 91–S–96

progeny. Sadly, although Ling-Ling did manage to conceive a few times, none of the baby pandas lived more than a day or two, dying young from infection and other complications. Ling-Ling is now thought to be too old for motherhood. But all hope is not lost: Hsing-Hsing has contributed to the equivalent of a panda sperm bank, a deposit which, it is hoped, will successfully fertilize a younger female panda at another zoo.

Another famous inhabitant of the National Zoo is Smokey Bear, whose symbolic leadership in the fight against forest fires has inspired many a youngster to stamp out thoughtlessly-tossed cigarette butts. Today's Smokey (whose middle name is *not* "The," contrary to popular belief) is the symbolic namesake of the original Smokey—the little Brown Bear rescued from a roaring fire in New Mexico's Capitan National Forest in 1950, who lived at the zoo until his death in 1976.

Now gone from the park, but not forgotten by its once-loyal membership, was a unique dining organization called the "Anteater's Association." Founded in 1941, the club started by offering twice-weekly meals of big game delicacies at the zoo cafeteria during November and December. Soon, the luncheons had become so prestigious that more than 850 VIPs avidly awaited the yearly dining extravaganzas, which featured menus that ran the gamut from antelope to zebra (but excluded endangered species). When club founder Gordon Leech left his job at the zoo to open a restaurant in Maryland in the 1950s, the Anteater's Association turned up its nose and died.

The National Zoo came about through the efforts of Smithsonian Secretary Samuel P. Langley. The first residents of the zoo had originally been exhibited on the Mall—the result of a request by Smithsonian taxidermists for live models. The public soon became attached to the animals (the collection of which had grown to include 225 species by 1888), and plans were laid to create a permanent home for them on the outskirts of the city. The zoo's first head keeper, William Blackburne (of the Barnum and Bailey Circus, which wintered in the nearby Falls Church area of Virginia), borrowed a circus wagon and carted the zoo's first 185 animals from the Mall to their new home.

The zoo at first acquired animals quite slowly—a good thing, too, as the building of permanent animal housing dragged on for decades. In the 1920s, however, the zoo had the equivalent of an open (cage) door policy, when the Smithsonian-Chrysler expedition swelled the zoo's animal population by a third.

The zoo's administration building, Holt House, is listed on the National Register of Historic Places. According to the National Register, the present building dates from 1827. Other sources date the house to 1805 (diamond-etched writing on upper windows tell that the house was a popular summer retreat for President Andrew Jackson). In 1842, the house became the home of Dr. Henry Holt, a local physician. The house was sold to the Federal Government in 1890.

The first animal house completed at the zoo was the Lion House, which was finished in 1892. The Elephant House followed in 1903, but was torn down in 1938. The first permanent bird house opened in 1928, and the reptile house slithered into being in 1931. During the 1960s, the zoo opened its great flight cage, and buildings and complexes for hoofed animals.

The National Zoo has long been heralded for its excellence in animal environments as well as for its educational programs. It led the vanguard of the movement to build more natural habitats for animals, rather than just warehousing them in exhibit cages and houses. In fact, the site for the zoo was chosen for its mixed terrain of hills and valleys, woods and fields—a forward-thinking real estate selection that simplified the development of natural habitat enclosures in later years.

See Also: The Mall (Chapter 4)

---

45 | Open to the Public | **Omni Shoreham Hotel (2500 Calvert Street, NW; 202/234–0700)**

The old Shoreham Hotel (now run by Omni International) has loomed over Rock Creek Park and Connecticut Avenue with a daunting, even haunting presence since its opening in 1930. In fact, its opening gala was held on Halloween—and just for kickers, Rudee Vallee and his orchestra were flown in on a chartered plane to perform at the grand event. The hotel was one of the first in the city to become handicapped accessible when it installed ramps in 1932 so that President Roosevelt could attend functions at the hotel with ease. The hotel's Blue Room, now used as a conference hall, was once one of the swankest nightclubs in the city, drawing sold-out audiences to hear the likes of Judy Garland and Frank Sinatra.

See Also: Sheraton-Washington Hotel

---

46 | Open to the Public | **Sheraton-Washington Hotel (2660 Woodley Road, NW; 202/328–2000)**

This Harry Wardman masterpiece was originally known as the Wardman Park and was Washington's largest and grandest hotel when it arrived on the scene in the 1920s. The hotel that stands here today is still the largest—filling some twelve acres just off Connecticut Avenue—although it is not the original that stood for so long as a vanguard of Washington

luxury hotels. When Harry Wardman lost his fortune in the 1929 Stock Market Crash, the
Wardman Park was seized by creditors, along
with Wardman's other holdings (including the
equally luxe Carlton Hotel—now the Sheraton
Carlton—and the Chastleton). The Sheraton Corporation bought the Wardman Park and its
apartment annex in 1953, transforming the complex into the Sheraton-Washington. In 1978,
Sheraton began building an even more enormous
hotel at the site of the old Wardman Park. When
the new hotel opened in 1980, the old one was
torn down.

See Also: Omni Shoreham Hotel and **Wardman
Tower;** Sheraton Carlton (Chapter 7); Chastleton
(Chapter 9)

Ad from the B.F. Keith playbill
of Feb. 5, 1928.

**47 Wardman Tower (At the Sheraton-
Washington) (2600 Woodley
Road, NW)**

Now part of the **Sheraton-Washington
Hotel,** this luxury building designed by Mihran
Mesrobian was constructed in 1928 by Harry
Wardman as a residential annex to the adjoining
Wardman Park Hotel. Wardman lost his consid-
erable fortune and real estate holdings in 1929. Both the Wardman Park and its apartment
annex were purchased by the Sheraton Corporation in 1953.

According to James Goode's 1988 book on Washington apartment buildings, *Best Addres-
ses,* the Wardman Tower was home to more top-ranking government officials than any other
apartment building in Washington. The presidents who lived here included Lyndon Johnson,
Dwight Eisenhower, and Herbert Hoover, while vice presidential residents included Spiro
Agnew, Henry Wallace, and Charles Curtis. Writer and Congresswoman Clare Booth Luce,
Senator Barry Goldwater, Secretary of State John Foster Dulles, Senator Millard E. Tydings,
U.N. Ambassador (and two-time presidential candidate) Adlai E. Stevenson, Washington
socialite-turned-diplomat Perle Mesta, and Chief Justice Earl Warren were also among the
many greats who lived at the Wardman Tower apartments.

The Wardman Tower was originally known by a number of other names, including the
"Annex" and the "Eastern Wing" because of its linkage (via a long, windowed corridor) to the
Wardman Park Hotel. In 1978, the building was renamed in Harry Wardman's honor when
Sheraton launched a full-scale renovation of the building.

See Also: The Elms, Omni Shoreham Hotel, and **Sheraton-Washington Hotel**

PLACES: Cleveland Park

Named for President Grover Cleveland, who established a "Summer White House" at
Oak View, the Cleveland Park neighborhood was part of a much larger parcel of land
known as "Pretty Prospects," which was developed into smaller estates and land tracts by
its owners as the city crept upward. When streetcars reached the neighborhood in the
1890s, it was transformed from a warm-weather retreat to a year-round residential area.

Most of the original Victorian summer homes have since been replaced with smaller brick and clapboard houses and apartment buildings. The neighborhood continues to draw an impressive mix of old and new power and money, with residents running the gamut from writers and artists to congressmen, lawyers, and military officers.

(48) John Foster Dulles Home (2740 32nd Street, NW)

This was the last residence of the masterful Cold Warrior, who served as secretary of state under Eisenhower. Dulles lived here from 1953 until his death in 1959.
See Also: John Foster Dulles Birthplace (Chapter 3)

(49) Samuel Gompers's Second House (3501 Ordway Street, NW)

This was the only house that labor leader Samuel Gompers ever owned. He lived here from 1919 until his death in 1924. Gompers had previously lived in a rented house at 2122 1st Street, NW. In 1886, Gompers helped found the American Federation of Labor (AFL), and he remained its leader until his death. In 1933, the AFL erected a memorial to Gompers at the northwest corner of Pennsylvania Avenue and 10th Street.
See Also: Samuel Gompers's First House (Chapter 9)

(50) Oak View Site (3500 block of Newark Street, NW)

Oak View (also known as Red Top) was the "Summer White House" refurbished by President Grover Cleveland in 1868. Cleveland transformed the simple farmhouse into a Victorian summer home complete with wrap-around porches, and the wave of homes built here during the next decade reflected the same summer-mansion style. Most of these Victorian homes are gone now, with the exception of **Twin Oaks** on Woodley Road. Oak View itself became so dilapidated that by 1927 it was considered a blight on the neighborhood. It was razed, and a new brick home was built on the site. All that remains of Oak View is a wall, made from the house's original stones, that still stands just past the home that replaced it at 3518 Newark Street.
See Also: Rosedale; The White House (Chapter 1)

(51) Open to the Public The Park and Shop (Connecticut Avenue at Ordway)

This little old shopping plaza was actually the first "stop and shop" mall in the country, pioneering the idea of parking and then doing all the shopping in a central location. Arthur B. Heaton designed the mall, which opened in 1931, as a Colonial Revival tribute to America's love of retail. For the first time, a parking lot was combined with a slew of convenient and pleasant stores. Among these were a Piggly Wiggly, and the first discount Dart Drugstore. The Park and Shop was allowed to deteriorate for many years, but recent preservation efforts saved it from destruction. A new renovation completed in late 1991 has given the strip mall an updated appearance that preserves something of its venerable heritage as the stop-and-shop forebear of today's shopping malls.

(52) George S. Patton House (3117 Woodland Drive, NW)

World War II hero General George S. Patton lived in this house from 1928 to 1931 while working at an army desk job. Patton had previously lived nearby at **Rosedale.**
See Also: Rosedale

53 Rosedale (3501 Newark Street, NW)

Rosedale (also called Woodley) is one of the oldest houses in Washington. It was built around 1794 as the manor home for the estate of General Uriah Forrest. Forrest, a gentleman farmer, counted among his friends George Washington and Pierre L'Enfant—both of whom were probably guests here during the planning and building of the city. (L'Enfant is even rumored to have designed Rosedale's gardens.) Forrest was so dedicated to the city growing below his estate that he mortgaged Rosedale to raise money as a Capitol investment. Unfortunately, the mortgage-holding bank went under, and Rosedale was sold at auction to Forrest's brother-in-law, Philip Barton Key (whose young nephew, Francis Scott Key, spent many a summer's day here).

The mansion became a favorite summer place for presidents Martin Van Buren through Grover Cleveland, and went on to become the home of Colonel E. M. House (who lived here during the first World War), George S. Patton, (who lived here in the early 1920s), and Henry Stimson (Roosevelt's secretary of war, who bought the house in 1929). The property was purchased by the Maret School in 1940, which continues to use it as a campus.

See Also: George S. Patton House and **Oak View Site**

54 Tregaron (3100 Macomb Street, NW)

The land upon which Tregaron was built was once part of another influential Cleveland Park estate, **Twin Oaks.** The land for Tregaron was sold in 1911 by Gardiner Hubbard's son-in-law, Alexander Graham Bell, to financier James Parmelee. Parmelee named his estate The Causeway, and hired Charles Adams to design the house. When Joseph Davies bought the property, he renamed it Tregaron after his Welsh ancestral home. Davies served as Soviet Ambassador during the 1930s, and his wife, socialite and cereal heiress Marjorie Merriweather Post, was a famed hostess and fundraiser. The estate was split up in 1980, and half is still being developed, while the other half (including the manor house) belongs to the Washington International School.

See Also: Twin Oaks and **Hillwood;** National Geographic Society (Chapter 7)

55 Twin Oaks (3225 Woodley Road, NW)

The last remaining true Victorian in the area, Twin Oaks was built by Gardiner Greene Hubbard, the founder of the National Geographic Society. Frequent visitors included Hubbard's son-in-law, Alexander Graham Bell (whose telecommunications efforts were financed by Hubbard). The house was sold to the Chinese government in 1947.

See Also: Tregaron; Alexander Melville Bell House, Alexander Graham Bell Laboratory, and Volta Bureau (Chapter 6); Bell-Morton House, Bell Experimental School Site, Alexander Graham Bell House Site, and National Geographic Society (Chapter 7)

56 Open to the Public Uptown Theater (3426 Connecticut Avenue, NW; 202/966–5400)

The Uptown is a rare and vanishing breed: a genuine Movie Palace. Theater architect John Jacob Zink designed a true Art Deco wonder in the Uptown, from its streamlined aluminum awning to the geometric lines of its facade. The theater opened with a gala celebration in 1936, its premier film the now-forgotten "Cain and Mabel," starring Clark Gable and Marion Davies.

Now run by the Cineplex Odeon Company, the Uptown shows films worthy of its grandeur. When the revamped and uncensored *Spartacus* re-premiered at the Uptown in April of 1991, two of its stars—Burt Lancaster and Jean Simmons—were in attendance.

57 | Open to the Public | **Yenching Palace Restaurant (3524 Connecticut Avenue, NW; 202/362–8200)**

One of Washington's long-established Chinese restaurants, the Yenching Palace also played an important role in international relations, for it was here that the secret negotiations to end the Cuban Missile Crisis took place in 1962. Representatives for President Kennedy and Premier Kruschev held incognito talks here, and a potentially nuclear confrontation was averted. (Perhaps the won-ton soup made the difference?)

PLACES: North of the Cathedral

The neighborhoods north of the Cathedral are a mixture of ritzy new malls and restaurants, schools and parks, with residential pockets of quiet, tree-lined streets scattered throughout. The various neighborhoods, including Friendship Heights, Van Ness, Tenleytown, Chevy Chase, and Forest Hills, often got their names from long-gone estates or prominent citizens of these heights that were once located far into the countryside beyond Washington. A major section of the area between Wisconsin and Connecticut Avenues has been set aside for diplomatic development, and such countries as Israel (which has one of the most heavily fortified embassies in the city) have now placed embassies in this area.

58 **4701 Connecticut Avenue (Corner of Connecticut Avenue and Chesapeake Street, NW)**

This elegant 1927 apartment house, built by developer Harry Bralove, was home to Harry S Truman and his family from 1941 until April of 1945. Truman moved in as a senator from Missouri; by the end of his tenancy, he was vice president of the United States. His vice-presidency—and his tenancy at 4701 Connecticut Avenue—was cut short by the sudden death of President Franklin Roosevelt. The Trumans moved from this building to Blair House for a few day's transition, and then into the White House on May 7, 1945. The apartment in which the Trumans lived, Number 209, has a brass plaque on the door commemorating their residency.

See Also: Sedgwick Gardens; Blair House and the White House (Chapter 1)

59 **Fort Reno (Near 39th and Ellicott Streets)**

The remains of one of the sixty-eight forts that ringed Washington during the Civil War can be found here beneath the reservoir. (The city waterworks were placed here at the turn-of-the-century.) The placement of a fort here made perfect sense, as this is also the highest point in the city. Following the Civil War, this area became one of the city's largest settlements of black immigrants from the south. The Fort Reno area remained a black enclave until the mid-twentieth century, when mostly white development finally pushed even long-time black residents out of the neighborhood.

See Also: Fort De Russey; "The Civil War Forts of Washington" (Chapter 10)

60 | Open to the Public | **Hillwood (4155 Linnean Avenue, NW; 202/686–5807)**

The home of the late Marjorie Merriweather Post—the heiress to the Post cereal fortune—is one of the last great remaining estates in Washington. Hillwood was built during the Jazz era, and while the estate was well-known, it didn't truly come into its glory days until Post acquired it in 1955. Her grand lifestyle and the additions she made to the estate (including the landscap-

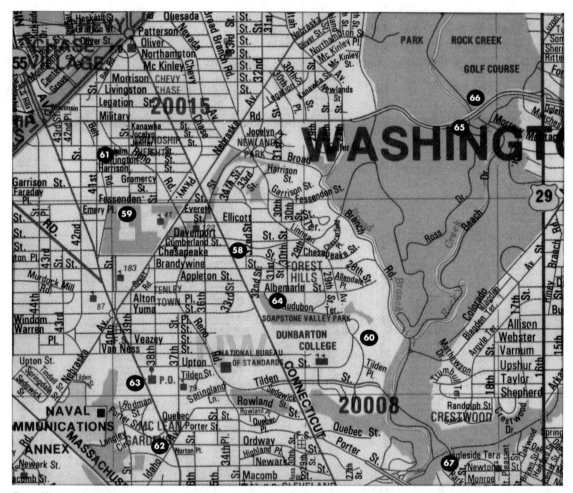

From Champion's Washington D.C. Street Map © 1991 by Rand McNally, R.L. 91–S–96

ing of formal Japanese and French Gardens, and the installation of a Russian dacha) made Hillwood the talk of Washington social and architectural circles.

Japanese garden on the grounds of Hillwood. (Jack Looney)

The forty-room, red brick Georgian mansion and its landscaped grounds can now be toured as a museum. (A film about Hillwood, narrated by Post's daughter, actress Dina Merrill, is included in the admission price). Post's personal fascination with Imperial Russia is evident in the displays of her collections of icons and other religious pieces, elaborate metalwork and porcelain, Faberge eggs, and even the royal dinner service of Catharine the Great.

See Also: Tregaron

61 | Open to the Public | **Randall Jarrell House (3916 Jenifer Street, NW)**

One of America's great poets, Randall Jarrell, lived at this house from 1956 to 1958 while working as a poetry consultant to the Library of Congress. Jarrell's experiences in Washington found their way into his writing, including his famous poem "The Woman at the Washington Zoo" (1960).

See Also: Library of Congress (Chapter 2)

---

62 **McLean Gardens (Friendship site) (3600 Wisconsin Avenue)**

McLean Gardens was built as a community for war workers during the Washington housing crunch of World War II. It was constructed by the federal government on the site of one of Washington's most renowned estates, Friendship.

Friendship had been so-named because of the congenial relationship between a pair of earlier landowners who between them owned about 3,000 acres in this area. The estate was best known during its tenancy by the McLean family. John McLean, the patriarch of the clan (and publisher of the Washington *Post*), died in 1919, passing the estate and the paper on to his son, Edward, and daughter in-law, Evalyn Walsh McLean. The couple, who also had houses in town, used Friendship as their country home, giving lavish entertainments and weekend parties here. They were a dazzling couple: She was the owner of the glamorous Hope Diamond and a leading society lady; he was publisher of the *Post* and a close friend of President Harding and his cronies. Edward McLean was so chummy with Harding that he even had an eighteen-hole golf course installed on the grounds of Friendship (importing the sod from Switzerland!) so that the president could play his (second) favorite game on the McLean's greens.

But all was not fun and games for the McLeans, especially at Friendship. Their cosseted young son, Vinson McLean, (dubbed the "million dollar baby" for the fortune he would inherit) was killed in a fluke traffic accident at the estate. The death of Vinson McLean was just the latest in a series of tragedies the family had experienced. Edward McLean's mother had died mysteriously only a few years before (amidst swirling rumors about the legendary curse of the Hope Diamond, which the lady had been handling soon before her death).

Meanwhile, through his friendship with Harding, Edward McLean became embroiled in the Teapot Dome scandal, which involved the illegal leasing of oil lands in Wyoming. The scandal, which would have brought down Harding himself had the president not died before the oil hit the fan, ruined McLean and his family. His marriage in tatters and his paper on the verge of bankruptcy, McLean was declared insane in 1931 and was committed to a Maryland mental hospital, where he died in 1947. The *Post* was sold to Eugene Meyer, whose daughter and grandson still own the venerable paper. And Friendship disappeared beneath the bulldozers; all that remains of the famous estate are the entry gates.

See Also: The Washington *Post* Building (Chapter 2); General Services Administration Building (Chapter 5); Walsh-McLean House, McLean House Site, and Teapot Dome Scandal House Site (Chapter 7)

---

63 **Sedgwick Garden Apartments (3726 Connecticut Avenue, NW)**

Built in 1931, this famous group of Art Deco luxury apartments was designed by Mihran Mesrobian, who also designed the **Wardman Tower** building. Harry S Truman and his family lived at Sedgwick Gardens in 1936. During World War II, tenants established a Victory Garden on the grounds.

See Also: Wardman Tower

64 Soapstone Valley Park (Connecticut Avenue and Linnean Streets, Audubon Terrace and Yuma Street)

This park has preserved a few of the strings of ancient soapstone quarrying areas where, some 2,000 to 5,000 years ago, local Native Americans mined stone to carve shallow vessels for cooking and eating. The largest of these quarries, Rose Hill, was discovered by archeologist William Henry Holmes in the early 1890s.

Holmes identified the soapstone (or, as the experts call it, steatite) quarries after examining the exposed rockbeds in the area, parts of which had already been commercially quarried for road paving. Holmes made the elementary discovery of old, pitted indentations—some as deep as six feet—dotting the crests of two hills every few hundred feet. After further study, Holmes theorized that the natives actually carved rough versions of the vessels while they were still attached to the stone face, then detached the cups and bowls and finished them back at the campsite.

Rose Hill was located just north of this park along Albemarle Road; it was later developed into the Forest Hill neighborhood. But the soapstone quarries in this park were preserved, along with several in Rock Creek Park. To this day, ancient pieces of soapstone vessels are sometimes unearthed here and along another major soapstone quarrying area: The cliffs overlooking the Potomac near the Chain Bridge.

See Also: Rock Creek Park

PLACES: Rock Creek Park

The Algonquin Indians once lived in this central section of Washington, fishing for herring and other species in the Rock Creek and hunting in the wilds of the hills and valleys. Evidence of the once-prevalent native population can be found in the soapstone (steatite) quarries on several hills, where tribes people once mined the rock to create cooking and serving vessels. Similar quarries can be found in **Soapstone Valley Park,** just west of Rock Creek Park.

Modern convenience came earlier to Rock Creek than to any other body of water—but only briefly, when, as legend has it, Robert Fulton tested a model of his revolutionary steamship, the *Clermont*, in Rock Creek. In 1807, he launched the full-scale version in the Hudson River, changing the course of shipping forever.

In 1890, Congress—at the urging of Charles Glover and other local business leaders—purchased the 1800 acres that form Rock Creek Park for the purposes of setting aside and preserving natural land within the rapidly developing urban landscape of Washington. President Theodore Roosevelt, probably the greatest outdoorsman to sit in the highest office, set the pace for recreation in the park, for he often escaped from the pressures of White House life by hiking through the park and fording the creek. He started a trend that continues to this day, as several fords are still popular crossing places along the Creek.

Over the years, the land has been developed for recreational purposes to include a golf course, nature trails, and bike and bridle paths. Two older historic sites have been preserved within the park—**Pierce Mill,** a working grist mill, and **Fort De Russey,** one of Washington's Civil War defenses. Another landmark within the park, the **Joaquin Miller Cabin,** was moved here from what is now Meridian Hill Park.

Winding through the park is Rock Creek Parkway, the road that drives some drivers mad with its shifting lanes and sudden right-of-way intersections, but nevertheless is one of the prettiest roads in the Washington area. Rock Creek Parkway was conceived by the 1901 McMillan Commission, not so much as an easy way to cut through the congested traffic of upper Northwest (as it has become today), but as a perfect driving experience. Elegant couples drove their Model A's through the park, as if they were out on a constitutional rather than behind the wheel of a car. These early road-trippers understood what some Washingtonians may have forgotten: Rock Creek Parkway is more about the pleasure of the trip than about the necessity of the destination.

65 | Open to the Public | ### Fort De Russey (Oregon and Military Roads)

When Washington became a city of forts during the Civil War, Fort De Russey was built as a northern defense. In 1864, President Lincoln was brought here for protective keeping when the Confederates were said to be on the verge of invading the capital city during the siege of Fort Stevens by General Early's forces.

See Also: Fort Reno; "The Civil War Forts of Washington" (Chapter 10)

66 | Open to the Public | ### Joaquin Miller Cabin (Beach Drive and Military Road)

The "Poet of the Sierras," as Joaquin Miller was known, lived in this cabin during the early 1880s while seeking government work in Washington. He later gained fame in England for his *Songs of the Sierras* (1871), and was only then embraced by America as a great poet. The cabin in which he lived was originally situated at 16th Street and Crescent Place, but was moved to this location when Meridian Hill Park (aka Malcolm X Park) was created at the site in the 1920s. Poetry readings and other literary events are now held in the cabin.

See Also: Meridian Hill Park (Chapter 9)

67 | Open to the Public | ### Pierce Mill (Tilden Street and Park Road; 202/426–6908)

The waterwheels of more than twenty mills once churned up and down the banks of Rock Creek Park, and eight of those mills operated within the bounds of Rock Creek Park. Only one remains. Washington's last operating grist mill was built by Isaac Pierce in the 1820s. The mill passed down through his family, but by the 1880s its old-fashioned millstone process had become outdated. Pierce Mill was purchased by the Federal Government when the parkland was acquired, and the mill continued to operate for another five years before being shut down. It was restored in the 1930s by the WPA, and was used to grind corn and flour for government cafeterias until 1958. The mill is now operated as a historic site, where visitors can watch the mill at work and purchase flour, grits, and cornmeal ground at the site. The carriage house of the old mill has been transformed into the Art Barn, a gallery exhibiting the work of Washington-area artists.

Chapter 9

UPPER NORTHWEST
16th Street and East

From 16th Street eastward, Upper Northwest is a decidedly different place than the neighborhoods to the west. While there are a few upper-middle-class neighborhoods, especially near the Maryland border, the heart of this section of Washington throbs in the inner-city neighborhoods in the lower eastern section.

Like neighborhoods to its west, Upper Northwest along 16th Street and to the east has its roots in tracts of gentry-owned land. Much of this area was originally part of a large estate called "Pleasant Plains," which stretched west to Georgetown.

The heart of the 16th Street plateau that looks down over D.C. is Meridian Hill, where a narrow and once very affluent wedge of a neighborhood traces the street up its sharp ascent. Meridian Hill gains its name from the area where Florida Avenue crosses 16th Street, which is believed to be the spot where the harder crust of the Piedmont Plateau gives way to the sandier, moister coastal plain on which most of Washington is built. The area has also been known as Columbia Heights, a name still attached to the neighborhood north of the park; Columbia College, now George Washington University (in Foggy Bottom), opened here originally in the 1820s. From 1888 to 1931, Mary Henderson, a Senate wife who lived in **Henderson's Castle,** almost single-handedly transformed this swath of 16th Street into an avenue of mansions.

Beyond Scott Circle, the true 16th Street Corridor begins. Bordered to the east by the Shaw neighborhood, and to the west by Dupont Circle, Adams Morgan, and Mount Pleasant, 16th Street is both a microcosm and a dividing line of race and class and culture. To the west, there is an eclectic mix of mostly white and hispanic middle- and lower-class neighborhoods. To the east, are the historic black neighborhoods of Shaw, and the adjoining areas of Logan Circle and LeDroit Park.

Seventh Street, once called Seventh Street Pike, is another main artery around which neighborhoods were built and commercial ventures crowded. One of the earliest major thoroughfares into Washington, the pike was constructed by a private company in 1820. Tolls were charged at gate-houses erected at Rock Creek Church Road (where a fire station now stands) and Piney Branch Road. (The toll-gate site is marked with a plaque identifying it as the closest point to the city of Washington reached by Confederate troops, under the command of Jubal Early.) Seventh Street changes its name to Georgia Avenue after it crosses "out of Washington" over Florida Avenue. Florida Avenue, called Boundary Road until 1890, was once the major northern boundary line between Washington and the Maryland suburbs.

The area south of the **Soldiers' and Airmen's Home** (around LeDroit Park and **Howard University**), long ago had a nasty reputation. Known as "Hell's Bottom" during the nineteenth century, the neighborhood was aswarm with saloons, gambling parlors, and houses of prostitution, especially after such dens of iniquity were pushed northward out of

Downtown in the 1880s and '90s. Hell's Bottom had gotten so hot with sin by 1891 that Congress passed a law prohibiting the sale of alcoholic beverages within a mile of the Soldiers' Home—so as to protect the elderly veterans from the temptations of fast living.

As 16th Street heads northward above these neighborhoods, it passes through Columbia Heights, with its middle-class houses and fascinating mix of churches. Rock Creek Park is a prominent neighbor, and it abuts 16th Street for much of its way. The street passes alongside the neighborhoods of Brightwood and Shepherd Park (the latter named for Boss Shepherd), as well as **Walter Reed Army Medical Center** before feeding out into one of the earliest of the modern, development-heavy Maryland suburbs, Silver Spring.

Most of the neighborhoods east of 16th Street have a history both triumphant and tragic, twice-scarred by riots and still struggling to be reborn. The neighborhood of Shaw, whose southern fringes include Logan Circle and its Victorian homes, was mainly farmland until the post-Civil War building boom swept through this section of the city, transforming it into a bustling enclave of markets and homes. Seventh Street Pike became an important avenue in Washington, and its side streets and alleys were popular settlements for the waves of European immigrants who flooded into the Eastern United States in the late nineteenth century.

Black families settled here too, and the ethnic diversity of the neighborhood lasted for a few years until the immigrant families slowly moved on. By the turn of the century, Shaw, which had effectively radiated out from this central Seventh Street corridor, was populated almost entirely by blacks. The neighborhood spread south to Logan Circle, which had appeared on L'Enfant's plans for the city as one of the original traffic circles, and north to the U Street corridor, which was to become one of the great black nightclub circuits on the East Coast.

The area has been hard hit by rioting, first in 1919 and again in 1968. The "Red Summer" riots of 1919 resulted from the racial tension sparked when returning black soldiers found they had been better treated in Europe than they were in America. Although bloody and destructive, these riots had little long-term impact. Indeed, within a few years, the neighborhoods had rebounded into their heyest-days yet, with the "Great Black Way" of U Street earning Shaw a national reputation as a center for black culture and talent. The 1968 riots, following the assassination of the Rev. Dr. Martin Luther King, Jr., were far more destructive, both in the breadth and impact of the violence. The twelve days of rioting destroyed much of black northwest, and to this day, the neighborhoods affected still live in the shadow of those violent days in April. The long-overdue arrival of the Green Metro Line in Shaw has at last sparked development and economic hope in a neighborhood long besieged by poverty and endless subway construction.

Northeast of Logan Circle is LeDroit Park. Originally developed into a neighborhood of mini-mansions for whites in the 1870s, it was promoted as the perfect compromise between city living and country leisure. One of the city's first truly planned neighborhoods—a nineteenth-century subdivision—the entire LeDroit Park development remained under private ownership until 1901. Around the turn of the century, LeDroit Park was transformed into an essentially black neighborhood, strengthening the black cultural explosion that was underway in nearby Shaw, especially along the U Street Corridor.

Just east of LeDroit Park is Howard University, the most prestigious black-oriented university in the country. Howard's history is one of triumph over racism, strength of will, and dedication to the development of intellect above all else.

Above Howard University are three remnants of older Washington—**McMillan Reservoir,** which once provided the water for the city, the **Soldiers' and Airmen's Home,** where old soldiers went to live and die (and presidents went to get out of the kitchen of Washington), and **Rock Creek Cemetery,** where such Washington notables as historian Henry Adams and local department store mogul Julius Garfinckle lie buried. The fringes of Upper Northwest are also dotted with other historic sites, including several Civil War forts, most notably **Fort Stevens,** and **Walter Reed Hospital,** home to the infamous old collection of the Army Medical Museum.

PLACES: 16th Street Corridor and Meridian Hill Area

Meridian Hill, the crown of 16th Street, was originally known as Peter's Hill, named for Robert Peter, the Mayor of Georgetown, who pieced together plots of land to build his estate there in 1760. In 1867, a land speculator named Isaac Messmore who had bought up much of the land on the hill, divided it into lots for building (the price: a mere 10–cents a square foot). The area was slow to develop at first, but by the turn of the century, the hill and the street became prime real estate for mansions and apartment buildings.

Thanks in part to the boosterism of Mary Henderson, of **Henderson's Castle,** nearly fifteen mansions were built along 16th Street. So, too, were such renowned places as the old **Cairo,** once a residential hotel before being redeveloped into apartments by Arthur Cotton

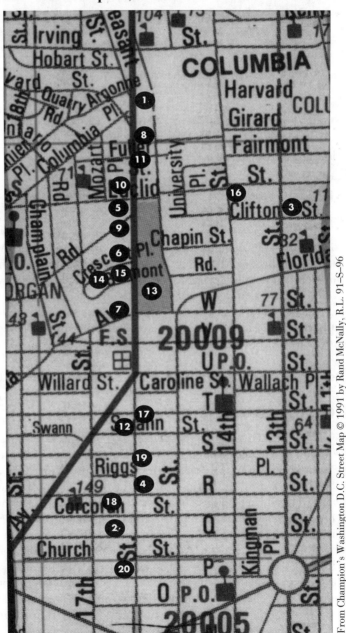

From Champion's Washington D.C. Street Map © 1991 by Rand McNally, R.L. 91–S–96

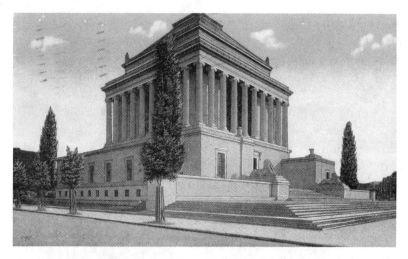

The Scottish Rite Temple, as shown on a 1920s postcard.

Moore; the Gothic **Chastleton Apartments;** and the Art Deco **Dorchester House,** where John F. Kennedy lived during a brief stint at the Office of Naval Intelligence. Further up on 16th Street, in the Columbia Heights neighborhood where George Washington University got its start, are a number of unique buildings, including John Russell Pope's **Scottish Rite Temple** and a trio of impressive churches. As 16th Street heads northward, it traces the border of Rock Creek Park and then continues on toward Maryland.

---

1 Open to the Public   **All Souls Unitarian Church (16th and Harvard Streets, NW; 202/332–5266)**

All Souls has an illustrious history of famous parishioners and pastors. Over the years, the congregation has included Presidents Millard Fillmore and William Howard Taft (Taft's funeral was held at All Souls as well), as well as John C. Calhoun, Daniel Webster, and Charles Sumner. Among those who served as pastors for the church were Transcendentalist Ralph Waldo Emerson, and author Edward Everett Hale.

This landmark church was built in 1924. Originally organized in 1821 as the First Unitarian Church, the congregation's first church was located at 6th and D Streets, NW. It moved in 1877 to 14th and L Streets, changing its name to All Souls Unitarian at that time.

Beekman Place Condominiums. *See* Henderson's Castle Site

---

2 The Cairo (1615 Q Street, NW)

The Cairo Hotel is the most renowned of the 2,000 some buildings built by Thomas Franklin Schneider throughout Washington. Built in 1894, the Cairo was originally a posh residential hotel serving the denizens of Downtown and Embassy Row. According to James Goode's 1988 *Best Addresses*, among the many elegant refinements offered at the original Cairo were an English basement featuring a bowling alley and billiards, and a rooftop garden where residents gathered to partake of refreshments and the view during the warm months. Visitors to the roof often tossed pebbles over the ledge to time their fall—causing carriages down below on Q Street to career out of control when the pebbles hit the street (lodging in wheels or frightening horses). The traffic accidents became so frequent that the police forced the hotel to close the open-air garden. Midway through the twentieth century, the building lost much of its luster and was nearly demolished, but was saved from that fate by its redevelopment into regular apartments in the mid–1970s. Arthur Cotton Moore oversaw the Cairo's transformation back to its former self. It re-opened as an apartment building in 1976 and was converted into condominiums three years later.

③ Calumet Place (Mount Pleasant Estate) Site (northeast corner of Clifton and 13th Street, NW)

A mansion known as Calumet Place once stood on this site. The house was erected in 1840, and was originally called Mount Pleasant by its builder, British native William Stone. Stone had come to Washington in 1815 to start an engraving business, but is probably best remembered as the bungling artisan who accidentally removed most of the original ink from the *Declaration of Independence* while engraving a copper plate to reproduce the document. Despite this mishap, Stone was one of the city's most eminent engravers, creating hundreds of architectural and city scenes of mid-nineteenth-century Washington. His son became a prominent physician who counted President Lincoln among his patients.

During the Civil War, Stone donated Mount Pleasant to the Union Army for use as a hospital, which came to be called "The Stone General Hospital." Following Stone's death in 1865, the property was sold to Ohio Senator John Sherman, who divided the land into separate tracts and built through-roads across the estate to make the area accessible for development. But the house itself remained intact, and was later owned by Senator John Logan, who renovated it and renamed the mansion "Calumet Place." Logan died in 1886, just a year after buying the house; his wife later rented the house out to a variety of Washington notables, including orator William Jennings Bryan. The house was torn down in 1925 and replaced by the Highview Apartments, but in remembrance of one its most famous occupants, the nearby Iowa Circle was renamed Logan Circle in 1930.

④ The Chastleton Apartments (1781 16th Street, NW)

Architect Philip Jullien designed this amazing Gothic Revival castle of an apartment building, which opened in 1920. For the first three years of its existence, it was the city's largest apartment building. The building passed through the hands of several owners before local hotel king Harry Wardman bought the Chastleton in 1926 and transformed a quarter of the units into hotel rooms. Wardman lost the Chastleton, along with his other posh hotel-apartment buildings, when the stock market crash of 1929 cleaned out his pockets and swept away his real estate.

Over the years, the Chastleton was home to a host of luminaries ranging from the soon-to-be Duchess of Windsor, Wallis Simpson, to an old soldier in his younger days, General Douglas MacArthur. During World War II, the residents of the building held protests when the Navy announced plans to take over the Chastleton as housing for WAVES (the Navy's version of the WACS). Finally, Secretary of the Navy Frank Knox chose to seek housing for his women's auxiliary elsewhere.

In the years that followed, the Chastleton continued to pass from owner to owner, becoming a transient hotel in 1946 before it was re-converted into apartments again in 1958. The building underwent its most recent renovation in 1986.

See Also: Sheraton Carlton Hotel (Chapter 7); Sheraton-Washington Hotel (Chapter 8)

⑤ Dorchester House (2480 16th Street, NW)

John F. Kennedy lived in Apartment 502 from October 1941 to January 1942, while serving as an ensign with the Office of Naval Intelligence. His residence was cut short when he was transferred out of Washington after becoming involved with Danish newspaperwoman Inga Arvad, who was suspected of being a German spy. JFK's older sister, Kathleen, who worked with Arvad on the *Herald-Tribune* then took over the apartment. Others to call the Dorchester home included golden-throated singer Eddie Fisher and Secretary of Labor Francis Perkins.

Then as now, Dorchester House was one of Washington's largest apartment buildings and featured the city's longest apartment building lobby. Constructed in 1941 by architect Francis Koenig, Dorchester House was built in a cross pattern that makes efficient use of space while remaining true to its geometric Art Deco roots.

See Also: Washington *Herald-Tribune* (Chapter 2)

6 The Envoy (2400 16th Street, NW)

Originally known as Meridian Mansions, this luxury complex cost just under a million dollars to build in 1919, making it the city's most expensive apartment building at the time. Residents of the building have included George Catlett Marshall, who lived here from 1919 to 1921 and went on to become army chief of staff during World War II, and writer Frances Parkinson Keyes, who lived here during the 1920s with her husband, New Hampshire Senator Henry Wilder Keyes.

By the late 1950s, the building was falling into hard times, like the surrounding neighborhood. In 1962, the controversial black New York Congressman Adam Clayton Powell tried to buy Meridian Mansions for use as housing for poor senior citizens. Neighborhood groups opposed the plan, and Powell finally abandoned his efforts when he fell from power amid allegations of financial corruption.

Shortly after the units were renovated and turned into condominiums in 1979, the building returned to a rental property.

7 Henderson's Castle Site (Beekman Place Condominiums) (Northwest Florida at 16th Street)

This elegant group of condominiums known as Beekman Place was once the site of an honest-to-good castle. Originally called Boundary Castle, because it was situated on Boundary Road (now Florida Avenue), the castle soon came to be known by the same name as its powerful owners, Mary Henderson and her husband, Missouri Senator John Brooks Henderson. The Hendersons moved to Washington for good in 1872, after the senator had already served his term and lost his bid for re-election. Although he was renowned for drafting the 13th Amendment, which abolished slavery, he was also roundly chastised for casting a "nay" on the vote to impeach President Andrew Johnson, and did not win re-election.

When the Hendersons decided to relocate to Washington permanently, Mary Henderson began casting an eye about for the perfect place for a palace. She found her pedestal, Meridian Hill on 16th Street, which was then farmland and estate country owned by a few landowners and speculators. The site offered a spectacular view of the city below, and of the White House in particular. With a valley like that, it seemed as if all of Washington were her fiefdom. In 1888, the main house of the castle was completed, and a servants' wing was added in 1892. Henderson's Castle had it all—turrets, a medieval gateway, and courtyard. And as for royalty, well—Mary Henderson (aka the "Queen of Sixteenth Street") lorded it like crazy over the servants and her family. Until her death in 1931, all female employees were required to dress demurely in ankle-length skirts.

Mary Henderson loved the view from 16th Street so much that she tried for years to have it renamed "Avenue of the Presidents." She pushed for the relocation of the White House to Meridian Hill, and even offered one of the homes she owned nearby to the government for use as the Vice President's Mansion. Through her efforts, too, Meridian Hill Park was built just across from her castle. And, in conjunction with her "personal" architect George Oakley Totten, Mary Henderson designed and built nearly fifteen mansions along the street, a real-estate speculation scheme aimed at bringing embassies and other wealthy Washingtonians to her hill. She may have been more driven by self-interest than by her interest in the good of the city. She didn't want noisy buses to come up 16th Street because she felt they would bring the wrong sort of people to her neighborhood, and she even tried to stop Harry Wardman from putting up his apartment buildings along 16th Street because she feared they would obstruct her view of the White House.

Despite her reputation as the ultimate Washington sophisticate, the Queen of Sixteenth found herself the star of one of Washington's great scandals when she tried to disinherit her granddaughter. It began when Henderson's only heir, her granddaughter Beatrice Henderson Wholean, tried to have her grandmother declared insane, for fear that the old woman would give away all her property. (Mrs. Henderson was offering one of her nearby mansions to the government for use as the vice president's house.) Mary Henderson fought back with a bitter disinheritance battle, revealing that her granddaughter had been adopted by her son, and therefore was not a blood relative. Henderson died in 1931 at the age of ninety, leaving her entire estate to her Japanese secretary. Beatrice Wholean contested the will, and eventually settled out of court for the bulk of the estate.

After Mrs. Henderson's will was straightened out, the furnishings and artifacts of the mansion were sold in 1935. Until it was razed in 1949, the castle served as a boarding house. The fortress-like stone columns which serve as the entrance to the Beekman Place condos are all that remain of the castle.

Henderson-Totten Houses

Mary Henderson and her faithful architect, George Oakley Totten, transformed 16th Street into an avenue of rich architecture in the hope that it might become the best address in town. Among the amazing buildings this pair put up here:

8 **2801 16th Street** (part of the Mexican Embassy complex): Built in 1923, when Mrs. Henderson still had high hopes about Meridian Hill becoming the new seat of power, this was the house she offered the government for use as the vice president's mansion. The building was also the site of the Spanish Embassy before becoming annexed as part of the Mexican Embassy complex.

9 **Embassy of Ghana Chancery** (2460 16th Street, NW): The first Henderson and Totten collaboration in their bid to redesign 16th Street was this house, now the Embassy of Ghana Chancery.

10 **Inter-American Defense Board** (2600 16th Street, NW): The so-called "Pink Palace" of the Inter-American Defense Board is another prominent house built by the team of Henderson and Totten. It is a pink stucco confection that was originally occupied by Oscar Straus, Teddy Roosevelt's Secretary of Commerce and Labor, and later by Mrs. Marshall Field, department store queen, before serving a long stint as the local headquarters of Order of the Eastern Star.

11 **Warder-Totten House** (2633 16th Street): George Oakley Totten believed in recycling building materials nearly a century before it became environmentally correct. This house, which was his own home, was rebuilt from the remnants of an earlier building, designed by H.H. Richardson, that had stood at 1509 K Street, NW until it was razed in 1923. The only Richardson house surviving in Washington, this home was built in 1855 for Benjamin H. Warder, a magnate who made his money manufacturing farm tools. The house is listed on the National Register of Historic Places.

12 Charles Evans Hughes's First House (Embassy of Bulgaria) (2100 16th Street, NW)

Now the home to the Bulgarian Embassy, this house was built by Charles Evans Hughes in 1910. A leader in the Progressive Movement, Hughes was appointed an Associate Justice to the Supreme Court in 1911. He lived here while serving that first stint on the high court; but in 1916, Hughes sold the house, hung up his robes, and ran for president. He lost (barely) to Woodrow Wilson.

See Also: Charles Evans Hughes House (Chapter 8)

13 | Open to the Public | Meridian Hill (Malcolm X) Park (16th Street, between Florida Avenue and Belmont Road)

Having failed to convince Congress to relocate the White House to this twelve-acre slice of real estate, Henderson successfully lobbied for the purchase of the land as a public park. Congress voted to pay Mrs. Henderson $490,000 for the land in 1910 and construction began on the park in 1917. Nineteen years, one landscaper (George Burnap), and an architect (Horace

Meridian Hill (Malcolm X) Park. (Jack Looney)

Peaslee) later, the park was completed and opened to the public in 1936. The park features a graduated cascade of waterfalls meant to denote the site as the fall line (meridian) of the nation's capital. The park has been officially renamed for the slain black power activist Malcolm X, a hero to many of the blacks who live nearby.

The upper terrace of the park was the site of the first campus of George Washington University, then called Columbian College. The college buildings, erected in the 1820s, were later used during the Civil War as hospital wards for Union wounded. This was also the site of an early black college, Wayland Seminary, which was established here in 1865 and moved to Richmond, Virginia, twenty-five years later.

See Also: Henderson Castle Site; George Washington University (Chapter 5)

Meridian House International Complex (Crescent Place):

This block of famous houses is home to Meridian House International, an organization that promotes and presents cultural events to the area's international community and visiting dignitaries:

14 Laughlin House (1630 Crescent Place, NW): Since 1961, this townhouse has served as the main administration building to Meridian House International. John Russell Pope built the house in 1915 for former U.S. Ambassador to Spain and steel heir Irwin Boyle Laughlin.

15 White-Meyer House (1624 Crescent Place, NW): Built by John Russell Pope three years before the Laughlin House, the White-Meyer House was the home of career diplomat Henry White, who served as ambassador to France. The house was later occupied by Washington *Post* publisher Eugene Meyer. For a time, it was used by the Antioch School of Law.

16 Olympia Flats (SE corner of Euclid and 14th Streets, NW)

In honor of Admiral George Dewey's victory at Manila Bay during the Spanish-American War, this 1898 building was named for the U.S.S *Olympia*, Dewey's flagship.

Perhaps the most prominent tenant of the apartment building was Ambrose Bierce, the jaunty if jaundiced newspaperman best known for *The Devil's Dictionary* (1906). Bierce came to Washington to write features for the Hearst papers, and was soon a Newspaper Row regular. He left Washington in 1913 to find himself (or so it seemed) in Mexico during the Mexican Revolution, and disappeared, never to be heard from again.

17 Roosevelt Hotel for Senior Citizens (2101 16th Street, NW)

The Roosevelt was originally a luxury apartment complex, one of several Harry Wardman erected on the 16th Street corridor. (The **Chastleton** and 2001 16th Street are also Wardman buildings.) Built in 1919, the Roosevelt was popular with members of Congress. From the 1920s through the mid-1950s, the Roosevelt Ballroom drew crowds to hear performances by the likes of Benny Goodman, Nat King Cole, and Ray Charles. But the posh place fell on hard times, and was closed in 1956 because of plumbing problems. In 1963, the Roosevelt was transformed into housing for the elderly.

See Also: Chastleton Apartments

18 Elihu Root House Site (1626 R Street, NW)

This site was once home to Elihu Root, who served as President Theodore Roosevelt's Secretary of State, and later, of War. Root moved often during his Washington years, also living on Lafayette Square, and in the Bell-Morton House just a few blocks south on Scott Circle.

See Also: Jackson Place Houses: 722 Jackson Place (Chapter 1); Bell-Morton House (Chapter 7)

19 Scottish Rite Temple (1733 16th Street, NW)

Also known as the House of the Temple, this true stop-and-stare John Russell Pope building is the final resting place of a famous Washingtonian: Albert Pike, the poet, adventurer, and scholar of Freemasonry who died in 1891 is interred in the crypt within the temple. Although Pike's will instructed that his remains be cremated and his ashes sprinkled among the acacia trees that grew in front of the first Temple of the Supreme Council of Freemasonry, the Temple Council thought it best that he be interred at Oak Hill Cemetery in Georgetown. But in 1944, Pike was re-interred in the crypt of the new temple building. To this day, he is said to haunt the building, perhaps in search of his acacia trees.

The cornerstone was laid in 1911, and the Masonic temple was dedicated in 1915. Pope designed the building as an ode on a Grecian shrine (one major influence was the Mausoleum of Halicarnassus, one of the Seven Ancient Wonders of the World). A closer look reveals the temple to be an early variation on the theme he would carry to even greater heights in his masterpiece, the Lincoln Memorial.

See Also: The Lincoln Memorial (Chapter 4)

20 Washington Foundry United Methodist Church (1500 16th Street, NW)

A church built on a prayer answered by a thunderstorm, the Washington Foundry United Methodist Church was originally built in 1815 at 14th and G Streets. It was given to the city by local foundry owner Henry Foxall, whose Foxall Ordnance Foundry west of Georgetown was a known target of the British during their invasion of Washington in August of 1814. Foxall anxiously awaited the enemy attack on his famed cannon factory, all the while praying that if God would spare his foundry, he would build a church in thanks. Before the enemy could make it to Georgetown, a massive thunderstorm struck, forcing the sackers to retreat before doing in the foundry. Foxall immediately went to work on his end of the deal by building the Foundry Chapel.

The church instantly became the presidential pulpit of choice, as President Madison attended soon after the church was completed. President Hayes and his wife also attended the church, walking over every Sunday morning from the White House.

The original church was razed to make way for a larger one (with pews to seat 1,200) during the Civil War. The building costs were so expensive that the church was forced to raise money by selling off its private cemetery lot (which was once located one block southeast of today's Meridian Hill Park) as real estate, moving the more than 1,500 graves to the Glenwood Cemetery in Northeast. In 1902, the second Foundry Methodist Church was razed to make way for an office building, and the congregation relocated to this site.

See Also: Epiphany Church (Chapter 2); Foxall Foundry Site (Chapter 6); Glenwood Cemetery and "The Burning of Washington" (Chapter 10)

PLACES: Shaw

When it first became a real neighborhood, Shaw was colloquially known as "Fourteenth and U," after the busiest intersection in the area. But slowly the name Shaw (adapted from nearby Shaw Junior High School) came into common usage. The school from which Shaw got its name was itself named after a Civil War hero, a young white Colonel named Robert Shaw, who died while leading his black regiment against the Confederate Army in a suicide mission. The story of Colonel Shaw and his regiment, the 54th of Massachusetts, was later depicted in the 1990 film *Glory*.

The neighborhood was slowly transformed from an immigrant enclave to a black social center, with the theaters and dinner clubs of the U Street corridor drawing blacks and whites alike to hear the great jazz musicians and singers of the 1920s and 1930s. Not only was Shaw a showcase of black talent; it was also a testing ground for the non-violent methods of the Civil Rights movement. During the 1930s, a group of black activists led by Howard University professor John Aubrey Davis led a fight against the discriminatory hiring practices of neighborhood establishments. The group became known as the New Negro Alliance, and their battlefield became Shaw, where they staged protests at neighborhood stores and restaurants that hired only whites but served mainly blacks.

The New Negro Alliance picketed establishments ranging from Mom and Pop groceries to larger targets like the High's Ice Cream Store and Peoples Drug Stores. The establishments tried to shake off the protesters, but to no avail—in some cases, the protests continued unabated for several years. The targeted companies gleefully thought the Alliance had met its match when the Sanitary Grocery Company (now known as Safeway) at 11th and U Streets got an injunction against the protesters to stop them from picketing the store. But the Alliance fought the injunction all the way to the Supreme Court, winning a surprising, dramatic decision in 1938 that affirmed the Alliance's rights to use protest as a means of exerting consumer pressure against companies that refused to employ blacks. *New Negro Alliance v. Sanitary Grocery* set a precedent that was built upon in later decades, culminating in the successful non-violent protests of the 1960s civil rights movement.

Ironically, the antithesis of these non-violent protests—the race riots of 1968—destroyed much of Shaw. After local landmarks, stores, and homes burned, there followed tough economic times that stymied what efforts there were to rebuild. The 1970s saw a recession, and the 1980s and early 1990s found the area hard hit by violent crime, drug abuse, low employ-

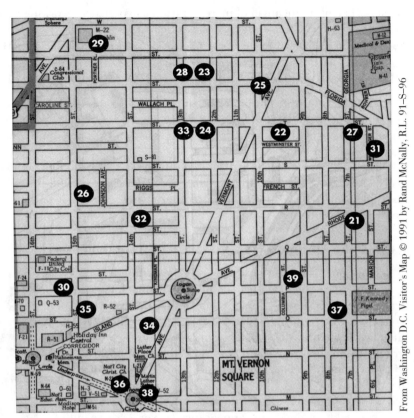

From Washington D.C. Visitor's Map © 1991 by Rand McNally, R.L. 91-S-96

ment, and high illiteracy, all contributing to the continued erosion of a once-great neighborhood. The worst may be over, however, as the long-awaited arrival of Metro's Green Line, which was heralded with a day of parades and speeches in May of 1991, is already stimulating new business development in the area.

㉑ Asbury Dwellings (Old Shaw Junior High School) (Rhode Island Avenue at Seventh Street, NW)

This huge Romanesque edifice was originally built in 1902 for use as the Technical High School (where white students learned vocational trades). The school was later renamed McKinley Technical, then finally turned over to the local school district for use as a black school, Shaw Junior High School. This school, which gave its name to the whole neighborhood, remained in use until the late 1970s, when the New Shaw Junior High School opened at Rhode Island Avenue and Tenth Street. Debates raged over whether the dilapidated old Shaw school should be demolished, but community activists managed to raise more than six million dollars to renovate the site as the Asbury Dwellings, where handicapped and elderly Washingtonians have found a much-needed home.

㉒ Clara Barton House (926 T Street, NW)

Clara Barton bought this house in 1878, but rented it out to others until 1886, when she finally moved in. She lived here until 1892, and then moved on, renting it out again to other tenants. The ultimate angel of mercy, Barton's experiences working as nurse during the Civil War inspired her to found the American Red Cross in 1881.

See Also: Clara Barton's Boarding House (Chapter 2); American Red Cross National Headquarters (Chapter 5)

---

23 | Open to the Public | **Ben's Chili Bowl (1213 U Street, NW; 202/667–0909)**

This restaurant was built on the site of the Minnehaha Theater, the city's first silent movie house, which opened in the early 1900s. Its facade is still clearly visible behind the restaurant sign, and the back dining room of Ben's is called the Minnehaha Room, in commemoration of its theatrical forebear.

The Chili Bowl opened in 1958, and its cheap and heaping chili dogs are legendary, as is its clientele. When in Washington, comedian Bill Cosby considers himself a regular—he even took his future wife, Camille, on secret dates here before their parents approved of the courtship.

---

24 **Duke Ellington Home (1212 T Street, NW)**

This house is typical of the turn-of-the-century townhomes occupied by Shaw's middle-class black families. It was the boyhood home of one of the country's greatest jazz composers and performers, Duke Ellington (born Edward Ellington). Ellington, who was born in 1899 at his grandparents' home on 22nd Street, lived here until the age of twenty-one, when he and his band, the "Washingtonians," headed for New York. Ellington attended local public schools, where he got his nickname from schoolmates who noticed his almost regal attention to his appearance (never a crease out of place or a spot to be seen on his wardrobe). He dropped out of high school to pursue piano lessons, and spent his adolescence playing in the numerous clubs and theaters for which the neighborhood was renowned. At the age of twenty-one, he and, the "Washingtonians," packed up and headed for New York, where they quickly made a name for themselves, soon playing the Cotton Club and the Apollo Theater. But Ellington never forgot his hometown—he often returned to play at the theaters along the Great Black Way.

Duke Ellington's boyhood home. (Jack Looney)

See Also: Howard Theater

---

25 | Open to the Public | **Evans-Tibbs House (1910 Vermont Avenue, NW; 202/234–8164)**

Wilson Bruce Evans, a leader in black education who served as the principal of the Armstrong Technical High School, purchased this house in 1904. The house was passed on to his daughter, Lillian Evans-Tibbs, who rose to stardom as the first truly world-renowned black opera singer. Lillian Evans-Tibbs (she married her singing coach, Roy Tibbs) performed under the stage name Madame Evanti, playing in opera houses around the world—but she still called the house on Vermont Avenue home. The Evans-Tibbs House, built in 1894, now serves as a museum and archive of historical materials on development and achievements of Washington's black community.

26 | Open to the Public | **Fifteenth Street Presbyterian Church (1705 15th Street, NW; 202/234–0300)**

The congregation of the Fifteenth Street Presbyterian Church has a remarkable heritage in black history. The church was first established in a school building on Fifteenth Street (between I and K Streets) in 1841 by John F. Cook, a black educator and leader who was the city's first black Presbyterian minister. Cook's sons, also community leaders, carried on their father's legacy of religious and educational excellence. In fact, the roots of Washington's black public schools were planted in the basement of the Fifteenth Street Presbyterian, with the establishment there of the Preparatory High School of Negro Youth in 1870. The school was the first high school for blacks in the nation, and its enrollment during the first year was a mere four students. (Dunbar High School, formerly the M Street School, is a direct descendant of this first institution.)

The Fifteenth Street Presbyterian has other claims to fame as well. Francis Grimke, the famous abolitionist, served as the church's pastor for more than fifty years, and his wife, Charlotte, helped found the Colored Women's League, which was operated out of the church, and was the first such national organization for black women in America.

In 1866, civil rights history was made when the Convention of Colored Men met at the church and drafted a formal request that Congress pass legislation promising "impartial suffrage" to all citizens, regardless of their ethnicity. When the convention's request was made public, white hardliners were indignant that blacks, so newly freed from slavery, were already demanding the right to vote.

The Fifteenth Street Presbyterian Church took over the former home of the Christian Science Church in 1918, and it was on this site that the Fifteenth Street Presbyterian Church built its new home in 1979.

---

27 **Howard Theater (624 T Street, NW)**

The theater where the "Great Black Way" was born is now a dilapidated shell of its former self, although restoration is at last underway and there are plans to re-open. The Howard officially opened its doors in 1910, with a premier list of performers that included Washington's own Abbie Mitchell, who went on to star in "Porgy and Bess" on Broadway.

The Howard was soon considered second only to New York's famed Apollo Theater. Its success sparked a growth industry in black theaters along the nearby U Street corridor during the next two decades.

The Great Black Way

As a key stop on the "Chitlin Circuit"—the highest echelon of the black entertainment circuit—the U Street Corridor often had more stars on stage than could be seen on a clear night in the skies overhead. Eubie Blake, Pearl Bailey, Duke Ellington, Ella Fitzgerald, Sammy Davis Jr., The Supremes, Smokey Robinson—virtually every major black entertainer (and more than a few white performers) of the twentieth century played here at one time or another. Large theaters such as the Howard, which started it all, regularly drew standing-room-only crowds, while clubs like the Poodle Dog Cafe, and social organizations like the True Reformers Hall, were other popular venues for local talent hoping for a big break. And what talent was born at these clubs! Pearl Bailey first danced on stage at the Jungle Inn at 12th and U Streets, Harry Belafonte started his career at a restaurant in the same block, and the teenaged Duke Ellington and his band had their first gig at the True Reformers Hall, which often held dances during World War I.

Nightclubs like the Jungle Inn, the Parrot Room, and the Bohemian Caverns stood shoulder to shoulder with the Club Bengasi, the Capitol Pleasure Club, the Casbah, and dozens of other cabarets. The combination of so many theaters with so many great performances earned the U Street Corridor its nickname, "The Great Black Way."

The Howard was a magnificent theater, with its ornate architecture that blended Beaux Arts flair with Italianate elegance. The theater featured seats for 1200, and a backstage dressing area that could accommodate dozens of performers. At a time when the city's white theaters rarely, if ever, booked blacks—and never allowed them to share the theater with white patrons—the Howard not only booked white performers, but often drew white audiences. But when the stock market crashed in 1929, so too fell the fortunes of the Howard Theater. It closed as a public theater that year, and was leased for two years as an evangelical revival hall. The Howard re-opened as a theater in 1931, under new management (including the brilliant booking skills of Shep Allen, who was soon to gain the nickname "D.C.'s Dean of Showbiz"). The inaugural performance was a no-holds-barred show by local hero Duke Ellington. Ellington was to return again and again to the Howard in the decades to come, while such greats as Billy Taylor, Billy Eckstein, Lena Horne, Ella Fitzgerald, Sarah Vaughn, as well as the mostly white big bands of Artie Shaw and Woody Herman headlined at the Howard through the 1940s. Sammy Davis, Jr. and Bill "Bojangles" Robinson also entertained spellbound audiences with their dancing, and such sports superstars as Jackie Robinson, Joe Louis, and Sugar Ray Robinson showed up on the stage from time to time to try their hand at stand-up comedy, or to emcee gala performances.

The theater also saw the debuts of Diana Ross and the Supremes, who played their first theatrical engagement at the Howard in October of 1962. And Pearl Bailey got her "big break" here; she danced as a Howardette showgirl, having been stage-struck at an early age after seeing Ethel Waters perform at the Howard.

When the 1950s rolled in and out, rock and roll seized the day and the stage. The big bands and jazz combos made way for Smokey Robinson, Martha and the Vandellas, Johnny Mathis, Patti LaBelle, James Brown, Marvin Gaye, and virtually every other major black performer of the times. But as the city and the country changed, theaters that had once been all-white were desegregated, while television, home stereo systems, and other personal amusements began siphoning off the once-avid audience of young and eager fans who had filled the Howard for six decades. In 1970, the Howard Theater was closed; a revival effort a few years later failed to draw the promised crowds, and the theater never regained its once-stellar role in the musical and cultural life of Washington's black community.

See Also: Duke Ellington Home, Lincoln Theater, and **"The Great Black Way"**

28 Lincoln Theater (1215 U Street, NW)

In its heyday in the 1920s and 1930s, the Lincoln was one of three movie palaces along the U Street Corridor. The 1,600–seat theater drew crowds to see first-run films, and, in the silent era, to hear the renowned playing of the theater's organist, Louis Brown, who accompanied the films on a Manuel Mohler organ.

The Lincoln also drew some controversy—in 1939, Howard University student activists picketed the theater during its run of *Gone with the Wind*. The protestors, led by Ralph Bunche (who later became the first black recipient of the Nobel Peace Prize), were infuriated that a theater serving the black community would show a film romanticizing the Southern side of the Civil War. The protesters boycotted the film and picketed the theater, often engaging audience-goers in heated debates about the content of the film. Although unsuccessful, the boycott was another indication that politically savvy blacks were becoming practiced at non-violent protest.

Gala events were sometimes held at the Lincoln as well: A March of Dimes rally, attended by First Lady Eleanor Roosevelt and boxing champ Joe Louis, attracted stellar crowds. And just behind the theater itself was a swank dance hall, The Lincoln Colonnade, the site of some of Shaw's most elegant balls and banquets.

The Lincoln Theater. (Jack Looney)

The Lincoln Theater opened in 1922 under the operation of Harry Crandall, who operated many of Washington's finest theaters, including the infamous Knickerbocker Theater. Five years later, the Lincoln was sold to the owners of the **Howard Theater.** Two other movie palaces shared U Street with the Lincoln—the Booker T. Theater (which once stood at the site of the Reeves Center for Municipal Affairs) and the elegant Republic Theater (which stood in the 1300 block of U Street), one of a chain of black theaters in the Washington area. Both were torn down in 1976, while the Lincoln has only survived through strenuous community efforts, often stalled, to renovate it for use as a performing arts complex.

See Also: Howard Theater; Knickerbocker TheaterSite (Chapter 8)

---

29 ⬛ Open to the Public ⬛ **St. Augustine's Catholic Church (1419 V Street, NW; 202/265–1470)**

This imposing neo-gothic church is home to the oldest black Catholic congregation in Washington. Founded in 1858 by a group of freed slaves, St. Augustine's originally occupied a chapel on 15th Street (between L and M Streets). In the 1860s, funds were raised to build a permanent church, which was opened in 1867 at the site of the present-day Washington Post Building. When the church was demolished in 1948, the congregation moved on to an interim church. Then in 1961, it joined forces with St. Paul's Catholic Church, which has been on this site since 1893. While St. Paul's congregation consisted mainly of whites and St. Augustine's mainly of blacks, the combined congregation is now predominantly, but not exclusively, black.

See Also: Washington *Post* Building (Chapter 2)

---

30 ⬛ Open to the Public ⬛ **St. Luke's Episcopal Church (1514 15th Street, NW)**

St. Luke's was built in 1879 by Calvin T. S. Brent, Washington's first black architect of note, who constructed the church using locally quarried bluestone. The church was founded by Reverend Alexander Crummell, whose passionate pulpit style and indomitable support of black rights was legendary throughout the eastern U.S. Legend had it that Crummell's father was an African king, sold into American slavery. Crummell's own regal bearing seemed to support just such a heritage, and he pursued a British education (graduating from the prestigious Queens College in Cambridge in 1853) to further his ability to lead his people. He established St. Luke's as the first black, independent Episcopal church in Washington, and later went on to head the American Negro Academy, an elite organization of black leaders. His church also went on to make history: It is now one of the oldest remaining churches in Washington built for a black congregation.

Shaw Junior High School. *See* Asbury Dwellings

Washington Riots

Washington has seen some of the most violent riots in the country's history. The riots of the nineteenth century erupted when the white majority began to fear that the growing awareness and education of blacks was threatening the status quo. The first of two major riots, the "Snow Riot" of 1835, bubbled up over white resentment that blacks were becoming educated and gaining the ability to purchase their freedom. The rioters attacked a boarding house/school run by a freed black man named Beverly Snow (who was luckily nowhere to be found at the time). The second riot, referred to as the "Pearl Riot" or the "Drayton Affair," occurred in 1848. On this occasion, angry crowds attacked the offices of the abolitionist *New National Era* paper after a Captain Drayton and his compatriots tried to spirit a number of Washington slaves to freedom aboard their vessel, *The Pearl.* (The ship was becalmed in the Potomac and the slaves recaptured.) There was one later riot of note in that century: The Know-Nothing Riots of 1857 at the Northern Liberties Market (now Mount Vernon Square), during which the archly conservative political party, the Know Nothings, hauled out a cannon to engage in a fight at a polling place in the public market.

The riots of the twentieth century have been exponentially worse than those of the previous century. There have been three of note in this century, two of which (the riots of 1919 and 1968) took place east of 16th Street; the third, the Cinco de Mayo riots of 1991 in Mount Pleasant, roared up and down 16th Street but were mainly contained to the west.

In the summer of 1919, a maelstrom of racial and social tensions began bubbling to the surface. Black veterans, trying to readjust to life in the U.S., were distraught that they were once again being treated as second-class citizens in their homeland. (They had been hailed as heroes in less-racially divided Europe.) Whites, threatened by the heightened sense of self-worth that many black soldiers had gained during the war, became increasingly nervous and reactionary. The white media sensationalized black crimes, while blacks grew more and more frustrated by the hard-line segregation policies of the Wilson Administration. White soldiers began roving the streets of black neighborhoods as if martial law had been declared. In July of 1919, the tension exploded, touching off riots and mob attacks by both blacks and whites. More than twen-

---

31 Waxie Maxie's (Quality Music Shop) Site (1836 7th Street, NW)

This empty lot was once the site of a musical landmark not only for Shaw but for the whole country: Waxie Maxie's, the pre-eminent record store for those who loved jazz and blues. The store opened in 1938, and was an instant mecca for neighborhood kids and music mavens alike. Major talents such as Sarah Vaughn, Buddy Rich, and Margaret Whiting, in town to perform on the Great Black Way, broadcast live radio performances from the store. Among those who regularly haunted the store to hear the latest music and hottest new performers was Ahmet Ertegun, the son of the Turkish Ambassador. Ertegun grew up to found Atlantic Records, a label that went on to represent many of the artists Ertegun grew up hearing at the Quality Music Store. While the Waxie Maxie's chain still survives with outlets throughout the

(Continued)

ty cities in the U.S. were fraught with violence, but Washington was home to the bloodiest battles, with barricades and bullets and bodies strewn through the landscape of Shaw. The hardest-hit intersection, at T and Seventh Streets, saw a string of riots within several days.

After five days, the military regained control of the city, as a heavy rain fell to drench the violence. Washington's "Red Summer" of 1919, as the bloody riot-torn days came to be known, resulted in the deaths of thirty people, with countless others injured.

The riots of 1968, although less deadly than those of 1919, seared the soul of the nation in a way the earlier conflict had not. Perhaps it was the contrast between the non-violent protests led by Reverend Dr. Martin Luther King, Jr., and the sheer force of violence that swept the nation in the wake of his assassination in Memphis. Or perhaps it was the bitter explosion of frustration over white America's resistance to the Civil Rights movement. Theory aside, the reality of the 1968 riots—which first ignited the day of King's murder (April 4)—was one of physical destruction as well as emotional wreckage. In twelve days of rioting, much of the Shaw neighborhood was burned to the ground or at least badly damaged. Local landmarks ranging from famous theaters to the Waxie Maxie record store were destroyed in the flames. Northeast Washington also suffered, notably the H Street corridor from 3rd Street to Bladensburg Road, which, like the 14th Street and 7th Street corridors of Shaw, have never fully recovered from the riots. The final tally of the riots ran in the tens of millions of dollars, with more than a hundred people injured and a dozen dead.

In contrast to the 1919 and 1968 riots, the Cinco de Mayo riots of 1991 were an odd exercise in carefree mob violence that cost no lives. The riot was sparked by an incident on May 5th that served as a magnet for all the frustrations of the large immigrant population of Mount Pleasant. A white police officer shot and wounded a hispanic man she was trying to arrest for being drunk and disorderly. Unfounded rumors soon spread that the man had been in handcuffs before the shooting and that he had been killed, and the streets were suddenly filled with angry youths who burned police vehicles and forced the closing of 16th Street. The riots, which ended up becoming a public "wilding" in which bored youths looted stores for the fun of it, lasted several days, until curfews and cooler heads prevailed. But the press took note, and Washington's reputation as a riot-prone city again made headlines around the world.

Washington area, the flagship Seventh Street store that made musical history was destroyed in the flames of the 1968 riots.

---

32 | Open to the Public | **John Wesley A.M.E. Church (1615 14th Street, NW)**

This African Methodist Episcopal church built in the 1850s was the site for major civil rights gatherings and events during the mid-twentieth century. The landmark 1954 Supreme Court case *Brown v. Board of Education*, in which Thurgood Marshall successfully argued for the desegregation of America's separate but unequal schools, might never have come to pass had it not been for the meetings of the Committee for School Desegregation, a Washington-based civil rights group that met at the John Wesley A.M.E. Church. The group's meetings, during which strategy and reasoning for achieving desegregation were clearly formulated, laid some of the foundation for Marshall's successful argument before the Supreme Court.

Although badly damaged in a 1979 fire, the church was painstakingly restored, and even improved upon in the process, with the installation of a stunning stained glass mosaic known as the Victory Skylight, which casts a dancing spectrum of light filtered through its 12,000 pieces of colored glass.

---

33 The Whitelaw (1839 13th Street, NW)

The Whitelaw was the first hotel-apartment building for blacks in Washington. Opened in 1919, at a time when the Shaw neighborhood was heading into its golden era (but when segregation was bitterly felt throughout the city, as evidenced by the race riots that same year), the Whitelaw was not only built for blacks—it was built by blacks. Developer John Whitelaw Lewis had arrived in Washington in 1894 as part of Coxey's Army of the Unemployed, a group of men desperate for assistance, who marched on Washington in the vain hopes of finding federal aid. Architect Isaah Hatton was born and raised in Washington, attending Dunbar (then the M Street) High School. The successful collaboration between the black architect and developer made all of black Washington proud; and it gave the community a much-needed and long-overdue apartment-hotel building to call its own. The Whitelaw is now a gutted shell of a building, surrounded by hurricane fencing and up for sale at the time of publication.

PLACES: Logan Circle and Thomas Circle

Logan Circle dates back to L'Enfant's original plans, although he drew it as a triangle. Originally called Iowa Circle, during the Civil War it became infamous as an executioner's square, where the hangman's gallows often swung with the bodies of deserters or spies.

The circle was renamed in 1930 for Civil War General John A. Logan, who had lived nearby in the former **Mount Pleasant** mansion. By the time it was renamed, the neighborhood's nearly all-white occupants of the late nineteenth century had given way to a nearly all-black society of middle-class families. In the late 1940s and early 1950s, the neighborhood went into a steep decline; many of its beautiful Victorians were transformed into seedy boarding houses, or simply boarded up and abandoned. But in the 1980s, young professionals and families, both black and white, began returning to the elegant old Victorian houses that surround the circle. Now designated as a Historic District, Logan Circle is in-

Thomas Circle as it appeared in the 1920s.

deed a time capsule of Washington's past. It is also home to a number of important churches, several of which—**Grace Reformed** and **National City Christian**—were the chosen houses of worship for a number of U.S. presidents.

To the southwest is Thomas Circle, named for Civil War General George H. Thomas. Washington's first open-space public demonstration of electric lighting took place at Thomas Circle on November 19, 1879, at the unveiling of the General's statue. The neighborhood surrounding Thomas Circle was once similar to the eight blocks around Logan Circle that have been so well preserved. But many of the historic buildings (including the city's first luxury apartment building, **Portland Flats**) were demolished to make way for new development.

34 | Open to the Public | ## Bethune Museum and Archives (Council House) (1318 Vermont Avenue, NW; 202/332–1233)

Also known as Council House, this Victorian home was both the last residence and final office of Mary McLeod Bethune, who founded and ran the National Council of Negro Women out of her home until her death in 1955. Bethune played an integral role in developing black political clout (with an emphasis on promoting women's rights). She led the "Black Cabinet," a group of powerful black leaders who lobbied on behalf of blacks during the New Deal years. Bethune also served under Franklin Delano Roosevelt as the National Youth Administration's Director of Negro Affairs, and held other high-level posts during various administrations, further serving the needs of the black community through her work. But she is probably best known as the founder of Bethune-Cookman College in Daytona Beach, Florida, the first black women's college in the country.

The Bethune House and Archives. (Jack Looney)

This house was witness to both social and political history. In its capacity as Bethune's home, many VIP's, including Eleanor Roosevelt and civil rights activist and Nobel Peace Prize winner Ralph Bunche, were entertained here. In its role as the headquarters of National Council of Negro Women, the site saw the fermentation of movements to support and preserve the rights and heritage of black women. The home is still owned by the organization Bethune founded. Now operated as a historical museum dedicated to preserving and promoting the history of black women, the building also houses the National Archives for Black Women's History, a comprehensive collection of manuscripts and papers relating to black women in America.

35 | Open to the Public | ## Grace Reformed Church (1405 15th Street, NW; 202/387–3131)

The cornerstone for Grace Reformed Church was laid by President Teddy Roosevelt, who practically made a career out of laying church cornerstones in Washington. (He also laid the cornerstone for the Washington National Cathedral.) Roosevelt's pew, in the third row from the front, is marked with a plaque. Built in 1903, the church has also attracted other presidents (as worshippers, rather than construction workers), notably Presidents Nixon and Eisenhower.

See Also: Washington National Cathedral (Chapter 8)

36 Open to the Public **National City Christian Church (5 Thomas Circle; 202/667–1377)**

Here Presidents Lyndon Johnson and, in its previous incarnation, President Garfield, attended church services. The present church was designed by John Russell Pope and constructed here in 1930, with an addition built in 1952.

37 Open to the Public **O Street Market (Northwest corner of 7th and O Streets, NW)**

The O Street Market is one of the few surviving public marketplaces that once served most neighborhoods of Washington. This building, erected in 1888, became home to the merchants displaced when the Northern Liberties Market (at 5th and K Streets) was ordered shut down by Alexander "Boss" Shepherd, the governor whose controversial improvements and corrupt administration were legendary. Although the 1968 riots damaged the site, the market was restored and re-opened as a public marketplace.

38 **Portland Flats Site (1129 Vermont Avenue, NW)**

The city's first luxury apartment building was opened at this location in 1879. Elegant beyond compare, the Adolph Cluss-designed building was a Victorian gem that filled the block with its tall and narrow lines. The six-story building featured amenities normally found only in hotels—a public dining room, drugstore, maid service—yet offered the smaller scale of residential living that had previously been available through boarding houses and inns. Each apartment even featured *its own telephone*, an extraordinary offering for the times. Portland Flats was transformed into a hotel in 1926, and then into an office building just before World War II. It was demolished in 1962 to make way for yet another modern office building.

39 Open to the Public **Shiloh Baptist Church (1500 9th Street, NW; 202/483–7901)**

The original members of this church migrated to Washington from Fredericksburg, Virginia, in 1862—just before the Union Army attacked the Confederate stronghold. The congregation held services in a variety of non-traditional sites (including private homes and a horse barn) before making this site its permanent home in 1924. The site had previously belonged to another church, and the displacement so angered one member of the earlier congregation that he set fire to the building a year after the Shiloh Baptist congregation had moved in, forcing them to hold services at the Howard Theater while the church was being rebuilt. Another fire in 1991 did less damage, but destroyed the church's historic organ.

Today the Shiloh Baptist has ten choirs and is famed for its rocking gospel services. The services are so popular that overflow crowds are often accommodated in the basement.

PLACES: LeDroit Park

The historic houses in LeDroit Park date back to the 1870s and 1880s, when developers began building mini-mansions in the rural area. At the time, the surrounding area was known as Hell's Bottom for its low-down vices, but this particular section was cleaned up and protected from such sins by its careful development plan.

Original plans called for a road known as Harewood Avenue to connect LeDroit Park to the **Soldiers' and Airmen's Home.** Harewood Avenue was to be the extension of 3rd Street at the other end of the traffic circle which is now officially known as the Anna

Cooper Memorial Circle, in honor of educator Anna Cooper, whose home still stands nearby.

Although Harewood Avenue never developed into a sophisticated boulevard lined with LeDroit's most pricey mansions (nor did it ever connect to the Soldiers' and Airmen's Home), some fine homes still cluster around the circle. Dotted between and beyond these houses are the rowhouses—some quite elaborate in their own right—that began replacing the earlier homes at the turn of the century. LeDroit Park is still a popular residential area with middle- and upper-class blacks. Past and present residents include Mary Church Terrell, an activist for women's suffrage and public education; Walter Washington, the first elected mayor in Washington; and the Rev. Jesse Jackson, who relocated his family to Washington in 1990 before running for a shadow office in the Senate.

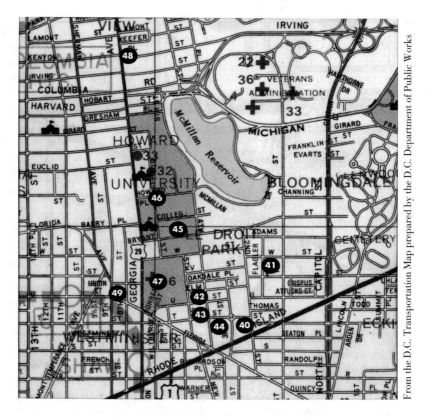

From the D.C. Transportation Map prepared by the D.C. Department of Public Works

40 Anna Cooper Home/Freylinghuysen University (201 T Street, NW)

The home of one of Washington's most influential educators also served as the home of one of the city's most important educational institutions. Dr. Anna Cooper (who received her Ph.D. at the Sorbonne) taught night school at Freylinghuysen University, founded in 1906 and dedicated to the classical education of black students. Dr. Cooper ended up sharing more than her teaching skills with the school: When the university found itself without a home, she offered her house on T Street to the school. The university continued to operate out of Dr. Cooper's home until it was closed in the 1960s.

41 Samuel Gompers's First House (2122 1st Street, NW)

American Federation of Labor (AFL) founder Samuel Gompers rented this house from 1902–1919. He spent most of his time in Washington working to further the cause of organized labor through lobbying and other methods of political persuasion.
See Also: Samuel Gompers's Second House (Chapter 8)

McGill Houses (throughout LeDroit Park):

The original houses of the LeDroit Park development, designed by James McGill, were masterpieces of urban/suburban residential architecture. Many still stand, and their richness of detail and abundance of flourishes seem almost whimsical in comparison with today's simpler architectural styles. The block that has best retained the overall flavor of what LeDroit Park looked like in the 1870s is the 400 Block of U Street. Another good McGill-watching block is that of 1900 3rd Street, which is now partially devoted to Howard University dormitories, and was also the location of the (now gone) homes of both James McGill and LeDroit Park developer Amzi Barber. One of the best-preserved examples of a typical LeDroit Park home can be seen at 1901–1903 3rd Street, while other beautifully preserved McGill houses stand at 517 T Street and at 519 Florida Avenue (the latter of which has been restored inside as well for use by the neighborhood preservation society).

Among the McGill Houses that became homes to prominent Washingtonians are:

42 **DePriest House** (419 U Street, NW): The home to the first black congressman elected in the twentieth century, Oscar DePriest, who was elected in 1928.

43 **Taliaferro House** (414 U Street, NW): The home of Clara Taliaferro, whose father, John Smyth, became the minister to the African nation of Liberia in 1890.

44 **Mary Church Terrell House** (326 T Street, NW): A designated historic landmark, this private house was the home of famed women's suffrage leader Mary Church Terrell, who went on to further distinction by serving as the first black woman appointed to the D.C. Board of Education. One of the first blacks to move into the then all-white LeDroit Park, Mary Church Terrell saw and fought first-hand the initial animosity of whites toward blacks in the neighborhood. She died in 1954, but her legacy lives on in the D.C. school system.

PLACES: Howard University and Vicinity

Howard University was established in 1867 as the country's pre-eminent black university. Its founder was General Oliver Otis Howard, a renowned civil rights advocate. Howard headed the Freedmen's Bureau, which had been formed by the federal government in 1865 to promote the mainstreaming of former slaves into American life through education, housing, and employment opportunities. The main campus now sprawls over seventy-five acres, bounded by Georgia Avenue to the west and the **McMillan Reservoir** to the east.

Howard alumnae, both black and white, have gone on to achieve greatness in the fields of politics, medicine, law, the arts, and virtually every other profession. Among the most famous alumnae of this most famous school are: Ralph Bunche (the first black American to win the Nobel Peace Prize, and the first black to serve as an undersecretary of the United Nations); Supreme Court Justice Thurgood Marshall (who distinguished himself while an NAACP lawyer by successfully arguing before the Supreme Court the *Brown v. Board of Education* decision of 1954 that ordered the desegregation of America's public elementary and high schools); Andrew Young (former mayor of Atlanta and U.S. Ambassador to the U.N.); Patricia Harris (former Secretary of Health and Human Services); former D.C. Council Chairman David Clarke; and dancer Debbie Allen and her sister, actress Phylicia Rashad.

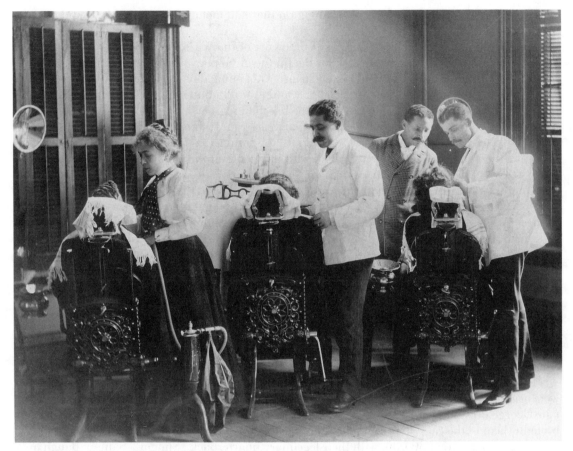

A dentistry class at Howard University, 1900. (Library of Congress)

The following on-campus sites are of particular historic significance:

45 Freedmen's Hospital Site (4th Street, between College and Bryant Streets)

Now used as spare laboratory facilities and school office space, this section is all that remains of the original site of the Freedmen's Hospital, the first hospital for blacks in Washington.

46 Howard Hall (607 Howard Place)

Howard Hall is the site of the first classes held at the University in 1867.

47 Howard University Hospital (Griffith Stadium site) (Georgia Avenue, between W and Elm Streets)

A full-service teaching and community hospital, this facility was built on the site of Griffith Stadium, the homebase for Washington's professional baseball and football teams from 1912 until the 1960s. Griffith Stadium, in turn, had been built on the site of Maryland House, an early resort on the (then) outskirts of Washington that had included bowling greens and a baseball field.

The stadium was named for Clark Griffith, owner of the Washington Senators, Washington's American League Team. But the first team to play at Griffith Stadium was the Washington Nationals, the National League team. At opening day in 1912, President Howard Taft tossed out the first ball from a special box in the stands, and in doing so created the tradition of presidents throwing the first pitch of the baseball season.

The stadium was a mecca for Washingtonians black and white (for it was one of the few places in the city that remained unsegregated). In the summer of 1916, the Washington Nationals kept the capital's residents so enthralled with its chance at the pennant that locals focussed more on the pending pennant games than on the ever-worsening war in Europe. In 1924, it was the Senators' turn to draw huge crowds, when the Senators won the World Series against the New York Giants. The Senators made it to the World Series again the next year, but lost to the Pirates. In 1960, the Senators skipped town to become the Minnesota Twins; the team was soon re-formed, though, and stayed in Washington—playing at the new D.C. stadium (now called RFK), which opened in 1961. In 1972, when the Senators again left Washington, this time to become the Texas Rangers, Griffith's team was history for good.

But the Senators weren't the only game in town. Washington had a bevy of black baseball teams, including the LeDroit Tigers, the Washington Pilots, and the Washington Elite Giants, all of whom played at Griffith Stadium. In the 1920s and '30s, the teams of the National Negro League also played at the stadium, often outdrawing the Senators. And starting in 1937, the Homestead Grays, another popular black team, made Griffith Stadium their home while the Senators were on the road.

Probably Washington's most famous sports team of all is the Washington Redskins, who were originally formed in 1932 as the Boston Braves. (Their owner, Washington laundry magnate George Preston Marshall, changed their name to the Boston Redskins in 1933.) Marshall brought them to the capital city and debuted Washington's new team at Griffith Stadium in 1937 before a crowd of 30,000, with their legendary quarterback "Slingin'" Sammy Baugh at the helm. The team won two NFL championships (in 1937 and 1942) while calling Griffith their home.

While Griffith Stadium itself was integrated, the same could not be said for the Redskins. The team was the last NFL team to hire a black player, and no black player ever touched down in a Redskins uniform at Griffith Stadium. It was not until the team moved to the D.C. Stadium in 1961 that they brought in a black player—and even then, only because the federal government, which owned the stadium, told Marshall it would deny the Redskins the use of the new stadium unless he integrated the team. Grudgingly, Marshall acquired wide receiver Bobby Mitchell from the Cleveland Browns in a trade in 1962. Mitchell, the first black Redskin, turned out to be one of the greatest players in the team's history.

Aside from the sporting events held at Griffith, the stadium was also the site of everything from concerts to mass baptisms (these last, performed by the famed radio preacher Elder Michaux, who had a church nearby, required canvas tanks filled with water with which to douse the converts). Today, all that remains of the famous arena is a commemorative plaque on display on a wall in the hospital—which happens to be inside a doctor's office, so that the plaque can only be viewed by appointment when the doctor is in.

See Also: Temple of Freedom Under God, Church of God; RFK Stadium (Chapter 11)

---

48 Schuetzen Park Site (East side of Georgia Avenue at Kenyon Street)

During the 1880s and 1890s, Washington's tight-knit German immigrant community used this site as a place to celebrate their traditional Schuetzenfest ("Shooting Festival") every

The Washington Historical Atlas . 261

August. The Schuetzen Park was used as a shooting range and gathering place for the various Shuetzengilds (*shooting skills clubs*) that were popular with German immigrants in the late nineteenth century.

---

49 | Open to the Public | **Temple of Freedom Under God, Church of God (2030 Georgia Avenue, NW; 202/387–6419)**

The modern church building that stands here today is the latest version of an earlier, historic church that dated from 1928: The Radio Church of God. The Radio Church had a congregation of millions of listeners who tuned in to hear its famous leader, Elder Solomon Lightfoot Michaux, preach the Gospel on CBS Radio. Michaux's flamboyance was legendary, his oratory astounding. And his back-up singers, the equally famous Cross Choir, were downright inspiring. Elder Michaux liked to do everything in a big way, especially his baptismal ceremonies. Sometimes he rented a boat to take the faithful out on the Potomac for the ritual; other times, he filled Griffith Stadium with those to be baptized, and drenched them in water stored in giant canvas tanks. Once, he even had the water for the stadium event imported from the River Jordan.

Reverend Michaux gained friends in high places. He was an advisor to President Franklin Roosevelt, and even was given the honor of symbolically nominating Eleanor Roosevelt for vice president at the 1940 Democratic Convention. Michaux died in 1968. His original church was destroyed in 1958 to make room for the grand new model that stands today.

The following is an account of Elder Michaux's Radio Church of God, as published in the WPA's 1937 guidebook, *Washington: City and Capital:*

> "The congregation usually numbers about 600, with the choir dressed in gray. While the theme song "Happy Am I" is sung, an electric cross is slowly lowered over the pulpit. The Elder is the chief attraction. He is middle aged, kindly, and one of the most powerful Negro leaders in the District. The audience is increased many times by a radio station, whose local call letters, WJSV, the Elder has taken to mean 'Willingly Jesus Suffered for Victory.' During the Summer the Elder occasionally holds camp meetings on Sherman Avenue, NW, attended by as many as 15,000 people. The annual baptism service in the Potomac is watched by more thousands. At the 1935 service 250 converts were immersed at a charge of $5 a head."

PLACES: Upper 16th Street and Eastern Northwest

The fringes of Upper Northwest, while mainly a mix of residential neighborhoods, are also home to a variety of important historic sites. This is the location of both the city's oldest cemetery, **Rock Creek Cemetery,** and the nation's smallest national cemetery, **Battleground National Cemetery.** These outer edges are also home to such military stalwarts as the **Walter Reed Medical Center,** where soldiers young and old still go for treatment, and the **Soldiers' and Airmen's Home,** the nation's oldest veterans' home.

---

50 | Open to the Public | **Battleground National Cemetery (6625 Georgia Avenue, NW)**

This tiny graveyard is the final resting place of the forty-one Union Soldiers from Wright's Sixth Division who gave their lives in the defense of Washington at the battle of **Fort Stevens** on July 12, 1864. Confederate General Jubal Early's attack, although ineffective against the city's defenses, was deadly enough to fill one cemetery, albeit a tiny, one-acre graveyard (the city's smallest).

See Also: Fort Stevens; "The Civil War Forts of Washington" (Chapter 10)

---

51 Open to the Public **Fort Stevens (Piney Branch Road and Quackenbos Street, NW)**

On July 12, 1864, Washington was aghast at the news that Confederate General Jubal Early and his army were marching on the capital from the north—heading right for Fort Stevens, a mere five miles above the city boundaries. The Union Army rushed in reinforcements, and hordes of spectators headed in the same direction. Even President Lincoln rushed out to Fort Stevens, bent on witnessing what could prove to be the first true test of Washington's defenses. Upon his arrival, Lincoln climbed atop the parapet of the fort to gain a better vantage point. There he stood, his trademark stovepipe hat in hand and his unmistakable height spotlighting him as the perfect target. The cannons roared all about him, and it was only after a soldier standing beside the president was shot in the leg and fell from the parapet that he reluctantly gave in to the pleas of the officers nearby—one of whom, Lt. Colonel Oliver Wendell Holmes (assigned as a presidential military escort), reportedly bellowed at the president "Get down, you fool." Lincoln is said to have responded to the upstart soldier who saved his life, "It's a good thing you know how to talk to civilians." A historic marker designates the spot where Lincoln stood.

The forty-one soldiers from Wright's Sixth Division who died in battle that day are buried in **Battleground National Cemetery** on Georgia Avenue. A small restored section is all that remains of the fort.

See Also: Battleground National Cemetery; "The Civil War Forts of Washington" (Chapter 10)

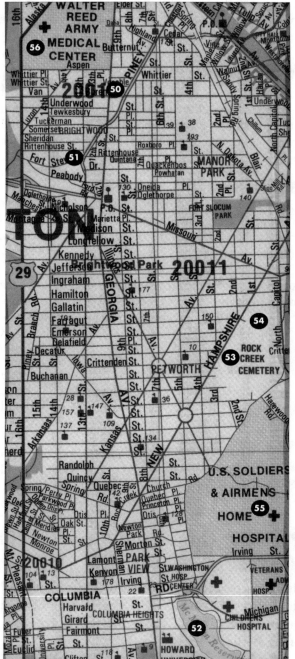

From Champion's Washington D.C. Street Map © 1991 by Rand McNally, R.L. 91-S-96

52 Open to the Public ## McMillan Reservoir (just east of Howard University on Reservoir Road)

This reservoir was built at the turn of the century, (with landscaped grounds designed by Frederick Law Olmsted, Jr.) as a water storage and filtration site. It is named for Senator James McMillan (of the McMillan Plan that altered the face of the city in the twentieth century). In 1991, plans to build a retail and office complex on part of the 92–acre grounds were put on hold by court order after preservation groups asked for an appraisal of the site's historic significance. The caverns of the underground facilities with their vaulted ceilings are one of the city's lesser-know architectural gems.

53 Open to the Public ## Rock Creek Cemetery (Rock Creek Church Road, NW; 202/829–0585)

Rock Creek Cemetery is the oldest cemetery in Washington, and is attached to the oldest church, **St. Paul's Episcopal Church.** It is also the site of the best-known graveside memorial in the city: Augustus Saint-Gaudens's statue at the grave of Mrs. Henry Adams. Henry Adams, a renowned historian and author, hired Saint-Gaudens to create the memorial for his wife, Marion "Clover" Adams, who committed suicide in 1883. Adams requested that the memorial consist only of a statue that reflected elements of Eastern mysticism, with which Adams had become fascinated during his travels in Japan. The statue that resulted from this commission is that of a draped woman, transfixed by emotion. It is often identified as "Grief," probably thanks to Mark Twain, who saw in the statue a symbol for all the grief of mankind. Adams himself abhorred the colloquial name, preferring to call it "The Peace of God," while Saint Gaudens referred to the statue as "The Mystery of the Hereafter." Whatever the name, the statue seems to have a profound effect on anyone who views it, and that effect is not always a pleasant one. It is said that the Japanese Ambassador once visited the statue out of curiosity, having heard about Adams' mystical instructions to the sculptor. After examining the memorial in silence for some time, the ambassador reportedly stormed off in a rage, proclaiming it a great insult to Japan.

The cemetery grounds were designed by architect Stanford White, and Henry Adams's grave resides here as well. Others buried in the cemetery include Washington's own department store king, Julius Garfinckel, as well as Lincoln's Postmaster General.

See Also: St. Paul's Episcopal Church; Adams House Site and Hay-Adams Hotel (Chapter 1)

54 Open to the Public ## St. Paul's Episcopal Church (within Rock Creek Cemetery; 202/726–2080)

Built in 1775, St. Paul's is the oldest church in Washington. Its congregation goes back even earlier, having begun meeting at a makeshift church on the same site in 1712. A fire gutted St. Paul's in 1921, and the church was rebuilt on the same spot, incorporating what was left of the original brick walls into the new version.

See Also: Rock Creek Cemetery

55 ## Soldiers' and Airmen's Home (3rd and Webster Streets, NW)

The oldest veterans' retirement home in the nation, the Soldiers' and Airmen's Home was built between 1843 and 1852. Legend has it that the original, fortress-like Scott Building was erected with the ransom money General Winfield Scott got his hands on in Mexico City during the Mexican-American War. During the Civil War, the crenelated tower of the Scott Building, one of the city's highest points, was manned by Union Army look-outs, who used signal flags to communicate with the ring of forts surrounding the city.

The home was equally famous as a presidential retreat. Anderson Cottage, one of the earliest buildings on the grounds, was used as a getaway by President Lincoln during the summer of 1864. Presidents Arthur and Hayes also used the cottage as their Summer White House, while President Buchanan used Quarters No. 1 as his hideaway.

Lincoln's frequent visits to Anderson Cottage did not go unnoticed by John Wilkes Booth and his band of conspirators. As legend has it, they initially attempted to kidnap the president one day as he rode to the Old Soldiers' Home. But they were thwarted, and so later drew up plans to kill him instead.

The Soldiers' Home had its heyday in the late nineteenth and early twentieth centuries, when it overflowed with

The Soldiers' Home as it appeared in the late nineteenth century.
(*Picturesque Washington*)

Civil War veterans and their visitors. Indeed, when LeDroit Park was being promoted to downtowners, its developers took great pains to point out how close the neighborhood was to the veterans' home, and how easily accessible the coming trolley car line would make it. Most everybody in Washington in those days either had a relative or a friend at the Soldiers' Home, and it was one of the city's main social centers for seniors.

---

56 Open to the Public **Walter Reed Army Medical Center (16th Street at Alaska Avenue, NW—enter on Georgia Avenue; 202/576–3501)**

Established in 1909, Walter Reed is the Army's top medical facility, and it is here that federal VIPs (including Congressmen, Senators, Supreme Court Judges, and U.S. Presidents, as well as military men) come for treatment. This was Dwight D. Eisenhower's hospital of choice when he was president, and it was here that Eisenhower died on May 28, 1969. General John "Blackjack" Pershing also came here to fight the final battles of old age. Pershing lived at Walter Reed in a third-floor suite for the last eight years of his life. Pershing, the World War I commander who led one of the city's great victory parades (in 1919), died at Walter Reed in 1948.

During the attack of Jubal Early's Confederate forces against Fort Stevens in July 1864, some of Early's men took up positions in a tree that stood just inside what are now the Georgia Avenue entrance gates to the hospital grounds. They acted as snipers from that vantage point, picking off the defenders of the fort. The Rebels' "sharpshooters tree" was designated by a historic marker when it was later removed.

A Stroll through the Army Medical Museum

For sixty-five years, the Armed Forces Medical Museum was located in a vast building on the Mall, where the Hirshhorn Museum and Sculpture Garden now stand. The following description of a visit to that grand old museum appeared in *Thirty Years in Washington*, edited by Mrs. John Logan, which was published in 1901:

"Close by the National Museum stands the large and handsome brick building now occupied by the Army Medical Museum, a grewsome [sic] place which, however much it may excite our interest and wonder, leaves a decidedly unpleasant impression on the nerves of sensitive people. It may be a heaven of delight for physicians and surgeons, but the unscientific shrink from the close observation of such an extensive display in wax and preserved flesh of the effects of the ravages of various diseases and of gunshot wounds.

". . . If you are scientific, you will linger with breathless interest over the long array of tumors, evidences of tuberculosis, of leprosy and so on; but if not scientific, you will have a curious feeling that your entire scalp is about to rise in revolt, and you will go away with a vague fear that you may have caught the diseases of the whole collection, and ought to hurry to the nearest doctor.

"To the unscientific mind doubtless the most interesting and the least disagreeable specimens are those which have been in the museum for a long time and show the wonderful effects of rifle bullets and shrapnel fragments after entering the human body. Here are skulls pierced by arrow heads without being fractured and others that have been broken by tiny bullets, that, after entering, plowed their way along in eccentric furrows. . . .

"Those who have seen General Sickles slowly making his way on crutches can not fail to be interested in his leg, or rather, a strong white bone which was once a part of his anatomy, and which bears the following official description:

'The right tibia and fibula communited in three shafts by a round shell. Major-General D.E.S., United States Volunteers, Gettysburg, July 2, 1863, amputed in the lower third of the thigh by Surgeon T. Sim, United States Volunteers, on the field. Stump healed rapidly and subject was able to ride in carriage July 16; completely healed, so that he mounted his horse in September, 1863. Contributed by subject.'"

Another historic site that once stood here was "Bleak House," the summer estate of "Boss" Alexander Shepherd, whose pioneering (and corrupt) public works overhaul of the 1870s transformed Washington into a liveable city at last. Bleak House was torn down in 1916 to make way for further additions to the medical complex.

The Army's major research and medical facility, the complex was rebuilt and reorganized in 1979, but has long been the site of a medical care facility and study center. Walter Reed was himself an Army physician who studied the causes and treatment of the illnesses—including

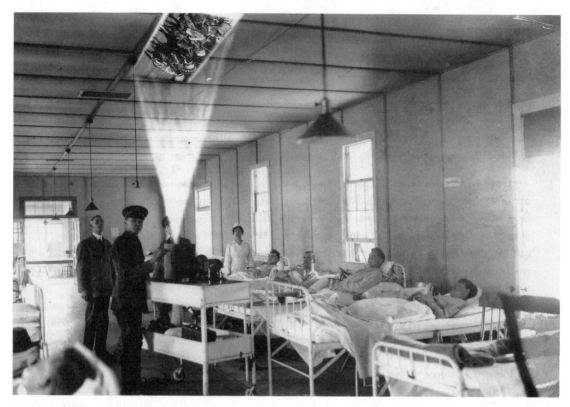

Early patients at Walter Reed watch motion pictures projected on the ceiling. (Library of Congress)

cholera, dysentery, and especially yellow fever—that often took more military lives than actual battle.

Buildings of historic importance at Walter Reed include:

The Armed Forces Institute of Pathology Building (6900 Georgia Avenue, NW): This windowless building, constructed in the 1940s to be able to withstand an atomic blast, was heralded by military architects, who predicted it would become the prototype for most future Washington buildings. The advent of the H-bomb made the building obsolete, and it now serves as a kind of memorial to the youngest days of the Cold War.

National Museum of Health and Medicine (Building 54; 202/576–2348): Formerly known as the Armed Forces Medical Museum, this famous "gross-out" museum was previously housed at various other locations in Washington (including a building on the site of the present-day Hirshhorn, and Ford's Theater). The collection grew out of the Army's decision in 1862 to gather specimens for the study of battlefield pathology—hence the limbs and other body parts on display, many of which date to the Civil War.

Probably the most famous bit of a soldier on exhibit is the leg bone of Major General Daniel Sickles, who lost his limb to a fly-by cannonball at Gettysburg. Sickles gave the leg, and the cannonball that removed it, to the museum. He had already become a legend in Washington when he murdered Attorney General Philip Barton Key II in a jealous rage over an affair Key was having with Sickles's wife. (Sickles was acquitted on a plea of temporary insanity—a first in the U.S. Court system.) He became even more famous after losing his leg, for later in life he began paying an annual visit to his lost leg on the anniversary of its removal. Even after his death his ghost was still said to drop by for a spell. After the museum moved to Walter Reed, however, the ghost apparently stopped haunting his phantom limb.

Other displays of historic note include pathological evidence from the assassinations of Presidents Lincoln and Garfield. It takes a strong stomach and a curious mind to appreciate this museum, but for those who can take it, it's an eye opener.

See Also: "A Stroll Through the Army Medical Museum"; Ford's Theater (Chapter 2); Hirshorn Museum of Modern Art (Chapter 4)

Chapter 10

UPPER NORTHEAST
(EXCLUDING ANACOSTIA)

While the area of Northeast above and around Capitol Hill may not percolate with political intrigue, it has had a bit of excitement over the years. During the War of 1812, when the British routed the Americans at the Battle of Bladensburg on August 24, 1814, this was the section of Washington that the enemy marched through en route to Capitol Hill and the burning rampage that followed. But at least they met some resistance as they marched down the turnpike that has since become Bladensburg Road—notably from Barney's Battery, a small group of sailors who set up a defensive post at what is now the Washington-Maryland border. The same site would later be transformed into Fort Lincoln, one of the sixty-eight Civil War forts that once surrounded Washington. And it was in this section of Washington that sculptor Clark Mills built his foundry and cast, among other pieces, the statue of "Freedom" that still tops the Capitol Dome.

But if anything defines Northeast Washington, it is its institutions: Some of the city's most renowned colleges and religious sites are located in this sprawling quadrant, which is less a place of neighborhoods than it is a place of space. Lower Northeast (on Capitol Hill), has been the site of more exciting scandal and political intrigue than has this region; and the sections of Northeast in Anacostia have a particular history all their own. (See Chapters 2 and 11 for these areas of Northeast.) But the wide open spaces of upper Northeast have their own appeal and historic importance.

Unlike Upper Northwest and the closer-in neighborhoods of Southeast and Southwest, Northeast Washington never quite caught on with developers of the bedroom communities within an easy trolley car ride of downtown. By the late nineteenth century, the rolling hills and flatlands of Northeast made up the largest section of wide-open space left in the Washington area. True, a few major estates called this out-of-town countryside home. For example, on the present-day site of **Gallaudet University** once stood the estates of Brentwood and Kendall Green. But for the most part, the area was undeveloped. It seemed the perfect place for building colleges such as **Catholic University** and **Gallaudet** and the **Franciscan Monastery,** and for putting aside space for special parks, like the **National Arboretum.**

Even today, the neighborhoods of Northeast are interspersed with empty plots of land and overgrown fields, as if the edges of residential neighborhoods could never quite stretch themselves to blend together, as have the tightly packed neighborhoods of Northwest. Likewise, commercial districts are few and far between, another indication that the flow of life and society in Northeast has remained as insular as its neighborhoods.

This is not to say that Northeast lacks dramatic sights or special communities—indeed, each neighborhood and institution stands out all the more here, defined as much by the in-between spaces as by the size of the places. The southernmost section of Northeast fills up fully half of Capitol Hill, claiming such inhabitants as Union Station and the Folger Shakespeare Library.

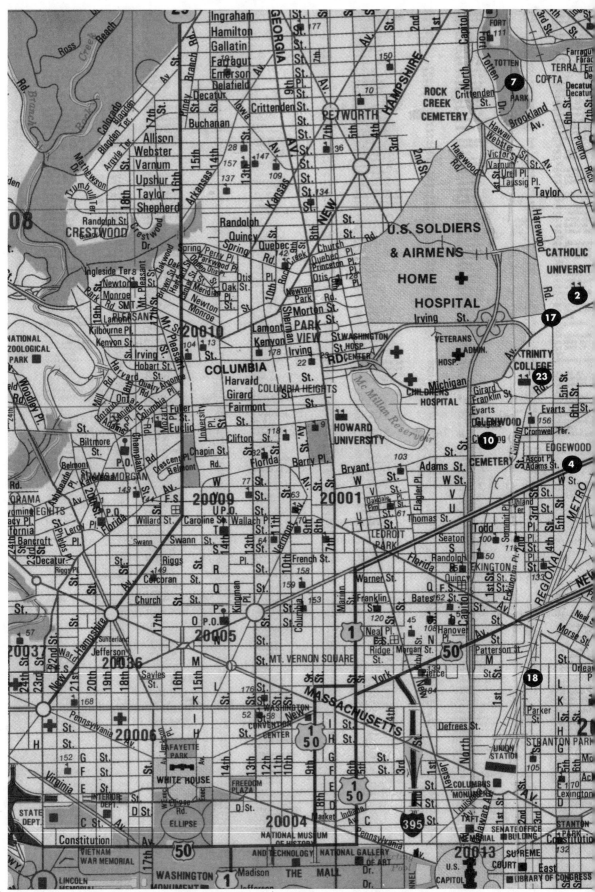

From Champion's Washington D.C. Street Map © 1991 by Rand McNally, R.L. 91–S–96

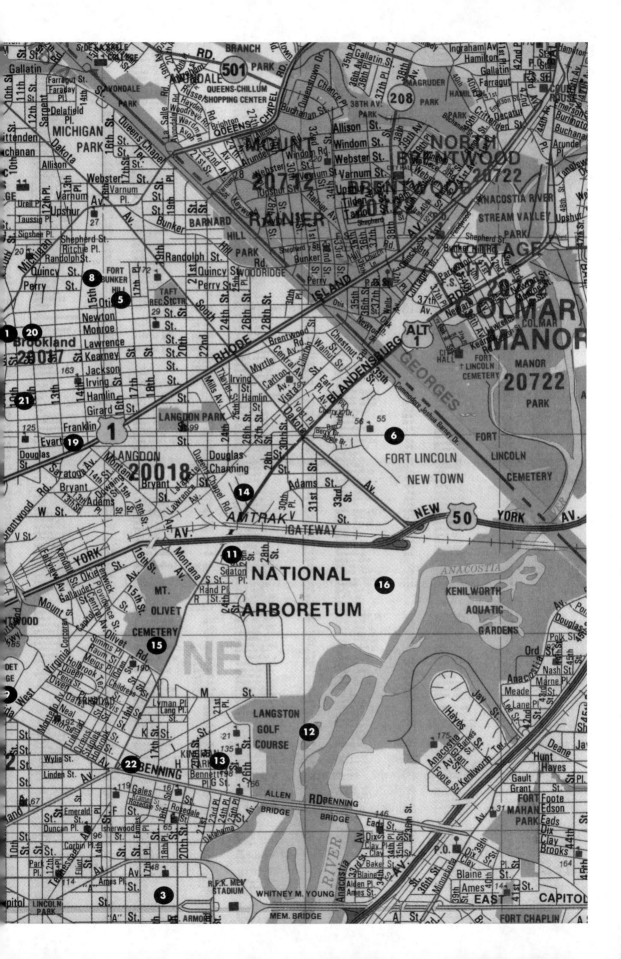

Higher up, around Catholic University, sits quiet little Brookland, a neighborhood founded on the site of the old Brooks farm that was originally settled in 1840 and is still dominated by Bellair, the old **Brooks mansion.** An eclectic yet pleasant enclave that mixes store-bought houses with clapboard classics, Brookland has stood against the tide of development and urban blight that has swept away many a similar neighborhood in the area.

PLACES:

Brentwood. *See* Gallaudet University

❶ Brooks Mansion (Bellair) (10th and Monroe Streets, NE)

Built in 1840, this was the manor house of the "Bellair" estate of the Brooks family. The house was built by Colonel Jehiel Brooks for his bride, Anne Queen (daughter of Richard Queen, who was the master of the **Haddock's Hills**estate for a time). After Brooks died in 1887, Bellair was sold to a development company, which transformed most of the estate into the neighborhood now called Brookland. The house itself remained, and was used first as an early building of the newly founded **Catholic University;** and after 1905, as a grammar school, St. Benedict's Academy, established by the Order of Benedictine Sisters. Since 1970, the house, which is adjacent to the Red Line Brookland Metro Station, has been the property of the Washington Metropolitan Area Transit Authority (or, as Washingtonians know it best, Metro).
See Also: Catholic University and **Haddock's Hills**

❷ Open to the Public | Catholic University of America (620 Michigan Avenue, NE; 202/635–5000)

The only university in the U.S. that answers directly to the Roman Catholic church, the Catholic University of America was founded at this site in 1877. The school's most visible landmark, the **National Shrine of the Immaculate Conception** (which is the seventh largest church in the world), was built under the auspices of the University between 1914 and 1959.

Although the university is naturally known for its theological education, it is also renowned for its theater department, which has turned out such stars as Susan Sarandon and Jon Voight. The success of the theater department is in large part due to the teaching methods of the school's famed acting teacher Father Hartke, after whom the University's Hartke Theater was named.

In the past decade, Catholic University has been torn by internal strife. It has found itself embroiled in the cultural problems of modern-day society—from the sexual and religious politics of birth-control, abortion, and gay rights, to the less clearly defined areas of broad philosophical discourse. Both teachers and students at the university have gotten into thorny disputes with the church hierarchy over the rights and necessities of educators to preach what they practice (as opposed to what the church dictates).

The most infamous such episode occurred in the mid-1980s when Father Charles Curran, a professor of Roman Catholic morality at the university, was censured by the Vatican for making statements about sexual behavior that were inconsistent with Roman Catholic teachings. Curran, a tenured theologian who had been teaching at Catholic University for twenty years, revealed the censure in 1986 after refusing to retract his statements on everything from masturbation to abortion. The Vatican revoked Curran's teaching credentials, and Catholic University stripped Father Curran of his tenure, banning him from teaching theology at the school. Curran fought the Vatican action, and brought a breach of contract suit against Catholic University. The Vatican reviewed its decision and upheld its verdict in 1987; the lawsuit made its way to the D.C. Superior Court, where the judge ruled against Curran in 1989. Catholic University offered Father Curran non-theological courses to teach; Curran declined the offer.

Not all campus scandals are as dramatic, or taken as seriously. In fact, the university has a relatively benign sense of humor about such events as student pranks—as evidenced by an anecdote sheet released by Catholic University that relates how "an immense marble statue of Pope Leo XIII at one of the university's main entrances was found on a recent holiday holding a can of 'Rolling Rock' in its upraised hand."

See Also: National Shrine of the Immaculate Conception; Georgetown University (Chapter 6)

---

3 Eastern High School (17th Street and East Capitol Street, NE; 202/724–8405)

One of the city's oldest public high schools, Eastern High School was established, along with Western High School (now the Duke Ellington School for the Performing Arts in Georgetown) in 1890 when the Central High School became overcrowded. The school's original location was at 8th Street and Pennsylvania Avenue, SE, in the building that now houses Hine Junior High School.

See Also: Duke Ellington School for the Performing Arts (Chapter 6)

---

4 Edgewood Site (Area around Rhode Island Avenue and Fourth Street, NE)

This area is still called Edgewood, even though the grand thirty-acre estate of that name disappeared in the 1920s. Originally known as Metropolis View, the house was built in 1830 by General Washington Berry. According to James Goode's 1979 work on the lost sites of Washington, *Capital Losses*, Edgewood became the last home to Salmon P. Chase, Chief Justice of the Supreme Court, in 1869. Chase died suddenly in 1873, and his youngest daughter, Kate Chase Sprague, moved into Edgewood after her seemingly ideal marriage to Senator William Sprague of Rhode Island ended in a nasty public divorce in 1882. Amidst rumors that she had been carrying on with another senator, Roscoe Conkling, Mrs. Sprague holed up at Edgewood and lived out her days in seclusion, with her daughter with mental retardation and a few aging servants as her only companions. She died in 1899. Edgewood was sold for use as a Catholic orphanage after World War I, and in 1920 it was razed to make way for roads.

---

5 Open to the Public Fort Bunker Hill (Otis Street at 16th Street, NE)

Fort Bunker Hill, one of the sixty-eight forts that ringed Washington during the Civil War, is partially preserved here.

See Also: Fort Lincoln Park, Fort Totten, and **"The Civil War Forts of Washington"**

---

6 Open to the Public Fort Lincoln Park (31st Street and Lincoln Drive, NE)

Fort Lincoln, now a park and recreation area, was one of the forts hastily erected around Washington during the Civil War. Like many other city forts, Fort Lincoln was purchased by the National Capital Parks and Planning Commission, which helped preserve the site and turn it into a public park.

Fort Lincoln, which sprawls over the line into Bladensburg, Maryland (where the Fort Lincoln Cemetery is located), resides in an area that was once a massive complex called the National Training Center for Boys—a federally-operated rehabilitation center for delinquent boys. But the Fort also stands at the location of an even older institution: Barney's Battery.

Commodore Joshua Barney knew it would be futile to set his tiny naval forces against the might of the British invaders in August of 1814, as it appeared the British would soon win the War of 1812. Rather than allow the British to capture and use his tiny flotilla of ships docked in the Potomac, Barney had his men burn the ships. Then they marched out Bladensburg Road and set up a last-ditch defensive line. (At the time, all land north of Florida/Benning Road was part of Maryland; the site is now in Washington, at the Maryland border.) This point became the area farthest west where the Battle of Bladensburg raged (the rest of the battlefield is on the Maryland side). Barney, badly wounded, was captured along with his gallant men. He was taken to a nearby spring up the road and treated for his wounds. The road that passes through the site is named for Commodore Barney.

See Also: "The Civil War Forts of Washington" and **"The Burning of Washington"**

Company E, 4th U.S. Colored Infantry, as photographed at Fort Lincoln in 1863. (Library of Congress)

---

❼ | Open to the Public | **Fort Totten (North of the Old Soldiers Home, off of Rock Creek Church Road, NE)**

This is one of Washington's few Civil War forts that is still relatively intact.

See Also: "The Civil War Forts of Washington"

The Civil War Forts of Washington

When Washington went to war against the South in April of 1861, the city created makeshift or hastily assembled fortresses as quickly as possible. Some, like Battery Cameron (the historic mansion Uplands, located at 1500 Foxhall Road, west of Georgetown), were actually private homes that took in artillery companies, becoming instant fortifications. In the early days of the war, even the Treasury, U.S. Capitol, and City Hall were transformed into heavily armed camps while Washington anxiously awaited reinforcements from the north to build and man the forts that would soon ring the city.

Most of the new forts were constructed at high points on the fringes of the city, in Maryland and in the quickly captured Northern Virginia suburbs. Thanks to the engineering expertise of General George McLellan, almost fifty forts were in place within a year of the start of the war. By the war's end in 1865, Washington was encircled by a thirty-seven square-mile defense loop made up of sixty-eight forts.

The Civil War forts of Washington saw little action. The only engagement of consequence between the Confederates and a Washington fort occurred at Fort Stevens on April 11 and 12, 1864, when the fort was attacked by General Jubal Early's men. President Lincoln came out to watch the battle, standing brazenly atop the parapets as bullets whizzed all around him.

1892 map of the Civil War defenses of Washington. (National Archives)

After the Civil War ended, Washington de-commissioned its forts as quickly as it had built them. By the summer of 1866 there were only four forts in operation. Today, only one—Fort Whipple in Arlington (now known as Fort Myer) remains an active-duty military facility. And even there, the old fort has long since disappeared beneath its modern successor.

Today, there is little evidence of the forts that once surrounded the city. Most were earthen fortresses to begin with, utilizing moats and natural hills or rocky outcroppings

(Continued)

as natural barriers behind which cannons were positioned. With few exceptions, all have long since been grown over, although at many there are historical markers.

A few forts in Washington and its suburbs have been preserved or restored. The most pristine is Fort Ward in Alexandria, Virginia, which has been perfectly restored and is also the site of a small Civil War museum. Probably the best preserved of the forts in Washington is Fort De Russey (in Rock Creek Park, where Lincoln was taken when it appeared that the city was about to be invaded by rebels). Others, including Fort Stevens, Fort Totten, Battery Kemble, Fort Dupont, and Fort Slocum, have been surrounded by parkland and, in some cases, partially restored.

In 1925, the National Capital Park and Planning Commission began acquiring the sites of the forts in the district, with plans to build a scenic drive linking many of them together. The road was to have commenced at Nebraska Avenue's westernmost edge (at the Potomac River), and ended twenty-three miles to the southeast at Blue Plains (in Anacostia). Although Fort Drive was still being discussed into the 1950s, nothing ever came of the plans. But the listing of the forts that would have been linked by Fort Drive still offers one of the best references to these sites. This listing of the Fort Drive forts (and descriptions of their state in the mid-1930s), appeared in the 1937 WPA guidebook, *Washington: City and Capital:*

"Battery Kemble: East side of Chain Bridge Road and south of its intersection with Little Falls Road NW. Part of the old fortifications still exist.

Fort Reno: Near Thirty-ninth and Ellicott Streets NW, east of Wisconsin Avenue. The original site of the fort is occupied by reservoirs. This is the highest point in the city.

Battery Terrill: On the hill on the side of Broad Branch Road at 30th Street NW. Can be reached by Thirtieth Street and Garrison Street.

Fort De Russey: In Rock Creek Park at its highest point just northeast of intersection of Military Road and Daniel Road NW. The fort is in exceptionally good state of preservation.

Fort Stevens: On the east side of Thirtieth Street between Quackenbos and Rittenhouse Streets NW. A small portion of the ramparts is standing and the remaining portion will be restored. A monument to President Lincoln commemorates the occasion of his being under Confederate fire here.

Fort Slocum: Between Madison and Oglethorpe Streets and Third Street and Kansas Avenue NW.

Fort Totten: North of Soldiers Home. Can be reached by Bates Road and Allison Street within Lincoln Cemetery. Just east of Bladensburg Road and Eastern Avenue NE.

Fort Lincoln: Partly within National Training School grounds and partly within Lincoln Cemetery. Just east of Bladensburg Road and Eastern Avenue NE.

Fort Mahan: Just north of Benning Road and west of Forty-second Street NE.

Fort Chaplin: On East Capitol Street at Forty-second Street extended. (Inaccessible to vehicles at present.)

Fort Dupont: Just east of Alabama Avenue between Massachusetts Avenue and Ridge Road SE. Fort is in excellent preservation. Adjoining area of 315 acres is

(Continued)

being acquired, which will make this, next to Rock Creek Park, the largest in the District of Columbia.

Fort Davis: Northwest corner Alabama and Pennsylvania Avenues SE.

Fort Stanton: Fifteenth Street and Morris Roads, Anacostia SE. (Approach from Nichols Avenue.) A portion of the old fort is still in existence.

Battery Ricketts: Bruce and Fort Place SE, Anacostia, immediately east of Fort Stanton. (Approach from Alabama Avenue.) Only a small part of the old battery remains.

Fort Snyder: In St. Elizabeth's Hospital grounds near Alabama Avenue and Thirtieth Street SE.

Fort Carroll: Immediately south of Nichols Avenue at First Street SE, Congress Heights.

Fort Greble: Between Raleigh Street and Fourth Street about Elmira Street extended SE, in Congress Heights. Remains of this fort are still visible.

The following forts acquired by the Commission but not connected with Fort Drive are:

Fort Raynard: Between River Road and Fessenden Street at Western Avenue.

Fort Bunker Hill: Perry Street between Thirteenth and Fourteenth Streets NE.

Fort Foote: On Potomac River near Oxon Hill."

---

8 | Open to the Public | **Franciscan Monastery (Commissariat of the Holy Land for the United States) (1400 Quincy Street, NE; 202/526–6800)&&:**

The Monastery, whose official name is the Commissariat of the Holy Land for the United States, was established in 1897, and its church, an ode to Italian Renaissance religious architecture, was completed in 1899. The main work of the monks is to raise money for the restoration and preservation of Christian shrines in the Holy Land. The Order of the Friars Minor runs the monastery and maintains its grounds, which feature a lovely rose garden.

---

9 | Open to the Public | **Gallaudet University (800 Florida Avenue, NE; 202/651–5000; TDD: 202/651–5104)**

Gallaudet University is the only accredited liberal arts university in the world devoted to the education of students with hearing impairments. It was founded in 1864 on the site of one of Washington's most venerable estates, Kendall Green. The founder of the school, Amos Kendall, was Postmaster General under President Andrew Jackson and went on to make a fortune as the business manager for Samuel F. B. Morse. In 1856, Kendall set up a small school at his estate to tutor five orphaned children who were deaf and mute. A year later, the school was chartered as the Columbia School Institute for the Deaf and Dumb, which became a four-year college in 1864. Kendall died five years later, but his legacy of learning lived on at his estate. The college was renamed in honor of the school's first teacher, Edward Miner Gallaudet, in 1894.

1894 was also the year the Gallaudet University entered the annals of football trivia. That year, its football team, the Bison, found they needed to prevent opposing teams from reading the sign language they used to call on-field plays. By forming a tight circle around their quarterback, they were able to communicate within the privacy of a human wall. Thus was born the huddle—one of the game's most ingrained traditions.

Another important event in the history of Gallaudet occurred in 1989, when the school's Board of Trustees appointed a new university president. Like her predecessors, she had solid academic and management credentials, but no hearing impairment. She couldn't even speak sign language. The student body revolted, boycotting classes, picketing the Administration building, and blocking access to the school grounds. Gallaudet students made international headlines by effectively shutting down the school to demand that their world of silence be heard loud and clear: They wanted a hearing-impaired president who understood *them*, not merely their fundraising needs. Finally, the new president stepped down, and King Jordan, a deaf educator and long-time leader for the rights of the handicapped, was named the new president. Since Jordan took office as the first deaf president of a major university, his work has been highly praised and his life heavily profiled in the major media.

The wonderful Victorian Gothic architecture and landscaping of the campus was the work of Frederick Law Olmsted (also responsible for the landscaping of the Capitol grounds) and Calvert Vaux.

Although Kendall Green is usually noted as the primary estate from which Gallaudet was carved, another major estate, Brentwood, also stood here once (at Florida Avenue and 6th Street, NE). Brentwood was a wedding gift from the Mayor of Washington, Robert Brent, to his daughter Eleanor on the occasion of her marriage to South Carolina congressman Joseph Pearson. Benjamin Latrobe was hired to design the house, which was completed in 1817. Brentwood was considered one of the city's finer country estates, but it slowly decayed as the family grew up and moved on, eventually abandoning the home altogether. The Ivy City Railroad Yards were built on part of the estate's land in 1916, and the federal government turned the site into Camp Meigs the following year for use as a training ground for soldiers heading into World War I. What remained of the house, as well as the camp barracks, were torn down in 1919.

---

10 **Glenwood Cemetery (2219 Lincoln Road, NE; 202/667–1016)**

One of Washington's little-known burial grounds, Glenwood Cemetery has several of the most unusual memorials in the city. The cemetery was founded in 1854, just as the Victorian era of overblown emotion and ornament was taking hold, which could explain some of these grave markers. One of the most notable is the figure of a small girl seated in a rocking chair, which memorializes the death by burning of Teresa Vasco, age two. Another remarkable monument was erected in memory of Benjamin C. Grenup, the first D.C. fireman to die in the line of duty. His memorial captures the circumstances of his death. (He was crushed by heavy equipment being hauled to a fire.)

During the Civil War, Glenwood Cemetery took in some 1,500 instant residents, when the Washington Foundry Methodist Church downtown was forced to sell its burial grounds to raise money, and transferred its graves here.

See Also: Washington Foundry Methodist Church (Chapter 9)

---

11 **Haddock's Hills Site (southeast corner of Bladensburg Road and New York Avenue, NE)**

This industrial area was once home to one of the earliest plantations in the area, Haddock's Hills, which dated back to a 1685 land-grant of 500 acres made by Lord Baltimore to Benjamin Haddock. According to James Goode's *Capital Losses* (1979), later owners of the plantation included Richard Queen, for whom nearby Queen's Chapel Road, which bounds the old estate site, was named; and Jonathon Slater, who expanded a small tenant house on the land into a grander Federal house in 1800. That house served as home to several prominent locals, notably Dr. Charles Nichols, who lived there in the 1850s while overseeing the construction of St. Elizabeth's Hospital. Nichols went on to serve as the facility's first curator. Anton Ruppert, a German immigrant who became one of the city's leading butchers, purchased the estate in 1865. The house—which came to be known as Ruppert House—and its attendant buildings were razed in 1938 to make way for development by the United Brick Corporation.

See Also: St. Elizabeth's Hospital (Chapter 11)

Kendall Green. *See* Gallaudet University

12 Langston Golf Course (26th Street and Benning Road)

This is the city's oldest golf course for blacks. It was opened in 1934 by the National Park Service as a blacks-only golf course. At the time, segregation laws prohibited blacks from playing golf at any of the city's other courses. Recently, the golf course has been threatened by the possible construction here of a new stadium to replace RFK. The people of Kingman Park, which is one of Washington's oldest and best established black neighborhoods, have been fighting the new stadium plans—to protect Langston Golf Course, as well as to avoid the added traffic and congestion that an even larger stadium would bring to their neighborhood.

13 Langston Terrace Apartments (2101 G Street, NE)

Completed in 1938 as part of President Franklin Roosevelt's New Deal, this apartment project gained national attention as a model development for public housing (in this case, public housing for blacks). At the time Langston Terrace was built, the city was filled with lower-income families, mostly black, who lived in the alleys of the city, often in makeshift houses and huts. Alley life was such a prevalent problem that a bureaucratic department—the Alley Dwelling Authority—was established in 1934 to regulate and attempt to eradicate this housing lifestyle. Langston Terrace was considered to be the prototype for a solution.

Roosevelt's interior secretary, Harold Ickes, ceremoniously laid the cornerstone of the project—which had been designed by Hilyard Robinson. Afterwards, the federal government continued to promote Langston Terrace with great fanfare at every occasion. (Queen Wilhel-

A WPA photographer captured these alley dwellers on film, circa 1937.

mina of the Netherlands even took a tour of the complex in 1940.) The Works Progress Administration, which was charged with the construction and running of the building, also had plans to build a similar complex for low-income whites, but funding ran out before the project could be started.

See Also: "The Alley Life" (Chapter 2)

14 Clark Mills Home and Foundry Site (2350 Bladensburg Road, NE)

Here, where Metro bus yards now sprawl, Clark Mills, one of the great sculptors of Washington's statuary, built a foundry, home, and studio in the late 1850s. Mills had been working in a temporary foundry set up on the grounds of the Treasury Department Building, in which he had cast the bronze statue of Andrew Jackson that still stands in Lafayette Park. The statue was considered one of the great engineering feats of its time when it was unveiled in 1853, for it depicted Jackson astride a rearing horse (thus the weight of the statue is carried entirely upon the horse's rear legs). It was the largest bronze work ever cast to date in America, and made Mills famous overnight.

The fame and fortune Mills won for his Jackson statue allowed him to buy part of the Meadow Bank Spa Springs farm, and set up shop here. Animal models (including buffalo and elk) roamed the farm grounds while Mills worked on his sculpture. Among the works Mills cast at his new foundry were the equestrian statue of George Washington that stands in Washington Circle (dedicated in 1859), and the famous figure of "Freedom" atop the Capitol Dome, which Mills completed in 1862. The foundry building, with its crenelated brick walls, was the only octagonal commercial building constructed in the city.

See Also: Lafayette Park and U.S. Treasury Building (Chapter 1); "A Dome for the Capitol" (Chapter 2)

15 [Open to the Public] Mount Olivet Cemetery (1300 Bladensburg Road, NE; 202/399–3000)

One of Washington's great old cemeteries, Mount Olivet is located just across the way from the National Arboretum. The seventy-five acre cemetery was founded in 1858, on the grounds of the former Fenwick Farm, purchased by the Roman Catholic Church for use as Washington's official Catholic burial ground. Catholics buried in other cemeteries around the city were disinterred and reburied here, so that Mount Olivet started out with quite a collection of notable tenants. Among those buried here are James Hoban, White House architect; and Constantino Brumidi, Capitol dome painter. Mount Olivet also has the graves of two notorious nineteenth-century figures—Henry Wirz, the evil commandant of the Confederate Andersonville Prison in Georgia, where hundreds of Union soldiers died; and Mary Surratt, hanged for her questionable role in the conspiracy to murder President Lincoln. Her grave, overgrown and nearly anonymous, is number 12F in lot 31, and is designated with a simple gravestone reading only "Mrs. Surratt."

16 [Open to the Public] National Arboretum (R Street off of Bladensburg Road, NE; 202/475–4815)

Nearly 450 acres of blooming, towering flora overlooking the Anacostia River, the National Arboretum resides upon what was once known as Hickey Hill, former site of the ancestral home of Captain William Hickey. Hickey was the brave young officer who led the only organized resistance to the British attack on Washington in 1814, a futile attempt that nonetheless made Hickey a local hero. Congress established the park in 1927, as a place for research into plant growth and development, and since that time the Arboretum has become a living laboratory for the study of (and not to mention the sheer enjoyment of) hundreds of plant species. One of the Washington area's favorite flowering shrubs, the azalea, is heavily represented here—some 70,000 bushes of every conceivable color paint a vivid springtime landscape at the park.

There are a number of surprising sights on the grounds of the arboretum, most notably the neo-classical columns of the U.S. Capitol, which were removed during the building's renovation in 1958 and left, forgotten, in storage until they were recovered and put on display at the Great Meadow of the National Arboretum. On June 14, 1990, Secretary of Agriculture Clayton Yeutter dedicated the display of twenty-two columns at the Arboretum that once graced the Capitol's East Portico. The landscaping around the columns includes a reflecting pool and water stair and fountain, all designed to add a classical flair to the elegant columns in the field.

A stir was created at another Arboretum highlight, the National Bonsai Collection, when it was discovered that a rare little tree worth $75,000 had disappeared from the collection. When the word spread about the bonsai caper, an embarrassed college student showed up, tree in hand; he had snitched the tiny tree with an eye to decorating his apartment, having no concept of the worth of the tree. The Arboretum quickly installed a security system to protect the multimillion dollar collection of fifty Japanese Bonsai trees (some dating back 350 years), which had been given to the U.S. by Japan in 1976 as a Bicentennial token of admiration.

See Also: U.S. Capitol (Chapter 3)

---

17 | Open to the Public | **National Shrine of the Immaculate Conception (Michigan Avenue at 4th Street, NE; 202/526–8300)**

When the National Shrine of the Immaculate Conception was completed in 1959, it made news around the world. To begin with, it was the main church in the United States devoted to Marianism (the worship of the Virgin Mary, by papal declaration the patron saint of America). In addition, it was the largest Catholic church in the Western Hemisphere.

The shrine's crypt gallery features the coronation crown of Pope Paul VI, who removed the gold and silver headpiece after his 1963 coronation and placed it on the altar in a gesture meant to symbolize unity with the world's poor. Through the efforts of Cardinal Spellman's office, the crown (the last to be worn by a Pope) was given to the shrine as a holy relic. To this day, pilgrims from around the world visit the crown and make donations to support the work of Mother Theresa in Calcutta.

Now the seventh largest church of any denomination in the world (the Washington National Cathedral is the sixth), the shrine has a lavishly decorated Byzantine dome that can be seen for miles. Although formerly part of the Catholic University of America, since 1973 the National Shrine of the Immaculate Conception has been owned by the National Conference of Catholic Bishops.

The National Shrine of the Immaculate Conception. (Jack Looney)

See Also: Catholic University of America; Washington National Cathedral (Chapter 8)

---

18 | Open to the Public | **Old Washington (Uline) Coliseum (Washington Miracle Faith Center) (Between 2nd and 3rd Streets and L and M Streets, NE; 202/544–0313)**

Long before the Capital Centre, and even before RFK, the old Washington Coliseum (also called the Uline Arena) was the place to come see everything from ice hockey games and the circus to rock and roll concerts and the Ice Capades. Perhaps the most historic event to take place here occurred on February 11, 1964, when the Beatles performed their first American concert date here. Although they had performed earlier in the week on the Ed Sullivan show, that appearance was in a television studio, so it doesn't really count as the first concert appearance. But the Washington Coliseum gig sure does.

A recently released documentary, *The Beatles: The First U.S. Visit* (MPI Video, 1991) records this historic concert date. The film shows the Beatles arriving at Union Station in a mild snowstorm (but with hundreds of screaming fans lying in wait for the band anyway), and then shows scenes from the performance at the Coliseum. The most striking thing revealed in this rare live footage is the low-tech nature of the band and their entourage. The audience was packed to the rafters on all four sides of the arena, so, to accommodate the crowd, the band would play a few songs, then rotate their instruments and amps a quarter-turn and play to the folks on that side, then rotate again, going around and around in this fashion throughout the show. Ringo and his drums were on a revolving dais that simply spun around, but John, Paul, and George moved their own instruments and equipment at each turn.

Although the old Uline Ice Company next door is long-gone, the old Washington Coliseum still exists. But it goes by a different name and use today: The Washington Miracle Faith Center, where crowds pack in to save or be saved.

See Also: Union Station (Chapter 3)

---

⑲ Rammed Earth House Site (1300 Rhode Island Avenue, NE)

One of Washington's most unusual architectural wonders stood for more than two centuries at this site: The Rammed Earth House, built here in 1773. The 1937 WPA guidebook, *Washington: City and Capital*, describes the house's construction thus:

"This curious house, to which has been added a Greek Revival front portico and wooden rear, was constructed of ordinary dirt from the excavation. The dirt was dumped into heavy wooden forms and pounded with a large iron-shod mallet until the earth was packed or "rammed" to a very hard consistency. These large blocks of stone-like earth, 4 feet long and 24 inches thick, and a foot or more high, were then laid like huge bricks. The lasting quality of this form of construction was amply tested when the owners recently attempted to demolish the house. The house has been studied as a type of construction by several Government agencies interested in low-cost methods of enduring construction."

A nondescript apartment/retail building now occupies the site.

---

⑳ Marjorie Kinan Rawlings House (1221 Newton Street, NE)

This house, still privately owned, was the childhood home of writer Marjorie Kinan Rawlings. Rawlings was born in Washington in 1896, and spent most of her youth here. (She attended Western High School, now the Duke Ellington School for the Performing Arts.) In her late teens, Rawlings moved with her mother to Wisconsin. She later lived in rural Florida, where she wrote her Pulitzer-prize winning novel, *The Yearling*, published in 1938.

See Also: Duke Ellington School for the Performing Arts (Chapter 6)

㉑ The Round House (1001 Irving Street, NE)

Brookland is filled with delightful architecture, including a number of Sears-and-Roebuck houses; but the house at 1001 Irving Street is really worth driving around (and around) the block to see. Built in 1901, the only completely round house in the area is a one-and-a-half story home with a polygonal roof, supported by columns, that overlaps a circular porch. The wooden-shingle-sided house is currently painted a vibrantly violet hue, making the home resemble an architectural Easter egg planted at the street corner.

The Burning of Washington

The War of 1812 brought home to Washington what no other war before or since has: destruction at the hands of the enemy. On August 24, 1824, the British, led by Admiral Cockburn and General Ross, took on the Americans, led by General Winder, in Bladensburg, Maryland (so close to Washington that President Madison rode out to see the fighting). The rout of the Americans, which took about half an hour, was dubbed the "Bladensburg Races," for the battle more resembled a foot chase, with the British hot in pursuit of the quickly retreating Americans.

That same day, the British marched to Washington, meeting virtually no resistance upon their arrival in the afternoon. Word of their approach had spread quickly, and many residents had already fled. As they neared the Capitol, however, a rebellious soul inside what was then called the Gallatin House (now the Sewall-Belmont House) shot the horse out from under General Ross. Ross went into hiding for the rest of the siege of Washington, certain that someone was out to get him in particular.

At the U.S. Capitol, the enemy caroused through the hallways, grabbing books from the tiny Library of Congress and using them to stoke the fires that they set throughout the building. The Capitol was quickly consumed with flames. The rest of the federal city underwent the same fate, with only one notable federal site being spared: The Patent Office, where William Thornton made a passionate plea for its salvation, which for some odd reason touched a chord in the British souls.

The White House was less fortunate. Dolley Madison had waited until the last possible moment to leave, as her husband had not yet returned home from Bladensburg. When word reached her that the British had entered the city, she finally fled the house, taking only a few valuables, including the famed Gilbert Stuart portrait of George Washington. One story has it that Mrs. Madison had planned a dinner party for that evening. When the British arrived at the White House, they found an elegant meal all laid out for them, which they enjoyed before torching the building. The fire gutted the interior, leaving only the exterior walls standing.

Other sites destroyed during the British attack included the U.S. Treasury, as well as the offices of a newspaper run by a British journalist, the *National Intelligencer.* According to Admiral Cockburn, this paper had helped fan the flames of war by printing scurrilous articles about the British commander. To make certain this would not happen again, Cockburn instructed his men to do away with all the letters "C" in the type boxes.

While the city burned around them, the British high-tailed it over to the Rhodes Tavern to toast their success. They had as yet suffered no severe casualties. The next day, however, when they set upon the fort at Greenleaf Point (now the Navy Yard), the British accidentally blew about forty of themselves up with a careless match tossed into a storage area where gunpowder had been hidden.

The fires set by the British, although mainly limited to federal buildings, might well have spread throughout the city. Fortunately, a violent thunderstorm struck the next

(Continued)

afternoon, putting out many of the fires. But the next day a strange tornado or cyclone is said to have whipped through the city, causing cataclysmic damage to many of the same buildings that the thunderstorm had saved.

The Madisons moved into temporary residence at the Octagon House near the ruined White House, while Congress was soon installed in the hastily constructed Brick Capitol. The spirit of the new capital city was not as easily replaced, however, and there was much talk of moving the government from the burned ruins of Washington. But Congress finally voted in 1815 to rebuild the lost structures where they had once stood, and to remain in the city designated by George Washington as the nation's capital.

While the British soldiers who burned Washington may have believed theirs was a great victory, they found a furious populace on their return to England. The British press, reflecting the general public outrage, strongly censured its own national militia. These words, published soon after the burning, appeared in the London *Statesman:* "Willingly would we throw a veil of oblivion over the transactions at Washington; the Cossacks spared Paris, but we spared not the capital of America!" And the British *Annual Register* stated: "The extent of the devastation practiced by the victors brought a heavy censure upon the British character, not only in America but in the Continent of Europe."

22 Toll-Gate Site (east side of Bladensburg Road at Benning Road intersection, NE)

The old country road that ran from Baltimore into the District (and down which the British marched to burn the Capitol in 1814) was turned into the Bladensburg Turnpike by a commercial road company in 1820. At this site once stood the old turnpike's toll-gate house, where travelers passing between the District and Maryland were required to stop and pay a toll. Disgruntled travelers used to quip that if the pay turnpike had been in place when the British attacked Washington, the city might have been saved, because the enemy army wouldn't have had the money to pay the toll. A gas station now stands at the site.

23 [Open to the Public] Trinity College (125 Michigan Avenue, NE; 202/939–5000)

Trinity College, a women's liberal arts college with strong ties to the Catholic Church, was founded in 1897 by the Sisters of Notre Dame de Namur. The college claims two area landmarks as part of its small campus: The Chapel of Notre Dame, which features a sixty-seven-foot-high Byzantine dome that is decorated with Barcel La Farge's mosaic depiction of "The Coronation of the Virgin," taken from a scene in Dante's *Divine Comedy*; and the school's Main Hall, built in 1899, which features a four-story atrium with stained glass windows.
See Also: Catholic University of America

Chapter 11

SOUTHEAST AND ANACOSTIA

S ome might say this is the most neglected corner of Washington, for it is here that some of the most run-down black neighborhoods have trudged on for decades, unnoticed by the glamorous world of national politics that thrives nearby. Yet this is a place of history, too: Captain John Smith, John Wilkes Booth, Frederick Douglass, and William Marbury (whose failed lawsuit, *Marbury v. Madison*, expanded the powers of the Supreme Court) all left their marks here.

Southeast Washington has a split personality. The section on the northern banks of the Anacostia River includes the lower eastern half of Capitol Hill and such landmarks as the **Navy Yard, RFK Stadium,** and **Congressional Cemetery,** while across the river lies Anacostia, with its ancient and modern history of diverse cultures, neighborhoods, and personalities.

The first residents of either side of the Anacostia were Native Americans, and the first white man to document an encounter with them was Captain John Smith, who sailed up the Potomac in 1608, reaching the Potomac's Eastern Branch on June 16. Leaving their ship behind, Smith and his crew continued their exploration by canoe, and landed on the eastern banks of the river. They entered an Indian village, where the natives lived in domed huts made of skins and branches supported by curved poles. Smith later identified this site on a 1612 map as the village of the "Nacotchtank." After leaving the village, Smith and his men continued traveling to the east inland on foot up The Trail of Fair Justice (now known as **Good Hope Road**).

Later that century, the English trader Henry Fleet visited the same region, referring to the natives as the Nacostines. During his travels through the region in 1632, Fleet described the abundance of beaver, turkey, deer, and sturgeon that could be found in the area. He eagerly traded with the natives, acquiring "800 weight of beaver." Two years later, Father Andrew White, a Jesuit priest who traveled in the area in the company of Leonard Calvert, sent reports of his journey back to Rome, and in these he called the natives the "Anacostines."

The natives were friendly to the English explorers, who reportedly established a trading relationship with them and the other tribes in the region. The village was already famed throughout the region as a kind of one-stop-shopping spot for trading, with tribes from as far away as New York (the Iroquois) traveling south yearly to do business with the villagers. In fact, the native word, "Anaquash-tank," meaning "Town of Traders," is likely the source of the name given the village by John Smith, which has garbled its way into modern-day parlance as "Anacostia."

Within sixty years of their first contact with John Smith and his men, the original village and its people had disappeared. They were wiped out by a combination of the white man's diseases (against which they had no natural immunity), and attacks by both whites and other tribes.

The Nacotchanks are believed to have been a splinter tribe that sprang from the Algonquins, who lived in the region of present-day Rock Creek Park. Tahoga Village (located in present-day Georgetown), was another major native village in the region which also traded heavily with the English. These first native Washingtonians were so friendly to the Europeans that they inadvertently traded away their land and were soon displaced from their homeland.

Small farming communities of white settlers began cropping up on the eastern banks of the Eastern Branch of the Potomac (as the Anacostia was then known) long before the capital city site was selected. As the City of Washington began to rise to the north, the land that would one day be called Anacostia developed into an agricultural community, with a few land-tilling barons owning most of the land. The Eastern Branch of the Potomac slowly took on the new name of Anacostia, the only remnant of the village that had stood on its banks for centuries.

The mainland portion of Southeast was originally part of the "ten-miles-square" plan for the City of Washington, as laid out by the surveying team of Andrew Ellicott and Benjamin Banneker. This section, much of which is considered part of Capitol Hill (and is covered in Chapter 3), was sold to the federal government by the various landowners, chief among whom was Daniel Carroll (whose lands spread across most of lower Northeast and upper Southeast).

While this "mainland" (northern) portion of Southeast was developed as part of Washington from the city's inception, the settlements on the southern banks of the Anacostia River were not incorporated into the City of Washington until 1854. This formal stamp of urban identification sparked the development of a new, planned community where once only the crazy-quilt landscape of farms and country estates had covered the land. Uniontown, as the planned community was dubbed, was created by a development group led by John W. Van Hook. The group acquired 240 acres belonging to the Chichester Tract of farmland, which had been originally awarded in 1663 to an English surgeon named John Meekes, in gratitude for his transport of six colonists to the Maryland colonies. They chose the site for its proximity to the Navy Yard, which employed hundreds of lower-middle-class workers who were having a hard time finding affordable and safe neighborhoods within an easy commute.

Uniontown grew rapidly as its targeted audience of working-class Washingtonians moved in. A burgeoning community of freedmen who were treated harshly in many of Washington's working class neighborhoods also moved across the river. But Uniontown itself remained a white community, until Frederick Douglass created a scandal in 1877 by taking up residence in **Cedar Hill.** As Uniontown grew, it spread its reach into several outlying neighborhoods, although its core remained a quiet, middle-class mini-town. This area is often referred to as "Old Anacostia," and has remained relatively unchanged since the late nineteenth century.

The Anacostia side of the river was also home to one of the area's largest Victorian resort parks—Giesboro, located at the site where the **Bolling Airfield** now sprawls. Giesboro was originally a sprawling tract of real estate granted to early landowner George

Thompson, who also received a grant of the Saint Elizabeth Tract (where the hospital would later be built). The two combined tracts stretched south from the modern-day Suitland Parkway, where the neighborhoods of Congress Heights and Washington Highlands were also developed on much of its former land.

Another major portion of the land in Anacostia was owned at one time by William Marbury. Marbury began buying up land on the Eastern Branch in 1802, acquiring the Blue Plains Tract (in the southernmost tip, where the sewage treatment plant of the same name now resides) and the tract known as Addison's Good Will. Five years later, he bought the Chichester estate upon which Uniontown was later built. In 1800, Marbury moved into a mansion in Georgetown, but used his real estate purchases as investments. At around the time Marbury began his investments in the area's real estate, he became embroiled in what has gone down as one of the most important Supreme Court cases ever: *Marbury v. Madison*. In 1801, just as President John Adams was about to leave office, he appointed Marbury as a local justice of the peace and gave similar small offices to several other individuals. The incoming president, Thomas Jefferson, balked at these last-minute appointments, and ordered Secretary of State James Madison not to deliver the commissions. Marbury and the other men who were denied their appointments sued Madison, but the Supreme Court held that Marbury's lawsuit was unconstitutional. The decision of the high court, handed down in 1803, was the first of its kind, and thus it expanded the role of the Supreme Court into the realm of judicial review (and determined its ability to declare presidential or legislative acts unconstitutional).

As the twentieth century dawned, Washington's black citizens were slowly transforming several middle-class neighborhoods such as Shaw and LeDroit Park into well-defined black communities with unique social and cultural institutions. They were following the example set by Anacostia, which had already developed into just such a neighborhood by the turn of the century.

In 1932, Anacostia was again transformed, at least briefly, but with shattering effect, by the Bonus Army of World War I veterans, who had marched on Washington to demand promised bonus pay from Congress. Part of this Army encamped on the Anacostia Flats (now part of **Anacostia Park**) for a long summer of waiting. Their wait ended on July 28 when they were routed from their encampment by General Douglas MacArthur's troops and brutally forced out of Washington. The nation was shocked, and the incident helped President Hoover lose the election that year to Franklin Roosevelt.

Today's Anacostia is a contradiction in terms of both society and history. Its neighborhood streets are lined with nineteenth-century townhouses and homes that have changed little in the past hundred years; yet the scourge of crack houses and the desensitizing level of violence have given Anacostia the reputation of being a no-man's land where frontier justice rules. It's a reputation that, perhaps by statistics alone, is well-earned. In 1991, 30 percent of the murders committed in Washington occurred in Anacostia. But no place is a statistic, no neighborhood the aggregate of drug-arrest tallies and chalk-outline figures. And in Anacostia, there are pockets of hope—citizens who patrol their streets to fight off the dealers, parents who walk the neighborhood children to and from school, people for whom home is more than a place to bar the door at night and pray the bullets don't come through the windows. Right now, Anacostia is sleepwalking through a long, dark night of

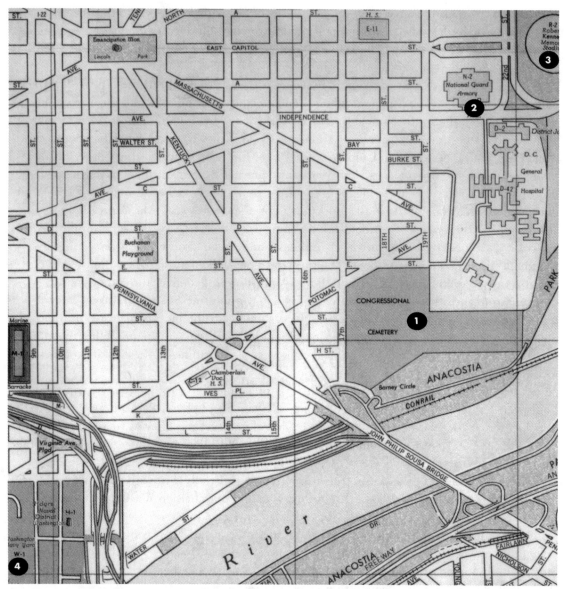

From Washington D.C. Visitor's Map © 1991 by Rand McNally, R.L. 91–S–96

violence. But fifty years ago, it was a neighborhood of dreams, and there are many residents who have chosen to hang on and wait for daybreak.

PLACES: "Mainland Southeast" (West of the Anacostia River)

Much of Southeast not located in Anacostia is located in the Capitol Hill area of neighborhoods and businesses that wrap around the federal seat of legislative power. Farther east of Capitol Hill is the neighborhood of Kingman Park, a long-established, middle-class black neighborhood which has been plagued since the 1960s with the scourge of traffic and pedestrian congestion generated by **RFK Stadium** and the **D.C. National Armory.**

The Starplex Armory complex (as the pair are sometimes called) sits at the far end of East Capitol Street, on the border between Northeast and Southeast. On the fringes of Southeast lie a number of historic sites—notably **Congressional Cemetery** and the **Navy Yard.**

---

① | Open to the Public | ### Congressional Cemetery (1801 E Street, SE; 202/543–0539)

Long before Arlington Cemetery was established as the nation's burial ground and VIP RIP place of choice, Congressional Cemetery was a desirable interment spot for many of Washington's greatest figures. Local residents created the cemetery in 1807, turning it over to the care of Christ Church (at 7th and G Streets, SE) in 1808.

Benjamin Latrobe designed the simple gravestones beneath which the great were to be buried, a selling point that was unpopular with many potential clients, who wanted the right to install elaborate tombstones or memorials. Still, the cemetery was popular enough that reservations were required for the one hundred original plots. By 1816 so many Capitol Hill crusaders were either already interred or had plots reserved here that the federal government began providing funds to preserve a section of the cemetery for Congressional movers and shakers.

The thirty-acre cemetery includes the final resting places of more than 150 senators and congressmen, along with many leading military men, artists, politicians, G-men, and more than a few just plain folks. Those buried here include Matthew Brady (famed Civil War photographer), J. Edgar Hoover, Benjamin Latrobe, Tobias Lear (Washington's close confidant), Robert Mills and William Thornton (both major architects of the Capitol), Pushmataha (the Choctaw Chief who fought the British), and John Philip Sousa (the March King who was born, lived, and died on Capitol Hill).

President Tyler's secretaries of state and the navy, who died in the gun explosion on the deck of the steamship *Princeton* in 1844, were buried here with

Secretary of State Abel Upshur and Secretary of the Navy Thomas Gilmer were among those killed when the *Princeton's* new "Peacemaker" gun exploded. Upshur and Gilmer were buried in Congressional Cemetery. (*Our First Century*)

great ceremony (which, perhaps inappropriately, included gun salutes!) following their White House funeral. Another tragic accident led to the installation in 1867 of one of the cemetery's most striking monuments. A twenty-foot-tall obelisk decorated with the figure of a mourning woman was built to mark the graves of the twenty-one women killed in an explosion at the Washington Arsenal (now Fort McNair) in 1864.

The cemetery also played a role in one of the great scandals of the nineteenth century, for it was here that the lovely Mrs. Daniel Sickles sometimes trysted with the Attorney General,

Philip Barton Key II. When the lady's husband discovered the infidelity, he stalked Key through Lafayette Park, murdering him on the steps of a prominent social club.

See Also: Rodgers House (Chapter 1); Key's Lovenest and Matthew Brady's Gallery Site (Chapter 2); Christ Church, J. Edgar Hoover's Home Site, John Philip Sousa Birthplace, and John Philip Sousa Home (Chapter 3); Fort McNair and "Washington Disasters" (Chapter 12)

---

2 | Open to the Public | **D.C. Armory (2001 E Street, SE; 202/457-9077)**

The Armory was built in 1947 as the headquarters and military staging ground for the D.C. National Guard and other local militia. The armory's size and crowd capacity made it a natural for inaugural balls and other official events. Perhaps the most famous was John F.

The D.C. Armory. (Jack Looney)

Kennedy's Inaugural Gala, held on January 19, 1960, the evening before his inauguration. A winter storm caused many ballgoers to desert their snow-bound limos and hike on their own formally shod feet to the Armory.

Today, the auditorium is mainly used for large-scale public events that range from mammoth antique extravaganzas and trade shows to the annual visit of the Ringling Brothers' Barnum and Bailey Circus.

One such circus visit, on April 1, 1991, resulted in one of Washington's most unusual robberies. As a longstanding April Fool's Day tradition, the Ringling Brothers' Barnum and Bailey Circus gives away elephant manure for use as fertilizer. A loading zone behind the Armory was stocked the night before with tons of bagged manure, in preparation for the expected hordes of eager gardeners. But when the circus crew went out the next morning to begin loading the colorfully bagged manure into waiting vehicles, they discovered that the joke was on them: Someone had already snuck in and taken the entire load of bagged manure. Since the fertilizer was marked for giveaway, the circus chose not to pursue a criminal investigation; and, as the elephants were obligingly making more fertilizer, the latest harvest was quickly bagged and distributed. The circus left town later that week without ever discovering who had availed themselves of the warehouse of pachyderm packets.

See Also: RFK Memorial Stadium

---

3 | Open to the Public | **RFK Memorial Stadium (2001 E Street, SE; 202/547-9077)**

RFK Stadium was built in 1961 to replace the crumbling Griffith Stadium, which once stood on the site of Howard University Hospital. Today the stadium is home only to the Washington Redskins football team, but the Washington Senators baseball team also played here until they left town in 1972 to become the Texas Rangers. The 55,750-seat stadium, originally called D.C. Stadium (and originally housing 55,004 seats), was renamed in honor of Attorney General Robert F. Kennedy, who was murdered in 1968.

The Redskins' first five years at the D.C. Stadium were lackluster; in fact, it was not until the 1966 season that the team broke its decade-long losing streak by finishing the year with a 7–7–0 record. But by the late 1960s, with a roster of fresh young stars like quarterback Sonny Jurgenson and running-back-turned-wide receiver Charley Taylor (both of whom joined the team in 1964), the team was poised for glory. The arrival of legendary coach Vince Lombardi in 1969 seemed to add the final ingredients necessary for a winning streak; then Lombardi died of cancer just before the start of the 1970. Two years later, George Allen finally coached the Redskins to win the 1972 NFC Championship, at home in RFK Stadium on New Year's Eve, whomping the rival Dallas Cowboys by a score of 26 to 3. Even the loss of the Super Bowl to the Miami Dolphins couldn't dull the glow of having a winning team at last.

Besides hosting Redskins games and other sporting events, the stadium has been the site of major rock concerts by such superstar performers as Madonna and the Grateful Dead. In 1971,

---

Hail to the . . . Boston Braves?

The triple Super Bowl champion Washington Redskins are as much a homegrown Capital tradition as Senate Bean Soup and jogging on the tow-path. Or are they? When it was formed in 1932, the team we now call the "Skins" was known as the "Braves." The *Boston* Braves at that. Their sister baseball team (established before the football team, but which shared Braves stadium with the upstart NFL team for the first year) eventually ended up in Georgia as the Atlanta Braves. Thus, when the 1991 fall sports season spawned politically correct protests against both the Braves' fans' symbolic "Tomahawk Chop" salute, and against the Redskins' team name, the activists were more on target than even they imagined, for the two teams were once allied by ties that were more than skin deep.

The team was re-located here in 1937, when owner George Preston Marshall, who was developing into quite a laundry magnate in the Washington area, decided to move his team closer to his business interests. He had already changed the team's name to the Redskins in 1933 after endless confusion with the Braves baseball team. Marshall liked to call himself the "Big Chief," and often appeared at games and team functions in war paint and headdress. Thus he chose to keep the Indian imagery in his team's name. He even hired a full-blooded Native American to coach the team in 1933, William "Lone Star" Dietz, who also often appeared in war paint and bonnet.

When Marshall moved the team to Washington in 1937, he made every effort to win over the team's new hometown. Marshall put together a large brass band to play at games and commissioned a fight song for the team's debut at Griffith Stadium. The composer was Barnet "Barnee" Briskin (at the time, the band-leader at the Shoreham Hotel). And the lyricist who penned the immortal lines "Hail to the Redskins, Hail Victory, Braves on the Warpath, Fight for Old D.C." was none other than Corinne Griffith, also known as Mrs. George Preston Marshall. The song has become one of the best-known professional sports anthems in American history.

In many ways, George Preston Marshall was the father of NFL spectacle. It was his idea to create half-time entertainment with marching bands and pom-pom girls. (His theory was that if he gave the girls some costumes and music in between the boys' game, he'd bring twice as many people to the stadium.) Another Marshall spectacle was the annual arrival of Santa Claus. During the half-time of the last regular season game, Marshall would have a fellow in a Santa suit arrive at the stadium by motorcycle, by balloon, or in some other surprising and amusing fashion. The only time he missed was the year he tried to float into the stadium via parachute: Snagged by a gust of arctic wind, Saint Nick was blown off course and forced to land on a nearby apartment house rooftop.

it even served as a giant jail when the May Day March on the Mall got out of hand and the police arrested more than a thousand protestors. With no place to put such a crowd, the police decided to corral the prisoners (mostly young adults) into RFK Stadium for an overnight stay. The protestors were left virtually to their own devices during their incarceration, so a full-scale party broke out, turning RFK into a scene out of Woodstock. To this day, the federal government is ironing out the multiple lawsuits that resulted from the mass arrest, the largest in the city's history.

Memorials outside of the stadium honor Clark Griffith, the long-time owner of the Washington Senator's baseball team, and George Preston Marshall, the founding owner of the Washington Redskins; both helped make Washington a true sports capital.

See Also: D.C. Armory and **"Hail to the . . . Boston Braves?";** Union Station (Chapter 2); Howard University Hospital (Chapter 9)

❹ | Open to the Public | **Washington Navy Yard (Entrance at 9th and M Streets, SE)**

The Washington Navy Yard was built in 1800, after a design by prolific architect Benjamin Latrobe, and served as the city's own personal naval base. During the Civil War, President Lincoln often visited the Navy Yard, chatting with the sailors and naval officers charged with defending the city from a river attack and with refurbishing such famous battleships as the *Monitor*, which docked at the Yard for repairs. The president used the Navy Yard as his point of departure for most river trips (in the same manner that modern presidents arrive and depart from Andrews Air Force Base).

The naval practice battery at the Navy Yard drilling during the Civil War. (*Harper's Pictorial History of the Civil War*)

According to Richard M. Lee's *Mr. Lincoln's City* (1981), the Navy Yard played a tragically dual role in April, 1865. Two weeks before his assassination, Lincoln took a relaxing cruise along the Potomac in the *Montauk*, a Union battleship docked here. The corpse of his assassin, John Wilkes Booth, was later brought for autopsy to the very same ship (still docked at the Navy Yard). The other Lincoln conspirators were at first held after their capture in a ship docked at the Navy Yard, before they were transferred to (now) Fort McNair, where they were tried and hanged for their crimes.

A sprawling complex that spreads along the waterfront from 1st to 11th Streets, the Navy Yard is now a historic site featuring two museums, the Naval Memorial Museum (202/433–4882) and Marine Corps Museum (202/433–3534). Both have fascinating military exhibits, but perhaps the most unique item at the Navy Yard is not found within a museum. It is found within the walls of the Foundry Building, where a plaque on the side of the building marks the location of the leg of Ulric Dahlgren, the son of then-Navy Yard Commander Admiral John Dahlgren. When young Dahlgren lost his leg in a Civil War battle near Gettysburg, his father

Of Life and Limbs

The leg of Colonel Ulric Dahlgren entombed in the wall of the Navy Yard is not as odd as it might seem: The missing limbs of other military men from the Washington area have been similarly memorialized. When Major General Daniel Sickles lost his leg at Gettysburg around the same time Dahlgren lost his, he generously donated the limb, and the cannonball that shot it off, to the Army Medical Museum (now the National Museum of Health and Medicine, located at Walter Reed Army Medical Center). Every year on the anniversary of his loss, Sickles would visit his limb at the museum and drink a toast in its honor, a tradition that was much tittered over in Washington's social circles.

When Stonewall Jackson was accidentally shot in the arm by his own men during the battle near Fredericksburg, Virginia, his personal physician amputated the wounded arm in a futile attempt to save his life. The arm was buried in a field behind the farm-house (called Elwood) where the surgery was performed, and a grave-marker, which still stands, was erected to memorialize the burial site of the "Arm of Stonewall Jackson."

Why this fascination with preserving limbs? The Civil War left more Americans severely maimed than any other conflict in American history, and the near-mythic number of limbs lost during the war may explain the sentimental devotion and even obsession about the missing parts. In fact, one of the most successful businesses in Washington during the post-Civil War era was the J.E. Hangar Company, which manufactured prosthetic limbs. To advertise its product line, the company published photographs documenting prosthetically equipped veterans at work and play throughout the Washington area.

Daniel E. Sickles.

See Also: Hirshhorn Museum and Sculpture Garden (Chapter 4); Walter Reed Army Medical Center: National Museum of Health and Medicine, and "A Walk Through the Army Medical Museum" (Chapter 9)

decided to commemorate his brave son's loss of limb by entombing the leg, with full military honors, in the wall of a foundry then under construction, where it still resides.

See Also: Fort McNair (Chapter 12)

PLACES: Anacostia (NE and SE) and Environs (East of the Anacostia River)

The original boundaries of the diamond-shaped Uniontown subdivision still enclose the historic district of Anacostia to this day: Fifteenth Street (east border), W Street (west border), Good Hope Road (north border), and Martin Luther King Boulevard (south border). Enclosed within these borders is the area developed as a planned community in 1854, and it is here that some of the city's greatest collections of un-retouched nineteenth-century architecture still stand. Sadly, many of the buildings are in poor condition, and the riots of 1968 left their mark here, but the Uniontown of old can still be seen, ghostlike, on every street and down every alleyway.

The Anacostia area also includes such neighborhoods as Congress Heights, which was developed on land that was part of the Giesboro Estate, and Good Hope, which was once part of the Chichester tract (along with Uniontown). These are fairly modern neighborhoods (built in the last century), as the lands they occupy were operating plantations and farms until the mid-to-late nineteenth century.

A number of Civil War fort sites also exist in Anacostia, several of which—**Fort Chaplin, Fort Davis, Fort Dupont, Fort Mahan,** and **Fort Stanton**—have been partially preserved as park areas. There's even a fort (Fort Snyder) on the site of **St. Elizabeth's Hospital.** Although these forts, which were among the sixty-eight that ringed Washington, never saw any action during the war, they played an important deterrent role by helping create kind of a "barbed wire" net of forts that kept the Confederates largely at bay.

---

⑤ | Open to the Public | **Anacostia Park (East Capitol Street, from Pennsylvania Avenue to the Naval Annex; 202/433–1190)**

Anacostia Park extends along the eastern banks of the Anacostia River, just across the water from the National Arboretum. Originally home to the Nacotchank village discovered by Captain John Smith, today's Anacostia Park fills some eight miles of woodlands and fields, and includes winding nature trails and a bird sanctuary.

Tucked away within the park is the Kenilworth Aquatic Gardens (900 Anacostia Drive, NE; 202/426–6905), which was founded within Anacostia Park in 1882 by Civil War veteran W.B. Shaw, who started the garden with water lilies imported from Maine.

In 1932, the Bonus Army—a group of Depression-buffeted World War I veterans who were pressuring Congress to pay them a cash bonus for their service—set up camp on the muddy flats along the eastern banks of the Anacostia which are part of Anacostia Park. They christened their settlement "Camp Marks," and built shacks and set up tents, decorating their temporary homes with angry messages. (One marcher built a mock graveyard to honor those who had died for their country.) Camp Marks was run like an army camp, with the men answering to roll calls, waking to reveille, and working mess detail. They built latrines (calling them "Hoover Villas") and set up a baseball diamond for organized games. The Bonus Army's credo said it all: "Stay until the bonus is granted; no radical talk; no panhandling; no booze."

On the evening of July 28th, General Douglas MacArthur, having driven the Bonus Army out of the rest of the city through teargas and intimidation earlier in the day, ordered the division of tanks under the command of Major Dwight Eisenhower to block the Anacostia Bridge. At eleven that night, the tanks crossed the bridge and destroyed Camp Marks, throwing the Bonus Army out of Washington in one of the city's darkest moments. Citizens watched, stunned, as their own army burned the makeshift village and forcibly ejected the veterans, kill-

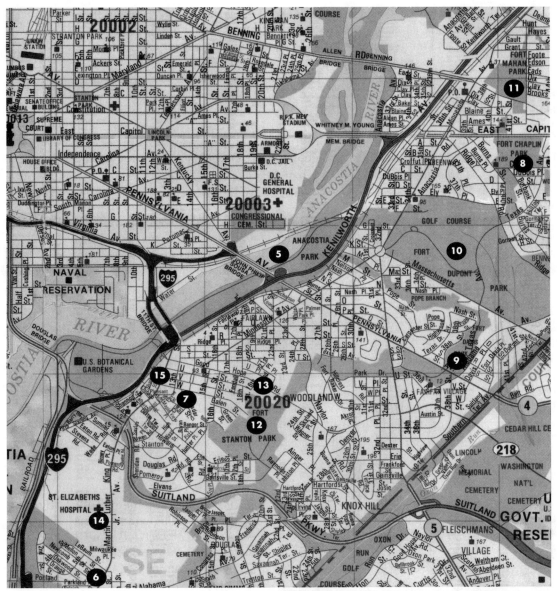

From Champion's Washington D.C. Street Map © 1991 by Rand McNally, R.L. 91–S–96

ing several. A horrified nation never forgave President Hoover for the episode. Franklin Roosevelt defeated the incumbent less than four months later.

See Also: "The Armies of the Mall" (Chapter 4)

⑥ Bolling Airfield (4 Portland Street, SE; 202/545–6700)

A major air force base near the branch of the Potomac and Anacostia Rivers, Bolling is located at the former site of Giesboro Point. A plantation-turned-fort-turned Victorian resort villa, Giesboro Point was once one of the area's most popular destinations for river excursions and Sunday outings. Over the years, four of the region's most important families had lived on the house estate, beginning with the Dent family, whose patriarch, Thomas Dent, received a land grant for 850 acres on the waterfront in 1663.

In 1833, George Washington Young, the area's largest slave-holder, bought the estate and developed it into a tobacco plantation. Then in 1863, the Union Army seized his estate for use as a defensive fort and massive stables. Camp Stoneman, as it was renamed, was the largest cavalry and work-horse stable in the area.

Following the Civil War, Camp Stoneman continued to operate at Giesboro until the Young family finally sold off the estate in 1877. Developers transformed the bucolic riverside landscape into a Victorian resort park, often called "Buena Vista," "Capitol View," and "City View," in various literature and guidebooks of the time. A typical day's outing might include a boat cruise up the river, picnic lunch on the grounds, and dancing in the Upper Giesboro house that evening. During one such dance in September of 1888, the building caught fire and was destroyed. The park was ruined and closed soon after.

The entire Giesboro Estate extended far beyond the bounds of the area that became the Victorian park, and much of this land was developed into the neighborhoods now known as Congress Heights and Good Hope. The site of the park was purchased by the military in 1917, after Billy Mitchell (then a Captain, soon to be a General, and now known as the Father of America's air force) convinced the secretary of war to buy the land for use as an airfield for the still-developing technology of flight. In 1918, the airfield was named for Col. Raynal Bolling, a supporter of peace-time military build-up, who died early in World War I.

---

7 | Open to the Public | **Cedar Hill (1411 W Street, SE; 202/426–5960)**

This brick homestead completed in 1855 was the home of black abolitionist and political advisor Frederick Douglass from 1877 until his death in 1895. When he purchased the house, Douglass broke a "whites only" covenant, angering many whites in Anacostia and the "mainland" alike. He raised even greater animosity in 1884 when he brought his second wife, Helen Pitts, home to Cedar Hill. (His first wife, Anna, died in 1882.) Pitts, a well-educated suffragette was twenty years younger than her husband. She was also white. The scandal soon faded, however, after Douglass pointed out that he was himself of mixed parentage, and that his first wife "was the color of my mother, and the second the color of my father."

Cedar Hill. (Jack Looney)

While in residence at Cedar Hill, Douglass entertained many of the leading political and social figures of his time; he also penned *The Life and Times of Frederick Douglass* (1882), the third volume of his autobiography. On February 20, 1895, Douglass collapsed suddenly and died at Cedar Hill while awaiting a carriage that was to take him to a speaking engagement.

Cedar Hill is preserved as a house museum and operated as the Frederick Douglass National Historic Site. Among the artifacts on display at the house and at the National Park Service visitors' center down the hill from the home are original furnishings and personal items from Douglass's life, as well as gifts from his friends and contemporaries, including abolitionist William Lloyd Garrison and author Harriet Beecher Stowe. One of the most unusual items at the visitors' center is a bone-handled walking cane used by President Lincoln. It was presented to Frederick Douglass by Mary Todd Lincoln, after her husband's assassination, in appreciation of Douglass's work in recruiting blacks to fight in the Union Army during the Civil War. Douglass's massive library of more than a thousand volumes is also on display at the house, and his beloved "Growlery," a one-room building that served as both a retreat and study has been reconstructed.

See Also: U.S. Treasury Annex (Chapter 1); Frederick Douglass Home (Chapter 3)

---

8 | Open to the Public | **Fort Chaplin Park (South of East Capitol Street at Fortieth Street, SE)**

One of the sixty-eight Civil War forts of Washington, Fort Chaplin was one of the Washington forts purchased by the National Capital Park and Planning Commission in the 1920s and '30s. The area was preserved as a city park. Just to the north sits another such fort park, **Fort Mahan Park,** while to the south, is **Fort Dupont Park,** another major preserved fort.

See Also: "The Civil War Forts of Washington" (Chapter 10)

---

9 | Open to the Public | **Fort Davis Park: (Northwest corner Alabama Avenue and Pennsylvania Avenue, SE)**

Just south of Fort Dupont Park, Fort Davis Park is one of the smaller fort areas protected as public parkland.

See Also: "The Civil War Forts of Washington" (Chapter 10)

---

10 | Open to the Public | **Fort Dupont Park (Randall Circle, SE; 202/426–7723)**

One of Washington's often forgotten Civil War forts forms the eastern boundary of this park, which offers an array of recreational facilities, including an indoor ice skating rink and a basketball court. After Rock Creek Park, it is the city's second largest park.

See Also: "The Civil War Forts of Washington" (Chapter 10)

---

11 | Open to the Public | **Fort Mahan Park (North of Benning Road and west of Forty-second Street, NE)**

This is yet another of Washington's Civil War Forts whose grounds have been preserved as a public park.

See Also: "The Civil War Forts of Washington" (Chapter 10)

---

12 | Open to the Public | **Fort Stanton Park (between Good Hope Road and Suitland Parkway at Sixteenth Street, SE)**

A portion of the old fort is still in existence at this parkland fort site which is the area's second largest (behind **Fort Dupont Park**).

See Also: "The Civil War Forts of Washington" (Chapter 10)

---

13 | Open to the Public | **Good Hope Road (Northern boundary road)**

After he had assassinated President Lincoln on the night of April 14, 1865, John Wilkes Booth made his escape along the Anacostia thoroughfare of Good Hope Road. Today, visitors and re-enactors retrace his (hobbled) steps as he fled the city with police and troops hot on his trail. Booth took Good Hope Road out of the city, heading deeper into the Maryland countryside, where Doctor Samuel Mudd set his broken leg and sent him on his way. Several days later, Booth was cornered and shot to death at a farm near Bowling Green, Virginia.

Good Hope Road dates back to the times when the Nacotchank Indians lived on the banks of the Anacostia, for Captain John Smith recorded in 1608 that he and his expedition explored inland along the route, which was then known to the natives as the Trail of Fair Justice.

See Also: Ford's Theater and Surratt Boarding House (Chapter 2); Fort McNair (Chapter 12)

---

⑭ Saint Elizabeth's Hospital (2700 Martin Luther King Avenue, SE)

Located to the south of old Anacostia is one of Washington's most infamous institutions, St. Elizabeth's Hospital. Today, the most famous patient at the hospital is undoubtedly John Hinckley, Jr., the man who shot President Reagan and his companions in 1981, in an attempt to gain the attention and affections of actress Jodie Foster. But perhaps the most famous patient ever to reside at St. E's (as it is often called) was the poet and political renegade Ezra Pound. Pound was incarcerated against his will in the hospital's Chestnut Ward from 1943 until 1958, although he continued to write and have his work published even from the asylum. He had been accused of treason against the United States, but was found mentally incompetent to stand trial. The charges stemmed from his denunciation of America's entry into World War II, and his vocal support for Italian fascist leader Benito Mussolini. Pound was finally freed from Saint E's after the treason charges against him were dropped.

Originally known as the U.S. Government Insane Asylum, Saint Elizabeth's opened in 1855 after a long campaign by reformer Dorothea Dix. Dix had moved to Washington in 1848 and stayed six years to work for more humane treatment of the mentally ill. Until the establishment of this hospital, Washington kept its mental patients in jail cells and treated them like criminals. The advent of the hospital provided the opportunity for patients to receive therapeutic care and treatment, rather than being warehoused.

During the Civil War, the name of the hospital was changed to St. Elizabeth's General Army Hospital, so wounded Union soldiers being treated there would not have to use the stigmatized "Insane Asylum" name on the return addresses of letters home. From that time on it has been known as St. Elizabeth's, so named from the original title of the land grant. (It is located on the old St. Elizabeth's tract.)

Also located on the grounds of St. Elizabeth's is the site of Fort Snyder, one of the city's Civil War forts, which was situated near Alabama Avenue and Thirtieth Street.

See Also: Washington Hilton (Chapter 6); "The Civil War Forts of Washington" (Chapter 10)

---

⑮ [Open to the Public] World's Largest Chair (Southwest corner of V Street and Martin Luther King Ave., SE)

Recently restored to its originally glorious lines, this, the "World's Largest Chair," was dedicated at this site on July 7, 1959, to honor the Curtis Brothers furniture company, which once stood here as well. The giant chair—made of solid mahogany from Honduras—was a gift from Bassett Furniture Industries, to honor, as a plaque notes, Curtis Brothers' ". . . outstanding leadership and service to the public."

So, is it truly the world's largest chair? Well, at 19.5 feet tall and 4600 pounds, it's got to be at least a contender. Curtis Brothers may be gone, but at least this wacky landmark has stood the test of time—and that makes it worthy of a sitting ovation.

"World's Largest Chair." (Jack Looney)

Chapter 12

SOUTHWEST

Southwest has seen its share of scandal and tragedy. A number of disasters have struck this area, including the Air Florida crash on the **Fourteenth Street Bridge** in 1982, and the deadly munitions explosion at the **Fort McNair** arsenal in 1864. The crimes of presidential assassins have been punished here, and the cries of victims long gone will be heard here yet, when the **U.S. Holocaust Museum** opens in 1993.

Today's Southwest is physically more than twice as large as the original quadrant, yet it is still Washington's smallest quarter. When the city was first planned by Pierre L'Enfant, those who moved here assumed that the area would be one of the most prominent in the new city—after all, it was close to the legislative seat and the Mall, as well as to the Potomac. But through the centuries, the scourge of technology (namely that of transportation) would again and again divide Southwest from the rest of the city.

This destiny of isolation was far in the future when the Greenleaf Syndicate, a group formed by Robert Morris (famous as the "Financier of the Revolution" who later fell on hard times), John Nicholson (Morris's friend and fellow financier), and James Greenleaf (a diplomat with an eye for real estate), saw Southwest as ripe for development. In the 1790s, the syndicate built a number of fine houses near the waterfront (a few of which still stand as part of the **Harbour Square** complex). At the time, the syndicate was banking on the planned Canal of Tiber Creek to enhance their development's value. This canal was to provide a commercial waterway connecting up-and-coming Southwest with the fashionable residential suburb and tobacco port, Georgetown. Georgetown, in turn, was to be connected to the rest of the northeast by an interstate canal system, according to George Washington's plans.

But the timing was all wrong: The canal system of George Washington's dreams never came to pass, and by the time the C&O Canal finally did make its way south to Georgetown in 1848, railroad technology had already begun supplanting the waterway transport system. The Canal of Tiber Creek saw little use as a social route, and the canal was soon a reeking morass of mud and algae. Completed around 1815, it was to become the great divide, not the great connector, for Southwest. The area, thus effectively cut off from the rest of the city by the canal, festered with petty crime and waterfront lowlife. By the time the canal was covered over in the 1870s, it had done almost irreversible damage to the reputation of the neighborhood that, cut off on all sides by bodies of water, came to be known as "The Island."

Because Southwest was isolated from the rest of the urban life of young Washington, the waterfront was its main source of income during the nineteenth century. Sailors and merchants docked at the Sixth Street wharf and strolled along the waterfront in search of food, gaming, and female companionship. Taverns and bawdy houses flourished, as did pick-pockets and con artists. Few Washingtonians would step into Southwest after dark, and most avoided it even in daylight.

Even as Southwest declined, a few wealthy and powerful citizens continued to build there, but they lined their homes as far north as possible, along B Street (now

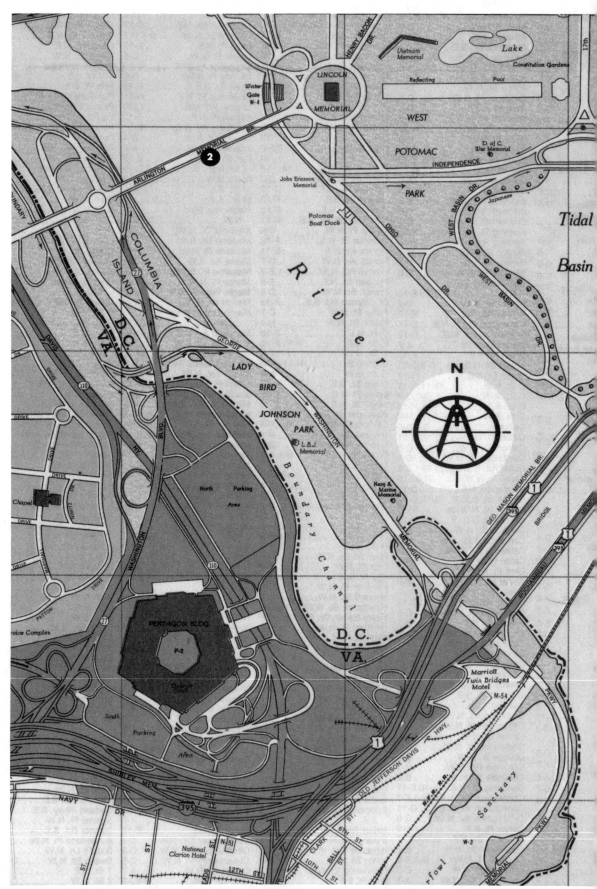

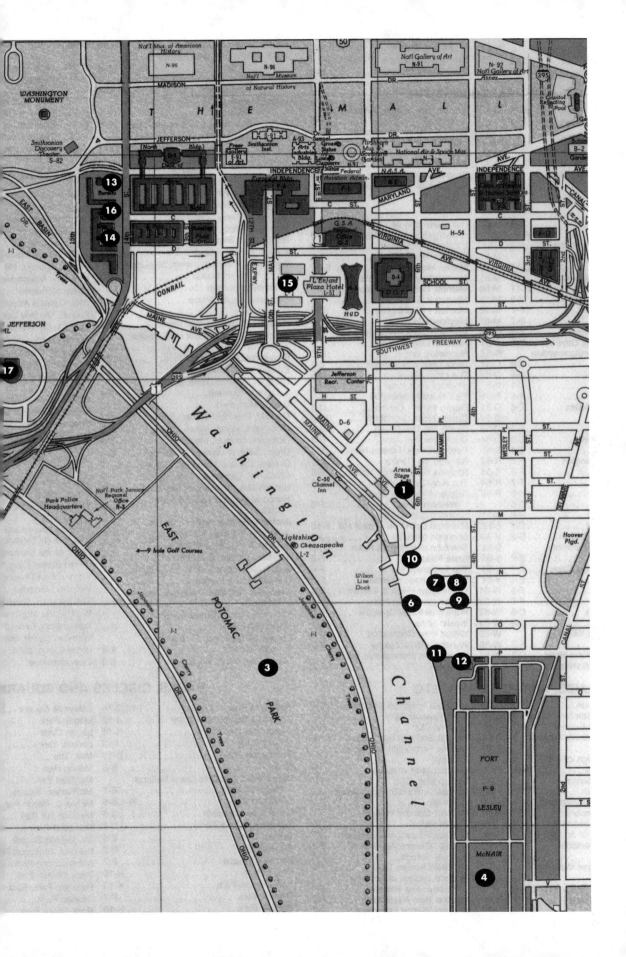

Independence Avenue). This northern area of Southwest, while a solid and stolid residential and commercial district, was not as clean-cut as it appeared—for here on B Street in the 7th and 8th Avenue blocks were two of Washington's most renowned slave pens, the Robey and the Williams. When slavery was at last abolished in the District, these institutions were immediately vilified by most Washingtonians, and more than a few citizens breathed a loud sigh of relief when the whole area was leveled to make way for railyards of the Baltimore and Pacific Railway.

When the Baltimore and Ohio Railroad also came through Southwest in 1873, the tracks effectively cut off the waterfront area of Southwest from the rest of the city. Once again, the miracle of transportation became a barrier to Southwest's development while allowing the rest of the city to expand its exposure. This dividing line was to be re-drawn yet again in the next century, when the Southwest Freeway was constructed, further isolating the residential and waterfront sections of the quadrant from the federal enclave on the other side of the highway.

As railroad transport rose in importance, the need for extensive port and canal facilities dried up. Washington was left with a waterfront blighted by tidal erosion that had allowed the Potomac to slowly encroach on the city, and a profusion of silt that had continually collected at the Long Bridge near the Southwest waterfront. In February of 1881, severe flooding scared Congress into appropriating funds to remedy problems caused by the creeping waters by dredging the areas south and west of the Washington Monument. Soon after, the Army Corps of Engineers began the massive effort to dredge the Potomac and transform the once-watery real estate into parkland. The end result of this dredging project includes the parks along the Potomac, the Tidal Basin area, and the West Mall with its monument grounds now enjoyed by millions of tourists a year. Indeed, virtually all of the waterfront property that juts out as park area across from the Washington channel, on up towards Memorial Bridge, resulted from the fill-in land created by the Army Corps of Engineers dredging project.

Maps spanning the years when the dredging and fill-in were progressing show the gradual extension of the land. First, the banks of the Potomac were extended southward from the Mall and the site where the Canal met the Ellipse, as the dredging crept southward like a pair of muddy sideburns. Then the land was filled in to the east and west, and finally the Tidal Basin was enclosed, creating the one pocket of water that remains where the Potomac once flowed freely. The Washington Channel was left open to the Potomac, allowing small vessels to continue sailing and docking at the long-established port.

The old Turkey Buzzard Point, also known as Greenleaf Point, was left intact, although its once-prominent position as the peninsula at the fork of the Potomac and Anacostia Rivers was all but erased by the extension of East Potomac Park even farther south than this original land-point extends. The Point was the home to the Washington Arsenal (now **Fort McNair**), Washington's earliest waterfront defense.

The concentration of parkland created by the dredging received mixed reviews at first, as locals complained that the city already had enough mud and soupy ground. But as the grass grew and the land firmed up, as the parks were landscaped and the monuments appeared, the newest section of the city was transformed by the 1940s into one of Washington's most beloved areas.

Yet, even while the parks and monuments of the fill-in were gaining a delighted following, the older residential section of Southwest was going through its worst times ever. The townhouses were falling apart, many homes were abandoned, and the whole area was seen as one big slum. The Redevelopment Land Agency, created by Congress in 1946, made the crumbling Southwest area one of its first targets for massive redevelopment. Hundreds of homes were bulldozed, the good along with the bad, and many historic sites were lost in the baby-with-the-bathwater approach to urban renewal. But the resulting groupings of townhouse communities and apartment houses, however homogenized and modern, has made the area more liveable for many of the area's residents.

Long before the creation of the Redevelopment Land Agency (which focused almost exclusively on residential areas in southwest), the federal government had promoted redevelopment of the area, especially for the purposes of new office space. Among these was the first of the major McMillan Plan projects to be enacted, the **Southwest Rectangle** development. Other efforts to revitalize the area have included an earlier redevelopment of the waterfront by the Army Corps of Engineers, the Town Center shopping district development (at the present site of **L'Enfant Plaza**), and a mixed-usage development of high- and low-rise buildings, undertaken in the 1960s.

Today's old Southwest is a conglomerate of clashing classes and lifestyles. There are federal buildings south of the Mall; residential areas, including public housing, extending to the southeast; the small commercial enclave of **Arena Stage** and the Waterside Mall; and the ritzy restaurants of the waterfront itself, where millionaires' yachts often sink anchor. The crime rate in the eastern reaches of the quadrant is flagrantly high, with drugs and shootings a fact of life for many of the residents of lower income housing areas in this section of the city. But history lingers on here, and with it, a hope that this section of Washington will someday be rescued from the blight of urban decay. There's always a future, especially in a place where traces of the past live on.

PLACES: The Waterfront and Environs

The waterfront of Southwest is diverse indeed. It encompasses not only the newest land in Washington—the waterfront of East Potomac Park—but also the older Washington Channel harbor area, where the Sixth Street Wharf and its various dens of iniquity once catered to sailors and dock workers. Today, the older waterfront area is home to seafood restaurants and an open-air market, parks and the renowned **Arena Stage** theater. The sailors of yore probably wouldn't recognize their bawdy old playground, but then again, they would probably be equally shocked to see how much land has been dredged out of the Potomac River, which once flowed all the way up to Constitution Avenue.

---

❶ | Open to the Public | **Arena Stage (6th and M Streets, SW; 202/554–9066)**

Since its founding in 1950 by Zelda Fichandler, Arena Stage has garnered national renown for the quality and diversity of its dramatic offerings. It has produced its share of stars—among them *L.A. Law* stars Michael Tucker and Jill Eikenberry, who met while members of the Arena company, and Robert Prosky, of *Hill Street Blues*—as well as such stage hits as *The Great White Hope* and *K2*.

"Bird's eye view of Sixth Street Wharf," as sketched in 1863. **(Library of Congress)**

The Arena moved here in 1961, after a five-year stint at the Heurich Brewery, which once stood at the site of the Kennedy Center for the Performing Arts. Before that, it had been housed in cramped quarters at the old Hippodrome Theater at 9th Street and New York Avenues, NW. The backstage area was so small at this first Arena site that actors exiting stage left had to run out into the alley and around the back of the building to re-enter at the other side of the theater before making an entrance from stage right!

When the Arena opened, it ignored the segregation policies of the city's other "white" theaters, choosing instead to seat blacks and whites side by side at any and all performances. The Arena did more than break the color code—it also broke the tedium of Washington's status as a "road show" town by producing shows developed for and at the Arena rather than waiting for the big Broadway road companies to come to town. In doing so, Arena created a role model for repertory theater in cities from Chicago to San Francisco.

See Also: Kennedy Center for the Performing Arts (Chapter 5)

---

② | Open to the Public | **Arlington Memorial Bridge (Crosses Potomac between Lincoln Memorial and Arlington)**

This elegant bridge was built as the result of a traffic jam. The bumper-to-bumper snarl-up that led to the construction of the bridge occurred on Armistice Day, 1921, as a long ceremonial procession was attempting to make its way from the Capitol Rotunda to Arlington Cemetery, for the official burial of the Unknown Soldier. The only way to get there was over the Highway Bridge (now called the Fourteenth Street Bridge), then along a back road past a dump and a race track (where Memorial Parkway now runs), and north again to the cemetery. Hundreds of dignitaries were trapped in their cars upwards of two hours as they waited to get over the bridge and through the woods for the ceremony. Some turned around and gave up. That same afternoon, the Fine Arts Commission held a special session and voted funds to construct a bridge directly linking the then-unfinished Lincoln Memorial with the cemetery.

Construction began on the bridge, designed by McKim, Mead & White, in 1926. Six years later, the structure was complete. Total cost: $14,750,000. President Hoover presided over the opening ceremonies, which were held on January 18, 1932.

See Also: Fourteenth Street Bridge

---

③ Open to the Public **East Potomac Park (Southern peninsula, south of the 14th Street Bridge; 202/426–6841)**

East Potomac Park was created when the Army Corps of Engineers dredged the Potomac in the 1880s. In the 1920s, the park was transformed into Hains Point, a popular tourist camp where travelers could park their cars and sleep over in rented tents (cost: $.50 a night) while visiting the local attractions. The camp included a miniature golf course, which is still in existence today, and a regular golf course. Today, the park's most famous feature is the startling aluminum statuary work, "The Awakening," created by Seward Johnson and installed here in 1980. The statue is divided into several parts, with the hands, knees, and face jutting up out the ground at different points, giving the illusion of a giant man bursting forth from the earth. In 1991, a car careened off the loop road and smashed into the giant's head. The head was hauled away for repairs in the fall of that year, leaving a decidedly decapitated appearance to the statue in the interim.

See Also: Fort McNair

---

④ Fort Leslie J. McNair (4th and P Streets, SW)

Pierre L'Enfant envisioned this military complex as the city's last and most important line of defense against attackers sailing up the Potomac. The original fort was erected in the early 1790s, and in 1804 the site became a major arsenal for the army. Although the Arsenal offered no resistance to the British invasion of Washington in 1814, it was here that the one major setback of the otherwise brutally successful sack of Washington occurred. Flushed with success from the Battle of Bladensburg, the British marched into Washington and in quick succession burned the Capitol, the White House, and almost every federal building in between. They then descended on the Arsenal, planning to pick it clean of weapons and other materials. Little did they know that, in hasty retreat, the defenders had hidden munitions in every nook and cranny. And so it happened that a British soldier carelessly tossed a match into one of the secret munitions storage areas—and KABOOM! Forty British soldiers were killed in the explosion, which also destroyed most of the fort. This explosion resulted in the greatest number of casualties suffered in a single incident by the conquering forces during their entire pillaging expedition.

In 1864, another explosion at the Arsenal cost the lives of more than twenty women and wounded another eighty. Military experts had already declared the munitions assembly operations at the Arsenal unsafe, when a rocket was accidentally ignited amidst a stockpile of fireworks, killing or maiming many of the women nearby who had been assembling rifle cartridges for Union troops. Twenty-one dead from the explosion were buried with solemn ceremony in the specially designed Arsenal Memorial at Congressional Cemetery, and soon after the tragedy, the Arsenal was closed down as a storage facility for explosives.

The site served for a time as the storage facility for the Army's Quartermaster Corps, and a prominent military hospital was also established at the site. It was here around the turn of the century that a dedicated Army Major, Dr. Walter Reed, spent a decade studying ways to ease the suffering of patients afflicted with the dreaded zymotic diseases, diphtheria and yellow fever. Dr. Reed's work with these patients helped lead to treatments for those once common and deadly diseases. The Walter Reed Army Medical Center in Northwest Washington was named in his honor.

Crowd watching hanging of the Lincoln conspirators, 1865. (Library of Congress)

Also on the grounds of Fort McNair is the site of the first U.S. Penitentiary, built in 1826. The Penitentiary attained national fame as the scene of the trial, imprisonment, and execution of four conspirators in the plot to assassinate President Lincoln and other top officials. After first being held in a ship at anchor in the Navy Yard, the conspirators were moved to the Penitentiary. On July 9, 1865, the day they were hanged, throngs of people clamored for prime viewing space atop the high wall overlooking the yard where the gallows stood.

Following the execution, the bodies were interred on the penitentiary grounds, where the remains of John Wilkes Booth had already been buried beneath one of the penitentiary cells. Booth's body was later removed and, on the orders of President Andrew Johnson, given to his brother, the famed Shakespearian actor Edwin Booth, for reburial in the family plot in Baltimore. This presidential favor would have caused a public uproar, but the event was kept quiet, and no one discovered the removal of the body until long after it had occurred.

Mary Surratt, the owner of the boarding house where the conspirators met, was hanged as a conspirator at the Penitentiary, the first woman so executed in Washington. Some historians still believe she was wrongly hanged; and it is said that the wailing voice of her ghost can be heard at the Penitentiary to this day, begging for help. The path she walked to the gallows has even been seen melted in the virgin snow, as if created by the solemn stroll of an unseen figure. The red brick house on the grounds where Mary Surratt nervously awaited her fate (in hopes that President Johnson might pardon her) still stands, although most of the penitentiary was demolished in 1869.

Surratt's is not the only ghost to haunt Fort McNair, for there have been reported sightings of the spirit of Dr. Walter Reed—perhaps forever searching for one last cure, a cure for his own mortality?

In 1908, the Army War College opened at the Fort, and the site soon became one of the country's eminent institutions for the development of an intelligent military. The Industrial College of the Armed Forces joined up later with the Army War College, and the two became the National Defense University, where would-be generals still come to study the tactics of great military strategists.

Today's Fort McNair has preserved a number of the early soldiers' barracks as well as the remains of the U.S. Penitentiary. The National Defense University still operates out of the original Beaux Arts building campus of the Army War College. Visitors are allowed on the grounds, although the buildings are closed to the public. One of the best views of the fort can be found across the Washington Channel at East Potomac Park, where the full, mile-long peninsula military installation can be seen.

See Also: East Potomac Park and **"Washington Disasters";** Ford's Theater and Surratt Boarding House (Chapter 2); Walter Reed Army Medical Center (Chapter 9); "The Burning of Washington" (Chapter 10); Congressional Cemetery and Washington Navy Yard (Chapter 11)

Washington Disasters

Washington has had its share of man-made and natural disasters. From the tornado that ripped through the city the day after the British nearly burned the city to the ground in 1814, to the floods caused when the Potomac periodically rose and engulfed Pennsylvania Avenue and Capitol Hill (as it did in 1881), and even to modern-day hurricanes like Hazel (October of 1954) and Agnes (June of 1972), the powers that be in the White House and Capitol have little control over the forces of nature.

The same holds true for man-made disasters, of which the city has seen its share. One of the worst and most dramatic took place on February 28, 1844, when there was an explosion aboard the battle steamship *The Princeton,* which was cruising the Potomac on its inaugural run, loaded with dignitaries (including President Tyler).

The explosion occurred just off Greenleaf Point, during the exhibition test firing of the ship's state-of-the-art weaponry, a pair of giant guns called the "Peacemakers." The disaster is described thus in *Our First Century,* a compendium of great events in American history, published in 1876:

"On firing the gun, a murderous blast succeeded—the whole ship shook and reeled— and a dense cloud of smoke enveloped the whole group on the forecastle; but when this blew away, an awful scene presented itself to the view of the hushed and agonizing spectators: The gun had burst, at a point three or four feet from the breech, and scattered death and desolation all around."

Among the dead were Secretary of State Abel P. Upshur and the newly appointed Secretary of the Navy, Thomas P. Gilmer. Also killed was the father of Julia Gardiner, the young woman President Tyler married in July of that year. (The president himself only missed death because he had been called back at the moment before the shot.) Of the survivors of the blast, the account reports, a Mr. Tyson of Philadelphia was perhaps

(Continued)

the most fortunate. He "was the only person who stood his ground, though a piece of gun, weighing about two pounds, had passed through his hat, about two inches from his skull, and fallen down by the side of him." Commodore Stockton was relatively uninjured, despite his position directly behind the exploding gun: "All of the hair on his head and face was burnt off; and he stood calm and undismayed, but deeply conscious, over the frightful wreck." Also among those spared was Secretary of War William Wilkins, who at the moment before the firing, jokingly dashed away from the scene, remarking, "Though Secretary of War, I don't like this firing, and I believe I shall run!" The dead of the *Princeton* are buried in the same cemetery—Congressional Cemetery—where twenty-one women killed in an 1864 munitions explosion at Fort McNair were also laid to rest.

Another famed Washington disaster occurred at the Knickerbocker Theater in what is now called Adams Morgan on January 28, 1922. A heavy snow caused the roof to buckle during a performance of a silent film, killing ninety-six patrons inside and causing the greatest loss of life of any disaster before or since in Washington.

Some of Washington's most startling disasters have happened in pairs. On January 13, 1982, in the mid-afternoon, Air Florida Flight 114 took off from National Airport, and promptly crashed into the southern span of the Fourteenth Street Bridge before plunging into the Potomac River. Seventy-eight people were killed (including seven on the bridge), and a hero was born in the form of Lenny Skutnick, a passer-by who dove into the icy waters of the Potomac to help slip a life-rope around a drowning woman.

That same afternoon, the Metro system's first and worst accident occurred, when a train derailed near Metro Center. Three people were killed in the crash and the ensuing crush of panicked passengers. All the emergency vehicles in Washington were at the site of the plane crash, so help was slow to arrive at the Metro accident. It was later debated whether swifter emergency response might have saved lives at that second deadly transportation accident of the day.

Earlier this century, Washington had another double-whammy day of disaster on January 15, 1953. The first accident of the day was the wreck of the Federal Express, a Pennsylvania Railway train from Boston filled with passengers bound for the pending inaugural of President Eisenhower. During the approach to Washington, the 200–ton locomotive lost its brakes and crashed into Union Station. The station-master had been warned in time to clear the concourse, so, although there were forty casualties (mainly on the train), there were no fatalities.

That same day, another disaster occurred within a few blocks of the first. The following description, recorded by Elizabeth Gertrude Clark, the Chronicler of the Columbia Historical Society (now the Historical Society of Washington) from 1951–1961, relates the details: "Just a few hours after [the train wreck] . . . there was a terrific blast at the Standard Tire and Battery Co. store, 10th and H Streets, NE. The blast, preceded by a stubborn basement blaze, hurled a number of injured firemen out through plate glass windows. The street was covered with refrigerators, television sets and other store appliances. In spite of the heroic work of police, bystanders and firemen 'who rushed in even before the rubble had settled,' 25 persons were injured. Fire chief Millard Sutton was critically injured. Both of his legs were broken."

5 Open to the Public | **Fourteenth Street Bridge (At 14th Street, feeding onto 395 to Virginia)**

One of Washington's oldest and most heavily traveled bridges, the Long Bridge, once stood at approximately this site. (The Chain Bridge and Georgetown's Aqueduct Bridge were smaller and less stable.) Long Bridge was originally built in 1834. It saw its heaviest usage during the Civil War, when it became the standard route south for the Union Army. After the war, the railroad tracks were laid across the bridge. It was used first as a bridge for the Baltimore and Potomac Railroad (which was stationed where the National Gallery of Art now stands), and in 1870, for the Baltimore and Ohio Railroad (which had its station at the site of the present Union Station).

Around 1905, the Long Bridge was replaced by the Fourteenth Street Bridge (early on called the Highway Bridge). The Fourteenth Street Bridge gained national fame when it became the site for the horrific Air Florida crash on January 13th, 1982. It was a cold, snowy day, and the pilots of flight 114 joked around in the cockpit about how long they thought the de-icing of their wings would last. As it happened, not long enough; in the time it took between the de-icing and the clearance for take-off, enough ice had already formed again on the plane's wings that it rose only slightly from the runway before crashing into the bridge span. The plane plummeted into the icy Potomac, drowning seventy-one passengers who were still strapped in their safety belts when they died. Another seven fatalities were caused by the accident on the

Advance guard of the Army of the United States crossing the Long Bridge, May 24, 1861, as sketched for *Harper's Pictorial History of the Civil War*.

bridge. Only a few survivors were plucked from the freezing river water. The accident has gone down in Washington history as the worst aircraft disaster the city has ever seen.

See Also: "Washington Disasters" and **Arlington Memorial Bridge**

---

⑥ Harbour Square (bounded by 4th Street, O Street, the waterfront and N Street, SW)

Harbour Square is a development of high- and low-rise apartment buildings and townhouses that dates to the 1960s efforts to revitalize the waterfront area. Although mainly comprised of new buildings, the complex also incorporates some historic houses:

⑦ **Duncanson Cranch House** (468–470 N Street, SW): Built in 1794, this was one of the original houses built by the early real estate speculators known as the Greenleaf Syndicate.

⑧ **Edward Simon Lewis House** (456 N Street, SW): This single-family townhouse, probably built in 1817, was broken up into apartments during the 1920s. During the 1930s, the Lewis House apartments were popular homesteads for journalists—both Ernie Pyle and Lewis Heath lived here during that decade. The apartment was more of a home-base than an actual home for Pyle, however. He spent most of the decade traveling through America with his wife, writing a syndicated column about the country and its people. The house was restored to a single home again when included in the Harbour Square development during the 1960s.

⑨ **Wheat Row Houses** (1315–1321 4th Street, SW): These four federal townhouses were built in 1794 by the Greenleaf Syndicate, and the group is thought to comprise one of the earliest preserved housing blocks in the city.

---

⑩ Thomas Law House (1252 6th Street, SW)

Real estate speculator and literary wanna-be Thomas Law lived in this house, built in 1795, with his wife, Elizabeth Parke Custis (Martha Washington's granddaughter). The house, also known as the "Honeymoon House" (possibly because the couple honeymooned there), was their home from 1796 to 1800. During that time, the Laws entertained a number of important people here, including the future King of France, Louis Philippe, and his brothers, and the popular French writer Volney. Law was one of the speculators who later won a contract to build the Canal of Tiber Creek, which eventually helped turn Southwest into a much-derided "island."

In 1800, the couple moved to a home on New Jersey Avenue, and the house became the residence of Richard Bland Lee, a Congressman from Virginia who served in the first, second, and third terms of the House. The house is now a community center for a group of nearby apartment buildings.

---

⑪ P Street Wharf Site (P Street at the Waterfront)

Like the rest of the original wharves, the old P Street Wharf no longer exists. But it did have a small role in the drama of the Civil War, for it was here that Union reinforcements under General Wright arrived to aid the city in its defense against rebel raiders. So relieved was President Lincoln at their arrival in July of 1864 that he himself rode down to the wharf to greet the fresh supply of soldiers.

12 Open to the Public

Waterside Park (At the waterfront, between P Street and Fort McNair)

Built in 1967 as part of the last major effort to revitalize the waterfront neighborhoods, Waterside Park is the scene of the annual Harborfest weekend, which celebrates Washington's heritage as a river city. The park is home to one of Washington's least known and most unusual monuments: The Titanic Memorial (near the seawall in the southwest corner of the park). The memorial to those who died when the famous ocean liner struck an iceberg on April 15, 1912, was sculpted by an artist who could well appreciate the impact of the tragedy, Gertrude Vanderbilt Whitney. Her brother, Alfred Gwynne Vanderbilt, died when German U-boats attacked the luxury liner the *Lusitania* in 1915. Whitney, who crafted the memorial in 1931, later donated her fortune and art collection to create New York's Whitney Museum of Art.

**The Titanic Memorial.
(Jack Looney)**

For an elite few, the Titanic Memorial is the focal point for an annual night on the town. The Titanic Society is a group of twenty men (and is limited to that number and gender) in the broadcast industry, who gather once a year to honor the men who gave their lives as the *Titanic* sank so that women and children would have seats on the lifeboats. The men of the society, dressed in full formal attire, gather at a designated dining place and engage in a memorial ritual that includes reading the Captain's log of names and ringing a ship's bell. The men then sup on one of three multi-course meals that were served the night the ship went down (the menu rotates yearly). Afterward, they take limousines to the Titanic Memorial, where they lay a wreath at the foot of the monument, and each man gives a toast to the lost souls who went down with their ship.

Washington Reacts to Sinking of the Titanic

Initial newspaper reports of the sinking of the *Titanic* included erroneous but momentarily encouraging rumors that the ship had been towed to port with little loss of life. At first Washington society reacted in shock, but still held out hope that these reports might be true. In her journals, later published as a collection entitled *Washington Wife* (1962), Congressional wife Ellen Maury Slayden gave an account of the mood in the city as the news sank in:

"(April 16, 1912) . . . A day of strange quietness, a spiritual numbness, a sense of mysterious horror at the loss of the *Titanic*. There has been no loud display of grief, nor crowding around telegraph offices even among those who knew their loved ones were on the great leviathan, but people moving softly and speaking low as if at a funeral. . . .

(Continued)

"All day there were 'extras,' but no news. Last night [my husband, a friend and] I attended the opening of a part of the Freer Collection at the Smithsonian and had a quietly pleasant evening, laughing as we drove home at the varying cries of 'Extree,' 'Extree,' and 'E-C-extry,' that had redoubled but never thought of buying one. The papers cry 'Wolf' too often, and extras are a common catch-penny device.

"All night I was wakeful, and about six I went down for the paper and waked [my husband] to tell him the incredibly awful facts.

"Later at Rigg's market, my faith in the brotherhood of man was renewed. Usually a noisy, sociable place, it was noticeably quiet. Even errand boys spoke gently. . . . In the afternoon there were groups on the street, not only the kind that usually show collective interest in great events, but small-shop people, schoolgirls with plaited hair and boys in knickers intent on the evening papers, trying to understand the plan of the ship from the pictures.

"(April 29, 1912) Nothing, not even Roosevelt and the deplorable spectacle of a President and an ex-President hurling accusations against one another from the stump, diverts our thoughts or talk from the *Titanic.* Every company is shadowed by it. The senatorial investigation is a farce and a horror combined. The chairman, who doesn't know the rudiments of marine science or travel, has insisted on knowing why the passengers were not in the watertight compartments and made the survivors describe the shrieks of the drowning. I have not been to the hearings, but must try to go once for the historical interest and the 'experience that shall live in memory'—the motive that so often impels me."

PLACES: Southwest Rectangle Area

Until the Baltimore and Potomac (B&P) railroad arrived here in 1873, this was Southwest's middle- and upper-class enclave. Then the area was leveled to make way for the railyards. In the following decades, it was a relatively barren area, although a few major federal buildings, including the red-brick **Auditors Building,** were erected here. The area fringing the Mall became an extension of the Victorian resort-like atmosphere where the Smithsonian buildings were rising, and here, near the present-day Department of Agriculture, there once stood one of Washington's truly unique tourist attractions—the General Noble Redwood Tree House.

During the 1930s, in an effort to homogenize this area just south of the Mall with the Federal Triangle area being built to the north of the Mall, several major government edifices were built in the quagmire of the 14th Street corridor. In its report in the early twentieth century, the McMillan Commission had originally suggested that this area be developed as part of its plan for a monumental center at the heart of the federal city. The South Building of the Department of Agriculture was the first of the Southwest Rectangle structures completed; it was followed by the **Bureau of Engraving and Printing** and the first Department of Health and Human Services building (which was originally built for the Social Security Administration). The entire, cohesive Federal Rectangle project was never completed as originally envisioned, but it did lay the groundwork for the development of L'Enfant Plaza, as well as the plethora of government buildings that now line Independence Avenue.

13 Auditors Building (14th Street and Independence Avenue, SW)

This building served as the first home of the Bureau of Engraving and Printing from its construction in 1879 until 1914. Designed with security in mind, it has only one real entrance: the main doors facing Independence Avenue. In 1978, the building was officially designated a historic landmark.

See Also: Bureau of Engraving and Printing and **U.S. Holocaust Museum**

14 Open to the Public Bureau of Engraving and Printing (14th and C Streets, SW; 202/447–9709)

One of Washington's more popular bureaucratic attractions is this site, where all the paper money in the U.S. is printed. The Bureau of Engraving and Printing has resided here since the 1930s when it moved here from temporary quarters at the site of the new **U.S. Holocaust Museum.**

The free tour of the Bureau includes a glimpse of the giant presses that work around the clock to spit out giant sheets of bills, as well as an exhibit of some of the finest and strangest works of forgery uncovered by the Secret Service (which was first created to combat counterfeiters). The collection on view is a mere fraction of a much larger exhibit that had been a major attraction at the U.S. Treasury Building until officials there removed it for fear it might give inspiration to would-be currency crooks.

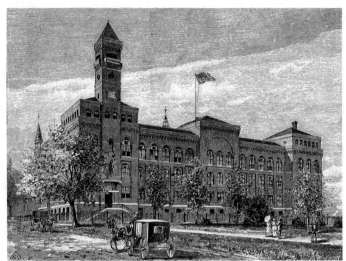

In the late nineteenth century, 250 presses in the first Bureau of Engraving and Printing (now the Auditors Building) churned out five million dollars worth of small bank notes approximately every twenty-eight days. (*Picturesque Washington*)

See Also: Auditor's Building and **U.S. Holocaust Museum;** U.S. Treasury Building (Chapter 1)

15 Open to the Public L'Enfant Plaza (Frontage Road and D Street, SW)

I.M. Pei's 1966 attempt at a mixed-use urban environment has been a mixed blessing for Southwest. The underground mall complex is badly oriented in relation to the surrounding office and hotel buildings, and tourists using the Metro stop here are often left scratching their heads in confusion.

One of the highlights of the plaza is the 10th Street Mall, a kind of pedestrian Main Street that features the Benjamin Banneker Fountain, a memorial to the black mathematician who worked with surveyor Andrew Ellicott to lay out the boundaries of Washington.

16 | Open to the Public | ### U.S. Holocaust Museum (Raoul Wallenberg Place; 202/822–6464)

Slated to open in 1993, the U.S. Holocaust Museum will be the first museum in the country devoted to those who died, those who survived, and those who saw inside the Nazi Holocaust. Among the exhibits on view will be displays of diaries and artifacts found at the concentration camps; an oral history videotape archive of Holocaust survivors and the GIs who liberated them; and a railroad car used to transport Polish Jews to the death camp at Treblinka.

The section of 15th Street running behind the museum has been renamed Raoul Wallenberg Place to honor the Swiss savior of hundreds, or perhaps thousands, of Jews and others targeted for extinction by the Nazis. Wallenberg, who is believed to have perished in a Soviet prison, helped smuggle Nazi victims out of danger through Switzerland.

From 1914 to 1930, this site held the temporary buildings of the Bureau of Engraving and Printing.

See Also: Auditor's Building and **Bureau of Engraving and Printing**

PLACES: Tidal Basin Area

The area around the Tidal Basin is one of the most famous spots in Washington, both for the view it offers of the **Jefferson Memorial** at the Basin's south side, and for the Japanese cherry trees that line the banks around the basin.

The world-famous flowering cherry trees were a gift from the Empire of Japan in 1909. Although the original shipment was badly infected and had to be destroyed, Japan sent a second, healthier shipment, which was duly planted in 1912. In 1952, the trees went full circle when cuttings from the originals were sent to Tokyo, to be planted in place of the parent trees which had been dying off due to neglect.

The Cherry Blossom Festival, Washington's biggest hometown celebration, first took place in 1934. Since then, the festival's timing has rarely managed to coincide with the bloom's peak week, which usually happens in late March or early April.

The Cherry blossoms aren't the only floral stars of the Tidal Basin. Several embankments around the Basin were planted with thousands of tulip bulbs on the orders of Mrs. Lyndon Johnson while she was First Lady. The flowerbeds, known as the Tulip Library, represent one of the many successful beautification and landscaping efforts Mrs. Johnson undertook throughout the Washington area.

17 | Open to the Public | ### Jefferson Memorial (South side of the Tidal Basin; 202/426–6822)

The Jefferson Memorial has come to be appreciated by locals and tourists alike, but when its construction was planned, a group of female activists were so angry at the notion that their perfect loop of cherry blossoms might be ruined by a presidential memorial that they chained themselves to the trees in protest!

President Franklin Roosevelt presided over the dedication of the Jefferson Memorial on April 13, 1943, the 200th anniversary of Jefferson's birth. Designed by architect John Russell Pope in a Roman Parthenon style, the monument reflected Thomas Jefferson's love of this round, columned style. (In fact, it harkens back to Jefferson's own (rejected!) plans for the President's House, as well as to his Virginia homestead, Monticello). Standing in for the statue of Thomas Jefferson at the ceremony was a plastic cast of the figure created by Sculptor Rudolph Evans. Because bronze was in short supply and reserved strictly for military use, the nineteen-foot-tall statue could not be cast in its intended metal until several years after World

War II. The landscaping of Frederic Law Olmsted, Jr., adds formal yet delicate grace to the memorial grounds.

See Also: The White House (Chapter 1)

 Tidal Basin (Bordered by East Potomac Park and West Potomac Park, and the Mall)

The Tidal Basin is renowned as the place where one of the biggest sex scandals ever to hit Washington did so with a splash. At 2 a.m. on October 7, 1974, Arkansas Congressman Wilbur Mills, the powerful chairman of the House Ways and Means Committee, was pulled over by police while enjoying a moonlight spin around the Tidal Basin with local stripper Fanne Foxe and a masseuse. In the confusion that followed, Fanne Foxe somehow ended up in the water and the trio was arrested.

Reports quickly surfaced that Mills frequented the Silver Slipper, the downtown nightclub where Fanne Foxe performed. The married Mills didn't help his case by seeming publicly unabashed about his relationship with Foxe, even appearing on

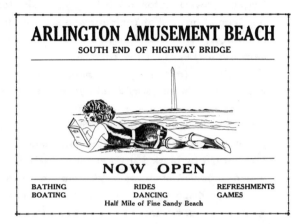

Ad appearing in the B.F. Keith program, August 27, 1923.

Slavery in Washington

Washington, situated as it is between the industrial north and the agricultural south, stood astride the spiritual boundary of slave states in America until 1850. The tempest that eventually erupted into the Civil War brewed for years in Washington before spreading out into the entire nation.

Two of Washington's most infamous slave pens, the Williams and the Robey, were located in Southwest Washington along B Street (now Independence Avenue), at 7th and 8th Streets. They resembled regular brick homes from the outside; but within those houses were basements filled with newly arrived, captured, or re-captured slaves. And upstairs in the parlor, men came to deal in the slave trade, as if haggling over the purchase of a few sheep or a new buggy. The Robey and the Williams did their business in relative discretion compared to the free-wheeling open slave block markets held at such sites as the Center Market and the courtyard of the Decatur House. But the behind-closed-doors dealings of the slave trade was all the more offensive to the city's freed blacks and abolitionists trying to bring freedom to Washington.

Despite being a slave "state," Washington was considered a very progressive southern city. One of the most influential abolitionist newspapers, Gamaliel Bailey's *National Era* (which first published Harriet Beecher Stowe's *Uncle Tom's Cabin*), was

(Continued)

published out of offices located in downtown Washington. And a fair number of free blacks operated successful businesses in Washington long before slavery was abolished. Blacks escaping from the southern states along the underground railroad passed through numerous "railway stations" in Washington churches, private homes, and boarding houses on their way to freedom in the north. Harriet Tubman was said to be a frequent, covert visitor to Washington as she led expeditions of escaping slaves. Indeed, one legend has it that Tubman, who suffered from narcoleptic fits caused by a childhood head injury, once dozed off in a public park in Washington directly beneath a poster advertising a reward for her capture.

Despite the (relatively) large population of freed blacks and abolitionists in Washington, the majority of whites in the city still feared and resented the movement to free the nation's slaves. Two major riots erupted in Washington as a result of these fears. The first, known as the "Snow Riot," occurred in 1835, when whites attacked the popular Snow's Epicurean Eating Establishment at 6th Street and Pennsylvania Avenue, NW, owned by black entrepreneur Beverly Snow. The mob, frightened by the recent, violent rebellion of slaves in Virginia led by Nat Turner, was fueled by rumors that Snow had made disparaging remarks about a white woman. Snow escaped the would-be lynch mob, but his escape so angered the mob that it went on to destroy other black-owned businesses in Washington, including Mrs. Wormley's Boarding House.

The second riot, known as the "Pearl Riot," occurred in 1848, after abolitionists tried to whisk seventy-seven slaves out of the city. When their ship, the *Pearl,* was captured, becalmed at the mouth of the Potomac, the captain and crew were returned to Washington. Angry mobs attacked the offices of the *National Era,* which they blamed for the escape attempt.

The Pearl Affair brought much-needed attention to slavery in Washington. Until then, too many legislators had turned a blind eye to the goings-on in the nation's capital, even while haggling over solutions to the problem on a national scale. The Compromise of 1850 helped stave off the Civil War for another decade by offering small victories to both the pro- and anti-slavery forces. The anti-slavery forces won the banishment of the slave trade in Washington (the first such ban in a slave state in the nation), while the pro-slavery forces gained a toughening of the Fugitive Slave Act laws.

The Civil War dealt a death blow to the institution of slavery in America. And Washington, the first slave state to banish the practice, served as a kind of mirror held up to the future. While Washington was hardly heaven on earth for freed blacks, it was considered by many to be a gateway to the promised land.

stage with her later that fall at a Boston nightclub (where he reportedly called her his "G-String hillbilly"). Mills didn't last much longer in the redlight limelight, and in December he was hospitalized for a nervous breakdown. The House Ways and Means Committee had already secretly voted him out as chairman when he resigned the post on December 10, 1974. The next year, Mills left politics for good, blaming his woes on alcoholism. Fanne Foxe made money and headlines for a few years by billing herself as the "Tidal Basin Stripper," being arrested on morals charges for removing her G-String while stripping, and finally, by publishing her account of the whole affair in *The Congressman and the Stripper.*

The Tidal Basin was originally created by the Army Corps of Engineers in 1897. Its purpose was to provide a constant source of water for the nearby Washington Channel, in case the estuary waters of the Potomac receded, leaving the boats docked there stranded. Thus it was, in effect, created as a reservoir from which more water could be channeled into the harbor. But the Tidal Basin quickly became a recreational area instead. In fact, from 1917 until 1925, it even boasted a popular beach at about the site where the Jefferson Memorial now stands. The whites-only beach featured a bath-house and room to stretch out on imported sand. In the waters of the Tidal Basin itself, there was a floating platform for lounging and diving.

See Also: U.S. Capitol (Chapter 3)

Appendix A

Washington Homes of the Greats

NOTE: This listing is relatively selective; most sites listed appear elsewhere in the book. Where hotels are listed here, the reference means that the individual was a resident, not merely a guest, at the hotel. Also, to preserve the privacy of those still living, residences of current Washingtonians are not normally included (with the exception of official residences such as The White House and the Vice President's House). An asterisk (*) after a listing indicates that the site no longer exists.

Acheson, Dean: 2805 P St., NW.

Adams, Charles Francis: Caldwell-Monroe House/Arts Club of Washington (2017 I St., NW).

Adams, Henry: 1607 H St., NW*; 1603 H St., NW.*

Adams, John Quincy: 1333 F St., NW*; The White House.

Agnew, Spiro: Wardman Tower (2600 Woodley Rd., NW).

Arthur, Chester: The White House; Anderson Cottage (Soldiers' and Airmen's Home—summer White House).

Bankhead, Tallulah: The Norwood (1868 Columbia Rd., NW); The Anchorage (1900 Q St., NW).

Barkley, Alben: 2101 Apartments (2101 Connecticut Ave., NW).

Barney, Alice Pike: 2306 Massachusetts Ave., NW.

Barton, Clara: 488½ 7th St., NW* (boarding house); 926 T St., NW; Clara Barton House (Glen Echo, MD).

Bell, Alexander Graham: Bell-Morton House (1500 Rhode Island Ave., NW); 1355 Connecticut Ave., NW*; 3414 Volta Place (laboratory).

Bethune, Mary McLeod: Bethune House (1318 Vermont Ave., NW).

Bierce, Ambrose: Olympia Flats (SE corner of Euclid Ave. and 14th St., NW).

Blaine, James G: 736 Jackson Place; 2000 Massachusetts Ave., NW.

Bliss, Robert Woods and Mildred: Dumbarton Oaks (31st and R Sts., NW); McCormick House (1785 Massachusetts Ave., NW).

Borah, William: 2101 Apartments (2101 Connecticut Ave., NW).

Brady, Matthew: National Hotel (Northeast corner of Pennsylvania Ave. at 6th St., NW)*; 937 Pennsylvania Ave., NW (studio).

Brandeis, Louis: California House (2205 California Ave., NW).

Brumidi, Constantino: 326 A St., SE.

Bryan, William Jennings: Calumet Place (Northeast corner of Clifton and 13th St., NW).*

Buchanan, James: The White House; Quarters #1 (Soldiers' and Airmens' Home—summer White House).

Burnes, David: Burnes House (OAS Building site)*.

Burnett, Frances`Hodson: 1219 I St., NW*; 1730 K St., NW*; 1770 Massachusetts Ave., NW.

Bush, George: Vice President's House (Naval Observatory grounds); The White House.

Calhoun, John C: Dumbarton Oaks (1703 32nd St., NW); Hill's Boarding House (Supreme Court site)*.

Carroll, Daniel: Duddington Manor (Between 1st St. and 2nd St., SE, at Duddington Place).*

Chase, Salmon P.: Edgewood (Rhode Island Ave. and 4th St., NE).*

Clark, Tom: 2101 Apartments (2101 Connecticut Ave., NW).

Clay, Henry: National Hotel (Northeast corner of Pennsylvania Ave. at 6th St., NW).*

Cleveland, Grover: The White House; Oak View (3500 block of Newark St., NW—summer White House).*

Curtis, Charles: Wardman Tower (2600 Woodley Rd., NW).

Davies, Joseph and Marjorie Merriweather Post: See also Post, Marjorie Merriweather; Tregaron (3100 Macomb St., NW).

Davis, Jefferson: 1736 I St., NW.*

Dirksen, Everett: Mayflower Hotel (1127 Connecticut Ave., NW).

Douglas, Stephen A.: 201 I St., NW.*

Douglass, Frederick: 316 A St., NE; Cedar Hill (1411 W St., SE).

Dulles, John Foster: 1401 I St., NW (birthplace)*; Wardman Tower (2600 Woodley Rd., NW); 2740 32nd St., NW.

DuPriest, Oscar: 419 U St., NW.

Eisenhower, Dwight, and Mamie: Wardman Tower (2600 Woodley Rd., NW); The Wyoming (2022 Columbia Rd., NW); The White House.

Ellington, Edward "Duke": 1212 T St., NW.

Evans-Tibbs, Lillian: 1910 Vermont Ave., NW.

Fisher, Eddie: Dorchester House (2480 16th St., NW).

Forrestal, James E.: Prospect House (3508 Prospect St., NW).

Frankfurter, Felix: 1727 19th St., NW.

Gallatin, Albert: Sewall-Belmont House (144 Constitution Ave., NE).

Garfield, James A: Northeast corner of 13th St. and I St., NW*; The White House.

Goldwater, Barry: Wardman Tower (2600 Woodley Rd., NW).

Gompers, Samuel: 2122 1st St., NW; 3501 Ordway St., NW.

Grant, Ulysses S.: 205 I St.*; The White House; Scott-Grant House (3238 R St., NW; summer White House).

Graham, Katherine: White-Meyer House (1624 Crescent Place, NW).

Haldeman, H.R.: 3402 R St., NW.

Hale, Edward Everett: 1739 N St., NW (now Tabard Inn).

Hamilton, Edith: 2448 Massachusetts Ave., NW.

Hammond, John Hayes, Jr. : 2221 Kalorama Ave., NW; Bell-Morton House (1500 Rhode Island Ave., NW).

Hannah, Mark: Tayloe House (21 Madison Place).

Harding, Warren G.: 2314 Wyoming Ave., NW; The White House.

Harriman, Averell and Pamela: 3038 N St., NW.

Hart, Gary: 517 6th St., SE.

Hayes, Rutherford B.: The White House; Anderson Cottage (Soldiers' and Airmen's Home—summer White House).

Hearst, William: 722 Jackson Place.

Henderson, Mary: Henderson Castle (Northwest corner of Florida at 16th St.).*

Henry, Joseph: Smithsonian Institution (Castle) Building (1000 Jefferson Drive, SW).

Heurich, Christian: Heurich House (1307 Rhode Island Ave., NW).

Hinckley, John, Jr.: St. Elizabeth's Hospital (2700 Martin Luther King Ave., SE).

Holmes, Oliver W.: 1720 I St., NW.*

Hoover, J. Edgar: 413 Seward Square, SE.*

Hoover, Herbert: Wardman Tower (2600 Woodley Rd., NW); 2300 S St., NW; The White House.

Hopkins, Harry: 3340 N St., NW.

Hubbard, Gardiner Greene: Twin Oaks (3225 Woodley Rd, NW).

Hughes, Charles Evans: 2100 16th St., NW; 2223 R St., NW.

Jarrell, Randall: 3916 Jenifer St., NW.

Jefferson, Thomas: Mrs. Conrad's Boarding House (C St. and New Jersey Ave., NE)*; The White House.

Johnson, Lyndon Baines and Ladybird: Kennedy Warren Apartments (3133 Connecticut Ave. at Devonshire Place, NW); Wardman Tower (2600 Woodley Rd., NW); The Elms (4040 52nd St., NW); The White House.

Kendall, Amos: Kendall Green (Gallaudet University site)*.

Kennedy, Jacqueline: See also Kennedy, John F. and Jacqueline; 3017 N St., NW.

Kennedy, John F.: See also Kennedy, John F. and Jacqueline; Dorchester House (2480 16th St., NW).

Kennedy, John F. and Jacqueline: 3271 P St., NW; 3307 N St., NW; The White House.

Kennedy, Kathleen: Dorchester House (2480 16th St., NW).

Kennedy, Robert F.: The Anchorage (1900 Q St., NW); 3214 S St., NW.*

Key, Francis Scott: The Maples (619 D St., SE); Key House (3518 M St., NW).*

Keyes, Francis Parkinson: The Envoy (2400 16th St., NW); The Anchorage (1900 Q St., NW).

La Follette, Robert M: 2112 Wyoming Ave., NW.

Lincoln, Abraham: Mrs. Sprigg's Boarding House (Library of Congress site)*; The White House; Anderson Cottage (Soldiers' and Airmen's Home—summer White House).

Lindbergh, Charles: The Anchorage (1900 Q St., NW).

Lippmann, Walter: 1727 19th St., NW; Alexander Melville Bell House (1525 35th St.); 3525 Woodley Rd., NW.

Lockwood, Belva: 619 F St., NW.*

Lodge, Henry Cabot, Sr.: 1765 Massachusetts Ave., NW.*

Logan, John: Calumet Place (Northeast corner of Clifton and 13th St., NW).*

Long, Huey: Mayflower Hotel (1127 Connecticut Ave., NW).

Longworth, Nicholas, and Alice Roosevelt: 20009 Massachusetts Ave., NW; 1736 M St., NW.

Luce, Clare Booth: Wardman Tower (2600 Woodley Rd., NW).

MacArthur, Douglas: The Chastleton Apartments (1780 16th St., NW).

McCarthy, Joseph: 335 C St., SE; 20 3rd St., NE.

McKinley, William: Ebbitt House (14th St. and F St., NW)*; The White House.

McLean, Edward and Evalyn Walsh: Walsh-McLean House (2020 Massachusetts Ave., NW); McLean House (1500 I St., NW)*; Friendship (3600 Wisconsin Ave.).*

McLellan, George: 334 H St., NW*; 1801 F St., NW.

Madison, James and Dolley: 1333 F St., NW; The White House; The Octagon House (1799 New York Ave., NW); 1801 F St., NW; The Seven Buildings (northwest corner of Pennsylvania Ave. and 19th St., NW).*

Madison, Dolley: See also Madison, James and Dolley; Cutts-Madison House (1520 H St., NW).

Marbury, William: Forrest-Marbury House (3350 M St., NW).

Marshall, George C.: The Envoy (2400 16th St., NW).

Marshall, John: 1801 F St., NW.

Mellon, Andrew: McCormick House (1785 Massachusetts Ave., NW).

Merrill, Dina: Hillwood (4155 Linnean Ave., NW).

Mesta, Perle: The Elms (4040 52nd St., NW); 2300 S St., NW; McCormick House (1785 Massachusetts Ave., NW); Wardman Tower (2600 Woodley Rd., NW).

Meyer, Eugene: White-Meyer House (1624 Crescent Place, NW).

Miller, Joaquin: cabin (moved to Rock Creek Park, at Beach Drive and Military Rd.).

Mills, Clark: 2350 Bladensburg Rd., NE.*

Mondale, Walter: Vice President's House (Naval Observatory grounds).

Monroe, James: 1801 F St., NW; Caldwell-Monroe House/Arts Club of Washington (2017 I St., NW); The White House.

Morton, Levi: Bell-Morton House (1400 Rhode Island Ave., NW).

Murrow, Edward R: 5171 Manning Place, NW.

Page, Thomas Nelson: 1759 R St., NW.

Palmer, A. Mitchell: 2131 R St., NW.

Patterson, Eleanor "Cissy": Patterson House (15 Dupont Circle, NW).

Patton, George S.: Rosedale (3501 Newark St., NW); 3117 Woodland Drive, NW.

Paul, Alice: Sewall-Belmont House (144 Constitution Ave., NE).

Pearson, Drew: 2820 Dumbarton Ave., NW.

Peary, Robert E.: 1831 Wyoming Ave., NW.

Perkins, Francis: Dorchester House (2480 16th St., NW).

Pershing, John: Sheraton Carlton Hotel (923 16th St., NW);Walter Reed Army Medical Center (16th St. at Alaska Ave.,NW).

Phillips, Duncan and Marjorie: 1600 21st St., NW (now Phillips Gallery).

Post, Marjorie Merriweather: See also Davies, Joseph and Marjorie Merriweather Post; Hillwood (4155 Linnean Ave., NW).

Porter, Katherine Anne: 3601 49th St., NW.

Pound, Ezra: St. Elizabeth's Hospital (2700 Martin Luther King Ave., SE).

Quayle, J. Danforth: Vice President's House (Naval Observatory grounds).

Rawlings, Marjorie Kinan: 1221 Newton St., NE.

Rayburn, Sam: The Anchorage (1900 Q St., NW).

Rockefeller, Nelson: 2500 Foxhall Rd., NW; Vice President's House (Naval Observatory grounds).

Roosevelt, Franklin D. and Eleanor: 2131 R St., NW; The White House

Roosevelt, Theodore: 1215 19th St., NW*; The White House; 736 Jackson Place, NW.

Root, Elihu: 722 Jackson Place; Bell-Morton House (1400 Rhode Island Ave., NW); 1626 R St., NW.

Seward, William: Rodgers House (17 Madison Place).*

Shepherd, Alexander "Boss": 1601 K St., NW*; Bleak House (Walter Reed Army Medical Center grounds site).*

Sherman, William Tecumseh: 205 I St., NW.*

Simpson, Wallis: The Chastleton Apartments (1780 16th St., NW).

Sousa, John Philip: 636 G St., SE (birthplace).

Sprague, Kate Chase: Edgewood (Rhode Island Ave. and 4th St., NE).*

Stanton, Edwin: 1323 K St., NW.*

Stevenson, Adlai: 1904 R St., NW; Wardman Tower (2600 Woodley Rd., NW).

Stimson, Henry: Rosedale (3501 Newark St., NW).

Straus, Oscar: 2600 16th St., NW.

Surratt, Mary: 604 H St., NW (boarding house).

Taft, Robert A: 1688 31st St., NW.

Taft, William Howard: The White House; 2215 Wyoming Ave., NW.

Taylor, Elizabeth (with John Warner): 3230 S St., NW.

Terrell, Mary Church: 326 T St., NW.

Thurber, James: 2031 I St., NW.*

Totten, George Oakley: Warder-Totten House (2633 16th St., NW).

Truman, Harry S: Sedgwick Garden Apartments (3726 Connecticut Ave., NW); 4701 Connecticut Ave.; The White House; Blair House (1653 Pennsylvania Ave., NW).

Tydings, Millard E.: Wardman Tower (2600 Woodley Rd., NW).

Tyler, John: Tyler House (National Gallery of Art site)*.

Wallace, Henry: Wardman Tower (2600 Woodley Rd., NW).

Warren, Earl: Wardman Tower (2600 Woodley Rd., NW).

Westinghouse, George: Blaine House (2000 Massachusetts Ave., NW).

Whitman, Walt: Numerous boarding houses (including: 1405 M St., NW*; 1407 L St., NW; 502 Pennsylvania Ave., NW*; 5335 15th St.).

Wilson, Woodrow, and Edith Galt: The White House; Woodrow Wilson House (2340 S St., NW).

Appendix B

Bibliography

Adler, Bill, ed. *Washington: A Reader*. New York: Meredith Publishing Company, 1967.

Alcott, Louisa May. *Hospital Sketches*. Boston: James Redpath, 1863.

Applewhite, E.J. *Washington Itself*. New York: Alfred A. Knopf, 1981.

Babb, Laura Longley. *Keeping Posted: One Hundred Years of News from The Washington Post*. Washington: The Washington Post Company, 1977.

Borchert, James. *Alley Life in Washington*. Urbana and Chicago, Ill.: University of Illinois Press, 1982.

Brinkley, David. *Washington Goes to War*. New York: Alfred A. Knopf, 1988.

Britton, Nan. *The President's Daughter*. New York: Elizabeth Ann Guild, Inc., 1927.

Carpenter, Frank G. *Carp's Washington*. Edited by Frances Carp. New York: McGraw-Hill, 1960.

Chaffee, Kevin, ed. *50 Maps of Washington, D.C.* New York: H.M. Gousha, 1991.

Clapper, Olive Ewing. *Washington Tapestry*. New York: McGraw-Hill, 1946.

Clark, Elizabeth Gertrude. *Reports of the Chronicler from Records of the Columbia Historical Society, Washington, D.C., 1951–1961*. Washington, D.C.: Columbia Historical Society, 1976.

Clark, Marion and Rudy Maxa. *Public Trust, Private Lust*. New York: William Morrow and Company, 1977.

Coleman, Edna. *White House Gossip: From Andrew Johnson to Calvin Coolidge*. New York: Doubleday, Page & Co., 1927.

Cutler, David. *Literary Washington*. Lanham, Md.: Madison Books, 1989.

Daniels, Jonathon. *Frontier on the Potomac*. New York: Macmillan, 1946.

Devins, R.M. *Our First Century*. Springfield, Mass.: C.A. Nichols & Co., 1878.

Dickens, Charles. *American Notes*. London, 1842.

Dole, Bob. *Historical Almanac of the U.S. Senate*. Washington: U.S. Government Printing Office, 1989.

Durbin, Louise. *Inaugural Cavalcade*. New York: Dodd, Meade & Co., 1971.

Eastman, John. *Who Lived Where*. New York: Bonanza Books, 1983.

Evans, James Matthew. *The Landscape Architecture of Washington, D.C.* Washington, D.C.: Landscape Architecture Foundation, 1981.

Ewing, Charles. *Yesterday's Washington, D.C.* Miami: E.M. Seemann Publishing, Inc., 1976.

Exton, Peter and Dorsey Kleitz. *Milestones into Headstones*. McLean, Va.: EPM Publications, Inc., 1985.

Federal Writers' Project. *Washington: City and Capital*. American Guide Series, Works Progress Administration. Washington: Government Printing Office, 1937.

Fitzpatrick, Sandra, and Maria R. Goodwin. *The Guide to Black Washington*. New York: Hippocrene Books, 1990.

Fleming, Thomas. *Around the Capital with Uncle Hank*. New York: The Nutshell Publishing Co., 1900.

Garment, Suzanne. *Scandal: The Culture of Mistrust in American Politics*. New York: Random House, 1991.

Gold, Gerald, Editor. *The White House Transcripts*. New York: Viking, 1973.

Goode, James M. *Capital Losses*. Washington, D.C.: Smithsonian Institution Press, 1979.

_____. *Best Addresses*. Washington, D.C.: Smithsonian Institution Press, 1988.

Greene, Constance McLaughlin. *Washington: A History of the Capital, 1800–1950*. Princeton: Princeton University Press, 1976.

Gutheim, Frederick. *The Federal City: Plans and Realities*. Washington, D.C.: Smithsonian Institution Press, 1976.

Hazelton, George C. *The National Capitol: Its Art and Architecture*. New York: J.F. Hazelton, 1897.

Hogarth, Paul. *Walking Tours of Old Washington and Alexandria*. McLean, Va.: EPM Publications, 1985.

Hutchinson, Louise Daniel. *The Anacostia Story: 1608–1930*. Washington, D.C.: Smithsonian Institution Press, 1977.

Junior League of Washington. *The City of Washington: An Illustrated History*. New York: Alfred A. Knopf, 1985.

Kelly, Tom. *The Imperial Post*. New York: William Morrow & Co., 1983.

Kohn, George C. *Encyclopedia of American Scandal*. New York: Facts on File, 1989.

Lait, Jack and Lee Mortimer. *Washington Confidential*. New York: Crown Publishers, 1951.

Lee, Richard M. *Mr. Lincoln's City: An Illustrated Guide to the Civil War Sites of Washington, D.C.* McLean, Va.: EPM, 1981.

Leech, Margaret. *Reveille in Washington, 1860–1865*. New York: Harper & Brothers, 1941.

L'Enfant Trust. *Dupont Circle Revisited: A Walker's Tour*. Washington, D.C.: L'Enfant Trust, 1987.

Leupp, Francis E. and Lester G. Hornby. *Walks About Washington*. Boston: Little, Brown, 1915.

Levin, Peter. *Seven by Chance: The Accidental Presidents*. New York: Farrar, Straus and Company, 1948.

Logan, Mrs. John A., Ed. *Thirty Years in Washington*. Hartford: A.D. Worthington, 1901.

Lomax, Elizabeth Lindsay. *Leaves from an Old Washington Diary, 1854–1863*. Edited by Lindsay Lomax Wood. New York: E.P. Dutton, 1943.

Lowry, Edward G. *Washington Close-Ups*. New York: Houghton Mifflin, 1921.

Melder, Keith, Ed. *City of Magnificent Intentions: A History of the District of Columbia*. Washington, D.C.: D.C. History Curriculum Project, 1985.

Mitchell, Mary. *Chronicles of Georgetown Life, 1865–1900*. Washington, D.C.: Seven Locks Press, 1986.

Moore, Charles. *Washington Past and Present*. New York: The Century Co., 1929.

Moore, Joseph West. *Picturesque Washington*. Providence: J.A. & R.A. Reid, Publishers, 1886.

Oppel, Frank, and Tony Meisel, Eds. *Washington, D.C.: A Turn of the Century Treasury*. Secaucus, N.J.: Castle, 1987.

Page, Thomas Nelson. *Washington and Its Romance*. New York: Doubleday, Page and Co., 1923.

Pearson, Drew and Robert S. Allen. *More Merry-Go-Round*. New York: Liveright Inc. Publishers, 1932.

_____. *Washington Merry-Go-Round*. New York: The Cornwall Press, Inc. 1931.

Peters, James Edward. *Arlington National Cemetery: Shrine to America's Heroes*. Rockville, Md: Woodbine House, 1986.

Protopappas, John J. and Lin Brown, Eds. *Washington On Foot*. Washington, D.C.: APA and Smithsonian Institution Press, 1981.

Rash, Bryson B. *Footnote Washington*. McLean, Va.: EPM Publications, 1983.

Reynolds, Charles B. *The Standard Guide to Washington*. Washington, D.C.: B.S. Reynolds Co., 1903, 1924, 1939.

Ross, Betty. *A Museum Guide to Washington, D.C.* Washington, D.C.: Americana Press, 1989.

Shackleton, Robert. *The Book of Washington*. Philadelphia: The Penn Publishing Co., 1923.

Slayden, Ellen Maury. *Washington Wife* (1897–1919). Edited by Terrell W. Webb. New York: Harper & Row, 1962.

Slansky, Paul. *The Clothes Have No Emperor: A Chronicle of the American 80s*. New York: Simon and Schuster, 1989.

Smith, A. Robert and Eric Sevareid. *Washington: Magnificent Capital*. Garden City, N.Y.: Doubleday & Company, Inc., 1965.

Smith, Howard K. *Washington: The Story of Our Nation's Capital*. New York: Random House, 1967.

Smith, Kathryn Schneider, Ed. *Washington at Home*. Washington, D.C.: Windsor Publications, 1988.

Staten, Vince. *Unauthorized America*. New York: Harper & Row, 1990.

Street-Porter, Janet. *Scandal.* New York: Dell, 1983.

Walker, John and Katherine. *The Washington Guidebook.* Washington, D.C.: Metro Publishers Representatives, Inc., 1969.

Walton, William. *The Evidence of Washington.* New York: Harper & Row, 1966.

Wiencek, Henry. *Smithsonian Guide to Historic America: Virginia and the Capital Region.* New York: Stewart, Tabori, Chang, 1989.

Wilroy, Mary Edith and Lucie Prinz. *Inside Blair House.* Garden City, N.Y.: Doubleday & Company, Inc., 1982.

Worth, Fred L. *Strange and Fascinating Facts about Washington, D.C.* New York: Bell Publishing Company, 1988.

Washington Timeline

1608: Captain John Smith sails up Potomac, noting presence of Nacotchtank Indians at Eastern Branch of Potomac.

1622: Captain Henry Fleet sails up Potomac, noting (and being captured by) Native American tribe of Tohoga Village at modern-day Georgetown.

1742: Bladensburg established in Maryland.

1749: Alexandria established in Virginia.

1751: Georgetown recognized and mapped.

1765: Old Stone House is built in Town of George (now Georgetown).

1787: Constitution provides for creation of a separate national capital, and search begins for site.

1790: Congress asks George Washington to finalize site selection of city.

1791: George Washington announces the site for the nation's capital . . . Pierre Charles L'Enfant hired as city planner . . . local landowners meet with Washington at Suter's Tavern and agree to sell property to government . . . Andrew Ellicott and Benjamin Banneker begin surveying city boundaries.

1792: Pierre L'Enfant fired as city planner . . . Cornerstone of White House laid.

1793: Cornerstone of Capitol laid by George Washington.

1800: Congress meets for first time in unfinished Capitol . . . President John Adams and wife, Abigail, move into spartan White House . . . Washington Navy Yard established.

1801: Thomas Jefferson elected President by Congress, following tight vote with John Adams . . . Congress assumes jurisdiction over the District of Columbia . . . Supreme Court arrives in Washington from Philadelphia.

1802: City of Washington incorporated . . . Congress establishes local governing body for district (with a mayor and council).

1803: Treasury Secretary Albert Gallatin makes the Louisiana Purchase from Napoleon Bonaparte while living at (now-named) Sewall-Belmont House on Capitol Hill.

1805: First school board meeting held.

1806: First public schools (for whites) open.

1807: First public school (for freed blacks) opens.

1808: Construction of Canal of Tiber Creek begins.

1812: War with Britain begins.

1814: British burn Capitol, White House, and other buildings . . . President Madison and wife, Dolley, escape to countryside.

1815: Congress votes (barely) to keep Washington as nation's capital and votes funds for city's reconstruction . . . Treaty of Ghent signed at Octagon House, ending War of 1812 . . . Congress moves into temporary quarters in Old Brick Capitol.

1816: St. John's Church opens on Lafayette Square.

1817: President Monroe returns to rebuilt White House.

1819: Decatur House completed for occupancy by Admiral Stephen Decatur and bride . . . Congress moves back into Capitol.

1820: First White House wedding: Maria Monroe weds Samuel L. Gouverneur.

1821: Admiral Decatur slain in duel.

1824: Marquis de Lafayette fetted in city-wide ceremonies, and park where largest occurred is named for him.

1830: The "Great Debate" over states' rights in the Senate between Daniel Webster of Massachusetts and Robert Hayne of South Carolina transfixes Congress and the nation.

1833: Treasury Building burns to the ground.

1835: Baltimore and Ohio Railroad reaches Washington . . . would-be assassin makes attempt on life of President Jackson during a state funeral at the Capitol.

1836: Construction begins on new Treasury Building . . . Patent Office Building (old Blodgett's Hotel) burns, destroying entire patent collection.

1839: Construction begins on new Patent Office Building.

1841: William Henry Harrison delivers longest inaugural address in U.S. history, while standing in a cold drizzle . . . President Harrison dies from pneumonia, probably contracted during his inaugural, leaving office after the shortest presidential term in history.

1842: Charles Dickens makes famous visit to city, which he finds to be a foolish and pretentious village.

1844: Gun explodes on the battleship *Princeton* during festive sail down Potomac, killing several cabinet secretaries, legislators, and prominent Washingtonians. President Taylor barely escapes injury in incident . . . Telegraph inventor Samuel F.B. Morse transmifs first telegraph message, from Supreme Court Chambers in Capitol, to a waiting operator in Baltimore.

1845: National Theater burns down.

1846: Alexandria and other Virginia territory once part of Washington is returned to the commonwealth from whence it came . . . Smithsonian Institution is founded.

1848: Abolition debate intensifies when abolitionists free 77 Washington house slaves and spirit them away on a boat, only to be stopped and the slaves recaptured . . . A major voice of the movement to free slaves, the *National Era*, is attacked by angry mobs . . . Cornerstone of the Washington Monument is laid.

1850: Chesapeake and Ohio Canal is finally completed, too late to truly compete with railroad transportation . . . President Taylor dies in office . . . The Compromise of 1850 abolishes the slave trade in Washington, D.C.

1855: James Renwick's magnificent red castle is completed on the Mall to house the Smithsonian Institution.

1856: Massachusetts Senator Charles Sumner nearly caned to death in Senate chambers by angry South Carolina representative Preston Brooks.

1857: "Know Nothing" riots in Washington kill six people . . . House holds first session in new chambers.

1859: Daniel Sickles murders Attorney General Philip Barton Key II in jealous rage over Key's affair with Sickles's wife. Sickles becomes first defendant to use the temporary insanity plea in an American court. He is found not guilty . . . Senate holds first session in new chambers.

1860: A year of major international diplomatic relations, as Edward, Prince of Wales, visits city, and first Japanese delegation comes to Washington . . . Supreme Court moves from its basement courtroom in the Capitol to the former Old Senate Chamber.

1861: Abraham Lincoln sneaks into the city for his first inaugural . . . The War between the States commences . . . Julia Ward Howe pens the lyrics to the *Battle Hymn of the Republic* at the Willard Hotel.

1862: Slavery is abolished in the District of Columbia.

1864: Confederate General Jubal Early and his troops attack Fort Stevens. Lincoln nearly gets shot during battle as he stands watching from ramparts. The Southerners are repulsed in the closest attack they will ever make on Washington . . . New iron Capitol Dome put into place.

1865: Fire at Smithsonian castle destroys the Institution's collection of scientific artifacts . . . The war comes to a close . . . President Lincoln is assassinated while attending a melodrama at Ford's Theater . . . Lincoln's secretary of state, William Seward, is nearly killed by assassin that same night in linked conspiracy.

1867: The Lincoln Conspirators are hanged at Washington Penitentiary.

1868: President Andrew Johnson is impeached.

1871: Alexander "Boss" Shepherd begins city improvement program as head of the Public Works commission . . . Howard University is founded . . . Georgetown is annexed by Washington.

1874: "Boss" Shepherd's mismanagement and bankrupting of city's funds leads him to flee to Mexico, and the federal government revokes the city's home rule.

1876: Philadelphia's Centennial Exposition results in largesse of artifacts for Smithsonian, which houses items in newly erected Arts and Industries Building . . . Work recommences on the Washington Monument.

1877: Washington *Post* founded by Stilson Hutchins.

1879: Canal of Tiber Creek filled in . . . The Capitol gets electric lighting.

1881: Army Corps of Engineers begins dredging Potomac.President Garfield mortally wounded at B & P Railroad Station on Mall by crazed office seeker Charles Guiteau . . . Garfield lingers for several months before finally dying after being taken to recuperate at seashore.

1882: Assassin Guiteau goes on trial for murder in sensational court proceedings, is found guilt and executed.

1885: Washington Monument is dedicated before a crowd of thousands.

1886: President Cleveland marries the much-younger Frances Folsom in only presidential White House wedding. Society is atwitter.

1888: Severe blizzard in March closes down city . . . first electric streetcar introduced in Washington.

1889: Worst flood in city's history.

1890: National Zoological Park moves its animals from the Mall to its new home at the new Rock Creek Park . . . White House gets electric lighting . . . first cable cars begin service in city . . . Washington County annexed into Washington City, extending city boundaries beyond Boundary Road (now Florida Avenue).

1892: Grand Army of the Republic (GAR) encamps on Mall amidst much celebration.

1894: Coxey's Army arrives in Washington to demand financial aid for unemployed Americans. Congress is not amused.

1897: Library of Congress building opens . . . First automobiles drive on city streets.

1899: Post Office (now the Old Post Office) construction underway.

1900: Potomac dredging work leads to creation of Potomac Parks and Tidal Basin.

1901: President McKinley assassinated at Pan-American Exposition in Buffalo . . . McMillan Commission (Park Authority) commences study to recommend city planning direction.

1902: McMillan Commission reports findings, which become known as the McMillan Plan.

1907: President Roosevelt presides over ground-breaking for Washington National Cathedral.

1908: Union Station opens.

1910: Fine Arts Commission established to implement McMillan Plan and oversee city-wide development.

1917: America enters World War I and Washington's population swells with war workers . . . Suffrage demonstrations lead to large-scale arrests.

1918: Armistice Day celebrations turn city into giant party.

1919: Pershing Victory Parade winds along Pennsylvania Avenue with 25,000 soldiers marching . . . "Red Summer" riots tear city apart, kill thirty people, and leave race relations in tatters.

1922: Knickerbocker Theater roof caves in, killing 96 in city's worst tragedy . . . Lincoln Memorial dedicated.

1923: President Harding dies in office.

1924: Former President Wilson dies at his S Street home . . . Key Bridge opened . . . Washington Senators win the World Series.

1925: Washington Senators lose the World Series.

1931: Hunger Marchers come to Washington.

1932: Hunger Marchers return but leave peacefully . . . Bonus Army arrives in city, encamping in empty buildings and on banks of Anacostia . . . President Hoover refuses to meet with Bonus Army, and Congress turns down the marchers' demand for bonus pay . . . General Douglas MacArthur's troops chase marchers from city in day of sad and bitter violence . . . Folger Shakespeare Library opens.

1933: Eugene Meyer buys *Washington Post* at bankruptcy auction from McLean family.

1934: Alley Dwelling Authority established to rid city of alley slums and relocate alley dwellers to public housing.

1935: Both the Supreme Court and the National Archives buildings are completed . . . First Cherry Blossom Festival takes place.

1937: GPO publishes WPA Washington guidebook, the most comprehensive history and tour guide yet printed to the nation's capital.

1939: Marian Anderson gives free concert on the steps of the Lincoln Memorial after the DAR refuses to allow her to perform at Constitution Hall because she is black.

1941: National Gallery of Art opens, a gift from Andrew Mellon . . . Washington goes to war again after Pearl Harbor, and city's population once again surges.

1942: Massive construction takes place to fill wartime need for housing and office space.

1943: The Pentagon is completed in Virginia . . . Jefferson Memorial dedicated.

1944: Groundwork laid for United Nations at Dumbarton Oaks.

1945: President Roosevelt dies at Warm Springs, Georgia . . . World War II ends after explosion of atomic bombs over Hiroshima and Nagasaki, Japan.

1949: NATO Treaty signed at Departmental Auditorium.

1950: President Truman and family move to Blair House as White House renovation commences . . . Puerto Rican Nationalists attempt to assassinate Truman at Blair House, murdering a special agent instead.

1951: Capitol is modernized.

1952: White House renovation completed after a literal gutting and rebuilding.

1954: Supreme Court decision in Brown v. Board of Education leads to the desegregation of Washington's public schools.

1961: President Kennedy is inaugurated, and the city is rejuvenated with his youthful charm . . . First Lady Jacqueline Kennedy commences White House re-decoration program.

1963: President Kennedy's preservation push helps save buildings around Lafayette Square, and inaugurates new era of historic structure awareness . . . March on Washington culminates with Rev. Dr. Martin Luther King, Jr.'s delivery of his now-famous "I Have a Dream" speech from the steps of the Lincoln Memorial . . . President Kennedy is assassinated in Dallas.

1968: Rev. Dr. Martin Luther King, Jr. delivers his last Sunday sermon from the pulpit of the Washington National Cathedral . . . King is assassinated in Memphis within the week, setting off riots in Washington that kill several people and destroy much of the city.

1971: May Day protest leads to thousands of arrests and temporary internment at RFK Stadium . . . Kennedy Center for the Performing Arts opens to rave reviews.

1972: City loses Senators baseball team for a second time, as the team leaves Washington to become the Texas Rangers . . . Break-in at the Democratic National Headquarters at the Watergate office complex leads to greatest political scandal in nation's history, and Pulitzer Prize for the Washington *Post* . . . Republic of China gives America a pair of giant pandas, Hsing-Hsing and Ling-Ling, and they become the stars of the National Zoo.

1974: President Nixon becomes first President in U.S. history to resign, because of the Watergate scandal. Impeachment had been pending.

1975: Home rule is restored to Washington, D.C., and the people elect Walter Washington as the city's first twentieth-century mayor.

1976: Metro opens its first subway stations, on the Red Line . . . Former Chilean Ambassador Orlando Letelier and an aide are killed by a car bomb that explodes as they drive around Sheridan Circle . . . Bicentennial celebrations draw a million people to the Mall on the Fourth of July for city's greatest fireworks display in history . . . National Air and Space Museum opens on Mall.

1977: Hanafi Muslims attack District Building, B'nai B'rith, and Islamic Center, killing a young radio journalist and injuring Marion Barry.

1981: President Reagan shot and nearly killed in assassination attempt outside the Washington Hilton.

1982: Air Florida flight crashes into 14th Street Bridge, killing almost all on board. That same day, Metro suffers its worst accident, also resulting in several fatalities.

1989: President George Bush is inaugurated, and installs horseshoe pit on White House grounds.

1990: Mayor Marion Barry is caught smoking crack cocaine by surveillance team and goes to trial . . . Washington National Cathedral finally completed after 73 years of construction . . . Citizens vote in Sharon Pratt Dixon as new Mayor, the first black woman elected to head a major U.S. city.

1991: Gulf War rivets city, but ends quickly . . . Cinco de Mayo riots in Mount Pleasant and Adams Morgan cause unrest in city for several days . . . Queen Elizabeth II visits Washington.

1992: Redskin owner Jack Kent Cooke threatens to move football team across river to Alexandria, Va.

Index of Places

Index of Names